LIBRARY IN A BOOK

TERRORIST CHALLENGE TO AMERICA

Harry Henderson

Facts On File, Inc.

TERRORIST CHALLENGE TO AMERICA

Facts On File, Inc.
132 West 31st Street
New York NY 10001

Library of Congress Cataloging-in-Publication Data
Henderson, Harry, 1951–
Terrorist challenge to America/Harry Henderson.
p. cm.—(Library in a book)
ISBN 0-8160-4975-0
1. Terrorism—United States. 2. Terrorism—Government policy—United States. 3. War on Terrorism, 2001–4. Terrorism—Research—Handbooks, manuals, etc. I. Title. II. Series.
HV6432 .H46 2003
363.3′2′0973—dc21 2002014585

Facts On File books are available at special discounts when purchased in bulk quantities for businesses, associations, institutions, or sales promotions. Please call our Special Sales Department in New York at (212) 967-8800 or (800) 322-8755.

You can find Facts On File on the World Wide Web at http://www.factsonfile.com

Text design by Ron Monteleone
Maps by Sholto Ainslie and Jeremy Eagle

Printed in the United States of America

MP Hermitage 10 9 8 7 6 5 4 3 2 1

This book is printed on acid-free paper.

CONTENTS

PART I

OVERVIEW OF THE TOPIC

CHAPTER 1

The New War Against Terrorism

Throughout the 1990s and into 2001, the threat of terrorism to the United States and its national interests had become a growing concern; however, the threat had seemed rather remote and indirect, and the concern tended to be theoretical. Clearly, U.S. interests abroad could be targeted, as the bombings of American embassies in Kenya and Tanzania on August 7, 1998, and the attack on the destroyer *Cole* on October 12, 2000, had demonstrated. Beginning in 1996, the Saudi Islamic militant Osama bin Laden and his al-Qaeda terrorist network had become increasingly prominent on the intelligence radar screen as a threat to carry out large-scale, coordinated attacks against U.S. targets.

Earlier, on February 26, 1993, Arab terrorists had parked a bomb-laden van in the basement garage of the World Trade Center in New York City. The powerful explosion produced a crater about 150 feet across and five stories deep, killing six people and injuring more than 1,000. Despite events, however, there seemed to be little willingness to take seriously the possibility of a major attack on U.S. soil. After all, the most deadly terrorist attack in the United States—the 1995 bombing of the federal building in Oklahoma City, which had taken 168 lives—had been the work of two homegrown extremists without connection to international terrorism. Investigations into the World Trade Center bombing and indictments would grind on for years and produced little awareness that the attack might be the harbinger of a much larger, more coordinated terrorist campaign.

By the late 1990s, the counterterrorism community, while not dismissing the possibility of conventional bomb attacks against targets in the United States, was apparently much more concerned with the possibility of attacks using weapons of mass destruction—be they biological, chemical, or even nuclear. Such attacks might kill not hundreds or thousands but hundreds of thousands of people in major U.S. cities. Thus, much attention focused on finding ways to detect and forestall such weapons being developed by "rogue states" that often operate outside the usual norms of international conduct, such as Iraq, Iran, or North Korea, and potentially passed to their terrorist allies.

It took only about an hour on the morning of September 11, 2001 to demonstrate just what a "conventional" attack carried out by unconventional means could do. Four large jetliners were hijacked almost simultaneously by a team of 19 terrorists armed with nothing more than box cutters or small knives. At 8:45 A.M. the first Boeing 767 hit the north tower of the World Trade Center in New York City; at 9:06 A.M. a second 767 hit the south tower. Both were on fire. By the end of the second hour, the intense heat of the burning jet fuel had melted the buildings' support structures, and first one tower and then the other collapsed in on itself in an eerie semblance of a controlled demolition. It took weeks to tabulate an accurate estimate of the lives lost, but New York mayor Rudolph Giuliani almost immediately predicted that the casualty total would be "more than we can bear."

The second impact in Lower Manhattan had made it clear that this was no accidental tragedy: The nation had been attacked by terrorists. At 9:40 A.M. the Pentagon, the nerve center of the world's most powerful military, located in Washington, D.C., was gouged by a third jet,; flames pierced deep into the huge building, and 184 people were killed. Shortly after, a fourth jet crashed in a field in western Pennsylvania. It had apparently been hijacked, possibly for an attack on the U.S. Capitol building in central Washington, D.C.

By mid-morning, the situation began to take on the dimensions of a war—it seemed quite likely that such a resourceful and well-organized enemy had more attacks on the way. President George W. Bush, following contingency plans dating back to the cold war, boarded Air Force One, accompanied by an extra fighter escort. Traffic in Lower Manhattan was halted, bridge, tunnels, and all man transit out of the city were shut down, and the entire national air transport system was ordered shut down. Most Americans still vividly recall their feelings of shock, horror, and helplessness as morning passed into afternoon and evening on the day that would become known simply as "9/11."

THE IMMEDIATE AFTERMATH OF SEPTEMBER 11

The American people did not panic, despite the flurries of rumors and false alarms about possible additional terrorist attacks. The attackers proved to be members of al-Qaeda, a network of Muslim terrorists led by bin Laden and based in Afghanistan. President Bush, Mayor Giuliani of New York City, and other prominent leaders called for calm and resolve. American leaders thus urged not to strike out against fellow citizens who were Muslims or of Arabic descent. Although there were a number of assaults, vandalism, and other hate crimes against persons of Middle Eastern appearance in the ensuing weeks, they were scattered and did not lead to widespread violence. Meanwhile, week after week, emergency workers drawn from around the nation painstakingly removed the rubble and sifted through it, first for survivors, then later for human remains. The estimated death toll at the World Trade Center, which had initially been as high as about 8,000, eventually fell to 2,790.

Not surprisingly, the weeks following the attack brought an upsurge of patriotic feeling, with flags sprouting seemingly from every home and business. Americans found heroes to identify with, especially the hundreds of New York City firefighters who had died trying to rescue victims from the burning towers and the passengers of the fourth airliner who, it seemed, had fought the hijackers for control of the plane before it crashed.

For weeks or even months, the usual acrimony of political debate was muted if not entirely suspended. On October 8, 2001, former Pennsylvania governor Tom Ridge was appointed to head the new Office of Homeland Security, intended to provide leadership and to coordinate the effort to detect and prevent future terrorist attacks. By the end of October, the beginnings of a strengthened national security structure were coming into place. During October, Congress passed the USA PATRIOT Act, which greatly extended the investigatory powers of law enforcement agencies such as the Federal Bureau of Investigation (FBI). As is often the case in wartime, the president's approval ratings soared to the 80 percent range in late 2001 and continued at that level in January 2002. However, a poll released by the Pew Research Center for the People & the Press on September 5, 2002, showed that support for the president had dropped to 60 percent. Further, the responses indicated a return of partisanship: Support for Bush had dropped from 95 to 83 percent among Republican respondents but fell from 69 to 39 percent among Democrats.

At the same time, Americans continued in a state of high stress as 2001 drew to an end. In October and November, letters laced with anthrax spores were sent to media and congressional offices, leading to the temporary closing of the Senate offices and some postal facilities. (Anthrax is a highly infectious and potentially deadly disease.) The perpetrator of the attacks remains unknown, although most experts believe it is probably an individual with some scientific training and a personal agenda not related to international terrorism. Nevertheless, coming so closely on the heels of September 11, the anthrax attacks, which killed five people, raised the specter of bioterrorism, a scenario that had increasingly become a major concern of terrorism experts.

As with many risks today, hypersensitivity brought about by incessant media coverage may have led to many people perceiving a much higher level of risk from terrorism than actually warranted. The media quickly spread and amplified the series of nonspecific terrorism warnings that were issued by the federal government and by local officials, suggesting a bewildering assortment of threats, targets, and means such as crop-dusting planes, apartment buildings, power plants, and landmarks like the Golden Gate Bridge. Military and local security personnel, including armed National Guard troops, were deployed to many high-risk locations such as airports, while the Coast Guard patrolled harbors in Seattle, Los Angeles, Houston-Galveston, and Chesapeake, Virginia. Although this visible security presence may have reassured some people, to others it had the opposite effect. Interestingly, people who had the most exposure to the news media reported that they felt the least secure.

Although any shock lessens with time, surveys suggest that 9/11 may have had an enduring impact on how Americans think about their future and their security. A May 2002 poll by the Institute for Social Research at the University of Michigan found that 50 percent of the people surveyed did not feel more secure then than they had just after the September 11, 2001, attacks; 42 percent reported being more concerned about being injured or killed by terrorists than they had in September 2001; and 84 percent believed that there would be significant new attacks. With regard to specific activities, 69 percent felt more concerned about their safety when flying; 37 percent, while attending a sporting event; and 22 percent, while visiting a shopping mall.[1]

ECONOMIC IMPACT

Even the worst terrorist attack in U.S. history could not bring America's huge economic engine to a halt, but it could make the ride bumpier. The grounding of the airline fleet around the nation even though it lasted only a few days, stranded thousands of people, forced changes in business and vacation plans, and drastically slowed the carriage of mail and goods. Trading on the New York Stock Exchange was halted for a week, while markets around the world suffered sharp downturns.

Congress rushed to provide economic aid in the wake of the attacks. The first approved package provided $40 billion in funding, with the president given the discretion to spend the first half immediately and the second half to be allocated in consultation with Congress. The bill included $5.1 billion in immediate relief to victims, cleanup at the attack sites, and aid to businesses and workers who had suffered economic hardships. In addition, the Air Transportation and Systems Stabilization Act (ATSSA) provided $15 billion in grants and loans to the airlines, many of which had already been struggling economically before the attacks.

The terrorist attacks had not halted a growing U.S. economy, however. The economy had actually been in decline since 2000. In the second quarter of 2001, gross domestic product (GDP) had fallen 1.6 percent and industrial production, factory utilization, and job creation were also at low ebb. The Dow Jones average had lost 5 percent during the preceding year. Economic pundits were divided as to whether the nation was on the brink of at least a mild recession.

Many observers believed that the terrorist attacks would be the "tipping point" that would make a recession inevitable. Indeed, between September 11 and November 7,250,000 additional jobs were lost, with the airline, hotel, and tourism industries being most heavily hit. Durable goods sales were down 8.5 percent in September, though the GDP declined only 0.3 percent. The fourth quarter of 2001, however, showed surprising economic strength, with GDP growing by 2.7 percent and consumer sentiment and spending also increasing (by 6 percent). The economy's rebound from the slow growth and terrorist shock of 2001 would be threatened in 2002, nonetheless, not by further terror attacks but by structural problems exacerbated by a domestic crisis rooted in the revelation of large-scale corporate accounting fraud.

Meanwhile, the government continued its increased spending in the wake of the attacks. A new $28.9 billion appropriation package passed in July 2002 emphasized military and security aspects but provided another $5.5 billion to rebuild infrastructure, such as mass transit, in New York City.

The longer-term effects of the terrorist attacks on different sectors of the economy will become clearer in the years to come. Airline and other travel-related industries continue to struggle, whereas the "war on terrorism" has provided new opportunities for defense contractors, makers of security systems, and companies involved in the production of antibiotics, vaccines, and systems for detecting biological agents. The consumer market, too, can be expected to reflect changes in people's life concerns. The instinct of people under stress to "nest" and focus on home comforts may help the real estate and home improvement industries.

Furthermore, the U.S. economy continues to have a major impact on the world economy. In October 2001, the World Trade Organization revised its growth projection of 7 percent down to 1–2 percent. Markets that had already been suffering (such as Europe and particularly, Japan) were also hard hit.

WHO IS THE ENEMY?

As Americans and their government coped with the immediate aftermath of September 11, they also had to reflect on the terrorists and how to characterize the efforts to neutralize or deter them. In his address to Congress on September 20, 2001, President Bush turned to the possible motivation of the terrorists and declared that

> *Americans are asking, why do [terrorists] hate us? They hate what we see right here in this chamber—a democratically elected government. Their leaders are self-appointed. They hate our freedoms—our freedom of religion, our freedom of speech, our freedom to vote and assemble and disagree with each other.*

This sort of rhetoric strengthened U.S. resolve by imbuing the nation with a sense of moral purpose. Just as America was said to have fought to "make the world safe for democracy" in World War I, to liberate the world from fascism in World War II, and to save it from totalitarian communism in the cold war, the war against terrorism was declared by the Bush administration, British prime minister Tony Blair, and many other leaders around the world to be a struggle to preserve civilization itself.

Thoughtful leaders could also direct this sense of national purpose toward moderating possible excesses in the response to terrorism. As Harold Koh, assistant secretary of state for democracy, human rights, and labor under President Bill Clinton's administration noted:

> *The terrorists attacked more than the symbols of U.S. economic and military strength—they struck at the very nature of our society and the qualities that have made us strong at home and influential abroad. They were trying to provoke us into a spasm of vengeance and intolerance comparable to their own. All the more reason, then, that even as we defend our security, we ensure the preservation of the universal values they sought to undermine—democracy, rule of law, human rights and an open society.*[2]

However, some American observers—and many more in Europe and other parts of the world—saw these characterizations, although well intended and motivational, as being too simplistic and giving little regard to what the people conducting the attacks actually believed. In looking at the writings of Islamic militants and extremists, while there is often a sense of distaste for a secular and overly permissive Western culture, there are also specific grievances, including the stationing of U.S. troops near Mecca, Islam's holiest site, in Saudi Arabia and in particular what they view as America's one-sided support for Israel. In other words, as linguist and political writer Noam Chomsky and others have countered, bin Laden does not hate Americans because they are free; he hates them because of what they have done.

Chomsky dismisses another common observation that the terrorism of bin Laden and other extremists represents a reaction to economic globalization and the American culture that it is spreading throughout the world. Chomsky believes that

> *the bin Laden network [has] as little concern for globalization and cultural hegemony as they do for the poor and oppressed people of the Middle East who they have been severely harming for years. They tell us what their concerns are loud and clear: they are fighting a Holy War against the corrupt, repressive and "un-Islamist" regimes of the region, and their supporters, just as they fought a Holy War against the Russians in the 1980s (and are now doing in Chechnya, western China, Egypt . . . and elsewhere).*[3]

If disagreement exists about the true motivations of al-Qaeda terrorists, there is also the question of their objectives and the worldview in which they frame them. Scholars and researchers have created an extensive literature that has sought to characterize the elements of terrorism and distinguish between different types of terrorists. Walter Laqueur, for example, points to what he calls "new terrorism" (other writers call it "superterrorism"), distinguishable from traditional terrorism in both motives and methods:

> *Traditional terrorism, whether of the separatist or the ideological (left or right) variety, had political and social aims, such as gaining independence, getting rid of foreigners, or establishing a new social order. Such terrorist groups aimed at forcing concessions, sometimes far-reaching concessions, from their antagonists. The new terrorism is different in character, aiming not at clearly defined political demands but at the destruction of society and the elimination of large sections of the population. In its most extreme form, this new terrorism intends to liquidate all satanic forces, which may include the majority of a country or of mankind, as a precondition for the growth of another, better, and in any case different breed of human. In its maddest, most extreme form it may aim at the destruction of all life on earth, as the ultimate punishment for mankind's crimes.*[4]

Where do bin Laden and al-Qaeda fit in to all this? On a continuum where 1 represents a terrorist group that is fighting for specific, limited political objectives (in other words, traditional terrorism), as for example, the main body of the Irish Republican Army, and 10 represents apocalyptic fanatics (of the new terrorism sort), such as the Japanese cult Aum Shinrikyo, perhaps bin Laden and al-Qaeda reach a 6 or 7. In his taped statements, bin Laden has described his grievances against America but has not formulated demands that might form the basis for any sort of negotiation. Indeed, when facing a group whose worldview and agenda appears to be so much at odds with the Western world, there seems little possibility that negotiating directly with the terrorists would be productive or even possible as it turned out to be in Ireland.

Given an implacable group that makes no demands, the focus of diplomacy as part of the counterterrorist effort turns to an attempt to split an extremist group such as al-Qaeda off from moderate Islamic groups and societies. Thus, U.S. leaders insist that in the war against terrorism, they are not at battle with Islam but with a small group of fanatics who have distorted the teachings of the Qur'an (Koran).

TERRORISM: CRIME OR WAR?

From the characterization of the terrorists proceeds the characterization of the antiterrorist effort. Traditionally, terrorists have been viewed primarily as criminals; thus, counterterrorism has fallen within the purview of law enforcement agencies such as the FBI, which had the lead role in pursuing Timothy McVeigh and Terry Nichols (the Oklahoma City bombers) and Theodore Kaczynski (the Unabomber). Generally, America's homegrown terrorist groups, whether primarily on the left in the 1960s and early 1970s or on the right in the 1980s and early 1990s, have been small, isolated, and not well coordinated. In addition, they fall under "conventional," or traditional, terrorism, as characterized by political analyst Brian Jenkins:

> *All terrorist acts are crimes. Many would also be violations of the rules of war, if a state of war existed. All violence or threat of violence is generally directed against civilian targets. The motives of all terrorists are political, and terrorist actions are generally carried out in a way that will achieve maximum publicity. The perpetrators are usually members of an organized group, although increasingly lone actors or individuals who may have separated from a group can have both the motivation and potentially the capability to perpetrate a terrorist attack. Unlike other criminals, terrorists often claim credit for their acts. Finally, terrorist acts are intended to produce effects beyond the immediate physical damage that they cause.*[5]

The very desire for publicity often proves the undoing of the traditional terrorists, who become exposed and thus vulnerable to the planting of informers and the gathering of intelligence that leads to arrests. Al-Qaeda and other religiously motivated "new terrorism" groups, however, are less vulnerable to traditional police tactics that often work well against ordinary criminal gangs. As these terrorists are not motivated by greed, it is hard to recruit paid informers. Furthermore, people willing to die for their beliefs are hard to intimidate with threats of prison, and most Western nations have moral and legal inhibitions against the use of torture. Infiltration is difficult when dealing with a group bound together by ties of ethnicity and culture that are unlikely to be understood by outsiders.

The scale and scope of the attacks of September 11, 2001, were beyond anything that could be accomplished by a small group of criminals. The hijackers entered the United States, following detailed training and instructions that amounted to tradecraft akin to that used by foreign spies. The 9/11 terrorists patiently learned flying skills, were supplied with money and false documents, and carried on clandestine communications. Some perceptive analyst among them had discovered both a physical vulnerability in airport security that allowed them to bring low-profile weapons (box cutters and small knives) aboard four different aircraft and a psychological vulnerability. They knew that airline passengers would probably follow the standard "script" that the safest way to deal with a hijacking was not to resist with the good chance they would eventually be released unharmed. No one anticipated that the object of the hijacking would be not kidnapping but acquiring the aircraft and turning it into a devastating missile.

It became quickly obvious that defending against further attacks from a group this resourceful, with agents in many parts of the world, would require more effective intelligence services coupled with the kind of response that only the military can muster in order to strike at the states that nurture and protect the terrorists. Only the military had the capability to strike at terrorist bases or training camps halfway around the world, and in the short run, at least, only the army and reserve forces such as the National Guard had enough ready personnel to beef up security at airports and other vulnerable public facilities, or increase security along the nation's borders.

But if resorting to the language of war was virtually dictated by the nature of the threat, the military paradigm is also useful rhetorically. War represents the ultimate threat to a nation and calls upon the utmost commitment and sacrifice by citizens. The Bush administration and many in Congress began to respond to misgivings or challenges to certain measures by saying "This is wartime," echoing the World War II era rebuke "Don't you know there's a war on?"

However, the flip side of the unity conveyed by the language of war is the way it can polarize the prevailing political dialogue and marginalize dissent. When Representative Barbara Lee of Oakland, California, became the only member of Congress to vote against the authorization for use of force against the terrorists, some leftist critics of U.S. policy applauded her political courage. For defenders of the administration, however, she became a symbol of a reflexively "anti-American" left that was no longer relevant to the times.

Attorney General John Ashcroft told the Senate Judiciary Committee that "charges of kangaroo courts and shredding the Constitution give new meaning to the term 'the fog of war'" and insisted that such critics "aid terrorists" and "erode our unity." Some persons speaking against the war in public were shouted down or threatened, as had been the case during World War II. As the months passed, however, critics began to be heard with greater force. The attempt by the administration to portray the war on terrorism as a continuing campaign and to link it to other threats or targets (such as Iraq's Saddam Hussein) has led to questioning the coherence and the wisdom of administration policy.

Nonetheless the war paradigm also has considerable legal value to the administration. The Constitution gives the president the powers of commander in chief of the military. Although the power to declare war is reserved to Congress, that power has in fact not been used since World War II. Instead, Congress has, by resolution, authorized the president to use force in conflicts such as the Korean War, Vietnam War, and the Persian Gulf War. On September 14, 2001, a joint congressional resolution authorized the president to use "all necessary and appropriate force against those nations, organizations or persons he determines planned, authorized, committed, or aided the terrorist attacks."

Finally, there is a fundamental problem in that the nature of the enemy and thus of the struggle do not fit the war paradigm very well. Wars are carried on between states and at least to some extent follow certain rules designed to protect civilians and to allow for the proper treatment of prisoners. Wars are ended by surrender of the losing side or by some other form of negotiation. A war such as World War II therefore had a definable objective and an official end.

The "war on terrorism" involves a state targeting not another state but an *idea* and the groups that embrace it. There are usually no rules except those that the state pursuing the terrorists is willing to impose on itself. Although terrorist groups can be scattered and leaders killed or captured, there is no way that "terrorism" as such can surrender or negotiate. Unlike conventional war, therefore, the war against terrorism has only an indefinite objective (of reducing the threat of terrorism as much as possible), and it would be not be very meaningful to declare an official end. Thus, while the war rhetoric bolstered national morale and focused efforts in the aftermath of September 11, 2001, questions about the ultimate meaning of the war on terrorism and how to fight it will likely remain unresolved for many years to come.

The Military and Diplomatic Campaign

Almost immediately following the attacks, President Bush and other leaders warned the U.S. public to be prepared for a protracted conflict. They pointed out that while parts of that conflict might be visible in the form of air strikes or other military actions, much of the campaign would be in the shadows, conducted by intelligence agencies and special forces soldiers.

The first responses were diplomatic rather than military. The United States asked for and received overwhelming support from traditional allies such as Great Britain, France, and Germany, as well as former foes such as Russia and China. They received more cautious support from such countries as Saudi Arabia and, particularly, Pakistan that faced domestic threats from radical Islamists. Within a month of the attacks, more than 30 countries had offered the United States troops or military aid, and more than 40 have allowed passage through their airspace.

The immediate military objectives were relatively straightforward: first, to destroy the Taliban, the militant Islamic government that ruled Afghanistan and provided sanctuary to the al-Qaeda terrorists, and second, to kill or capture as many of the latter as possible, disrupting the group so that it could not launch another major attack on the United States. A third goal was to help the people of Afghanistan establish a new, relatively secular and liberal government that would make the country no longer conducive to fostering terrorism.

The campaign began on October 7, 2001, with missile and air strikes against military and command facilities associated with the Taliban. This was followed by the insertion of small U.S. special forces contingents who linked up with the anti-Taliban Northern Alliance. Thus aided, the Northern Alliance went on the offensive in November.

Although some observers thought the Taliban would resist fiercely out of their religious motivation, it crumbled quickly, members often fleeing into hiding. The city of Mazār-i-Sharīf, a Taliban stronghold, fell on November 9. Only four days later Northern Alliance forces entered the capital, Kabul. Hundreds of Taliban and al-Qaeda prisoners were captured. The ground war had pretty much wound down by the end of November, and many of the objectives had been met. The Taliban had been removed from power, replaced by an interim government that would be formalized in 2002 by the Loya Jirga, Afghanistan's traditional national council. Many hundreds of prisoners would be interrogated, and many of the al-Qaeda fighters would be sent to special facilities built on the U.S. base in Guantánamo Bay, Cuba.

The campaign, however, revealed some of the limitations and downsides of U.S. military doctrine. This doctrine was based on the idea (ascribed to the experience of the Vietnam War) that the American public would not accept a significant number of American military casualties. The military therefore relied heavily on airpower and other forms of technological superiority rather than extensive participation in ground combat. In Afghanistan, this tactic proved militarily successful, achieving the objectives with only a handful of

U.S. combat deaths. The use of special forces troops was intended to provide a liaison with the Northern Alliance and allow for the more precise targeting of air strikes as the situation on the ground dictated, but the lack of an extensive U.S. ground presence meant that the targeting of air power often depended on secondhand intelligence from the Northern Alliance or others. This led to deadly errors. In one case, a party traveling to a wedding was misidentified as a Taliban caravan and blasted by an air strike. The total number of Afghani civilians killed by such mistaken attacks is unclear but is probably in the hundreds. One result was an upsurge in anti-American sentiment among Afghans who had originally welcomed the ousting of the Taliban.

More than a year later, the new government of Afghanistan was still grappling with the threat of conflict between the ethnically based warlords who held most of the actual power "on the ground" and the lack of basic infrastructure, such as roads linking the capital in Kabul with other major cities or regions. In addition, little of the aid that the United States promised when entering Afghanistan has actually arrived in the country. Finally, the campaign has also thus far failed in its symbolic objective, the one not officially included but eagerly desired by many Americans—the capture or death of Osama bin Laden. As of late 2002 no one knew where Osama bin Laden was hiding, but most assumed that he was still alive after a tape was released in November 2002. When another tape surfaced in February 2003, little doubt remained that he was still alive.

A Changing American Role in the World?

The shape of the ongoing war on terrorism can also be viewed against shifts in the understanding of the role of the United States in the world. Historically the United States has held somewhat contradictory views of that role. On the one hand there is the centuries-old doctrine of "American exceptionalism," the belief that America (even before it was the United States) was a nation uniquely constituted to represent something new in the world, whether the "city on a hill" of the Puritans or the torch held out to the world by the Statue of Liberty. But at the same time America believes it shows a unique and redemptive face to the world, it has until this past century kept the world at arm's—or indeed, ocean's—length.

Starting in the late 19th century, the economic interests of what was rapidly becoming the world's leading industrial nation and the growing ties of communication and transportation began to impel the United States to begin to function as a world power. The U.S. entry into World War I combined exceptionalism and a sense of moral mission with the exercise of newly developed economic and military muscle. Yet the diplomatic failures that followed the war saw a strong isolationist reaction and an attempt to restore the old role of America being an example to the world without becoming entangled in it.

However, the Allied victory in World War II, by leading to the cold war, marked a change from an America that entered the world episodically to redeem it to an America that had to keep the world in continuous balance between one superpower and its allies against its counterpart superpower, the Soviet Union and its satellites. But while the ICBM (intercontinental ballistic missile) finally removed the oceans as a protective barrier allowing an isolated America, the cold war, however dangerous, was somewhat predictable. The Soviets, after all, tended to be cautious in promoting their interests, and although there were crises in Berlin, Cuba, Korea, and elsewhere, they were in a context usually understandable to both sides.

The end of the cold war in the 1990s seemingly brought the United States to a new historical crossroads. The Soviet Union was no more, and the successor Russian regime was too weak and disorganized to be considered a credible superpower. A newly confident European Union held potential to become an economic superpower but showed little interest in militarization. China, on the other hand, with its rapid industrialization and economic liberalization certainly showed the potential to be both an economic and a military superpower but probably is still a couple decades away from having both the wherewithal and the willingness to become thoroughly involved in the world.

Facing the choice between a new isolationism and world leadership as the sole remaining superpower, the United States under the administration of Bill Clinton opted for the latter, albeit with what most observers would have to see as mixed results—stopping genocide in Serbia but failing to intervene in the horror in Rwanda, for example.

A few years prior, George H. W. Bush had intervened decisively but not conclusively when Iraq occupied Kuwait in 1990–91, by containing Iraq but not removing Saddam Hussein. However, when his son George W. Bush assumed the presidency in 2001, he did so after a campaign that had signaled a turn back to isolationism. (In the presidential debates Bush had criticized the idea that the United States should become involved in "nation building" activities throughout the world, and he suggested that America, while powerful, needed to act "humbly" in the world.) In fact, before September 11, 2001, the Bush administration had shown little initiative in dealing with global issues, rejecting, for example, the Kyoto treaty on climate change and refusing to accept expanded jurisdiction for the World Court.

The September 11 attacks caused a drastic return to U.S. involvement in the world. It became clear that the United States could no longer rely solely on having the world's most powerful military to protect it from attack. Terrorists had, viruslike, commandeered the world's global circulatory system, with its free movement of people and ideas, to bring death on an unprecedented scale to American shores. They had used America's own planes to attack it.

Bush's response harkened straight back to that exceptionalism that has historically puzzled Europeans in particular. With language replete with moral terminology (*evildoers, axis of evil*), the United States entered a new kind of world conflict with a vehemence comparable to that of the two world wars and the cold war. As noted earlier there was diplomacy—surprisingly effective diplomacy, given the short time span—to prepare the successful effort to oust the Taliban and root out al-Qaeda in Afghanistan.

That achieved, however, the intent of the effort in the latter part of 2002 and into 2003 to finally deal with the threat of Iraq's possession and potential use of weapons of mass destruction has been much less clear. The early rhetoric of the Bush administration seemed to suggest that only a "regime change" (presumably replacing Saddam Hussein with some form of democratically elected leadership) would do; however, as European critics (and some at home) began to question whether regime change was a legitimate exercise of U.S. military power, the administration seemed to settle on a strategic doctrine that is at once more modest but perhaps even more problematic.

Under this new doctrine, the United States has the right to intervene, with force if necessary, if any nation has or is likely to acquire weapons of mass destruction (chemical, biological, or nuclear) and cannot sufficiently guarantee that it will not transfer such weapons to terrorist groups for potential attacks against the United States or other nations. Thus, the administration distinguishes for example between Pakistan—which definitely has nuclear weapons—and Iraq—which probably does not have any but is likely working on them—as follows: Pakistan has cooperated with the war on terrorism and has a government that is trying to keep radical Islamists in check, while Iraq has shown no desire to cooperate and cannot be trusted to show restraint.

The Bush administration has stated the new doctrine this way: "America is now threatened less by conquering states than we are by failing ones. As a matter of common sense and self-defense, America will act against such emerging threats before they are fully formed."[6]

However, just as the United States was gearing up its military and diplomatic efforts against Iraq, another member of the "axis of evil"—North Korea—had apparently decided in late 2002 and 2003 to take advantage of American preoccupations. The North Korean government reactivated a nuclear reactor that it had mothballed in the 1990s in exchange for oil and other aid. Although the North Koreans claimed they were simply restarting their nuclear power program, they refused to allow inspection of the process, leading to suspicion that they were intending to produce nuclear weapons. (Experts believe they probably already have a few nuclear bombs.)

Critics of the "Bush doctrine" were soon asking why Iraq was being threatened with war if it did not disarm, when most experts believe it was still fairly far from possessing nuclear weapons, while the Bush administration was downplaying the events in North Korea and suggesting that a diplomatic rather than a military solution could be found. The most likely explanation is based on political and military realities. North Korea has a large military that is probably much more effective than Iraq's, and massive amounts of North Korean artillery are zeroed in on Seoul, the capital of South Korea. Further, if North Korea already has a few nuclear weapons, they could be used against Seoul or against defending forces with devastating results. South Korea, Japan, and other neighbors are understandably reluctant to support military action against North Korea that could rebound so destructively against them.

Although it could be argued that the situation with North Korea makes preventing Iraq from achieving similar capabilities all the more urgent, this dilemma shows how the unambiguous language used in the war against terrorism and against weapons of mass destruction often runs into a jarring collision with the different realities in many parts of the world.

Practical considerations aside, while the right of nations (as of individuals) to self-defense when under actual or imminent attack has been generally recognized, the idea of preemption against nations who *may* be developing a threat and *may* be interested in arming terrorists is more problematic. The general criticism is that the Bush doctrine is unilateral. The decision in a case such as Iraq would ultimately be made solely by the U.S. president (who as of November 2002 had received both a congressional resolution authorizing military action and a UN Security Council resolution that can, at least, be construed as not preventing it).

This unilateral doctrine has aroused strong criticism from many European governments (with the notable exception of Great Britain under Prime Minister Tony Blair) that had expressed warm sympathy for the United States after September 11 and had also strongly supported the war in Afghanistan. Now, however, according to an article in *BusinessWeek*, "From Paris to Moscow and Beijing to Brasilia, genuine sympathy with America seems to have been transformed into a groundswell of unease about the nature of American power and how it is being projected."[7]

In late 2002 there were also signs that the Bush administration was trying to avoid going it alone. Indeed, Bush did go to the United Nations to make the case against Iraq, and the administration in November 2002 negotiated a Security Council resolution that took into consideration the concerns of Russia, France, and China about directly tying Iraq's conformance to the resolution with a go-ahead for a U.S.-led attack.

The situation became more problematic in early 2003, however. Iraq's cooperation with UN weapons inspectors was passive, with Iraq allowing inspections on demand but not volunteering significant information that would enable confirmation that it had actually destroyed the extensive stockpiles of chemical and biological weapons that it had apparently possessed at least as late as the early 1990s. Then, in February 2003 U.S. secretary of state Colin Powell came before the UN Security Council and laid out photographs, documents, and communications intercepts that he said showed that Iraq has been hiding weapons and "sanitizing" sites ahead of visits by inspectors. Powell also presented evidence of Iraqi links with al-Qaeda, including the harboring of an al-Qaeda cell in Baghdad and the creation of a terrorist camp in northeast Iraq (in an area controlled neither by Saddam Hussein nor the nearby Kurdish groups). This linkage to al-Qaeda suggests that the Bush administration wants to reinforce its case against Iraq by joining it more closely to the war against terrorism.

Nonetheless several principal members of the UN Security Council, including France, Germany, Russia, and China, have continued to express misgivings about the desire of the United States to in effect give Iraq an ultimatum to disarm immediately or face military force. Critics of the Bush policy, both domestic and foreign, generally concede that Bush has a strong case that Iraq has been cheating with regard to weapons of mass destruction, but they see why this requires immediate military action rather than stepping up diplomatic pressure and inspections. The links to al-Qaeda, on the other hand, might provide a more compelling reason to act immediately, but the evidence for the links seems much weaker than that for the weapons.

The original goals of the war on terrorism have also become entangled with the new objective of preventing the proliferation of weapons of mass destruction, and both must be considered in the context of ongoing regional conflicts. It is unclear to what extent al-Qaeda and other terrorist and radical Islamic groups might be able to exploit reaction in the Arab world against a U.S. attack of Iraq. If the attack were swift and successful and the successor government had legitimacy in Arab eyes, the effects might be minor, but there are of course no guarantees.

The longstanding conflict between Israel and the Palestinians also affects the war on terrorism. American support for Israel has been used as a major justification by terrorists for attacking the United States. Israeli leaders in turn have tried to justify what critics call harsh, repressive measures against Palestinians by linking their adversaries to the global war against terrorism.

Pakistan has supported the U.S. antiterrorism campaign in Afghanistan, but its regime faces pressure from its own militant Islamic groups as well as a conflict with its neighbor (and fellow nuclear power), India, which accuses it of not doing enough to stop cross-border terrorism such as the December 13, 2001, attack on the Indian parliament. In August 2002, Pakistan's president, Pervez Musharraf, gave himself broad new powers, but the ensuing election showed surprising strength for the Islamic parties. In the wake of this, if Fazal-ur-Rehman, prime ministerial candidate of the Muttahida Majlis-e-Amal party forms the new government, it will likely be less cooperative with U.S. antiterrorist operations in the region.

The Muslim world extends far beyond the Arab world, of course. Even before the end of the war in Afghanistan, plans were being made to send U.S. advisers and training cadres to the Philippines, where the government is fighting an Islamic extremist group called Abu Sayyaf, which is believed to have ties to al-Qaeda. Furthermore, the bombing attack in Bali, Indonesia, on October 12, 2002, that killed more than 190 people, many of them Australian tourists, has been tied to intelligence that suggests that al-Qaeda, working with local Islamic terrorists, may be preparing attacks throughout Southeast Asia.

Even in Latin America, intelligence reports in late 2002 suggested that Hezbollah and other terrorist groups with ties to al-Qaeda might be planning operations aimed at U.S. and Israeli interests in the region. (Meanwhile, it should be noted that the war on terrorism also encompasses non-Islamic terrorist groups such as Colombian leftist groups against which the United States has been providing the government with military aid and advisers.)

During the cold war, the United States was often accused of embracing regimes with poor human rights records (such as Iran under the shah or many right-wing regimes in Latin America) as long as they were anticommunist. Today in the war against terrorism similar questions also arise—whether, for example, the price for Russian cooperation in operations in Afghanistan and other parts of the region was U.S. acquiescence to the Russian suppression of Chechen rebels, or cooperation from China might be paid for by muting criticism of Chinese human rights violations.

FAILURES OF INTELLIGENCE

As the initial shock of the 9/11 attacks began to wear off, the question of whether they could have been detected and prevented naturally arose. The media in the process found a favorite catchphrase: "connecting the dots." What clues, had they been shared and acted upon in time, might have led to the team of 19 hijackers being rounded up before they could board the four planes on September 11? Amid investigatory reports and media revelations, Congress began a largely secret joint intelligence committee investigation.

In the preceding five years, the intelligence community had become increasingly concerned about the activities of bin Laden and al-Qaeda. Bin Laden was far from unknown to U.S. intelligence. While the extent of direct ties between the Central Intelligence Agency (CIA) and bin Laden during the 1980s is a matter of controversy, the United States had certainly backed the local Islamic fighters, or mujahideen, in their struggle to expel the Soviet invaders of Afghanistan. Bin Laden, a wealthy Saudi, forged extensive ties with these mujahideen and other extremist Islamic groups with an agenda of replacing moderate Islamic regimes with radical ones—including, ultimately, the grand prizes of Egypt and Saudi Arabia. This shadowy network began to be known as al-Qaeda, meaning "the Base."

By 1996, the CIA had become concerned enough about bin Laden's activities to set up a permanent task force to monitor him. Indeed, until a media leak revealed the secret, U.S. monitors were able to listen regularly to bin Laden's cell phone conversations. That same year, Sudan, which had become bin Laden's base of operations, offered to turn him over to either the United States or Saudi Arabia, which had revoked his citizenship. U.S. officials turned down the offer, in part because they did not think they had sufficient evidence to tie bin Laden to a specific crime.

In 1998, Ramzi Ahmed Yousef, a close associate of bin Laden, was convicted for the 1993 World Trade Center bombing. Bin Laden next unleashed a well-coordinated terrorist attack, the near-simultaneous bombings of the U.S. embassies in Nairobi, Kenya, and Dar es Salam, Tanzania. The Clinton administration retaliated by launching cruise missiles against al-Qaeda training camps in Afghanistan and Sudan, but the attacks caused little lasting damage to al-Qaeda, and one attack, on a pharmaceutical plant in Sudan, became an embarrassment when no evidence of the suspected chemical or biological weapons was found.

In February 1998, bin Laden in effect declared all-out war on America, urging Islamic activists to target U.S. territory and civilians. On December 14, 1999, an Algerian, Ahmed Ressam, was caught bringing explosives and bomb-making materials into the United States at Port Angeles, Washington. Further investigation suggested that Ressam was part of a larger al-Qaeda plan to greet the new millennium with coordinated attacks against a ship in Yemen, tourist sites in Jordan, and, apparently, unknown targets within the United States. Later, Robert M. Bryant, who retired as deputy director of the FBI in 1999, expressed his dismay at the failure to step up the investigation of al-Qaeda activities in the United States:

> *If you understood Al Qaeda, you knew something was going to happen. You knew they were going to hit us, but you didn't know where. It just made me sick on Sept. 11. I cried when those towers came down.*[8]

Indeed, an internal White House memo suggested that attention be paid to potential "sleeper cells" that might already be planted in the country. Despite urgings that a concerted antiterrorism campaign be organized, little was done.

Suggestions that the United States work with anti-Taliban forces such as the Northern Alliance to overthrow the Taliban and thus expose al-Qaeda were also considered but never acted upon. In early 2001, the Bush administration began to develop such plans further. Ironically, the plan to have the CIA arm and train the Northern Alliance was scheduled for final presidential approval on September 10.

Other problems made a coordinated response to the al-Qaeda threat more difficult. The National Security Agency (NSA), responsible for monitoring worldwide communications, had relatively few Arab-speaking technicians. The same was true of the CIA and FBI. As noted earlier, highly ideological groups whose culture is very different from that of most Americans are particularly hard to infiltrate or to recruit informers from. Although U.S. intelligence agencies have superb technological tools for satellite and aerial surveillance and for monitoring communications, capabilities for "humint"—human intelligence, such as from informers or agents in place—remain all too limited.

Thus, in the years leading up to September 11, 2001, there was abundant evidence that bin Laden and al-Qaeda were growing in both resolve and capabilities, and U.S. intelligence agencies were concerned about these developments. But somehow that concern could not be turned into an effective course of action. Summing up a dismal assessment, former CIA director James Woolsey stated that the multiple failures continued right up to the fateful hour on September 11:

> *[The attack] was a systematic failure of the way this country protects itself. "It's aviation security delegated to the airlines, who did a lousy job. It's a fighter aircraft deployment failure. It's a foreign intelligence collection failure. It's a domestic detection failure. It's a visa and immigration policy failure."*[9]

The FBI, the principal agency charged with domestic security, came in for especially harsh criticism. Coleen Rowley, an agent in its Minneapolis office, wrote a memo detailing multiple failures of the agency to understand and act on her office's findings before and after September 11, 2001 about Zacarias Moussaoui, who is now accused of being the last surviving would-be hijacker and possibly a key figure in planning 9/11. Rowley wrote that the agency had been derelict in not seeking a warrant to examine Moussaoui's computer after a flight school instructor had reported that Moussaoui had been interested in learning to fly large commercial jets. (The hijackers reportedly were interested primarily in steering the planes, not taking off or landing them—a fact that made some flight school personnel suspicious.)

FBI director Robert Mueller praised Rowley's initiative and promised Congress that she would not suffer for her whistle-blowing. He admitted, "We have to develop the capability to anticipate attacks. . . . We have to develop the capability of looking around corners.[10] The FBI, whose reputation had already been tarnished by quality control problems in its crime laboratories and problems with handling evidence relating to Timothy McVeigh and the Oklahoma City bombing investigation, faced still a greater and more urgent challenge.

REORGANIZING HOMELAND SECURITY

While the FBI and CIA tried to better coordinate the gathering of intelligence, the FBI and the many other agencies that had domestic security responsibilities were facing another threat that could strike almost anywhere in any number of ways. In an attempt to create a new structure for fighting terrorism, President Bush appointed former Pennsylvania governor Tom Ridge to head a new office, Homeland Security, on October 8, 2001. Ridge's primary duty was to create new ways to share intelligence and guard the United States while communicating information about terrorist threats to the American people.

This was only an interim measure, however, and the actual scope of authority of the new office was unclear, as it was not a full-fledged cabinet department. Although Ridge could try to get the heads of the CIA, FBI, U.S. Customs, and other agencies to adopt new policies, there was still little institutional structure for coordination among agencies that traditionally had very different responsibilities and spheres of operation.

The question was how radical a reorganization was necessary or desirable to achieve homeland security. At one extreme, all of the relevant agencies, from the CIA and FBI down to the Coast Guard and FEMA (Federal Emergency Management Agency), have been merged into one super agency. While this would eliminate a considerable amount of redundancy, such a superagency might itself be massive and unwieldy. Also, Americans, who traditionally are wary of highly centralized government power, might well feel that such a super agency would pose too great a threat to civil liberties and too much resemble the national police whose unbridled power had been a feature of Nazi Germany and the Soviet Union.

At the other extreme might be a minimal solution, in which the existing agencies would be essentially untouched, but some sort of liaison or coordination mechanism would be grafted on. Each FBI office might, for example, have a person charged with forwarding relevant information to the CIA or U.S. Customs, while passing on to local agents the information received from outside agencies. This minimalist approach seemed little different from what was supposed to be happening already but had failed disastrously.

As 2002 wore on, the administration and Congress groped toward a solution that would be somewhere in between. The resulting bill, the National Homeland Security and Combating Terrorism Act of 2002, whose passage became stalled over issues such as whether federal workers moving to the new department would retain their existing civil service protections. (Democrats supported their union constituency, while Republicans charged that the Democrats were placing "special interest" concerns ahead of national security.)

The surprising Republican victory in the November 2002 midterm election gave the GOP control of the Senate again and perhaps provided the needed political momentum to have the home security legislation passed a few weeks later. The following January, Tom Ridge easily won confirmation as the first head of the Department of Homeland Security.

The new department is divided into four major divisions: Border and Transportation Security; Emergency Preparedness and Response; Chemical, Biological, Radiological and Nuclear Countermeasures; and Information Analysis and Infrastructure Protection. Twenty-two existing agencies are scheduled to be incorporated into the new agency, including FEMA, the U.S. Customs Service, the U.S. Border Patrol, and the Coast Guard.

Critics have raised a number of points about the new agency, however; for example, the FBI and CIA are conspicuously absent from the roster of agencies to be incorporated. Evidently, the Bush administration felt that incorporating these two vast, complex agencies would be too difficult and lengthy a task. Senator Joseph Lieberman of Connecticut, nonetheless, proposed that the new agency include an intelligence directorate of sorts that would receive all terrorism-related information generated by the FBI and CIA. This proposal was later withdrawn.

If there were those who wanted the new agency to be larger, there were others who wanted it to be slimmer and less ambitious. A July 2002 report by the Brookings Institution recommended that the department focus only on border and transportation security, infrastructure protection, and intelligence and threat analysis. The Brookings analysts believed that FEMA, for example, should not be part of the new agency because of its broader focus on responding to disasters. This highlights another difficulty likely to be encountered as the new agency is implemented: How will it continue to perform the functions of the incorporated agencies that are not related to terrorism? The Coast Guard, for example, has major responsibilities for boating safety.

In officially unveiling the new plan, the president also emphasized a number of tasks to which the Homeland Security Agency should give high priority. These included making a detailed survey of the nation's infrastructure (including highways, pipelines, and power plants), analyzing vulnerabilities, and devising procedures to protect the installations. "Red teams" of simulated terrorists would also devise plots for attacking installations to test U.S. ability to defend them.

PROTECTING INFRASTRUCTURE

The protection of the facilities that provide the nation with vital resources and capabilities was a major emphasis of counterterrorism research even before September 11. Given the size of the country, the extent of its industrial facilities, and the concentration of its population into sprawling urban areas, developing a plan to adequately defend so many targets is a daunting task.

Airports and Transportation Infrastructure

Naturally, airports received the most immediate attention following September 11. A new agency, the Transportation Security Administration, headed by Admiral James M. Loy, who ultimately reports to Secretary of Transportation Norman Mineta, has since been created to protect air, rail, and bus transit facilities. Airport baggage and passenger screeners, who had been primarily the responsibility of individual airlines (under light supervision by the Federal Aviation Administration) are now federal employees. Screeners are being given more thorough background checks, and many have been found to have criminal or immigration violations. Unfortunately, tests continue to show that it is easy for weapons and simulated explosives to pass through the screening process. And while airline passengers have generally been cooperative and patient when delayed by the screening process, critics have suggested that many current measures such as the banning of tiny scissors or nail clippers are not particularly effective or sensible. Indeed, as of August 2002, the requirement that passengers be asked whether they had packed their own luggage or let it out of their sight was eliminated as being an unlikely question to trip up terrorists.

The question of ethnic profiling in this area has been particularly controversial. From the point of view of achieving the efficient allocation of resources and minimizing the inconvenience to the majority of citizens, heightened screening of persons who appear to be of Arab or Middle Eastern extraction might appear to make sense. However, putting the question of fundamental fairness aside, such "screening" is for many Americans uncomfortably reminiscent of the racial profiling experienced by minorities, particularly by African Americans and Hispanics. Thus airport screening now includes a mixture of nonethnic profiling, such as focusing on passengers who pay for their tickets in cash and selecting individuals randomly for more extensive screening.

Longer-term measures include the required installation of explosives-scanning machines at all airport gates by December 31, 2002. One such machine is a scanning device called the CTX 5000, deployed in some airports in the late 1990s, which uses the same techniques as a hospital CAT scan. Its 3-D imaging capability can make it much easier to identify weapons or other suspicious objects. Other devices under development will be able to chemically "sniff" for vapors given off by explosives. However, the expense of the machines, the need to redesign many airports to accommodate them, the potential creation of bottlenecks and congestion, and the need for training operators all threatened the ability to meet the deadline, although it turned out that requirements could be minimally met without serious disruption.

The use of smart card technology may make it possible to in effect prescreen frequent fliers who have undergone thorough background checks and to identify them using biometrics (devices such as scanners that "read" the unique pattern of veins behind a person's eye.) If such a system can be made sufficiently foolproof, it might restore something approximating the relatively easy access to airports available decades ago. However, any system used for identification can also be used for tracking the movements of citizens, raising civil liberties concerns.

If armed terrorists slip through the screening, despite these precautions, then the question of defending the aircraft itself becomes paramount. Since 9/11, the number of sky marshals, armed federal plainclothes security agents, aboard U.S. commercial flights has been increased. The cost of providing a sky marshal on every flight is considerable and thus far has not been mandated.

As hijackers now seek control of the plane, it is essential to keep them out of the cockpit at all costs. Two simple measures that have been taken are to lock the cockpit, prohibiting the flight crew from leaving it under any circumstances, and to reinforce the previously flimsy door. A more controversial measure is allowing cockpit crew to have firearms. Opponents to this idea, including some within the Bush administration, say that pilots should not be distracted from their primary task of safely landing the plane as soon as possible. They also point to possible damage from bullets hitting vital parts of the aircraft. Supporters of arming pilots, including many in Congress, point out that many pilots have military backgrounds that include knowledge of proper use of firearms, and that it would be better to give them a weapon that could prevent the plane from being diverted than to have to have a fighter jet shoot down the airliner. In November 2002 Congress passed a law allowing pilots to apply for licenses to carry firearms.

Although other forms of transportation such as trains and buses cannot easily be used as weapons for mass attacks, some attempt has been made to improve their security. Key points in the transportation system, including bridges, tunnels, and urban subway systems must also be protected from attacks that could seriously disrupt transportation and commerce.

Protecting Public Space

Many places besides airports need to be protected. Office buildings, schools, and shopping malls are vulnerable to truck or car bombs or even an individual suicide bomber. While the latter inflicts relatively few casualties, experience in Israel in the past few years has shown that such attacks are difficult to prevent. Large public gatherings such as concerts or sporting events like the Super Bowl are also obvious terrorist targets and have thus received heightened security measures by banning backpacks, coolers, and other objects that might contain bombs or weapons. But although a society in which all public spaces are under continuous surveillance might be more secure, many people do not want to live in such a culture in which individuals would be frequently required to show a national ID card or smart card or be scanned biometrically.

Critical infrastructure such as power plants, dams, and pipelines present additional problems. Some facilities, such as nuclear power plants, contain dangerous material that could be scattered in an attack or used by terrorists for their own purposes. Pipelines and power lines are hard to protect because the country is vast, and they stretch for hundreds or thousands of miles. Chemical plants, refineries, and liquefied natural gas (LNG) storage facilities are also attractive targets to terrorists because of the volatile and dangerous nature of their contents.

The electronic information infrastructure of online banking systems, e-commerce, and the Internet itself is vulnerable to cyberterrorism, either through the physical destruction of key routing facilities or the more likely hacker-style attacks such as the introduction of computer viruses or so-called denial-of-service messages that flood websites with bogus requests. The scenario of a terrorist-hacker taking over control of, for example, a chemical factory or an air traffic control center is, fortunately, unlikely, since these facilities are generally either not connected to the Internet or isolated behind layers of firewalls. Causing economic damage through denial of service is perhaps more likely.

Just as the architecture and engineering in new buildings incorporate seismic standards based on recent experience with earthquakes, standards could also be developed to strengthen office and apartment buildings against terrorist bombs. The objectives would be to resist or contain the blast, to minimize the amount of collapsing or falling material that could cause further casualties, and to make building spaces more accessible to rescue workers. Of course, increased safety also means increased cost.

Planners are faced with a difficult dilemma. Given limited financial and human resources, how much "hardening" of infrastructure targets is feasible without diverting too many resources from the more active, mobile effort to track down the terrorists and prevent them from attacking in the first place? The likely outcome is that infrastructure facilities will be more alertly and comprehensively defended than before, but in the long run there will be a combination of hardening and "point defense" (heightened security for key installations) and a more general alertness.

ULTIMATE TERROR WEAPONS

Besides infrastructure, the other main preoccupation of terrorism experts and indeed the general public is the possibility that terrorists might gain access to weapons of mass destruction (WOMD) that could destroy whole cities and potentially kill millions of people. These fall into three classes: biological, chemical, and nuclear (or radiological).

Bioterrorism

The as-yet unsolved anthrax attacks carried out through the U.S. mail that killed four people in October 2001 provoked more than 2,300 alleged incidents of contamination by anthrax or other dangerous substances during the first half of that month. Most were hoaxes, many others false alarms. While likely the work of a single individual and not terribly effective, the anthrax attacks caused considerable psychological stress for the general public and economic damage to the U.S. Postal Service, as well as shutting down Congress for several days.

The government response to the threat of biological attack has been significant. The National Institutes of Health fiscal 2003 budget includes $521 million for building new research labs, $440 million for basic research, $592 for research on vaccines and diagnostic tests, and $194 million for clinical research.

Biological warfare has been practiced on occasion. During World War II, the Japanese created Unit 731, which produced and tested biological agents in Manchuria. In Japan's war against China, fleas infected by Unit 731 with diseases such as plague, smallpox, and typhus were apparently spread across the area, in 1942 possibly causing hundreds of deaths. The United States has also conducted biological warfare research with the U.S. Navy in 1950 even spreading a supposedly harmless bacteria over San Francisco and other cities in the 1950s and 1960s in order to test the efficacy of biological weapons and possibly resulting in one or more deaths. (The United States renounced the production of biological agents in 1969, retaining a defensive biological warfare research program.)

Preparation of an effective form of agents such as anthrax requires specialized technical skills. The Soviet Union built up a very large stockpile of biological agents that could feasibly be obtainable on the black market. Most moderately developed countries, including Iraq and Iran, have the capability to create biological warfare agents. Possible bioweapons as identified by the *Journal of the American Medical Association* in 1997 include brucellosis, plague *(Yersinia pestis)*, Q fever, smallpox, viral encephalitis, viral hemorrhagic fevers (such as Marburg or Ebola), anthrax, and botulism. Large supplies of "weaponized" anthrax and botulinum spores were found in Iraq during the 1991 Gulf War.

Preventive measures include closer tracking of the distribution of biological agents, development of inexpensive detection systems, and stockpiling of vaccines in case a virulent disease such as smallpox is unleashed by terrorists. In the event of an attack, the initial containment and amelioration will depend on well-equipped local or regional hospitals with sufficient numbers of properly trained personnel. Investment in such facilities would also pay dividends by strengthening the overall public health infrastructure.

There have also been proposals to inoculate against smallpox selected, crucial personnel, such as paramedics and other "first responders" to terrorist incidents, or even larger sectors of the population ahead of time so they would have immunity to the disease. (Some areas, such as New Jersey have already begun to implement such plans.) However, a small number of people inoculated with the current smallpox vaccine will experience serious or even fatal reactions. Thus, inoculating 100 million Americans against smallpox might mean that several dozen die. Another concern is that those inoculated may pass on the disease to members of vulnerable groups (for example, those with a compromised immune system or custom of eczema or unimmunized children) during the brief period before inoculation before that area of their skin has healed. Trials in New Jersey, Texas, and other areas brought forth fewer volunteers than expected. Concern hightened in March 2003 when several people with prior histories of heart disease died after being inoculated. Concern over who would pay lost wages and medical expenses for those who experienced mild or severe side effects was another factor in low turnout. In addition, the risk of the vaccine and the likelihood of legal liability have made drug companies reluctant to produce new stocks. Although the government is likely to indemnify the producers against legal claims, the limited commercial market for the vaccines is also likely to mean that the government will have to fund both production and future research, at least unless the nation experiences further biological attacks. In 2000, the Centers for Disease Control and Prevention, the nation's top agency for tracking epidemics, began to study the bioterrorism issue. Other materials have recently surfaced as potential biological weapons. Ricin, a deadly toxin made from castor bean plants, was found in a London house occupied by four alleged Algerian terrorists in January 2003.

Bioterrorism need not necessarily involve a direct attack on human beings. Instead, the target might be livestock or even crops. Terrorists who were patient and organized on a large scale could wage a battle of attrition against the American economy and society. As one writer notes,

> *The U.S. has around a five-day supply of foods for the table. If food shipments were interrupted, it would be only a matter of a few days until many kinds of foods become unavailable. Hoarding would occur with an effective attack on a critical infrastructure such as the national power grid or telephone grid. And introducing a deadly zoonotic pathogen into a large number of meat animals could destroy domestic and foreign markets for that species. Attacking critical infrastructures with biological agents is quite feasible today.*[11]

Chemical Weapons

Like biological weapons, chemical weapons offer terrorists an accessible, potentially lethal agent. During World War I, chlorine and mustard gas were used by both sides in an attempt to overwhelm entrenched enemy forces. Despite the rapid adoption of crude gas masks, many thousands of soldiers died and many others led painful, shortened lives with ruined lungs. In World War II, however, chemical agents, though extensively stockpiled, were not used by either side, perhaps because any advantage gained would be quickly neutralized by counterattack.

Iraq under Saddam Hussein has developed extensive chemical weapons stockpiles. At the laboratories at Al-Muthanna inspectors have found 2,850 tons of mustard gas, 790 tons of sarin, and 290 tons of tabun. The latter two are nerve gases that can kill in very small quantities. In fact, the best-known terrorist chemical attack occurred when sarin was released in a Tokyo subway in 1995 by members of the apocalyptic Aum Shinrikyo cult, killing 12 persons and injuring about 5,000 to various degrees. (The cult also unsuccessfully experimented with biological attacks using aerosols of botulin and anthrax.)

One of the many unconfirmed threats following September 11 was that terrorists might use crop-dusting planes to spread chemical agents. However, both biological and chemical weapons require considerable technical skill to prepare, and their deployment is subject to the vagaries of wind and other conditions. A greater threat, instead, would be the introduction of such agents into the air circulation systems of large buildings. Such systems therefore become part of the infrastructure that should be "hardened" to whatever extent is feasible.

Nuclear Terrorism

Nuclear terrorism remains the biggest nightmare for many people. A nuclear explosion, after all, would fulfill the most fanatic terrorist's apocalyptic desires in the most visible possible way. But nuclear weapons are even more difficult for terrorists to handle than are chemical or biological agents. The possible terrorist acquisition of a ready-made nuclear warhead (perhaps from the former Soviet arsenal) through purchase or theft is a nightmare to any security agency, but warheads have complex safety interlocks, and it has been proposed that the weapons be fitted with devices that would allow them to be remotely destroyed or disabled if terrorists obtain them. One of the major goals of U.S. policy in the post–cold war era has been to help Russia safely secure its nuclear weapons, as well as reducing the number of warheads in both the U.S. and Russian arsenals. Indeed, considerable financial subsidies and even job offers have been used to try to prevent former Soviet nuclear scientists from being hired by "rogue states" such as Libya, Iraq, Iran, or North Korea, all of which have attempted or may currently be attempting to build nuclear weapons.

If terrorists cannot obtain a ready-made nuclear device, could they build their own? Building a nuclear weapon from stolen fissionable material would require considerable expertise if the terrorists want to avoid serious or fatal exposure to radiation. Refining the fissionable material from uranium is possible, given the resources of a rogue state. The possible development of nuclear weapons is often cited as a reason for the United States to attack Iraq and remove its current regime.

A perhaps more likely threat is that terrorists will create a radiological weapon, also known as a "dirty bomb." Such a weapon would not create the devastating explosion of a nuclear weapon but rather would use conventional explosives to scatter radioactive materials, such as waste from a nuclear reactor or a radiation source from a medical device, over a large area. Since such nuclear waste is currently stored at many nuclear power plants and other facilities, it is quite plausible that terrorists could obtain some, and it would then be a simple matter of creating a bomb that would disperse it. On June 10, 2002, Jose Padilla, a former Chicago gang member and Muslim convert, was arrested and accused of plotting to use a dirty bomb against an American city, although the actual extent of evidence of such a plot is uncertain.

Experts believe that a radiological weapon would have a mainly psychological effect rather than do extensive direct damage. Many Americans have a fear of radiation that is out of proportion to its actual danger. The Federation of American Scientists has estimated that if a bomb, perhaps containing a radiation source from a food irradiation machine, were exploded in Manhattan it would perhaps increase the chance of death from cancer for persons in the immediate area by one in 100. Given that everyone's chance of eventually dying from cancer is already about 25 in 100, this would mean merely raising it to 26. Even that risk would fall off rapidly with distance from the center of the explosion. Most deaths would likely be from the explosion itself (although some deaths would be from exposure of those closest to the radiation).

A dirty bomb attack might have considerable economic impact, however. If current EPA regulations were enforced after an attack, large areas might be declared uninhabitable and not be able to be decontaminated to a sufficient degree to allow reoccupation.

No matter the form, coping with a WOMD attack requires the training of "first responders"—the firefighters, police, paramedics, and other personnel who would be expected to contain the scene and render aid to victims. The first responder

> *needs to be taught and provided necessary equipment to manage a situation (such as in a weapons of mass destruction incident that could involve biological or chemical weapons). This includes confining and isolating an incident; detecting, decontaminating and treating large numbers of people on the scene; organizing regional capabilities; and having initial capabilities within the city or town for about 24 hours until federal assistance can arrive.*[12]

COUNTERTERRORISM AND CIVIL LIBERTIES

The policies and techniques used to combat terrorism necessarily come into conflict with concerns about civil liberty. The investigatory apparatus of surveillance and wiretaps that might uncover possible terrorist attacks could also be used to intimidate an administration's political opponents. On the other hand, procedural safeguards built into the legal system such as keeping communication between attorney and client privileged might also provide a conduit for communication between terrorists.

According to the previously cited survey by the Institute for Social Research, in May 2002, seven in 10 Americans said they were willing to give up at least some of their civil liberties if it would improve security. Not surprisingly, the survey respondents who said they were most concerned with their personal safety were also most likely to sacrifice some measure of liberty.

Just as the expansion of law enforcement powers embodied in the Antiterrorism and Effective Death Penalty Act of 1996 was a response to the 1995 Oklahoma City bombing, the September 11, 2001, attacks quickly resulted in a considerable expansion of the powers of such agencies as the FBI. The USA PATRIOT Act and subsequent legislation, for example, resulted in the following changes:

- The FBI can now conduct "preliminary investigations" without having evidence of a specific crime.
- Groups suspected of some possible terrorist activity can now be investigated at the initiative of local field offices without evidence of specific criminal activity.
- Earlier restrictions on investigating religious or political groups have been relaxed; now any group that is generally accessible to the public can be investigated and observed.
- In seeking evidence online, the FBI can now use the same Internet tools (such as search engines and data mining techniques) that are available to the general public.

Supporters of these expanded powers believe that they are necessary for timely detection and apprehension of terrorists. To argue their case, they cite restrictive policies and regulations such as those that prevented the FBI from accessing information developed by grand juries and hampered the investigation of the 1993 World Trade Center bombing suspects.

Civil liberties groups, meanwhile, point to a different history. During the 1970s, the FBI investigated left-wing political groups such as CISPES (Committee in Solidarity with the People of El Salvador), which opposed U.S. foreign policy in Latin America. Critics also point to COINTELPRO (Counterintelligence Program), which went beyond surveillance to activities designed to disrupt political groups and turn dissidents against one another. They worry that with broad new powers that will be exercised generally in secret and with little accountability, history may repeat itself.

In more subtle ways, such surveillance might also cast a chill on robust political debate and the exercise of First Amendment rights. One writer notes,

> *Suspicions that government infiltrators are reporting the discussions at meetings dampen the spontaneity or destroy the harmony of a political gathering. Thus many people will hesitate to attend a meeting where the police are taking down license numbers or engage in a demonstration where they are being photographed.*

However, a poll commissioned by the First Amendment Center and released in August 2002 suggests that there may not be as much opposition to narrowing the scope of the First Amendment as civil libertarians would desire. Earlier polls had already revealed that the number of respondents who believed that the First Amendment "went too far" in protecting the freedom of speech and other basic freedoms had doubled from 20 percent to 40 percent from 2000 to 2001, but by mid-2002, the number willing to support First Amendment restrictions had further risen to 49 percent. About an equal number agreed with the assertions that the media had been too critical of the government's antiterrorist efforts and that antiterrorism efforts should trump another First Amendment right, the freedom of groups to practice their religion.

The Fourth Amendment, which guarantees privacy in an individual's personal effects, also comes into play in the conflict between the struggle against terrorism and the Constitution. In 1972, as concern about abuses was heightening, Supreme Court Justice Lewis F. Powell, Jr., noted that

> *Security surveillances are especially sensitive because of the inherent vagueness of the domestic security concept, the necessarily broad and continuing nature of intelligence gathering, and the temptation to utilize such surveillances to oversee political dissent. We recognize, as we have before, the constitutional basis of the President's domestic security role, but we think it must be exercised in a matter compatible with the Fourth Amendment.*[13]

The proposed Terrorism Information and Prevention System (TIPS) program has also aroused controversy. TIPS encourages workers who are in a position to observe out-of-the-ordinary behavior in neighborhoods, such as letter carriers or meter readers, to report suspicious activities. To historically minded liberals the idea of the government encouraging citizens to spy on one another is reminiscent of the Soviet Union under Stalin. Supporters of the program, however, believe that safeguards against the harassment of political dissidents could be included and that information gathered could be used for proper, restrained investigation.

Another program that aroused controversy in early 2003 is called Total Information Awareness (TIA). Currently a research project in the Pentagon, this effort would use data mining technology to be able to sift through huge amounts of commercial, personal, and other data available in online databases. Supposedly, advanced software would be used to identify patterns that might indicate, for example, money being diverted to terrorists groups. However, civil libertarians and privacy advocates are not reassured by government statements that the data being processed would be "anonymized" and thus not directly traceable to individuals.

IMMIGRATION LAW

Since foreign terrorists must, in general, be physically present in the United States to carry out their attacks, the control of the entry of persons into the country is an obvious means in combating terrorism. Concern about immigration in general has ebbed and flowed throughout U.S. history, with relatively open access to some groups at some times and more restrictive policies at other times. Since the immigration reforms of the 1960s, legal access has been relatively easy, especially the obtaining of temporary visas, such as for students. There are also millions of illegal immigrants, and the thousands of miles of U.S. borders are largely undefended.

Border security has been considerably tightened since September 11, 2001, including the deployment of additional border patrol and customs agents. Hundreds or even thousands of people been rounded up although they may be guilty only of immigration violations. This largely secret dragnet has apparently snagged relatively few persons connected with al-Qaeda, although there may be legitimate reasons to hold persons whose activities are sufficiently suspicious; for example, a group of 22 Arabs who had fraudulently obtained permits for transporting hazardous materials turned out not to be connected to terrorism, but it certainly seems reasonable to have held them.

On the other hand, critics of indiscriminate roundups have pointed out that one of the best sources of intelligence about terrorism is the ethnic immigrant communities that exist in most large American cities. Indiscriminate "sweeps" of immigrants are likely to discourage people in these communities from cooperating with authorities and possibly passing on valuable information.

Responding to such concerns, the Justice Department established the Responsible Cooperators Program, which offered a fast track to citizenship to immigrants, including illegal immigrants, who provided information leading to the apprehension of terrorists. While immigrants do not have all the rights of citizens, the Supreme Court has declared,

> *There are literally millions of aliens within the jurisdiction of the United States. The Fifth Amendment, as well as the Fourteenth Amendment, protects every one of these persons from deprivations of life, liberty, or property without the process of law. Even one whose presence in this country is unlawful, involuntary or transitory is entitled to that constitutional protection.*[14]

In practice, however, because many immigrant suspects are being held in secrecy and without being charged or processed, they may not be able to avail themselves of legal rights. Further, in decisions such as *Reno v. Arab-American Anti-Discrimination Committee* (1999), the Supreme Court has apparently backed away considerably from its earlier expansive statements about due-process rights for immigrants. Writing for a 6-3 majority, Justice Antonin Scalia declared that "an alien unlawfully in this country has no constitutional right to assert selective enforcement as a defense against his deportation." Scalia went on to give great deference to the government's need to deport certain aliens quietly for reasons of national security.

MILITARY TRIBUNALS

Once suspected terrorists are arrested, how should they be tried? One of the most controversial developments from a civil liberties point of view is the use of military tribunals rather than civilian criminal courts, particularly in the cases of the hundreds of Taliban or al-Qaeda fighters who were captured on the battlefield in Afghanistan and transported to isolated, heavily guarded facilities in Guantánamo Bay, Cuba.

The argument for military tribunals does have some historical precedent. Generally, captives fit into two categories: lawful combatants and unlawful combatants. The former are uniformed soldiers who fight according to the internationally accepted rules of war and are entitled to the protections afforded by the Geneva Convention. The latter do not belong to a recognized army, have no uniforms, do not carry weapons openly, and engage in activities contrary to the laws of war, such as deliberate attacks on civilians. The United States declared al-Qaeda terrorists to be such unlawful combatants. The Taliban fighters, however, are a borderline case: They fought for a government that was not recognized by most nations.

The case of Zacarias Moussaoui, accused coconspirator with the September 11 terrorists, raised the issue of whether military tribunals might be used as a way to avoid the stricter evidentiary requirements of civilian courts. In early February 2003 Moussaoui's defense attorneys won a court order requiring that the government produce Ramzi bin al-Shibh, whom the government had accused of being the intermediary between Moussaoui and the hijackers. Because the intelligence agents interrogating bin al-Shibh do not want to make him available for fear of compromising the interrogation, prosecutors are reportedly contemplating trying Moussaoui before a military tribunal.

Another problematic case is that of Abdullah al-Muhajir, born Jose Padilla in Brooklyn, New York. Padilla was arrested for an alleged plot to set off a radioactive "dirty bomb" and was imprisoned in a U.S. Navy brig in Charleston, South Carolina. The court has allowed him access to a lawyer but also affirmed that the president has "the power to detain unlawful combatants and it matters not that Padilla is a United States citizen captured on United States soil."

In February 2003 the House of Delegates of the American Bar Association (ABA) voted overwhelmingly to support the right of U.S. citizens held as enemy combatants to have access to an attorney and to judicial review of their status. The ABA is also urging Congress to establish clear standards and procedures for designating individuals as "enemy combatants." This latter request is unlikely to be met, however, because of the political and institutional deference that Congress has historically given to the executive branch in matters pertaining to the conduct of war.

The latest string of decisions in the federal appeals court seems to follow in the historical tracks of the Supreme Court, which has also generally given great deference to the president's wartime powers as well as considering such measures to be "political questions" beyond the reach of the court. This track record and the government's apparent willingness to plea-bargain somewhat marginal cases (such as that of "American Taliban" John Walker Lindh) makes it difficult to say whether the highest court will review any of the cases arising from the war against terrorism.

SECRET EVIDENCE

Another troubling area from a civil liberties standpoint is the use of secret evidence that is not revealed to the defendant or his or her attorneys. The argument in favor of this practice is that if the defendant is in fact involved with terrorists, sensitive information about informants or methods used by counterterrorist agencies could be revealed to the terrorist group. However, the basic constitutional right to face one's accusers and present or rebut evidence at trial is inevitably compromised whenever evidence is withheld from the defense.

The 1996 antiterrorism act expanded the use of secret evidence and even provided for a secret "Terrorist Removal Court" to conduct deportation proceedings. However, critics have pointed out that use of such evidence did not result in the apprehensions of any of the 19 terrorists who later participated in the September 11, 2001, attack, and that three prosecutions that were successful did not rely on secret evidence.

Federal courts have come to differing conclusions in balancing the rights of persons being held in connection with the prosecution of terrorism. A key case involves terrorist suspect (and U.S. citizen) Yaser Esam Hamdi, who is being held incommunicado on a Norfolk, Virginia, naval brig. In June 2002, a Virginia federal district court ordered that Hamdi be given access to the public defender only to have its decision overturned a month later by the Court of Appeals of the Fourth Circuit, which cited the need to keep information out of the hands of terrorist groups.

Another interest that comes into play is that of the media under the First Amendment and the public's "right to know." Here, too, results have been mixed. In August 2002, a federal appeals court in Philadelphia ruled that the media can be barred from deportation hearings because of the danger that even seemingly innocuous pieces of evidence could reveal American vulnerabilities to terrorist groups. However, that same month sixth circuit court of appeals judge Damon Keith said in the case of Rabih Haddad, a Lebanese immigrant, that secret hearings should be a carefully considered exception, not the norm, and noted that "the executive branch seeks to uproot peoples' lives outside the public eye and behind a closed door. Democracies die behind closed doors."[15]

SEPARATION OF POWERS

Ultimately, the war against terrorism may well have an impact on the structure of the U.S. system of government itself. Traditionally, the design of the U.S. government has relied on separation of powers, checks and balances, and compartmentalization that avoids giving any one branch or agency too much power. Thus when the CIA was developed as a powerful foreign intelligence and intervention agency, it was, by statute, prohibited from becoming involved in domestic criminal investigation, a role of the Justice Department and FBI.

From the point of view of advocates of a strong war on terrorism, the firewalls between agencies that prevent abuse of power are obstructions to the sharing of information and resources needed to fight a new kind of battle against a formidable new kind of enemy. But while most critics of the proposed expansion of interagency cooperation acknowledge that better information sharing is indeed needed, they worry that

> *Congress may well have overcompensated, creating the risk that intelligence agencies such as the CIA will now have substantial access to domestic criminal law investigatory tools. And history suggested that when the CIA gets involved in domestic activity, abuses are likely to follow. The agency is simply not trained in adhering to domestic legal limits on its conduct, because its principal field of operation is espionage overseas, where domestic rules do not apply.*[16]

FACING THE FUTURE: THE HOME FRONT

More than a year after September 11, 2002, many observers have noted ways in which life in the United States has changed and not changed. The obvious change is the ongoing awareness of the continuing terrorist threat both at home and abroad. This threat is kept alive by a seemingly endless series of reports from intelligence sources of possible plans for attacks and warnings from government officials of particular forms of attack or general targets. The awareness of the terrorist threat, together with tighter security not only at airports but also at most major buildings and transportation and infrastructure systems, has become virtually institutionalized.

Although as of early 2003 there have been no further major terrorist attacks on American soil, two incidents triggered much of the same response that a terrorist attack would have engendered. One, of course, was the anthrax attacks of late 2001; the other was the series of sniper killings in the Washington, D.C., area in October 2002. In both cases, although there were only a handful of deaths, the random nature of the people targeted made the public feel if anything more helpless. While one might conceivably choose to move to a small town or not work in a large building, everyone handles mail and visits gas stations and restaurants. Although there is still no official suspect for the anthrax attacks and the two suspects in the sniper attacks have no known connection to terrorist groups, these incidents serve as a disturbing reminder that one can have terror without terrorists. The same vulnerabilities in modern society that can be exploited by al-Qaeda can be used at least on a small scale by small groups or deranged individuals.

The ongoing sense of vulnerability apparently had a decisive effect on the November 2002 midterm elections. The Republicans made terrorism and homeland security their main election issue, trying to translate the continuing high support for President Bush and his antiterrorist efforts to support for Republicans in general. In this they were aided by weeks of campaigning by the president himself up to election day.

The majority of Democrats, meanwhile, had virtually ceded foreign policy to Bush, supporting his major initiatives including the resolution authorizing possible war against Iraq. Democrats in the Senate did, however, temporarily succeed in blocking resolution of the legislation authorizing the Department of Homeland Security in response to labor unions' objecting to provisions that would make it easier for the department to dismiss workers. While the move is understandable in terms of traditional

Democratic issues, the Republicans were able to cast this action as obstructionism that threatened vital efforts to protect the nation against terrorism.

Domestic issues, particularly the economy, corporate corruption, and health care, would normally have given the Democrats promising opportunities, but the Democrats failed to make a coherent case or to differentiate theirs from similar-sounding Republican proposals. The focus on Iraq and terrorism also continued to mute the domestic debate.

The result was that an electoral struggle that was almost as tightly balanced as that in 2000 was tipped decisively into the Republican column. The Republican Party regained control of the Senate and gave President Bush if not exactly a mandate, at least a powerful new lever for furthering his agenda for the war on terrorism. The president wasted no time declaring his intentions: "The single most important item of unfinished business on Capitol Hill is to create a unified Department of Homeland Security that will vastly improve our ability to protect our coasts and our borders and our communities. The election may be over but a terrorist threat is still real."[17]

As 2002 ended and 2003 began, the president had gotten his Department of Homeland Security, and implementation of the new agency went under way. However, in February 2003, draft legislation for the Domestic Security Enhancement Act of 2003 leaked out of the Justice Department. Elements of the proposal include

- Routine collection of DNA samples from terrorism suspects, eventually creating a large database
- Automatic holding without bail of terrorism suspects
- Disallowance of Freedom of Information Act requests for information about detainees
- Ability to strip Americans who support any designated terrorist group in any way of their U.S. citizenship

While some provisions in the draft represent relatively modest extensions or clarifications of powers already granted in the USA PATRIOT Act, such actions as blocking information and particularly, removing citizenship (and attendant legal rights) would put suspects in an even more impenetrable legal limbo. This has naturally rung an alarm bell with civil libertarians. It is uncertain to what extent the Justice Department will proceed with the proposal or whether Congress will enact the more extreme provisions.

The ongoing debate about terrorism and security has become part of a political picture that includes more usual, domestic concerns such as a proposed budget with the largest deficit in U.S. history (in absolute terms), the president's tax cut program, Social Security, health care, and other important matters. There is no doubt, however, that the terrorist threat is indeed still real, as are its related challenges:

- Will the recently enacted homeland security measures be able to prevent significant attacks from both international and potential domestic terrorists?
- How will this latest episode in the American struggle between security and civil liberties be resolved?
- Will a global framework for containing terrorism emerge, or will the United States act mainly unilaterally or with small groups of allies?

---

1 Institute for Social Research, University of Michigan. "Homeland Insecurity: Survey Shows Many Americans Still Worried and Shaken." Available online. URL:http://www.umich.edu/~newsinfo/Releases/2002/May02/r050302a.html.

2 Harold Kongju Koh. "Preserving American Values: The Challenge at Home and Abroad." In Strobe Talbott and Nayan Chanda, eds. *The Age of Terror: America and the World After September 11.* New York: Basic Books/Yale Center for the Study of Globalization, 2001, pp. 143–169.

3 Noam Chomsky. *9–11.* New York: Seven Stories Press, 2001, pp. 31–32.

4 Walter Laqueur. *The New Terrorism: Fanaticism and the Arms of Mass Destruction.* New York: Oxford University Press, 1999, p. 81.

5 Quoted in "First Annual Report to the President and the Congress of the Advisory Panel to Assess Domestic Response Capabilities for Terrorism Involving Weapons of Mass Destruction." December 15, 1999, p. iii. Available online. URL: http://www.rand.org/nsrd/terrpanel/terror.pdf.

6 Quoted in *APS Diplomat Recorder*, vol. 57, September 21, 2002, p. 1

7 John Rossant. "Despite the Griping, Support for the U.S. Runs Deep." *Business Week*, September 16, 2002, p. 46.

8 Robert M. Bryant, quoted in Judith Miller, Jeff Gerth, and Dan Van Natta, Jr. "Planning for Terror but Failing to Act." *New York Times*, December 30, 2001, p. A1.

9 James Woolsey, quoted in ibid.

10 Robert Mueller, quoted in Michael Duffy and Nancy Gibbs. "How Far Do We Want the FBI to Go?" *Time*, vol. 159 (June 10, 2002), p. 24 ff.

11 James P. Lucier. "We Are What We Eat—and That Makes the United States Vulnerable." *Insight on the News*, vol. 14 (November 16, 1998), p. 6.

12 Juan Otero and Deborah Rigsby. "NLC Explains Local Role, Need for 'First Response' to Terrorism." *Nation's Cities Weekly*, vol. 21 (September 7, 1998), p. 1 ff.

13 *United States v. United States District Court*, 407 U.S. 297, 320 (1972).

[14] *Matthews v. Diaz*, 426 U.S. 67, 77 (1976).

[15] *Rabih Haddad et al. v. John Ashcroft et al.*, U.S. Court of Appeals for the Sixth Circuit (2002).

[16] James X. Dempsey and David Cole. *Terrorism and the Constitution.* 2d ed. Washington, D.C.: First Amendment Foundation, 2002, pp. 162–163.

[17] Presidential press conference, November 8, 2002.

CHAPTER 2

THE LAW AND THE "WAR ON TERRORISM"

The responses to the September 11, 2001, attacks include a number of pieces of important legislation that create new agencies and expand investigatory and law enforcement powers. This chapter is divided into three parts. The first part covers the basic legal structure, domestic and international, regarding terrorism as it existed prior to the attacks. The second part covers the major post-9/11 legislation. The third part provides a survey of cases (mainly in the Supreme Court) that involve issues that are emerging in the current prosecution of terrorism, including the use of military tribunals.

BASIC LEGAL FRAMEWORK

The U.S. Code consists of all legislation that has been passed by Congress. It includes a number of provisions concerning terrorism and related matters such as immigration.

DEFINITION AND CHARACTERIZATION OF TERRORISM

18 U.S. Code Sec. 2331 defines *international terrorism.*

> *— (1) the term "international terrorism" means activities that*
> *(A) involve violent acts or acts dangerous to human life that are a violation of the criminal laws of the United States or of any State, or that would be a*

criminal violation if committed within the jurisdiction of the United States or of any State;
(B) appear to be intended —
(i) to intimidate or coerce a civilian population;
(ii) to influence the policy of a government by intimidation or coercion; or
(iii) to affect the conduct of a government by assassination or kidnapping; and
(C) occur primarily outside the territorial jurisdiction of the United States, or transcend national boundaries in terms of the means by which they are accomplished, the persons they appear intended to intimidate or coerce, or the locale in which their perpetrators operate or seek asylum;

Domestic terrorism (such as that carried on by U.S. extremist groups) falls generally under the category of seditious conspiracy, which is defined in 18 U.S.C. Sec. 2384.

If two or more persons in any State or Territory, or in any place subject to the jurisdiction of the United States, conspire to overthrow, put down, or to destroy by force the Government of the United States, or to levy war against them, or to oppose by force the authority thereof, or by force to prevent, hinder, or delay the execution of any law of the United States, or by force to seize, take, or possess any property of the United States contrary to the authority thereof, they shall each be fined under this title or imprisoned not more than twenty years, or both.

18 U.S.C. Sec. 2385 deals specifically with advocating the overthrow of the government:

Whoever knowingly or willfully advocates, abets, advises, or teaches the duty, necessity, desirability, or propriety of overthrowing or destroying the government of the United States or the government of any State, Territory, District or Possession thereof, or the government of any political subdivision therein, by force or violence, or by the assassination of any officer of any such government; or

Whoever, with intent to cause the overthrow or destruction of any such government, prints, publishes, edits, issues, circulates, sells, distributes, or publicly displays any written or printed matter advocating, advising, or teaching the duty, necessity, desirability, or propriety of overthrowing or destroying any government in the United States by force or violence, or attempts to do so; or

Whoever organizes or helps or attempts to organize any society, group, or assembly of persons who teach, advocate, or encourage the overthrow or destruction of any such government by force or violence; or becomes or is a member of, or affiliates with, any such society, group, or assembly of persons, knowing the purposes thereof—

Shall be fined under this title or imprisoned not more than twenty years, or both, and shall be ineligible for employment by the United States or any department or agency thereof, for the five years next following his conviction.

If two or more persons conspire to commit any offense named in this section, each shall be fined under this title or imprisoned not more than twenty years, or both, and shall be ineligible for employment by the United States or any department or agency thereof, for the five years next following his conviction.

As used in this section, the terms "organizes" and "organize," with respect to any society, group, or assembly of persons, include the recruiting of new members, the forming of new units, and the regrouping or expansion of existing clubs, classes, and other units of such society, group, or assembly of persons.

Unlike domestic terrorism, international terrorism carried out on American soil often involves violations of immigration law. In general, aliens who engage in terrorist activities as defined in 8 U.S. Sec. 1182 of the U.S. Immigration and Nationality Act (INA) are excludable and deportable. *Terrorist activity* is defined as follows:

(I) *The highjacking [sic] or sabotage of any conveyance (including an aircraft, vessel, or vehicle).*
(II) *The seizing or detaining, and threatening to kill, injure, or continue to detain, another individual in order to compel a third person (including a governmental organization) to do or abstain from doing any act as an explicit or implicit condition for the release of the individual seized or detained.*
(III) *A violent attack upon an internationally protected person (as defined in section 1116(b)(4) of title 18) or upon the liberty of such a person.*
(IV) *An assassination.*
(V) *The use of any—*
  (a) *biological agent, chemical agent, or nuclear weapon or device, or*
  (b) *explosive or firearm (other than for mere personal monetary gain), with intent to endanger, directly or indirectly, the safety of one or more individuals or to cause substantial damage to property.*
(VI) *A threat, attempt, or conspiracy to do any of the foregoing.*

. . . . .

(iii) *"Engage in terrorist activity" defined*
As used in this chapter [of the U.S. code], *the term engage in terrorist activity means to commit, in an individual capacity or as a member of an or-*

ganization, an act of terrorist activity or an act which the actor knows, or reasonably should know, affords material support to any individual, organization, or government in conducting a terrorist activity at any time, including any of the following acts:

(I) The preparation or planning of a terrorist activity.

(II) The gathering of information on potential targets for terrorist activity.

(III) The providing of any type of material support, including a safe house, transportation, communications, funds, false identification, weapons, explosives, or training, to any individual the actor knows or has reason to believe has committed or plans to commit a terrorist activity.

(IV) The soliciting of funds or other things of value for terrorist activity or for any terrorist organization.

(V) The solicitation of any individual for membership in a terrorist organization, terrorist government, or to engage in a terrorist activity.

FOREIGN INTELLIGENCE SURVEILLANCE ACT, 1978

Much counterterrorism work involves the gathering of intelligence abroad. As a result of the 1975–76 Church Committee hearings into abuses of citizens' First Amendment and other rights by the CIA, FBI, and National Security Agency (NSA), Congress passed the Foreign Intelligence Surveillance Act (FISA) in 1978.

The FISA provides a legal procedure for obtaining authorization for surveillance, electronic eavesdropping/wiretapping, or surreptitious entry; however, since public authorization proceedings could tip off the people being investigated, warrants are issued by a secret court consisting of seven federal district court judges. In order to get a warrant, the entity being investigated must be "a foreign power or an agent of a foreign power." This requirement is intended to prevent the ordinary legal process from being circumvented in ordinary criminal cases. In addition, if the target is a "U.S. person" (a citizen or permanent resident alien), there must be "probable cause to believe that the U.S. person's activities may or are about to involve a violation of the criminal statutes of the United States." Although evidence gathered under FISA must be gathered primarily for "an intelligence purpose," the evidence can be used later in a criminal prosecution.

Following September 11, 2001, there have been attempts to loosen some of the restrictions imposed on the gathering and use of intelligence by FISA. Advocates of such loosening argue that the requirement that there be probable cause to believe an actual crime had occurred seriously hampered the investigation of Zacarias Moussaoui and possibly prevented the discovery of the 9/11 hijacking plot.

Antiterrorism and Effective Death Penalty Act of 1996

The Antiterrorism and Effective Death Penalty Act (AEDPA) of 1996 added or revised many provisions of the U.S. Code that define terrorist activity and deal with related matters such as deportation of immigrants and the regulation of chemical and biological weapons as well as explosives. The following is a summary of the provisions that deal directly with terrorism (material in quotes is from the legislative summary).

Jurisdiction for Lawsuits Against Terrorist States

Title II, Subtitle B gives victims of foreign terrorism greater ability to sue a foreign government that sponsored the terrorist attack in cases where "money damages are sought against a foreign government for personal injury or death caused by an act of torture, extrajudicial killing, aircraft sabotage, hostage taking, or the provision of material support or resources to terrorists," subject to a 10-year statute of limitations. (Such lawsuits have generally been barred on grounds of "sovereign immunity" in the past.) The right to sue can be limited in cases that "the Attorney General certifies will interfere with a criminal investigation or prosecution, or a national security operation, related to the incident that gave rise to the cause of action, subject to specified restrictions."

Assistance to Victims of Terrorism

Title II, Subtitle C, the Justice for Victims of Terrorism Act of 1996, amends the Victims of Crimes Act of 1984 to provide money for states "(1) to provide compensation and assistance to State residents who, while outside U.S. territorial boundaries, are victims of a terrorist act or mass violence and are not eligible for compensation under the Omnibus Diplomatic Security and Antiterrorism Act of 1986; and (2) for eligible crime victim compensation and assistance programs to provide emergency relief, including crisis response efforts, assistance, training, and technical assistance, for the benefit of victims of terrorist acts or mass violence occurring within the United States and funding to U.S. Attorney's Offices for use in coordination with State victims compensation and assistance efforts in providing emergency relief."

Prohibitions on International Terrorist Funding

Title III, Subtitle A "Amends the Immigration and Nationality Act (INA) to authorize the Secretary of State, in consultation with the Secretary of the Treasury (Secretary) and the Attorney General, to designate an organization as a terrorist organization upon finding that the organization is a foreign organization that engages in terrorist activity and such activity threatens the security of U.S. nationals or U.S. national security." The procedures for such designation are then given.

Section 303 "Sets penalties for knowingly providing, or attempting or conspiring to provide, material support or resources to a foreign terrorist organization. Requires any financial institution that becomes aware that it has possession of, or control over, any funds in which a foreign terrorist organization or its agent has an interest, to retain possession of or maintain control over such funds and report to the Secretary the existence of such funds, with exceptions. Establishes civil penalties for knowingly failing to comply with such provision."

Prohibition on Assistance to Terrorist States

Title III, Subtitle B "Imposes penalties upon U.S. persons who engage in a financial transaction with a country knowing or having reasonable cause to know that such country has been designated under the Export Administration Act as a country supporting international terrorism." Existing language is amended in section 323 so that "humanitarian assistance to persons not directly involved in violations" is no longer an exception to the prohibition, but "medicine or religious materials" are allowed.

Sanctions Against Terrorist Nations

The ability of the president to impose sanctions on terrorist states is substantially enhanced. Section 324 affirms the president's power to "use all necessary means, including covert action and military force, to destroy international infrastructure used by international terrorists."

Section 325 "Amends: (1) the Foreign Assistance Act of 1961 to authorize the President to withhold assistance to the governments of countries that aid (including providing military equipment to) terrorist states, with exceptions by presidential waiver when in the national interest; and (2) the International Financial Institutions Act to direct the Secretary to instruct the U.S. executive director of each international financial institution to oppose assistance by such institutions to terrorist states."

Subsequent sections define various types of assistance affected by the legislation and appropriate a small amount of funds for assistance to foreign countries in developing counterterrorism programs.

Terrorist and Criminal Alien Removal and Exclusion—Subtitle A: Removal of Alien Terrorists

This section provides additional powers to remove or exclude aliens who are associated with terrorism. Title IV, Subtitle A "Directs the Chief Justice of the United States to publicly designate five district court judges from five of the U.S. judicial circuits to constitute a court with jurisdiction to conduct removal proceedings."

A controversial provision allows for the use of secret (classified) testimony in courts closed to the public ("in camera"): "Allows a single judge of the removal court, in determining whether to grant an application, to consider, ex parte and in camera, in addition to the information contained in the application: (1) other (including classified) information presented under oath or affirmation; and (2) testimony received in any hearing on the application of which a verbatim record shall be kept."

Exclusion of Members and Representatives of Terrorist Organizations

Title IV, Subtitle B "Makes being a member or representative of a foreign terrorist organization a basis for exclusion from the United States under the INA."

Modification to Asylum Procedures

Title IV, Subtitle C "Prohibits the Attorney General from granting asylum to an alien excludable as a terrorist unless the Attorney General determines that the individual seeking asylum will not be a danger to U.S. security." It has various provisions that limit the rights of such aliens to appeal.

Nuclear, Biological, and Chemical Weapons Restrictions

Title V, Subtitle A "Revises Federal criminal code provisions regarding prohibited transactions involving nuclear materials to cover specified actions involving nuclear byproduct material and actions knowingly causing substantial damage to the environment.

"Expands jurisdiction by making such prohibitions applicable where an offender or victim is a U.S. national or a U.S. corporation or other legal entity. Repeals a requirement for jurisdiction that at the time of the offense the nuclear material must have been in use, storage, or transport for peaceful purposes.

"Modifies the definition of 'nuclear material' to mean material containing any plutonium (currently, with an isotopic concentration not in excess of 80 percent plutonium 238)."

Section 503 "Directs the Attorney General and the Secretary of Defense to jointly conduct a study and report to the Congress on the number and extent of thefts from military arsenals of firearms, explosives, and other materials that are potentially useful to terrorists."

Biological Weapons Restrictions

Title V, Subtitle B "Amends the Federal criminal code to include within the scope of prohibitions regarding biological weapons attempts, threats, and conspiracies to acquire a biological agent, toxin, or delivery system for use as a weapon. Authorizes the United States to obtain an injunction against the threat to engage in prohibited conduct with respect to such prohibitions."

Expanded definitions of biological agents and related items are given. Biological weapons are included in the category of "weapons of mass destruction" as used elsewhere in federal law. The secretary of Health and Human Services is directed to develop a list of biological agents that have the potential to be dangerous weapons and to develop safety procedures for the use and access to such materials.

Chemical Weapons Restrictions

Title V, Subtitle C specifies criminal penalties for any person who "without lawful authority, uses or attempts or conspires to use a chemical weapon against: (1) a U.S. national while such national is outside the United States; (2) any person within the United States; or (3) any property that is owned, leased, or used by the United States, whether the property is within or outside of the United States." It also provides for studying the feasibility of developing a test facility where the effects of chemical weapons can be analyzed.

Implementation of Plastic Explosives Convention

Title VI Implements a treaty commitment. This provision generally requires that all plastic explosives be manufactured with a "detection agent," or taggant, included. It also prohibits "any person (other than a U.S. agency or the National Guard of any State) possessing any plastic explosive on the effective date of this Act from failing to report to the Secretary the quantity of such explosives possessed, the manufacturer or importer, and any identification marks."

Criminal Law Modifications to Counterterrorism

Title VII, Subtitle A provides increased penalties for "(1) conspiracies involving explosives; (2) specified terrorism crimes, including carrying weapons or explosives on an aircraft; and (3) the use of explosives or arson."

Subtitle B expands jurisdiction over persons involved with offenses committed while aboard an aircraft in flight, as well as over persons involved with bomb threats. It also specifies increased criminal penalties.

Section 725 adds chemical weapons to the legal category of "weapons of mass destruction."

Section 726 "Adds terrorism offenses to the money laundering statute."

Section 727 "Sets penalties for: (1) killing or attempting to kill any U.S. officer engaged in, or on account of, the performance of official duties or any person assisting such an officer or employee; and (2) threatening to assault, kidnap, or murder former Federal officers and employees."

Section 728 "Includes among the aggravating factors for homicide that the defendant intentionally killed or attempted to kill more than one person in a single criminal episode."

Section 732 specifies research into tagging explosives or making them inert, as well as the regulation of the user of fertilizer in making explosives.

Roving Wiretap Provisions, 1999

Provisions in the Intelligence Authorization Act for 1999 expanded the ability of federal agents to use court-ordered wiretaps. Rather than specifying a particular phone or other instrument, agents are permitted in effect to follow the suspect and tap whatever instruments he or she is likely to use. These provisions are being opposed by civil libertarians and privacy advocates because they remove the specificity that the Fourth Amendment requires with regard to what is to be searched.

Limitations on Assassination

An executive order (12333, December 4, 1981) signed by President Ronald Reagan provides that "No person employed by or acting on behalf of the United States Government shall engage in, or conspire to engage in, assassination." This remains in force; however, *assassination* is generally interpreted as the intentional targeting of a specific person. As the attacks on Muammar al-Qaddafi in Libya in 1986 and Osama bin Laden more recently in Afghanistan seem to indicate, bombing or shooting missiles at an area where a foreign leader is likely to be residing is not interpreted as an attempt at assassination.

Use of the Military and Military Tribunals

The recent proposals to use military tribunals to try terrorist suspects captured in Afghanistan or elsewhere have increased interest in the underlying legal basis for such trials. The power to conduct military tribunals is generally held to flow from the president's constitutional role as commander in chief of the armed forces.

In the Civil War case of *Ex Parte Milligan* (1866), the Supreme Court ruled that military tribunals could not be used in states where the normal courts were available and functioning. However, the World War II case *Ex Parte Quirin* (1942) essentially reversed *Milligan*, holding that military trials could be used to try Nazi saboteurs who had landed in the United States from a submarine. Although World War II was a formally declared war, a declaration of war is not considered necessary to establish war conditions, and there have been no such declarations since World War II. Under the 1973 War Powers Act, a Congressional declaration authorizing the use of force has the general effect of a declaration of war.

The use of military forces within the United States has generally been restricted by the Posse Comitatus Act (18 U.S.C. 1385), passed during the post–Civil War Reconstruction era (1878). This law generally prohibits the use of military personnel for domestic law enforcement activities except where explicitly authorized by the Constitution or by Congress. However, the military has sometimes provided "assistance" or advisers (as at the 1993 siege of the Branch Davidian religious compound in Waco, Texas), and urgent needs such as the "war on drugs" and now the "war on terrorism" have been cited as justification for modifications to the Posse Comitatus Act.

A provision added to the 1977 Defense Appropriations Act (10 U.S.C. 382) allows the use of the U.S. military in response to an attack using a biological or chemical weapon of mass destruction.

TERRORISM AND INTERNATIONAL TREATIES

The United States is party to a number of multilateral international treaties relevant to terrorism. A selection of such treaties are presented, organized by subject. Citations following some treaty titles refer to the following:

Bevans Bevans, Charles. *Treaties and Other International Agreements of the United States of America, 1776–1949.* Washington, D.C.: U.S. Department of State, 1968–76.

LNTS *Treaty Series: Publications of Treaties and International Engagements Registered with the Secretariat of the League.* Geneva: League of Nations, 1920–46.

TIAS *Treaties and Other International Acts Series.* Washington, D.C.: Government Printing Office, 1946.

UNTS *United Nations Treaty Series.* New York: United Nations, 1946/47 –. Available online. URL: http://untreaty.un.org/ENGLISH/series/simpleunts.asp.

UST *United States Treaties and Other International Agreements.* Washington, D.C.: U.S. Department of State, 1952 –.

Aviation and Hijacking

Convention on International Civil Aviation (Chicago, December 7, 1944; entered into force April 4, 1947. 61 Stat. 1180; TIAS 1591; 3 Bevans 944; 15 UNTS 295)

This treaty resulted in the creation of the International Civil Aviation Organization (ICA). It established the general framework for international standards for the operation of civil aviation; later agreements added provisions specifically relating to hijacking, sabotage, and other terrorist acts.

Convention on Offenses and Certain Other Acts Committed on Board Aircraft (Tokyo, September 14, 1963; entered into force December 4, 1969)

This treaty did not specify particular criminal acts, but gave an aircraft's pilot in command the authority to act if he or she had "reasonable grounds" to believe that an act has been or is about to be committed that is a threat to "safety" or "good order and discipline on board the aircraft." Such actions can include restraining the threatening passenger and calling upon the assistance of crew or passengers.

Convention for the Suppression of Unlawful Seizure of Aircraft (The Hague, December 16, 1970; entered into force October 14, 1971)

This treaty covers the procedures for the detention and investigation of persons accused of having unlawfully seized or attempted to seize an aircraft (hijacking), including cooperation between the nation in which the person is apprehended, the state where the aircraft is registered, and the state where the accused person resides.

Convention for the Suppression of Unlawful Acts Against the Safety of Civil Aviation (Montreal, September 23, 1971; entered into force January 26, 1973. 24 UST 564; TIAS 7570)

This treaty is directed at a variety of forms of destruction or sabotage that would compromise the safety or operation of the civil aviation system, specified as:

Unlawfully and intentionally to perform an act of violence against a person either when that person is on board an aircraft in flight and the act is likely to endanger the safety of the aircraft or that person is at an airport serving international civil aviation and the act is likely to cause serious injury or death, to destroy an aircraft in service or to so damage it as to make flight unsafe or impossible; to place or cause to be placed on board an aircraft in service by whatever means a substance likely to destroy it or so to damage it that it cannot fly or that its safety in flight is likely to be endangered; to destroy damage or interfere with the operation of air navigation facilities if it is likely to endanger the safety of an aircraft in flight; to communicate knowingly false information thereby endangering the safety of such an aircraft; to destroy or damage the facilities or an airport serving international civil aviation or damage aircraft not in service located on such an airport or disrupt the services of such an airport.

PROTOCOL FOR THE SUPPRESSION OF UNLAWFUL ACTS OF VIOLENCE AT AIRPORTS SERVING INTERNATIONAL CIVIL AVIATION, SUPPLEMENTARY TO THE CONVENTION OF SEPTEMBER 23, 1971 (MONTREAL, FEBRUARY 24, 1988; ENTERED INTO FORCE AUGUST 6, 1989; FOR THE UNITED STATES, NOVEMBER 18, 1994)

This is a supplementary protocol to the Montreal Convention immediately preceding.

Biological and Chemical Weapons

PROTOCOL FOR THE PROHIBITION OF THE USE IN WAR OF ASPHYXIATING, POISONOUS, OR OTHER GASES, AND OF BACTERIOLOGICAL METHODS OF WARFARE (GENEVA, JUNE 17, 1925; ENTERED INTO FORCE FEBRUARY 8, 1928; FOR THE UNITED STATES, APRIL 10, 1975. 26 UST 571; TIAS 8061; 94 LNTS 65)

This is the original treaty against the use of poison gas (which had been extensively employed by both sides in World War I) and bacterial agents. In general, the treaty was adhered to during World War II.

Convention on the Prohibition of the Development, Production, and Stockpiling of Bacteriological and Toxin Weapons and on Their Destruction (Washington, London, and Moscow, April 10, 1972; entered into force March 26, 1975. 26 UST 583; TIAS 8062; 1015 UNTS 163)

This treaty prohibits the development, production, and stockpiling of bacteriological (biological) and toxin weapons and requires the destruction of existing stockpiles.

Convention on the Prohibition of the Development, Production, Stockpiling and Use of Chemical Weapons and on Their Destruction, with Annexes (Paris, January 13, 1993; entered into force April 29, 1997)

This treaty provides a rigorous schedule for the destruction of chemical weapons stockpiles among signatory nations. It was originally signed by 144 nations and as of October 2001, 18 more nations had added their signatures to the agreement.

Genocide and Human Rights

Convention on the Prevention and Punishment of the Crime of Genocide (Paris, December 9, 1948; entered into force January 12, 1951; for the United States, February 23, 1989)

This convention was enacted in the aftermath of the Holocaust and reflected the declaration of the crime of genocide in the Nuremberg Tribunal following World War II. It was applied in 1998 when the International Criminal Tribunal for Rwanda convicted a Rwandan army major for genocide for inciting Hutu mobs to rape and attack Tutsis. While it is unlikely this provision would be applied to ordinary terrorist groups, it could become relevant if the terrorist group is motivated by race hatred, or if a government attacked an ethnic group in the guise of counterterrorism.

HELSINKI FINAL ACT, CONFERENCE ON SECURITY AND COOPERATION IN EUROPE, 1975

This treaty was signed by most European nations as well as the United States and the Soviet Union. Besides dealing with the peaceful resolution of international disputes, the agreement provides the following:

> "*The participating States will respect human rights and fundamental freedoms, including the freedom of thought, conscience, religion or belief, for all without distinction as to race, sex, language or religion.*" It also provides that
>
> *The participating States on whose territory national minorities exist will respect the right of persons belonging to such minorities to equality before the law, will afford them the full opportunity for the actual enjoyment of human rights and fundamental freedoms and will, in this manner, protect their legitimate interests in this sphere.*

While not directly dealing with terrorism, this agreement could potentially both restrict suppressive counterterrorism and enhance the rights of ethnic minority groups, thus reducing the potential for terrorism. The agreement resulted in the creation of a network of national groups monitoring compliance with the agreement.

INTERNATIONAL COVENANT ON CIVIL AND POLITICAL RIGHTS (NEW YORK, DECEMBER 16, 1966; ENTERED INTO FORCE MARCH 23, 1976; FOR THE UNITED STATES, SEPTEMBER 8, 1992)

This fundamental document, ratified by more than 140 nations, specifies civil and political rights including political and social self-determination and equal and due process in legal proceedings. The agreement prohibits torture and scientific experimentation without a person's consent, as well as slavery. Theoretically, at least, it would prevent extrajudicial antiterrorism measures, though a clause in the agreement does allow for its abrogation "in time of public emergency."

Maritime

Protocol for the Suppression of Unlawful Acts Against the Safety of Fixed Platforms Located on the Continental Shelf (Rome, March 10, 1988; entered into force March 1, 1992; for the United States, March 6, 1995)

Similar to laws against sabotage of civil aviation, this agreement deals with offenses in which an individual or individuals seize a ship, attack personnel on board, damage a ship, or otherwise interfere with its safe navigation and operation. It specifies the taking into custody of persons suspected of such offenses, and the cooperation of the nation where the arrest is made, the nation to whom the ship is registered, and the nation where the suspects reside, and encourages the promotion of extradition for such offenses.

Nuclear Materials

Convention of the Physical Protection of Nuclear Materials, with Annex (Vienna, October 26, 1979; entered into force February 8, 1987)

This treaty, signed by 45 nations, restricts the transport of nuclear materials to or through nonsignatory nations and provides standards for protecting the integrity of shipments and recovering them in case of theft. Signatories are required to criminalize the theft or fraudulent obtaining of nuclear materials or the use of such materials in attacks or threatened attacks and to make these extraditable offenses. The treaty was further affirmed in 1992.

Treaty on the Nonproliferation of Nuclear Weapons (Washington, London, and Moscow, July 1, 1968; entered into force March 5, 1970)

This treaty, among other things, requires that

> *Each nuclear-weapon State Party to the Treaty undertakes not to transfer to any recipient whatsoever nuclear weapons or other nuclear explosive devices*

or control over such weapons or explosive devices directly, or indirectly; and not in any way to assist, encourage, or induce any non-nuclear-weapon State to manufacture or otherwise acquire nuclear weapons or other nuclear explosive devices, or control over such weapons or explosive devices.

By attempting to restrict the possession of nuclear weapons to those nations already having them, the treaty attempts to make development of nuclear weapons by "rogue states" (some of whom support terrorism) less likely.

Terrorism (General)

Convention to Prevent and Punish the Acts of Terrorism Taking the Form of Crimes Against Persons and Related Extortion That Are of International Significance (Washington, D.C., February 2, 1971; entered into force October 16, 1973)

This treaty requires that signatories take

all the measures that they may consider effective, under their own laws, and especially those established in this convention, to prevent and punish acts of terrorism, especially kidnapping, murder, and other assaults against the life or physical integrity of those persons to whom the state has the duty according to international law to give special protection, as well as extortion in connection with those crimes.

It provides for the extradition or prosecution of offenders.

Convention on the Prevention and Punishment of Crimes Against Internationally Protected Persons, Including Diplomatic Agents (New York, December 14, 1973; entered into force February 20, 1977. 28 UST 1975; TIAS 8532; 1035 UNTS 167)

This treaty deals with attacks against or kidnapping of government officials or diplomats, who are "internationally protected persons."

International Convention Against the Taking of Hostages (New York, December 17, 1979; entered into force June 3, 1983; for the United States, January 6, 1985. TIAS 11081)

This treaty deals with the taking of hostages "in order to compel a third party, namely, a State, an international intergovernmental organization, a natural or juridical person, or a group of persons, to do or abstain from doing any act as an explicit or implicit condition for the release of the hostage." Signatories are required to take measures against groups in their territory who may be planning such hostage taking, to facilitate the freeing and repatriation of hostages, and to extradite or prosecute alleged hostage takers.

International Convention for the Suppression of the Financing of Terrorism (Adopted by the General Assembly of the United Nations in Resolution 54/109, December 9, 1999)

This agreement defines and prohibits terrorist acts and prohibits individuals from participating in such acts or providing funds or other resources to groups known to be terrorist.

Torture

Convention Against Torture and Other Cruel, Inhuman, or Degrading Treatment or Punishment (New York, December 10, 1984; entered into force June 26, 1987; for the United States, November 20, 1994)

Article 5 of the Universal Declaration of Human Rights and Article 7 of the International Covenant on Civil and Political Rights provides that no one shall be subjected to torture or to cruel, inhuman, or degrading treatment or punishment. This agreement requires signatories to take legal measures to prevent the use of torture within its territory. Torture may not be justified under any circumstances, even national emergency. The prosecution and extradition of persons accused of committing acts of torture is specified.

Warfare

Convention Respecting the Laws and Customs of War on Land, with Annex of Regulations (The Hague, October 18, 1907; entered into force January 26, 1910. 36 Stat. 2277; TS 539; 1 Bevans 631)

Among other things, this agreement deals with the responsibilities of military forces, the treatment of prisoners of war, prohibition on the use of "poisoned weapons," and the responsibility of an attacker to avoid unnecessary damage to civilians or nonmilitary buildings.

Convention Relative to the Treatment of Prisoners of War (Geneva, August 12, 1949; entered into force October 21, 1950; for the United States, February 2, 1956. 6 UST 3316; TIAS 3364; 75 UNTS 135)

The famous Geneva Convention forms the basis for the rights of prisoners in modern war, specifying what may be demanded of prisoners and what treatment must be provided them. The treaty was reaffirmed and expanded in 1977.

Convention Relative to the Protection of Civilian Persons in Time of War (Geneva, August 12, 1949; entered into force October 21, 1950; for the United States, February 2, 1956. 6 UST 3516; TIAS 3365; 75 UNTS 287)

This agreement requires the humane treatment of civilians and also combatants whose injuries or other circumstances have removed them from active combat. Hospitals and other facilities for the treatment of such persons are not to be attacked.

POST–SEPTEMBER 11 LEGISLATION

The legislation passed in the wake of the September 11, 2001, attacks includes new funding for recovery and counterterrorism efforts, creation of new agencies, reorganization of existing ones, and a broadening of investigatory and prosecutorial powers considerably beyond the 1996 antiterrorism act.

VICTIMS OF TERRORISM TAX RELIEF ACT OF 2001

This act provides income tax exemptions and other tax relief to terrorism victims and their families. It includes additional tax relief (such as more favorable depreciation treatment) for the area of New York City around the former World Trade Center.

2001 EMERGENCY SUPPLEMENTAL APPROPRIATIONS ACT FOR RECOVERY FROM AND RESPONSE TO TERRORIST ATTACKS ON THE UNITED STATES

This provides $40 billion in funding for relief and recovery from the September 11, 2001, terrorist attacks, with allocation of half dependent on subsequent action by Congress. Funding is to be used for heightening federal, state, and local preparedness; investigation and prosecution of terrorists; providing increased transportation security; and repairing damaged transportation systems and other infrastructure.

AIR TRANSPORTATION SAFETY AND SYSTEM STABILIZATION ACT, 2001

The act provides up to $5 billion in grants and $10 billion in credit for airlines to compensate them for losses suffered as a consequence of the 9/11 terrorist attacks or the halt in operations ordered by the government after the attacks. Also, it establishes procedures for compensation for individuals killed or injured in the terrorist attacks.

PUBLIC HEALTH SECURITY AND BIOTERRORISM PREPAREDNESS AND RESPONSE ACT OF 2002

This directs the secretary of Health and Human Services (HHS) to develop and implement a "coordinated strategy" for dealing with bioterrorism and related public health emergencies. It provides assistance to states to upgrade infrastructure including public health laboratories, health monitoring systems, and training and protection for personnel who are called upon to respond to emergencies. In addition, it provides for a national stockpile of vaccines and drugs for treating disease outbreaks.

ENHANCED BORDER SECURITY AND VISA ENTRY REFORM ACT OF 2002

This provides for an increase of 200 Immigration and Naturalization Service (INS) inspectors and upgraded technology for INS and Border Patrol, including information and identification systems for immigrants. It also provides for monitoring of foreign students and exchange visitors.

Aviation and Transportation Security Act

The act establishes the Transportation Security Administration within the Department of Transportation. The new agency is responsible for airline security, including airport passenger and baggage screening (formerly supervised by the Federal Aviation Administration), which will now be carried out by federal employees. It expands use of air marshals aboard airliners and includes safety measures for rail, highway, and other forms of transportation.

Uniting and Strengthening America by Providing Appropriate Tools Required to Intercept and Obstruct Terrorism (USA PATRIOT) Act of 2001

This is arguably the most important legislation passed in response to the September 11, 2001, attacks. It broadens a variety of law enforcement, surveillance, intelligence-gathering, and prosecutorial powers. Some significant provisions of the USA PATRIOT Act include the following:

- The president may freeze U.S. assets of any country, organization, or person upon determining that there is a threat to U.S. national security.
- The legislation authorizes and promotes the sharing of foreign intelligence information between federal agencies, easing, for example, the traditional legal barriers between the CIA as foreign intelligence agency and the FBI's role in domestic intelligence and counterintelligence.
- The government can more easily "trap and trace" communications and extend these activities to e-mail and other computer-based communications, including stored files.
- "Roving" surveillance that is not tied to a particular communications device but follows the target is permitted.
- Anti–money laundering requirements are extended from banks and other financial institutions to securities brokers and dealers and prohibit various practices used to conceal the source of funds.
- The act expands the ability to deport aliens associated with terrorist groups or who advocate or otherwise support terrorist actions.
- Terrorist activity now falls under the category of "racketeering," allowing application of the RICO (Racketeer Influenced and Corrupt Organizations) statute.
- Penalties for terrorist activity are increased, "harboring a terrorist" is defined as a crime, and the statute of limitation for terrorist activity that "resulted in or created a foreseeable risk of death or serious bodily injury to another person" is removed.
- "Knowing possession" of a biological agent or toxin for other than legitimate purposes such as medical research is outlawed.

COURT CASES

The following court cases deal with legal issues that are particularly relevant to the prosecution of the war on terrorism following the September 11 attacks. Some cases, particularly those dealing with the use of military tribunals, date back to the 19th century but have become relevant in light of recent events. Some recent cases have not yet reached trial but are included because of their potential importance.

EX PARTE MILLIGAN, 71 U.S. 2 (1866)

Background

Lambdin P. Milligan was arrested in Indiana in 1864 by order of General Alvin B. Hovey, commander of the military district of Indiana. Although the Civil War was in progress, there was essentially no fighting in Indiana. Milligan was not a member of the U.S. armed forces and thus not ordinarily subject to military justice. Nevertheless, he was tried by a military commission on charges that he had attempted to aid and abet the Confederate rebellion by creating a secret military organization to attack Indiana and other Union states.

Legal Issues

Upon his conviction and death sentence, Milligan appealed to the U.S. circuit court in Indiana under the Habeas Corpus Act of 1863. He argued that he was not subject to the jurisdiction of the military court. The government's initial argument was that the federal courts did not have jurisdiction over appeals from military courts. The circuit court divided on the question, so the Supreme Court agreed to hear the matter. The Court began by deciding that Milligan could use the right of habeas corpus to appeal from the military to a civilian court.

In his opinion, Justice Davis went on to the question of whether the use of the military court was legitimate. He defined the crux of the matter as

> *Upon the facts stated in Milligan's petition, and the exhibits filed, had the military commission mentioned in it jurisdiction, legally, to try and sentence him? Milligan, not a resident of one of the rebellious states, or a prisoner of war, but a citizen of Indiana for twenty years past and never in the military or naval service, is, while at his home, arrested by the military power of the United States, imprisoned, and, on certain criminal charges preferred against him, tried, convicted, and sentenced to be hanged by a military commission, organized under the direction of the military commander of the military district of Indiana. Had this tribunal the legal power and authority to try and punish this man?*

Justice Davis stated the government's claim as follows:

> *It is claimed that martial law covers with its broad mantle the proceedings of this military commission. The proposition is this: that in a time of war the commander of an armed force (if in his opinion the exigencies of the country demand it, and of which he is to judge), has the power, within the lines of his military district, to suspend all civil rights and their remedies, and subject citizens as well as soldiers to the rule of his will; and in the exercise of his lawful authority cannot be restrained, except by his superior officer or the President of the United States.*

Decision

Justice Davis observed,

> *If this position is sound to the extent claimed, then when war exists, foreign or domestic, and the country is subdivided into military departments for mere convenience, the commander of one of them can, if he chooses, within his limits, on the plea of necessity, with the approval of the Executive, substitute military force for and to the exclusion of the laws, and punish all persons, as he thinks right and proper, without fixed or certain rules.*

He then concluded that this position was incompatible with the constitution and with the essence of "republican government."

> *The statement of this proposition shows its importance; for, if true, republican government is a failure, and there is an end of liberty regulated by law. Martial law, established on such a basis, destroys every guarantee of the Constitution, and effectually renders the "military independent of and superior to the civil power"—the attempt to do which by the King of Great Britain was deemed by our fathers such an offense, that they assigned it to the world as one of the causes which impelled them to declare their independence. Civil liberty and this kind of martial law cannot endure together; the antagonism is irreconcilable; and, in the conflict, one or the other must perish.*

Although the Court had generally held during the war that it had no jurisdiction to hear appeals from military tribunals, the Court now ruled that martial law could only be applied to American civilians under circumstances where, because of foreign invasion or insurrection, the regular courts were closed.

Impact

This decision is still referred to as an important affirmation of the supremacy of legal protection for persons under the normal judicial system except under the most extreme circumstances. However the following case, *Ex Parte Quirin*, at least in some aspects reversed the holding in *Milligan.*

Ex Parte Quirin, 317 U.S. 1 (1942)

The first military tribunal case *(Milligan)* arose from America's worst domestic conflict. The next case came in the midst of the nation's greatest international challenge, World War II.

Eight German saboteurs were landed from a submarine—four in Long Island and four in Florida. Although they had lived in the United States previously, they had returned to Germany in the 1930s, and all but one acknowledged German citizenship. They were under German military orders to attempt to disrupt or destroy key installations involved with the U.S. economy and war effort. The saboteurs proved to be quite inept and were quickly swept up by the FBI, which turned them over to the U.S. military for trial. The saboteurs filed habeas corpus petitions. The petitions were denied by the District Court for the District of Columbia and the matter passed to the Supreme Court for review. The Court held a special session to consider the petition in an expedited manner.

Legal Issues

The attorneys for the accused Germans argued that the military did not have jurisdiction because, among other things, as specified in *Milligan*, the regular U.S. courts were open and available for trial.

Decision

The Court rejected the habeas petition, first noting that

> *The Constitution thus invests the President as Commander in Chief with the power to wage war which Congress has declared, and to carry into effect all laws passed by Congress for the conduct of war and for the government and regulation of the Armed Forces, and all laws defining and punishing offences against the law of nations, including those which pertain to the conduct of war.*

Applying the laws of war, the Court also stated,

> *The . . . enemy combatant who without uniform comes secretly through the lines for the purpose of waging war by destruction of life or property, are familiar examples of belligerents who are generally deemed . . . to be offenders against the law of war subject to trial and punishment by military tribunals.*

Because the Germans were subject to the law of war and had violated it, the military jurisdiction was upheld.

Impact

Although this decision appears to reverse *Ex Parte Milligan*, there are some differences in the circumstances (for example, unlike the Germans, Milligan was a U.S. citizen). However, by upholding military jurisdiction over an "unlawful combatant" serving an enemy of the United States, *Quirin* has been cited as a strong precedent for upholding the use of military tribunals for trying terrorists captured by the U.S. military.

U.S. v. Wang Kun Lue and Chen De Yian, U.S. 2d Circ., 96–1314 (1996)

Background

This case arose from an "ordinary" kidnapping, not an act of terrorism. Wang Kun Lue and various coconspirators were charged with meeting in New York City and planning to kidnap another individual, Chan Fung Chung, for ransom. The actual kidnap attempt failed when the victim's cries attracted the attention of a nearby firefighter and an off-duty police officer. Defendant Chen De Yian originally pled guilty to "(1) violating 18 U.S.C. Sec. 1203, the Act for the Prevention and Punishment of the Crime of Hostage-Taking ("Hostage Taking Act"), Pub. L. No. 98–473, Title II, Sec. 2002(a), 98 Stat. 2186 (1984), and (2) carrying a firearm in relation to the hostage taking in violation of 18 U.S.C. Sec. 924(c)," as part of a plea bargain. He later sought review of his conviction from the appeals court.

Legal Issues

These U.S. code provisions implement the International Treaty Against the Taking of Hostages, signed in 1979. According to the court record,

> *Defendant first argues that the district court erred in holding that Congress has the authority to pass the Hostage Taking Act under the Necessary and Proper Clause of Article I, [1] as an adjunct to the Executive's acknowledged authority under Article II to enter into treaties, with the advice and consent of the Senate. [2] Chen contends that (1) the Hostage Taking Act is unconstitutional because the Hostage Taking Convention upon which it is based exceeds the Executive's authority under the Treaty Clause and (2) even if entry into the Convention is in accord with the treaty-making authority, the Hostage Taking Act is not a "plainly adapted" means of effectuating the Convention's ends and thus exceeds Congress's authority under the Necessary and Proper clause.*

Further, the defendant-appellant argued that because the federal legislation involved hostage taking that took place entirely within the United States and involved only U.S. citizens, Congress had gone beyond the proper subject of an international treaty.

Decision

The court quickly dismissed the challenge to the treaty-making power and Congress's implementation of it as being well-settled law. The court quoted constitutional expert Lawrence Tribe as observing in an example that while "The President and the Senate could not . . . create a fully operating national health care system in the United States by treaty with Canada, in the court's words, "within such generous limits, it is not the province of the judiciary to impinge upon the Executive's prerogative in matters pertaining to foreign affairs."

In interpreting the international law, the court stated that according to the *Restatement (Third) of the Foreign Relations Law of the United States*, Section 302,

> *Contrary to what was once suggested, the Constitution does not require that an international agreement deal only with "matters of international concern." The references in the Constitution presumably incorporate the concept of treaty and of other agreements in international law. International law knows no limitations on the purpose or subject matter of international agreements, other than that they may not conflict with a peremptory norm of international law. States may enter into an agreement on any matter of concern to them, and international law does not look behind their motives or purposes in doing so. Thus, the United States may make an agreement on any subject suggested by its national interests in relations with other nations.*

Having dismissed the challenge to the treaty-making and implementation powers, the court concluded that the argument that the hostage taking act was not a "necessary and proper" implementation of the treaty was not valid. The law needs only to have a "rational relationship" to the objectives of the treaty, and a law against hostage taking is rationally related to a treaty that is designed to deter hostage taking. A challenge under the Tenth Amendment (powers reserved to the states) was ruled immaterial, because the treaty power is one specifically given to the executive. Finally, a challenge on equal protection grounds argued that the hostage taking act, by treating citizens and aliens differently, impermissably discriminated. The court ruled, however, that this equal treatment provision bound only state and local governments, not the federal government, which has sole authority to regulate immigration and aliens.

Impact

This case implies that an attempt to overturn an antiterrorism law because it seems to be an overextension of an international treaty is likely to fail. The courts give great deference to the constitutional treaty-making power of the executive and to Congress's ability to implement treaties.

RENO V. AMERICAN-ARAB ANTI-DISCRIMINATION COMMITTEE, ET AL., 97-1252 (1999)

Background

In 1987, the INS began deportation proceedings against seven Palestinians and a Kenyan on the grounds that they were advocates of "doctrines of world communism" in violation of the cold war–era McCarran-Walter Act. When the constitutionality of this law was questioned, prosecutors replaced the charges with others relating to involvement with groups that engage in destruction of property or terrorist attacks.

The underlying reason for deporting the aliens, however, was that they had been distributing literature and carrying out other work for the Popular Front for the Liberation of Palestine, which has engaged in both terrorist and political activities.

Legal Issues

The defendants argued that the First Amendment protected their rights of association and political advocacy, and thus they could not be deported solely on grounds of their association with a particular group. They claimed they were engaged in lawful political activity and had no involvement with terrorism.

Decision

On the government's appeal from the Court of Appeals for the Ninth Circuit, the Supreme Court ruled by a 6-3 majority that the government can select illegal aliens for deportation on the basis of their political views or group associations. Writing for the Court, Justice Antonin Scalia said that "an alien unlawfully in this country has no constitutional right to assert selective enforcement as a defense against his deportation." Scalia further noted that government officials may well have legitimate but sensitive reasons relating to foreign policy or national security for wanting to deport certain aliens and that the government should not be obliged to have to make those reasons public. However, Justice John Paul Stevens in a concurring opinion asserted that there were limits to the government's discretion and that it could not punish otherwise innocent people simply for being members of a proscribed group.

The three dissenting justices said that the Court, which had previously decided not to take up the substantive issue, should have confined itself to the procedural issue of whether the Antiterrorism and Effective Death Penalty Act of 1996 had precluded the appeals courts from having jurisdiction over such deportation decisions. The dissenters thus criticized the majority for unnecessarily making such a broad ruling that would deny basic First Amendment protections for aliens.

Impact

Although the case was remanded to the lower courts on procedural grounds, the real impact comes from the willingness of the Court majority, as evidenced by Justice Scalia's opinion, to deny the First Amendment protections of freedom of association and of expression to deportable aliens. Combined with the acceptance of the 1996 law's restrictions on appeals, the result is that the government has very broad discretion in deporting aliens that it believes to be associated with terrorist groups and that such aliens will have little recourse to the courts in the future.

Kiareldeen v. Reno, 71 F. Supp. 2d 402, 419 (D.N.J. 1999)

Background

Hany Kiareldeen, a Palestinian resident of the United States since 1990 and a student at Rutgers University in New Jersey, married a U.S. citizen in 1997 and applied for permanent residency status. In March 1998, however, INS and FBI agents arrested Kiareldeen, charging him with having stayed in the country too long after completing his studies. He was detained without bail. In removal proceedings Kiareldeen acknowledged that he had overstayed his visa but said that he had earlier asked for a "discretionary adjustment" of his status based on a claim for political asylum (he faced the threat of persecution or torture if he returned to his homeland). The INS, however, presented secret evidence to the judge that claimed that Kiareldeen was a member of a Palestinian terrorist group and thus a threat to U.S. national security.

At the conclusion of the first removal hearing, the judge ordered a reconsideration of whether Kiareldeen should continue to be detained pending conclusion of the legal process. At the second removal hearing, the judge determined that "[a]n evaluation of the evidence by a person of ordinary prudence and caution cannot sustain a finding that this respondent has engaged in terrorist activity." On April 2, 1999, the judge ordered that Kiareldeen's immigration status be adjusted and that he be freed on $1,500 bail pending completion of the proceedings.

The government appealed to the Board of Immigration Appeals (BIA), which stayed the order for Kiareldeen's release and then voted 2 to 1 to deny his release. The FBI announced that it had closed its criminal investigation, and although Kiareldeen had never been charged with any crime, he remained in INS detention. After another hearing, the BIA reversed its ruling and ordered that Kiareldeen be freed, but the government appealed to the attorney general's office for review. Meanwhile, however, a habeas corpus petition that Kiareldeen had previously filed came before a federal district court in New Jersey.

Legal Issues

In the habeas petition, Kiareldeen argued that the use of secret evidence and hearings was not authorized by any of the immigration statutes. Further, he argued that even if the evidence was authorized, it would be unconstitutional under the Fifth Amendment, which guarantees due process of law in criminal proceedings.

The broader legal issue was whether the use of secret evidence was permissible under the U.S. Constitution. Civil libertarians argued that the constitutional right to confront one's accusers and the state's evidence cannot be exercised if evidence and even witnesses are concealed from the defendant. Defenders of the practice argued that in certain circumstances evidence must be kept secret in order to protect vital intelligence sources, while at the same time dangerous terrorists must be prevented from entering the country.

Decision

Judge William Walls granted the habeas petition, ruling that Kiareldeen was being held without justification, and freed him after 19 months of detention. He began by addressing the use of secret evidence:

> *[T]he court does not ignore the warnings of [the previous Rafeedie and Anti-Discrimination Committee cases] . . . Minimally, these cases teach that the INS' reliance on secret evidence raises serious issues about the integrity of the adversarial process, the impossibility of self-defense against undisclosed charges, and the reliability of government processes initiated and prosecuted in darkness.*

The court further noted that the unclassified summaries that the INS had provided were inadequate, because they were not specific enough for the defense to determine what evidence needed to be rebutted or countered.

Responding to the government's argument that national security required the use of secret evidence, the court replied, "even if the interest is argued to be the undeniably weighty one of national security, as the government maintains, the court must inquire whether that interest is so all-encompassing that it requires that [Kiareldeen] be denied virtually every fundamental feature of due process," which "the Constitution directs must be extended to all persons within the United States, citizens and resident aliens alike."

Impact

Although the decision was narrow, based on procedural considerations in this case, the court had clearly expressed misgivings about the use of secret evidence and its impact on due process rights. Nonetheless, the use of secret evidence was expanded by the 1996 antiterrorism act and is likely to increase in the wake of the September 11, 2001, attack. Up to that time, courts apparently viewed the practice with suspicion (for example, another district court in *Rafeedie v. INS* had come to a similar conclusion). On the other hand, in *Reno v. American-Arab Anti-Discrimination Committee et al.* the Supreme Court had refused to extend First Amendment rights to noncitizens. The question remains whether the high court, confronted with arguments based on fundamental due process and the Fifth Amendment, might agree with the lower courts that the use of secret evidence is unacceptable. As of early 2003, the Supreme Court had not resolved this issue.

Humanitarian Law Project, et al. v. Reno, U.S. 9th Circ., 98-56062 (2001)

Background

Under the Antiterrorism and Effective Death Penalty Act (AEDPA) of 1996, it is illegal, among other things, to provide "material support" such as "training" or "personnel" to groups that have been designated as terrorist organizations by the U.S. government. Two such groups are the Kurdistan Workers' Party (PKK) and the Liberation Tigers of Tamil Eelam (LTTE), commonly known as the Tamil Tigers.

Supported by the Humanitarian Law Project and other organizations, in 1998 two American citizens sued to prevent the enforcement of the relevant AEDPA provisions, saying that they feared they would be punished if they carried out their intention of providing support for nonviolent humanitarian and political activities of the PKK and LTTE.

Legal Issues

Plaintiffs argued that established case law (as in the case of *NAACP v. Claiborne Hardware Co.*, 458 U.S. 886) prevented the government from punishing people for simply being associated with a group. To be legally liable, not only the group has to have unlawful goals, but also the individual in associating with the group must have a "specific intent to further those illegal aims." Plaintiffs also argued that the AEDPA gave the secretary of state "unfettered and unreviewable authority to designate which groups are foreign terrorist organizations" in violation of the First and Fifth Amendments, which protect freedom of association and the right to due process.

The District Court denied most of the plaintiff's claims; however, the district judge did agree that the AEDPA was "impermissibly vague" in banning the provision of "personnel" and "training." The idea behind impermissible vagueness is that people should not be punished for violating a law that is so imprecise that it is not possible to know with reasonable certainty whether one's conduct is in compliance with the law.

Decision

The plaintiff appealed the district court's decision. The Court of Appeals for the Ninth Circuit rejected the plaintiff's claim that the AEDPA punished mere association with or membership in terrorist groups. Rather, the court declared that "What AEDPA prohibits is the act of giving material support, and there is no constitutional right to facilitate terrorism by giving terrorists the weapons and explosives with which to carry out their grisly missions."

The circuit court also rejected the plaintiff's argument based on *Reno v. American-Arab Anti-Discrimination Committee* that a specific intent to break the law was needed before the government could punish "advocacy." The court said that what was being punished was not advocacy but the giving of material support and that once a group receives such support the donor has no control over what it is used for, lawful or not. Thus, the court held, it is reasonable for the government to ban such support, and doing so does not violate the First Amendment, which deals with association and advocacy.

The court then dealt with the connection between advocacy and the giving of money. The Supreme Court ruled in *Buckley v. Valeo* (424 U.S. 1) in 1976 that the government cannot ban contributions to political campaigns because of the practical connection between advocacy and contributing to political activities that further that advocacy. However, the circuit court noted that *Buckley* did not prevent all limitations on campaign spending and that at any rate, the AEDPA was not trying to regulate expression but to prevent terrorist activity.

The appeals court agreed with the district court that the ban on providing support and personnel was impermissibly vague, noting that "when a criminal law implicates First Amendment concerns," the law must be "sufficiently clear so as to allow persons of 'ordinary intelligence a reasonable opportunity to know what is prohibited.'" The court noted that under the existing language of the law, someone who is merely advocating for the group might be construed as supplying it with "personnel" and freeing up resources for other activities. Similarly, although the government claimed that the ban against providing training had to do with such things as training in weapons use or tactics, the law itself did not say that, and conceivably even teaching a group about international law might be deemed a violation of the AEDPA.

Impact

The decision essentially left intact the government's ability to ban aid to terrorist groups. The problems that the court found with vagueness can apparently be satisfactorily addressed by adding more precise language. In the wake of September 11, 2001, and the USA PATRIOT Act, the government's powers to ban assistance to terrorist groups have been further expanded.

The October 2002 arrest and indictment of six Yemeni immigrants in Lackawanna, New York, may lead to a new challenge to language prohibiting giving material aid to terrorist groups.

U.S. v. John Philip Walker Lindh, U.S. District Court for the District of Eastern Virginia, Crim. No. 02-37A (2002)

Background

U.S. citizen John Walker Lindh, dubbed the "American Taliban," became a convert to militant Islam and went to Afghanistan, where he joined Taliban forces that were fighting the Northern Alliance. After the September 11 terrorist attacks, U.S. forces joined in the battle against the Taliban. Lindh was captured in the course of a battle. He was charged with a number of counts, including aiding the Taliban against U.S. forces and carrying weapons and explosives in the course of his activities.

Legal Issues

The primary issues brought by the defense revolved around suppression of incriminating statements made by Lindh after his capture. The defense argued that Lindh was not told of his legal rights and that wounded, medicated, and held under physically harsh conditions, Lindh was not in a condition to make a legally informed or voluntary statement.

Decision

The case was resolved by a plea bargain. Lindh agreed to plead guilty to fighting for the Taliban and the carrying of a weapon and explosives (grenades). He was sentenced to 20 years in prison.

Impact

Analysts suggest that both Lindh and the government were strongly motivated to come to a plea agreement. Lindh faced an unsympathetic jury pool and if convicted, appeals court. The government, on the other hand, may have questioned its ability to sustain all the counts of the case and might have had to deal with negative publicity if details of Lindh's harsh treatment in Afghanistan were publicized.

Hamdi v. Rumsfeld, U.S. 4th Circ., 026895Pv2 (2002, pending)

Background

Like John Walker Lindh, Yaser Esam Hamdi is a U.S. citizen who went to Afghanistan to fight for the Taliban. He was captured by U.S. forces and initially held at Guantánamo Bay, Cuba, though when authorities learned he had been born in Louisiana and might still be able to claim American citizenship, he was transferred to the naval brig at Norfolk, Virginia.

After a writ of habeas corpus was filed, the Eastern district court in Virginia ruled that "Hamdi must be allowed to meet with his attorney because of fundamental justice provided under the Constitution." The government moved to block the meeting, and the Court of Appeals for the Fourth Circuit issued a stay and agreed to hear the government's appeal.

Legal Issues

The fundamental issue was whether the usual legal rights available to U.S. citizens could be set aside in favor of the president's power to declare a person to be an "unlawful combatant" subject to the exclusive jurisdiction of a military tribunal.

Decision

The appeals court opined that the district court had been too hasty in ignoring the government's prerogatives in times of active military hostilities. In particular, the government asserted the right to hold an "enemy combatant" without trial or counsel for the duration of the hostilities. Further, the district court had not properly considered the government's argument that allowing Hamdi access to counsel might allow the passage of sensitive information to terrorists.

The appeals court expressed great deference to the power of the executive branch in wartime matters. It directed that

> *Upon remand, the district court must consider the most cautious procedures first, conscious of the prospect that the least drastic procedures may promptly resolve Hamdi's case and make more intrusive measures unnecessary. Our Constitution's commitment of the conduct of war to the political branches of American government requires the court's respect at every step. Because the district court appointed counsel and ordered access to the detainee without adequately considering the implications of its actions and before allowing the United States even to respond, we reverse the court's June 11 order mandating access to counsel and remand the case for proceedings consistent with this opinion.*

In late October 2002, the appeals court heard further arguments in the case. On January 8, 2003, the court again rejected defense contentions, reiterating the need to show deference to the government under wartime conditions:

> *The safeguards that all Americans have come to expect in criminal prosecutions do not translate neatly to the arena of armed conflict. In fact, if deference is not exercised with respect to military judgments in the field, it is difficult to see where deference would ever obtain.*

Again focusing on the constitutional issue, the court noted that "the constitutional allocation of war powers affords the president extraordinarily broad authority as commander in chief and compels courts to assume a deferential posture in reviewing exercises of this authority." The opinion also noted that "courts are ill-positioned to police the military's distinction between those in the arena of combat who should be detained and those who should not."

Impact

The government has been able to arrange that prisoners such as Lindh and Hamdi are brought into the jurisdiction of a circuit that is widely believed to be conservative and favorably inclined toward upholding the government position. Like the case of Lindh, this case may well be resolved by plea bargain. If not, the Supreme Court may have to decide whether to uphold the government's contention that its decision to consider someone to be an unlawful combatant is essentially unreviewable by the courts.

U.S. v. Arnaout, U.S. District Court for the District of Northern Illinois, Eastern Division, Crim. No. 02-892 (2003)

Background

Enaam Arnaout, a Syrian-born U.S. citizen, was charged with raising money through his Islamic charitable organization, the Benevolence International Foundation (BIF), for use by al-Qaeda as well as by Islamic militant groups in Chechnya and Bosnia. The indictment laid out what it alleged was a "pipeline" of associations with al-Qaeda operatives by which Arnaout and the BIF funneled money and supplies to various groups. According to prosecutors, e-mails, photos, and documents seized in the BIF's Bosnia offices showed that Arnaout had been communicating directly with Osama bin Laden.

Arnaout was charged with perjury (for filing false declarations to the government) and racketeering fraud, alleging that he had defrauded donors to the BIF by concealing the fact that some of their money was being used to support militants and terrorists rather than for charitable purposes.

Legal Issues

Much of the government's evidence against Arnaout was filed in the form of a detailed document called a proffer. The proffer quoted documents and other evidence purporting to show links between the BIF and al-Qaeda, as well as citing an al-Qaeda operative who allegedly was told by bin Laden in 1993 that the BIF was one of al-Qaeda's funding channels. However, many of these alleged links were tenuous, and the authors of most of the documents or statements could not be verified or made available for questioning. Although second-hand (hearsay) material is allowed in certain cases in which obtaining direct testimony is impracticable, the prosecution must still show that a "preponderance of the evidence" links the defendant to the alleged conspiracy.

Decision

The federal judge ruled that the proffer did not meet the required standards of proof and was "devoid of analysis linking proffered hearsay to a specific conspiracy." She also ruled that the prosecutor could not, in his opening statement, link Arnaout to one particular alleged al-Qaeda operative, Mohamed Loay Bayazid, because the relevant evidence had not been supplied to the defense in a timely manner.

Although the prosecution could theoretically prepare new filings of statements by the coconspirators, they realized that the judge's decision made it very unlikely that they would be able to sustain the charges relating to aiding al-Qaeda. The government therefore agreed to a plea bargain in which Arnaout pled guilty only to a single count of racketeering conspiracy involving using money raised under false pretenses to supply boots and uniforms to Muslim fighters. Although Arnaout faces a sentence of up to 20 years in prison, leniency may be recommended if he cooperates with the government in providing further information about the fund-distribution network.

Impact

This case shows that it can be hard for prosecutors to prove illegal ties or activities involving individuals and terrorist groups. In many such cases the main evidence comes from documents that cannot be independently verified and coconspirators who are not available to testify. The result in this case suggests that even the somewhat relaxed standards of conspiracy law may still be too hard to meet. This situation, combined with frustration at not being able to effectively prosecute terrorist networks may lead to laws that relax the standards of evidence even farther, in turn creating concern about potential abuses (as has already been the case with other aspects of RICO when applied to "nontraditional" conspiracies).

CHAPTER 3

CHRONOLOGY

1989

- Osama bin Laden appears to have established a loose-knit organization called al-Qaeda (the Base) in order to promote terrorist attacks against the United States and other Western nations.

1991

- ***April:*** Osama bin Laden is expelled from Saudi Arabia for supporting antigovernment Islamists. He moves to Sudan.

1993

- ***February 26:*** A 1,000-pound bomb concealed in a van explodes in the underground garage of the World Trade Center in New York City, causing moderate damage to the structure, killing six people and injuring 1,042. Al-Qaeda is suspected, but there is no hard evidence.

1996

- The CIA assigns a task force to monitor Osama bin Laden's activities, as leader of al-Qaeda. Although Sudan offers to turn over bin Laden to the United States or Saudi Arabia, both refuse. U.S. officials believe they lack the evidence to convict bin Laden of a crime.
- ***May 18:*** Sudan expels Osama bin Laden. He moves to Afghanistan, where he had made close ties with Islamic fighters while helping the anti-Soviet Afghan resistance in the early 1980s.

1998

- ***February 22:*** Osama bin Laden issues a decree calling for direct attacks on U.S. citizens and property.

- ***June 7:*** Ramzi Ahmed Yousef, a close associate of bin Laden, is convicted and sentenced to life without parole for masterminding the 1993 World Trade Center bombing.
- ***August 7:*** Near-simultaneous bomb attacks on the U.S. embassies in Nairobi, Kenya, and Dar es Salam, Tanzania, kill 224 people. Osama bin Laden is later indicted in absentia by a U.S. grand jury for these attacks.
- ***August 20:*** The United States launches retaliatory cruise missile strikes on suspected terrorist installations in Afghanistan and Sudan. The United States claims that one target, a Sudanese pharmaceutical company, is a chemical weapons facility, but this assertion later turns out to be unsubstantiated.

1999

- ***October 12:*** The United States plans to sponsor a team of 60 Pakistani commandos to kill or capture Osama bin Laden. The operation is called off when a military coup overthrows Pakistani prime minister Nawaz Sharif.

2000

- ***October 12:*** Two suicide bombers in a small boat filled with explosives pull up to the U.S. destroyer *Cole* while it is refueling in Aden, Yemen. The explosion kills 17 people and tears a large gash in the side of the warship. The attack is believed to be connected to Osama bin Laden.

2001

- ***May 29:*** A U.S. district court finds Osama bin Laden guilty in absentia for conspiring to kill Americans through such acts as the 1998 embassy bombings in Africa.
- ***September 11:*** In New York City, two hijacked airliners heavy with fuel slam into the twin towers of the World Trade Center, at 8:46 A.M. and 9:03 A.M. By 10:30 A.M., both towers have collapsed. The death toll, overestimated at first, will eventually be set at about 2,790, which includes 147 passengers and crew aboard the two airlines. A third airliner hits the Pentagon in Washington, D.C., badly damaging part of one of the building's five sides and killing 184 people, including the 40 passengers and crew members on the plane. A fourth airliner, with 40 passengers, crashes in a field in western Pennsylvania after passengers apparently struggle with four hijackers for control of the cockpit, killing all aboard. The United States halts all commercial air traffic, and many government and major private facilities are evacuated. President George W. Bush gives a speech in the evening vowing to hunt down and punish the terrorists.

- ***September 12:*** The North Atlantic Treaty Organization (NATO) invokes a treaty clause declaring that the previous day's attacks against the United States will be treated as an attack against all NATO member nations. The UN Security Council and General Assembly pass resolutions condemning the attacks.
- ***September 13:*** U.S. airports reopen, except for Logan (Boston) and Reagan (Washington, D.C.). The U.S. government warns citizens against harassing or discriminating against Arab Americans.
- ***September 14:*** President George W. Bush declares a state of emergency and calls up 50,000 reservists to join in homeland defense. Meanwhile, an appropriation of $40 billion for victim relief and counterterrorism efforts is rushed through Congress.
- ***September 15:*** Boston's Logan airport reopens.
- ***September 15:*** President George W. Bush explicitly declares Osama bin Laden the "prime suspect" in the attacks. The FBI reports that it has 4,000 agents sifting through more than 40,000 leads relating to the terrorist attacks.
- ***September 16:*** The federal government orders the grounding of all crop-dusting aircraft in response to intelligence reports suggesting that they may be used for biological or chemical attacks.
- ***September 23:*** President George W. Bush signs a bill giving airlines $5 billion in direct payments and $10 billion in loan guarantees to help them deal with the effects of the air shutdown and the ongoing decline in air travel.
- ***September 28:*** The UN Security Council passes a comprehensive antiterrorism resolution.
- ***October 5:*** Robert Stevens, a photo editor at American Media in Boca Raton, Florida, dies of inhalation anthrax. This rare disease last killed an American in 1976.
- ***October 7:*** U.S. and British forces begin the air campaign against Taliban facilities in Afghanistan. Polls report that nine out of 10 Americans support the air strikes.
- ***October 7:*** A videotaped statement from Osama bin Laden (made from an unknown location) praises the September 11 attacks and declares that "neither America nor the people who live in it will dream of security before we live it in Palestine, and not before all the infidel armies leave the land of Muhammad."
- ***October 8:*** Former Pennsylvania governor Tom Ridge is appointed to head a new federal agency, the Office of Homeland Security.
- ***October 8:*** The U.S. Coast Guard steps up harbor patrols.
- ***October 10:*** The FBI releases a list of 22 most wanted terrorists.
- ***October 10:*** Air strikes against Taliban forces and infrastructure continue.

- ***October 11:*** The Senate passes a bill called the USA PATRIOT Act that gives law enforcement agencies broader powers to fight terrorism, authorizing roving wiretaps, detention of aliens without specific charges, and more aggressive tactics to combat money laundering. The next day the House approves a similar bill by a vote of 227-79.
- ***October 12:*** Thirty-nine names are added to the list of 27 organizations linked to the financing of terrorist activities. U.S. financial institutions are ordered to freeze their funds.
- ***October 12:*** A letter sent to NBC news anchor Tom Brokaw tests positive for anthrax spores. An assistant to Brokaw contracts the milder cutaneous (skin) form of the disease.
- ***October 14:*** President George W. Bush asks Congress to allocate $1.5 billion to the Department of Health and Human Services to deal with bioterrorism threats.
- ***October 15:*** A letter sent to Senate Majority Leader Tom Daschle tests positive for anthrax.
- ***October 17:*** President George W. Bush releases another $50 million in aid to Pakistan, for a total of $100 million.
- ***October 17:*** The House of Representatives building is closed for five days to test for anthrax.
- ***October 17:*** Australia and Canada agree to contribute forces to the campaign in Afghanistan.
- ***October 17:*** The Pentagon admits that an errant U.S. bomb has struck Red Cross warehouses in Afghanistan.
- ***October 18:*** Secretary of Defense Donald Rumsfeld announces a stepped-up propaganda campaign in Afghanistan, including radio broadcasts and leaflets dropped from aircraft. Meanwhile heavy air strikes in Afghanistan increase the flow of refugees fleeing across the border into Pakistan.
- ***October 18:*** An assistant to a CBS news anchor and a New Jersey letter carrier both test positive for cutaneous anthrax.
- ***October 21–23:*** Two Washington, D.C., postal workers die of inhalation anthrax.
- ***October 25:*** "Operation Green Quest," a multiagency task force led by the U.S. Customs Service is announced. Its objective is to dry up funding for terrorist groups by preventing money laundering.
- ***October 26:*** President George W. Bush signs the consolidated antiterrorist bill passed by the House and Senate as the USA PATRIOT Act.
- ***October 31:*** Transportation secretary Norman Mineta announces new, stricter security policies at U.S. airports and other transportation facilities. He urges citizens to show their patriotism by exercising patience.
- ***October 31:*** A New York woman, Kathy T. Nguyen, dies of inhalation anthrax. Altogether the attacks have killed five people.

- ***November 3:*** The independent Arabic television network al-Jazeera releases a videotape showing Osama bin Laden and some of his associates in an undisclosed location. Bin Laden condemns Arabs who cooperate with Western nations.
- ***November 4:*** Both Great Britain and Pakistan release statements saying that they find the evidence of Osama bin Laden's involvement in the September 11 terrorist attacks to be credible and sufficient for indictment.
- ***November 9:*** Northern Alliance forces backed by the United States and other Western countries capture the Afghanistan city of Mazār-i-Sharīf, a Taliban stronghold.
- ***November 9:*** President George W. Bush announces a 25 percent increase in the number of the National Guard and reserve troops, who have become a common sight at airports.
- ***November 13:*** U.S.-backed Northern Alliance forces enter Kabul, the capital of Afghanistan, as Taliban fighters flee into the countryside.
- ***November 16:*** U.S. officials say they believe Muhammad Atef, one of Osama bin Laden's closest aides, has been killed in a U.S. air strike south of Kabul.
- ***November 19:*** President George W. Bush signs a package of airline security measures in a ceremony at Washington's reopened Reagan National Airport. Provisions include strengthening cockpit doors and posting a larger number of armed federal marshals on flights. It also orders the federalization of airport screening workers (who had previously been the responsibility of airlines), requiring them to be U.S. citizens and pass a security screening.
- ***November 25:*** Another major Afghan city, Kandahār, falls to allied forces. U.S. Marines establish a major base for further operations to seek out and destroy Taliban and al-Qaeda forces.
- ***November 26:*** President George W. Bush warns Iraq it must allow inspectors to return to verify that the country is not developing weapons of mass destruction.
- ***November 26:*** Taliban prisoners being held in a fort in Mazār-i-Sharīf revolt and kill Michael Spann, a CIA officer who had been questioning prisoners.
- ***November 27:*** The FBI begins a program of interviews of 5,000 men in the United States, primarily of Middle Eastern origin.
- ***November 27:*** Afghani leaders including the Northern Alliance and supporters of the former king, Zahir Shah, attend a meeting in Bonn, Germany, to begin the process of forming a new government for Afghanistan.
- ***November 28:*** Under mounting pressure from Congress and civil liberties groups, Attorney General John Ashcroft reveals that federal charges have been filed against 104 suspects, of which 55 are in custody. An additional

548 people are in custody for immigration violations. He vows to "use every constitutional tool to keep suspected terrorists locked up."

- ***November 29:*** The House overwhelmingly passes a $318 billion defense appropriations bill that includes $20 billion specifically for expenses relating to the war on terrorism.
- ***December 1:*** Singapore arrests 15 persons suspected of links to al-Qaeda. They are believed to be targeting embassies, military bases, and other important installations.
- ***December 3:*** The United States and Canada agree to reinforce their border, which has been only lightly guarded. The United States deploys an additional 400 National Guard troops to border checkpoints.
- ***December 6:*** Speaking before the Senate Judiciary Committee, Attorney General John Ashcroft defends the use of military tribunals rather than civilian courts for trying terrorist suspects.
- ***December 13:*** A new videotape of Osama bin Laden is released by the Pentagon. On it he expresses satisfaction with the September 11 attacks, noting that his engineering experience had led him to believe that at least several floors of the twin towers might be destroyed and that the towers might even collapse above the impact points of the planes.
- ***December 13:*** A federal judge binds Zacarias Moussaoui for trial on multiple conspiracy charges relating to the September 11 attacks. Moussaoui, a French-Moroccan citizen, was arrested for immigration violations after his suspicious actions had been reported by a Minnesota flight school.
- ***December 18:*** Defense secretary Donald Rumsfeld tells NATO defense ministers that the war on terrorism would not be limited to Afghanistan but would extend to other countries where terrorists operated or that sponsored terrorism.
- ***December 20:*** British peacekeeping forces arrive in Kabul, and Hamid Karzai takes over as the country's interim leader.
- ***December 22:*** Richard Reid, a British citizen, is subdued by fellow airline passengers and attendants on a flight from Paris to Miami when he allegedly attempts to detonate explosives hidden in his shoes.
- ***December 27:*** Al-Jazeera TV broadcasts a new videotape in which Osama bin Laden refers to the September 11 attacks as a "blessed terror." It is unclear, however, when the tape was actually made.
- ***December 27:*** Defense secretary Donald Rumsfeld announces that captured al-Qaeda and Taliban prisoners will be transferred to the U.S. naval base in Guantánamo Bay, Cuba.

2002

- ***January 2:*** The United States has about 180 suspected al-Qaeda and Taliban fighters in custody.

- ***January 2:*** Afghanistan confirms that a U.S. airstrike the previous week killed Qari Ahmadullah, one of the chief Taliban intelligence operatives.
- ***January 2:*** Zacarias Moussaoui refuses to enter a plea on terrorist conspiracy charges in a federal court in Alexandria, Virginia; a federal judge enters a plea of not guilty for him.
- ***January 12:*** Pakistani president General Pervez Musharraf bans four militant Islamic groups believed to be associated either with the December 13, 2001, attack on the Indian parliament or with terrorist attacks in Pakistan. Tensions along the border between the two nuclear-armed nations have been high.
- ***January 12:*** The first 20 al-Qaeda and Taliban detainees arrive in Guantánamo Bay, Cuba. A temporary detention center called Camp X-Ray has been built for them.
- ***January 16:*** The first contingent of U.S. troops arrives in the Philippines. Their mission is to train Filipino soldiers in counterterrorism tactics in the struggle against Abu Sayyaf, an Islamic fundamentalist group with links to al-Qaeda.
- ***January 16:*** "American Taliban" John Walker Lindh is charged with four criminal counts in the U.S. district court in Alexandria, Virginia. Treason, a capital crime for which the Constitution requires two separate eyewitnesses, is not included among the charges.
- ***January 18:*** Alleged "shoe bomber" Richard Reid is indicted in Boston for nine charges including attempted murder and attempted destruction of an aircraft.
- ***January 29:*** In his State of the Union address, President George W. Bush refers to Iran, Iraq, and North Korea as an "axis of evil," citing their support of terrorism and development of weapons of mass destruction.
- ***February 8:*** Administration officials attempt to differentiate between the status of Taliban detainees and those associated with al-Qaeda. While the former will be treated as prisoners of war in accordance with the Geneva Convention, the latter will not be given that status, although they may be given some of its benefits.
- ***February 9:*** The 2002 Winter Olympic Games begin in Salt Lake City, Utah, under very tight security and concern about possible terrorist attacks. The games will be completed without significant incidents.
- ***February 10:*** At his arraignment John Walker Lindh pleads not guilty to what are now 10 charges, including conspiracy to kill Americans abroad.
- ***February 22:*** Pakistani officials confirm that *Wall Street Journal* reporter Daniel Pearl, who was kidnapped by Islamic terrorists in the preceding month, has been killed by his captors.
- ***February 27:*** Pentagon officials announce that up to 200 U.S. troops supported by 10 UH-1H Huey helicopters may be sent to the Republic

of Georgia to train local troops to fight terrorists who are operating near the country's border with Russia.

- ***February 28:*** Senate Majority Leader Tom Daschle, a Democrat, praises the accomplishments thus far in the war on terrorism but questions whether ongoing efforts have "a clear direction." Senate Minority Leader Trent Lott calls Daschle's comments divisive.
- ***March 1:*** President George W. Bush approves the deployment of up to 100 U.S. troops to Yemen to train the local military in counterterrorist tactics.
- ***March 2:*** In Operation Anaconda, the first major ground engagement involving the U.S. army in Afghanistan, a special forces soldier is killed in the Shahi Kot valley south of Kabul. Later in the week six more soldiers die when their helicopter is hit by enemy fire and crashes; a U.S. Navy Seal also dies after falling from a helicopter into enemy territory.
- ***March 6:*** The U.S. military reports that forces in Operation Anaconda have killed several hundred al-Qaeda and Taliban fighters.
- ***March 6:*** Georgian president Eduard Shevardnadze approves the U.S. plan to send a special forces contingent to Georgia to provide counterterrorism training.
- ***March 6:*** Attorney General John Ashcroft announces an expansion of Neighborhood Watch, a crime fighting program, to include "terrorism detection and prevention."
- ***March 9:*** Afghani women in Kabul celebrate International Women's Day by appearing in public without the body-covering *burkas* that had been required by the Taliban.
- ***March 10:*** The *Los Angeles Times* reports that a leaked classified Pentagon report contains plans to use nuclear weapons against Libya, Syria, China, Russia, Iran, Iraq, and North Korea under certain conditions.
- ***March 11:*** At the six-month anniversary of the September 11 attacks, President George W. Bush announces that the second phase of the war on terrorism has begun. He hints that the United States will attack any country that is building weapons of mass destruction; observers suggest that he particularly has Iraq in mind.
- ***March 11:*** Memorial ceremonies are held at the Pentagon and at the World Trade Center site, where two columns of powerful searchlights symbolically represent the destroyed towers.
- ***March 12:*** Director of Homeland Security Tom Ridge unveils the Homeland Security Advisory System. It will use a range of colors to indicate the severity of the terrorist threat. For each level there are suggested responses to be made by federal, state, and local governments.
- ***March 13:*** After nearly two weeks of intense fighting, the U.S. military reports that it has secured the Shahi Kot Mountains in Afghanistan. The area had been a rallying point for al-Qaeda and Taliban fighters.

- ***March 14:*** Holding his first regular press conference of the year, President George W. Bush says, "We're going to deal with [Saddam Hussein]. The first stage is to consult with our allies and friends, and that's exactly what we're doing."
- ***March 17:*** Two Americans and three Pakistanis are killed in a grenade attack at a church in Islamabad. Pakistan president Pervez Musharraf orders authorities to find and arrest the terrorists.
- ***March 20:*** Attorney General John Ashcroft reports the results of interviews with aliens from Islamic countries who entered the United States since January 2000. Of the first 4,000 cases, about 1,700 had left the country or could not be found. Ashcroft announces plans to interview another 3,000 persons who may have information regarding terrorism.
- ***March 20:*** Operation Anaconda officially ends with Major General Frank Hagenbeck declaring that it has made the world safer from terrorism.
- ***March 21:*** Secretary of Defense Donald Rumsfeld announces the procedures to be used by military commissions that will try al-Qaeda and Taliban suspects. He says that detainees will be presumed innocent, cannot be forced to testify against themselves, and will be allowed to challenge the evidence against them. However, they will be tried before a panel of U.S. military officers, not a civilian jury, and will have no right to appeal, with the president having the final say on any convictions.
- ***March 22:*** Ahmed Omar Saeed Sheikh and 10 other suspects are charged in Pakistan for the kidnapping and murder of *Wall Street Journal* reporter Daniel Pearl. Saeed has also been indicted in absentia by a U.S. court.
- ***March 24:*** General Tommy Franks, head of U.S. Central Command, says that evidence found in more than 50 sites in Afghanistan shows that al-Qaeda has been "in hot pursuit" of chemical and biological weapons.
- ***March 25:*** A Department of Transportation memo says that 70 percent of knives, 30 percent of guns, and 60 percent of simulated explosives were not detected by security screeners in airport security tests.
- ***March 25:*** A report released by Massachusetts representative Edward J. Markey states that U.S. nuclear power plants have lax security and that terrorists could have feasibly gained employment at the plants.
- ***March 29:*** Federal prosecutors announce that they will seek the death penalty against Zacarias Moussaoui, who faces six charges relating to the September 11 attacks. In keeping with their policy on capital punishment, French officials refuse to provide evidence that might be used to argue for the death penalty.
- ***March 30:*** Pakistani authorities aided by CIA and FBI agents capture 35 suspected terrorists in Faisalabad and Lahore.

- ***March 31:*** Afghani leaders announce plans for the convening of the Loya Jirga. This 1,500-member national council is expected to create a new government for Afghanistan.
- ***April 1:*** U.S. officials confirm that Abu Zubaida, a top al-Qaeda leader, has been captured in the raids in Pakistan.
- ***April 9:*** Attorney General John Ashcroft announces the indictment of four people, including an attorney, for providing material support and resources to a terrorist organization. Specifically, they are accused of helping Sheikh Omar Abdel Rahman, convicted in 1995 of plotting to blow up various buildings in New York, of carrying out terrorist activities from his prison cell.
- ***April 9:*** Justice Department officials say they have no immediate plans to bring charges against Yaser Esam Hamdi, the second American citizen found to be fighting with the Taliban.
- ***April 11:*** Attorney General John Ashcroft announces a new shared database to fight terrorism by combining federal and state records with foreign intelligence sources.
- ***April 23:*** Under Operation Tarmac, federal authorities arrest hundreds of airport workers in the Washington, D.C., area and then at 15 other airports nationwide. The workers are accused of making false statements about their criminal background or of committing immigration violations.
- ***April 28:*** The Pentagon confirms that U.S. troops are helping Pakistan track down Taliban and al-Qaeda suspects who have fled from Afghanistan into Pakistan.
- ***April 30:*** Enaam Arnaout, executive director of the Benevolence International Foundation, a charity based in Illinois, is arrested by federal agents, who charge him and his organization with providing logistical support to al-Qaeda.
- ***April 30:*** An expanded prison facility at Camp Delta, Guantánamo Bay, is opened. Three hundred al-Qaeda and Taliban detainees are transferred there from the crowded facilities at Camp X-Ray.
- ***May 2:*** A British-led allied force begins to scour an area in southeastern Afghanistan for al-Qaeda remnants.
- ***May 3:*** Over a two-day period, several small pipe bombs are found in rural mailboxes in Illinois, Iowa, and Nebraska.
- ***May 7:*** Lucas Helder is arrested on suspicion of having planted the mailbox bombs and later charged with using explosives to destroy property. Further investigation suggests that he is a disturbed individual with no links to terrorist groups.
- ***May 9:*** A car bomb explodes in Karachi, Pakistan, killing 12 people and wounding many more. No group claims responsibility, but Islamic militants upset with Pakistan's cooperation with the United States are suspected.

- ***May 10:*** A bomb explodes during a Victory Day parade in Dagestan, a southern Russian republic. No group claims responsibility, but Islamic militants are suspected.
- ***May 10:*** Attorney General John Ashcroft announces a new computerized system for keeping track of whether persons admitted to the United States under student visas are actually attending school.
- ***May 13:*** The American Trucking Association announces that it will train up to 3 million truckers to detect and report possible terrorist activity involving trucks and drivers, in an effort to protect bridges, tunnels, and other infrastructure from possible terrorist attacks.
- ***May 15:*** The *New York Times* breaks the story of an FBI agent who wrote a memo before September 11 urging that Middle Eastern men enrolled in U.S. flight schools be investigated for possible terrorist links. The memo suggested that terrorists might be taking flight lessons in order to use planes for attacks.
- ***May 17:*** President George W. Bush denies that he failed to act on any prior knowledge of possible terrorist attacks.
- ***May 17:*** The FBI informs apartment building managers that based on information the agency had received, terrorists may be planning to blow up buildings.
- ***May 21:*** Transportation secretary Norman Mineta tells the Senate Commerce Committee that he will not authorize the use of firearms by pilots in the cockpit.
- ***May 21:*** The State Department issues its annual *Patterns of Global Terrorism* report. It lists Iran, Iraq, North Korea, Libya, Cuba, Sudan, and Syria as governments that continue to sponsor terrorism. Defense secretary Donald Rumsfeld testifies to Congress that many of these countries are attempting to obtain weapons of mass destruction and have relationships to terrorist groups that would be willing to use them.
- ***May 28:*** The last steel girder is cut down at Ground Zero, the former World Trade Center site, marking the official end of the 37-week-long recovery effort.
- ***May 31:*** The Justice Department files a motion asking a federal court to prevent American-born suspected terrorist Yaser Esam Hamdi from meeting with his attorneys. They argue that he is an unlawful combatant and that his communication could be used to frustrate intelligence-gathering efforts.
- ***May 31:*** Attorney General John Ashcroft announces new guidelines for the FBI that will allow the agency to take the initiative in investigations of possible terrorist activities rather than only responding to evidence from other sources.

- ***June 4:*** Congress begins joint intelligence committee hearings on the failure of U.S. intelligence agencies to detect and prevent the plot leading to the September 11 attacks.
- ***June 6:*** President George W. Bush announces a plan to create a new, unified department to provide for homeland defense and security. The proposed department would draw employees and resources from many existing agencies including the Secret Service and U.S. Coast Guard but not the FBI or CIA.
- ***June 8:*** U.S.-backed Philippine commandos attempt to rescue hostages being held by the Abu Sayyaf rebel group. Two hostages are killed in the action; one is rescued.
- ***June 10:*** Attorney General John Ashcroft announces the arrest of Jose Padilla, a former Chicago gang member who has taken the name Abdullah al-Muhajir. He is alleged to have plotted to explode a radioactive dirty bomb in an American city but is held merely as an unlawful combatant without charges being brought. Later, Secretary of Defense Rumsfeld suggests that Padilla may not be tried but rather interrogated to find out what he knows.
- ***June 11:*** Afghanistan's Grand Council, or Loya Jirga, gathers in Kabul to organize a new government.
- ***June 11:*** The federal district court for eastern Virginia orders that Yaser Esam Hamdi, a suspected terrorist being detained at the Norfolk Naval Station brig without access to counsel, be allowed unmonitored access by the public defender.
- ***June 12:*** A U.S. district judge denies Zacarias Moussaoui access to documents that she says may contain information about airport security measures that might assist potential terrorists.
- ***June 12:*** A New Jersey appeals court rules that federal authorities are not required to reveal the names of persons who were held in the state following the September 11 attacks. The judge cites the government's paramount interest in national security; the American Civil Liberties Union will prepare an appeal to the New Jersey Supreme Court.
- ***June 13:*** Hamid Karzai, who has been serving as head of the interim Afghan government, is overwhelmingly elected by the Loya Jirga to be the head of the country's new government, or Transitional Authority.
- ***June 13:*** A car bomb explodes outside the U.S. consulate in Karachi, Pakistan, killing 12 people and injuring 51 others. A previously unknown group called al-Qanoon claims responsibility.
- ***June 13:*** The judge in the Zacarias Moussaoui trial permits him to defend himself against charges of terrorist conspiracy, although expressing misgivings about his course of action and later appointing an attorney to assist Moussaoui and serve as a backup if he proves unable to defend himself adequately.

- ***June 14:*** By an 83-1 vote, the Senate passes a law that will bring the United States into compliance with two international terrorism treaties by harmonizing laws relating to terrorist financing and extradition of bombing suspects.
- ***June 16:*** Senate Majority Leader Tom Daschle and House Majority Leader Dick Armey announce their intention to approve the new homeland security agency before September 11, 2002.
- ***June 22:*** Canadian authorities arrest Adel Tobbichi and accuse him of providing forged passports and otherwise helping terrorists plan an attack on the U.S. embassy in Paris.
- ***June 24:*** A report by a committee of the National Academy of Sciences says that more must be done to protect nuclear power plants and the power grid from terrorist attacks, and that the country as a whole has "enormous vulnerabilities" to chemical or biological attack.
- ***June 26:*** FBI agents search the apartment of an unidentified scientist in connection with their investigation of the anthrax mail attacks. The scientist works for a contractor at the U.S. Army's biological warfare laboratory at Fort Detrick, Maryland.
- ***July 4:*** A lone gunman opens fire at an El Al ticket counter at Los Angeles International Airport, killing two people and wounding three others before he is shot dead by the Israeli airline's security agents. Investigations suggest that the gunman, a limousine driver named Hesham Mohamed Hadayet, was motivated by unknown personal reasons rather than being connected to a terrorist group.
- ***July 8:*** Federal health officials announce that they are considering a range of possible scenarios involving a terrorist attack using smallpox. Responses to be considered range from selective inoculations of about 500,000 health and emergency service personnel to the vaccination of millions of people.
- ***July 11:*** The U.S. district court in New York rules that "material witnesses" may be detained pending grand jury hearings. The decision lends support to use of this tool in terrorism investigations following the September 11 attacks.
- ***July 12:*** The U.S. Court of Appeals for the Fourth Circuit overturns the June 11, 2002, decision of the district court allowing Hamdi access to counsel. The circuit court rules that the district court did not properly consider the implications of its actions for national security.
- ***July 15:*** A Pakistani court sentences four terrorists for the death of *Wall Street Journal* reporter Daniel Pearl. Ahmed Omar Saeed Sheikh is sentenced to death; the other three receive life sentences. The defense intends to appeal on the grounds that the judge was acting under pressure from the United States.

- ***July 16:*** President George W. Bush sends Congress his new domestic security and homeland defense proposals. These include a coordinated plan to assess and protect critical infrastructure, using "red teams" to test defenses with mock terrorist attacks, and the loosening of legal restrictions on use of the military within U.S. borders.
- ***July 17:*** In the unclassified portion of its report, the House Subcommittee on Terrorism and Homeland Security urges U.S. intelligence agencies to be more aggressive in attempting to penetrate terrorist groups, pursue leads, and disrupt terrorist plots.
- ***July 17:*** The Treasury Department proposes regulations that would require financial institutions to obtain and maintain detailed verification of customers' identities, including drivers' licenses and Social Security numbers or taxpayers' ID numbers. A database link to the Social Security Administration would be used to verify Social Security numbers. However officials deny that this is a move toward a national ID number.
- ***July 17:*** Omar Shishani, a Jordanian American returning from Indonesia, is arrested at the Detroit airport after authorities find $12 million in fraudulent checks in his baggage. Authorities later reveal that he also was carrying passages from the Qur'an (Koran) referring to genocide and martyrdom and that he had offered to tell authorities about terrorism. He is held without bail.
- ***July 18:*** Zacarias Moussaoui attempts to enter a guilty plea in his federal trial for terrorist conspiracy but seems not to understand its implications, and the judge refuses to accept it. When Moussaoui continues to insist, the judge recesses the hearing for a week to see whether he will change his mind. The following week he enters a plea of not guilty, saying that it is his religious duty to "defend his life."
- ***July 24:*** Congress approves an antiterrorism package worth $28.9 billion. About half goes to pay and upgrades for the military and intelligence agencies; $5.5 billion is allocated for relief and rebuilding in New York City. Most of the rest goes to agencies involved in homeland defense (including the new Transportation Security Administration, the U.S. Coast Guard, and the FBI) and to "first response" training and protection of nuclear facilities.
- ***July 25:*** The National Conference of State Legislatures issues a call for state governments to take a greater role in gathering antiterrorism information and in training first responders to deal with possible terrorist attacks.
- ***July 25:*** The Bush administration threatens to veto the bill creating the Department of Homeland Security because it extends civil service protections to the new agency's employees. The administration argues that this would prevent the agency from getting rid of incompetent workers or giving merit pay to those who perform well.

- ***July 25:*** The House votes to create an independent commission to review the performance of U.S. intelligence agencies with regard to the September 11 attacks. The provision had been opposed by the Bush administration, which had wanted any inquiry to be conducted only by the existing House and Senate intelligence committees.
- ***August 8:*** A panel of the U.S. circuit court of appeals in Philadelphia rules 2-1 that the media can be barred from secret deportation hearings being held under 1996 antiterrorism legislation. The court noted, "Even minor pieces of evidence that might appear innocuous to us would provide valuable clues to a person within the terrorist network."
- ***August 26:*** An appeals court, affirming a ruling from the federal District Court for the Eastern District of Michigan rules that the decision whether to close deportation hearings involving terrorism issues must be made on a case-by-case basis. Judge Damon Keith also comments that "the executive branch seeks to uproot peoples' lives outside the public eye and behind a closed door. Democracies die behind closed doors." The conflicting opinion (see August 8) may have to be resolved by the Supreme Court.
- ***August 29:*** James Ujaama, an African-American citizen of Seattle, is arrested on his return to the United States after having spent five years in London. Authorities charge that Ujaama, who had been a respected entrepreneur in Seattle, had become a Muslim extremist, trained with al-Qaeda, sworn a loyalty oath to a radical cleric, and planned to set up a terrorist training camp in the United States. A number of prominent Seattle African Americans expressed puzzlement at these developments and offer support for Ujaama.
- ***September 11:*** After much nerve-wracking anticipation the first anniversary of the attacks on the World Trade Center and Pentagon passes without significant terrorist incidents.
- ***September 19:*** A bipartisan group led by four senators—Robert Torricelli (Democrat, New Jersey), Joseph Lieberman (Democrat, Connecticut), John McCain (Republican, Arizona), and Arlen Specter (Republican, Pennsylvania)—demand a comprehensive investigation by an independent commission into the failures leading up to the September 11, 2001, attacks. The Bush administration opposes the effort.
- ***October 4:*** Attorney General John Ashcroft announces the arrest of six members of an alleged terrorist cell in Portland, Oregon. They are accused of obtaining weapons and training in the United States after the September 11, 2001, attacks and then attempting to go to Afghanistan to fight with al-Qaeda and the Taliban against U.S. forces.
- ***October 4:*** Richard Reid, the so-called shoe bomber, pleads guilty to counts that include attempted use of a weapon of mass destruction, attempted

homicide, and placing an explosive device on an aircraft. He faces a sentence of from 60 years to life in prison.

- ***October 12:*** A huge blast in Bali, Indonesia, kills more than 180 people, most of them tourists from Australia and Western countries. Indonesian police later arrest a man identified only as Amrozi. According to Indonesian accounts, Amrozi is affiliated with a local radical Islamic school called Al-Islam, which in turn has allegedly had contact with Indonesia's leading Islamic extremist cleric, Abu Bakar Bashir. There are also reports from interrogations that al-Qaeda operatives plotted attacks against "soft Western targets" throughout Southeast Asia, possibly in cooperation with Indonesian radical groups such as Jemaah Islamiyah, of which Bashir is the spiritual leader.
- ***October 21:*** A federal grand jury indicts six Yemeni immigrants in Lackawanna, New York, near Buffalo. Federal authorities describe them as an al-Qaeda "sleeper cell" and say that two of the men had admitted receiving training from al-Qaeda and having attended a speech by Osama bin Laden. Although authorities admitted they had no evidence of planning for a specific attack, they said that their relationship to al-Qaeda could be considered providing "material support" to the terrorist group under a 1996 antiterrorism law.
- ***October 24:*** Three weeks of seemingly random sniper attacks in the Washington, D.C., area culminate in the arrest of two suspects, John Allen Muhammad and John Lee Malvo. The suspects are believed to have killed 10 people and wounded four, and several other murders in other parts of the country are subsequently linked to them. Although there are some reports of Muhammad making anti-American statements and possibly being connected to a fringe Black Muslim group, there is no evidence of connection to al-Qaeda or other foreign terrorist groups.
- ***November 3:*** A Predator unpiloted drone aircraft uses a Hellfire missile to destroy a vehicle in Yemen, killing Sinan al-Harethi (also called Abu Ali), a senior al-Qaeda leader and five associates. U.S. officials say that armed Predator drones had been flying missions in Yemen looking for targets of opportunity.
- ***November 5:*** In the 2002 midterm elections, the Republicans recapture the Senate while maintaining their margin in the House of Representatives. Republicans hail this unusual outcome (with the party in the White House gaining seats in a midterm election) as evidence of popular support for President George W. Bush's war on terror and militant stance toward Iraq.
- ***November 7:*** U.S. Drug Enforcement Agency (DEA) officials announce arrests in what they say are schemes to trade drugs for weapons for terrorist groups. One scheme is said to involve trading $25 million in cocaine and cash for a large number of weapons for the AUC, a Colombian

paramilitary group. The other plot is said to involve selling heroin and hashish in order to buy four shoulder-fired Stinger missiles for al-Qaeda.

- ***November 8:*** At a news conference President George W. Bush speaks modestly about the Republican victories but says that passing the stalled legislation for the Department of Homeland Security is his top congressional priority.
- ***November 8:*** Ronald Noble, head of the international police force Interpol, warns that many channels of intelligence are indicating that al-Qaeda is preparing a major operation that will attack the United States and a number of other nations simultaneously. Noble also says that he believes Osama bin Laden is likely still alive.
- ***November 8:*** After intense negotiations between the United States and France, Russia, and China, the UN Security Council passes a unanimous resolution declaring that Iraq is in "material breach" of past UN resolutions regarding the dismantling of Iraqi weapons of mass destruction. The resolution states that if Iraq does not accept a strict regime of inspections (including the ability to freeze movement in and out of areas being inspected), there will be "serious consequences." In that case, U.S. officials reserve the right to undertake military action against Iraq without need of UN authorization.
- ***November 20:*** U.S. Senate approves 90-9 the homeland security bill, merging 22 agencies with combined budgets of about $40 billion and about 170,000 workers. This is the largest U.S. government reorganization since World War II.
- ***November 22:*** U.S. authorities announce they have captured senior al-Qaeda leader Abd al-Rahim al-Nashiri, who is believed to have been chief of operations for the terrorist network in the Persian Gulf and the planner of the 1998 embassy bombings in Africa and the October 2000 attack on the USS Cole in Yemen.
- ***November 26:*** President George W. Bush signs legislation that allows commercial pilots to carry firearms in airliner cockpits.
- ***December 5:*** A federal judge rules that accused "dirty bomb" plotter Jose Padilla (Abdullah al-Muhajir) may have access to a lawyer, but he also rules that the U.S. government has "the power to detain unlawful combatants and it matters not that Padilla is a United States citizen captured on United States soil."

2003

- ***January 8:*** A federal appeals court hearing the case of Yaser Esam Hamdi rules that the president has the power "during wartime" to detain indefinitely a person captured on the battlefield and does not need to give him or her access to an attorney. Further, the determining of when the war has ended is to be left to the president.

- ***January 10:*** Federal prosecutors try to set aside a judge's ruling that accused "dirty bomb" terrorist Jose Padilla (Abdullah al-Muhajir) be allowed access to an attorney. The government argues that such access could compromise Padilla's interrogation; however, Judge Michael B. Mukasey expresses irritation at this latest government move.
- ***January 20:*** British police storm a London mosque that authorities have considered for some time a fertile ground for recruiting terrorists. Their raid was triggered by the discovery earlier in the month of a small quantity of the deadly toxin ricin in a London house where four Algerians were arrested. Abu Hamza al-Masri, the Egyptian-born radical cleric who heads the mosque, is later removed from his post by British authorities.
- ***January 25:*** Tom Ridge is sworn in as head of the newly established Department of Homeland Security. He had been confirmed by a 94-0 vote in the Senate.
- ***January 29:*** President George W. Bush announces the creation of a Terrorist Threat Integration Center to provide a single coordinated effort to analyze terrorist threats. The new unit, which will incorporate elements from the FBI, CIA, and other agencies, will be headed by George J. Tenet, currently director of central intelligence. Some critics are concerned that this marks a new involvement of the CIA in domestic intelligence affairs.
- ***January 31:*** Some relatives of victims of the September 11, 2001, attacks appear in a Hamburg, Germany, court to offer testimony about the impact of the tragedy on their lives. They hope to persuade a German judge to give a tough sentence to Mounir Motassadeq, accused of aiding a Hamburg al-Qaeda cell involved in planning the 9/11 attacks.
- ***January 31:*** Richard Reid, the "shoe bomber," is sentenced to life in prison for trying to blow up an airliner. At his sentencing he defiantly declares allegiance to Osama bin Laden and tells the judge that "I am at war with your country."
- ***February:*** Some time during the first week of February, a federal district court in Virginia secretly rules that defense attorneys for Zacarias Moussaoui, who has been charged with conspiracy in connection with the September 11, 2001, attacks, must be allowed to question Ramzi bin al-Shibh, an al-Qaeda operative accused of being the intermediary between Moussaoui and the hijackers. Because the military and intelligence agencies do not want to make bin al-Shibh available, prosecutors may be forced to hold a military rather than a civilian trial for Moussaoui. The government will appeal the ruling.
- ***February 2:*** Indonesian authorities arrest Mas Selamat Kastari, who is believed to be the leader of the Singapore cell of Jemaah Islamiyah. He

had been a fugitive since December 2001, when a plot to blow up the American embassy in Singapore was uncovered.

- ***February 3:*** President George W. Bush sends his $2.23 trillion fiscal 2004 federal budget to Congress. It includes about $36 billion for the new Department of Homeland Security and the budgets for agencies being absorbed into the new department. It does not include a budget for a potential war with Iraq.
- ***February 5:*** Speaking before the UN Security Council, U.S. secretary of state Colin Powell focuses on Iraq's concealment of weapons of mass destruction and also accuses Iraq of having harbored an al-Qaeda cell in Baghdad. Commanded by Abu Mussab al-Zarqawi, the cell is purported to have assassinated Lawrence Foley, an American diplomat, in Amman, Jordan, in October 2002. Powell also reveals the existence of an al-Qaeda training camp in northeastern Iraq, but it is in a Kurdish area outside Iraqi government control.
- ***February 6:*** British police arrest seven suspects in four cities in England and Scotland. They are believed to be connected to suspects arrested in January 2003 on suspicion that they had plotted to use the toxin ricin in terrorist attacks.
- ***February 7:*** Attorney General John Ashcroft announces that the nation's terrorism alert level is being raised from "elevated risk" to "high risk" based on undisclosed intelligence suggesting that al-Qaeda may be planning terror attacks during the Muslim religious observance of hajj, which takes place in mid-February. The higher alert level will automatically trigger increased security at many critical facilities such as bridges, highways, tunnels, and large office or apartment buildings.
- ***February 8:*** The revelation of Justice Department drafts for proposed legislation called the Domestic Security Enhancement Act of 2003 results in criticism from the American Civil Liberties Union and other groups. Supporters say that the new legislation, which was only in the discussion stage, represented a reasonable filling in of gaps in the USA PATRIOT Act. Critics, however, argue that the new law would significantly undermine basic rights. Provisions in the draft legislation make it easier, for example, to collect DNA routinely from terrorism suspects and allow terrorist suspects to be held automatically without bail. The most controversial provisions would allow anyone who provides any sort of support for a group on the government's list of terrorist organizations to be stripped of U.S. citizenship. Freedom of Information Act requests for information about detainees would be barred.
- ***February 10:*** Enaam Arnaout, head of the Islamic charity Benevolence International Foundation, pleads guilty to one count of racketeering conspiracy. He admits that his organization used money raised for supposedly

charitable purposes to supply boots and uniforms for Muslim fighters in Chechnya and Bosnia. Federal prosecutors had originally charged Arnaout with having provided support to al-Qaeda but then accepted the plea bargain. Arnaout's attorney says the government's decision amounts to an admission that Arnaout had no links with al-Qaeda, while prosecutors insist that they still believe Arnaout had such ties.

- ***February 10:*** The American Bar Association, at its midyear meeting, votes overwhelmingly to support the right of U.S. citizens held as enemy combatants to have access to an attorney and to legal review of their status. It also urges Congress to establish clear standards and procedures for designating individuals as enemy combatants.
- ***February 11:*** A statement believed to be from Osama bin Laden is broadcast on the al-Jazeera television network. It urges Muslims to "show solidarity and defend the Iraqi people." U.S. secretary of state Colin Powell tells a congressional committee that "This nexus between terrorists and states that are developing weapons of mass destruction can no longer be looked away from and ignored."
- ***February 13:*** After a plane goes down in rebel-held territory members of the Revolutionary Armed Forces of Colombia (FARC) announce they have taken three American passengers prisoner.
- ***February 19:*** A German court convicts Mounir Motassadeq, a Moroccan student, of belonging to an al-Qaeda cell and helping transfer funds to the September 11 hijackers. He is given the maximum sentence of 15 years in prison. The panel of seven judges rejects defense claims that lack of access to classified intelligence data and to witnesses in U.S. custody (such as key al-Qaeda leader Ramzi bin al-Shibh) had prevented Motassedeq from receiving a fair trial.
- ***February 19:*** Secretary of Homeland Security Tom Ridge announces a new publicity campaign to inform the public about measures it can take to prepare for possible terrorist attack. The campaign will include a government web site (http://www.ready.gov) a toll-free telephone line (800-BE-READY), and television and radio public service announcements.
- ***February 20:*** A Tampa, Florida, federal grand jury indicts eight members of the Palestinian Islamic Jihad, which is designated by the U.S. government as a terrorist organization. They are accused of racketeering, extortion, and other crimes in support of terrorist activities, as well as conspiracy to kill and maim people abroad. The alleged leader of the group is Sami Amin al-Arian, a Palestinian professor at the University of South Florida. Four members of the group remain at large.
- ***February 20:*** Pentagon officials announce the United States will be sending more than 1,700 troops to fight terrorism in the Philippines.

Their objective is "to disrupt and destroy" about 250 members of the Abu Sayyaf terrorist group in the southern part of the country.

- ***February 25:*** The FARC says that they will free three captured Americans if Colombia agrees to release a large number of their imprisoned members and to set up a "demilitarized zone." However, the Colombian government, which has received an increasing amount of military aid from the United States, seems unlikely to accede to the demands.
- ***March 1:*** Pakistan authorities arrest Khalid Shaikh Mohammed, the suspected chief planner of the September 11, 2001, hijackings, the 1998 bombings of American embassies in Africa, and other terrorist attacks. Mohammed is quickly transferred to U.S. custody for interrogation in an undisclosed location.
- ***March 4:*** An American missionary is killed at Davao Airport in the Philippines by a bomb probably set by terrorists.
- ***March 17:*** In an address to the American people President George W. Bush gives Saddam Hussein and his sons 48 hours to leave Iraq, or they will face "military action at a time of our choosing."
- ***March 17:*** Director of Homeland Security Tom Ridge raises the nation's security level to orange, indicating a high risk of terrorist attack. He also announces Operation Liberty Shield, a multiagency effort to reinforce border and transportation security and to protect infrastructure such as chemical and power plants. Meanwhile, asylum seekers from Iraq and a number of other Muslim countries will be detained until their applications are processed, and thousands of Iraqi and other immigrants are being asked to come in for "voluntary interviews."
- ***March 19:*** The U.S. offensive against Iraq opens with targeted cruise missile and "bunker buster" bomb attacks on a Baghdad bunker that U.S. intelligence believe is being used by top Iraqi officials including Saddam Hussein. However, subsequent television appearances suggest that the Iraqi leader survived and is likely still in control of the government.
- ***March 21:*** A "shock and awe" attack rocks Baghdad with hundreds of cruise missiles and B-52 bomb strikes concentrating on government facilities. Meanwhile U.S. and British forces cross from Kuwait into southeastern Iraq, taking control of key oil fields, entering the port city of Umm Qasr, and surrounding Basra.
- ***March 23:*** U.S. and British forces continue their northwest drive to within about 100 miles of Baghdad, but they meet increasingly heavy resistance, especially from the militia known as Fedayeen Saddam, as well as flare-ups of fighting in areas such as Umm Qasr that had been previously only partially secured. Iraqi television shows what are claimed to be several American prisoners of war.

- ***March 24:*** Bush administration officials announce that they will be asking for $75 billion to pay Iraq war-related costs for the rest of the fiscal year. Of this amount about $63 billion is for the war itself, $8 billion for humanitarian relief, and about $4 billion for homeland defense.
- ***March 25:*** U.S. forces approach to within 50 miles of Baghdad; Iraqi resistance continues. The advance is also hampered by a sandstorm.
- ***March 25:*** British troops surrounding the city of Basra carry out artillery and air strikes on installations in the city in hopes of aiding a reported Shiite rebellion against Saddam Hussein's government. UN officials warn of a looming humanitarian crisis in Basra and other Iraqi cities, which are running out of water and food supplies.
- ***March 25:*** Several hundred U.S. troops begin a hunt for Taliban fighters in the countryside around Kandahar, Afghanistan, following discovery of a large cache of weapons.
- ***March 26:*** The U.S. Third Infantry Division cuts off the city of Najaf, about 90 miles south of Baghdad, killing as many as a thousand Iraqi fighters and capturing hundreds more. Total U.S. and British deaths in the war thus far number about 50, with about half being victims of accidents or "friendly fire" incidents.
- ***March 30:*** Four U.S. soldiers are killed near Najaf by a suicide bomber in a taxi at a checkpoint. Iraqi officials say that thousands from across the Arab world are ready to become martyrs for Islam by defending Iraq.
- ***April 1:*** U.S. soldiers shoot and kill women and children in a van when its driver fails to stop at a checkpoint.
- ***April 1:*** U.S. special operations forces rescue Pfc. Jessica Lynch, one of the eight soldiers still missing since the 507th Ordnance Maintenance Co. took a wrong turn in Nasiriyah and was ambushed 10 days earlier. She is flown to Germany to be treated for injuries. Bodies are also recovered in the mission.
- ***April 3:*** Large sections of Baghdad lose power for the first time since the war began after huge explosions rock the capital. Coalition forces are now inside the so-called Red Zone radiating from Baghdad, the region in which commanders fear Saddam's forces might use chemical or biological weapons. Some U.S. forces fight to within 20 miles of the city.
- ***April 5:*** A suicide bombing kills three U.S. soldiers, a pregnant woman, and the driver at a checkpoint near Baghdad.
- ***April 7:*** As antiwar demonstrations continue, police use non-lethal bullets to fire on a protest in Oakland, California. In addition to protesters, they hit longshoremen going to work.
- ***April 8:*** With U.S. force now inside Baghdad, fighting intensifies. More civilians are wounded and killed. Three journalists are killed: two when the press hotel is fired on by U.S. forces, and one—from the Arab network al-Jazeera—when a U.S. plane attacks its offices.

- ***April 8:*** After taking control of Basra, British put a sheik in power, to begin forming a new government. U.S. general Jay Garner is appointed by the Pentagon to form an interim postwar administration in Iraq.
- ***April 8:*** The Department of Homeland Security, having been criticized for not providing local governments with enough money, announces that seven major U.S. cities will get $100,000 million for antiterror security.
- ***April 9:*** Baghdad falls and Saddam's reign ends, although it is still unclear if he is dead. U.S. forces pull down statues of him; people celebrate in the streets of Baghdad. Mohammed al-Douri, Iraqi ambassador to the UN, says that "the game is over," meaning that the war is over. Many in the Arab world are shocked at the quick fall and concerned about the future, especially when a U.S. marine draps an American flag over the face of a statue of Saddam.
- ***April 9:*** Looting starts in Baghdad, beginning with the palaces of Saddam and his sons and other government buildings but soon spreading widely. UN offices are looted and vehicles taken. Representatives call on U.S. forces to take responsibility for securing the environment for the civilian population.
- ***April 9:*** The International Committee of the Red Cross (ICRC) suspends humanitarian operations in Baghdad, saying that the city is "chaotic and unpredictable." Alarmed at the high number of civilian casualties, the ICRC expresses frustration at not being able to remove wounded from the streets to treat them. Their hospital in the center of the city is ransacked by armed looters who strip it of beds, medical equipment and supplies, and anything else they can carry.
- ***April 10:*** Another suicide bomber kills U.S. soldiers at a checkpoint near Baghdad.
- ***April 10:*** Iraqis tell U.S. Marines where they can find seven P.O.W.s in Samara. Five members of the 507th maintenance company and two Apache helicopter pilots are rescued.
- ***April 15:*** In Ur the United States holds a forum of Iraqi opposition leaders to discuss the postwar government. Many Iraqis boycott the meeting to protest the installation of Gen. Garner.
- ***April 15:*** U.S. forces open fire on a crowd in Mosul, killing at least 7 and wounding many. The crowd was becoming hostile toward the U.S. new govenor. Across Iraq and the Arab world concern grows about who will run the interim government. There is strong opposition to Americans governing Iraq, even if only temporarily.
- ***April 15:*** A total of 118 Americans have been killed in the war, 37 in noncombat or friendly fire situations. Untold thousands of Iraqis have been killed, including civilians.

- ***April 16:*** U.S. forces in Baghdad capture Abu Abbas, the Palestinian behind the 1985 hijacking of the Italian cruise ship *Achille Lauro*, during which Leon Klinghoffer, an elderly American, was murdered.
- ***April 16:*** The United States begins to pressure Syria, accusing the country of harboring escaped high-ranking Iraqi leaders and/or WOMD transferred from Iraq. Damascus denies these charges.
- ***April 17:*** Martin Sullivan, head of the U.S. presidential panel on cultural property, resigns in protest of the U.S. forces' failure to protect museums, libraries, and other cultural institutions and sites in Iraq from looters. UNESCO had provided U.S. officials with location information prior to the war. Within the Arab world, some express the belief that the United States wanted Iraqis to lose their history and cultural heritage.
- ***April 17:*** The State Department lifts travel warnings to Bahrain, Oman, Qatar, and the United Arab Emirates. The day before, the Department of Homeland Security had lowered the domestic terrorist alert level from high, where it had been since March 17, to elevated.
- ***April 18:*** With fighting mainly over, U.S. air and naval forces begin to leave the area.
- ***April 22:*** Brig. Gen. Vincent Brooks, deputy operations director at Central Command, confirms that U.S. troops have negotiated a cease-fire with the People's Mujahedeen, a Hussein-supported group that has been fighting to overthrow the Iranian government for 17 years.
- ***April 22:*** Hundreds of thousands of Shiites from Iraq, Iran, and other countries head to Karbala, Iraq, on an important Shiite pilgrimage for the first time since 1977. Under Saddam Hussein and the ruling Sunni Muslims this had been banned. U.S. troops avoid the city and the road there, trying to avoid provoking further anti-U.S. sentiment over its occupation.

CHAPTER 4

BIOGRAPHICAL LISTING

This chapter provides brief biographical sketches of important individuals involved with terrorist attacks against the United States or with leadership in the subsequent response. It should be noted that in some cases, pending allegations of an individual's involvement in terrorist attacks have not yet been resolved in a court of law. More information about many of the individuals discussed in this chapter can be obtained from the Internet resource sites discussed in Chapter 6 and listed in the bibliographies in Chapter 7.

John Ashcroft, attorney general of the United States (2000–). Born in Chicago on May 9, 1942, he is a former governor and senator of Missouri. Ashcroft's nomination as attorney general proved to be the most contentious of George W. Bush's cabinet picks. Many liberals opposed Ashcroft because they believed that his strong conservative Christian beliefs would prevent him from protecting rights such as that of abortion choice. Conservatives, meanwhile, pointed to his intelligence, personal integrity, and principles. After the attacks of September 11, 2001, Ashcroft, as the nation's chief law enforcer, pledged to uphold civil liberties but also suggested that critics who raised constitutional issues were aiding terrorism. He has espoused stronger power for law enforcement (such as outlined in the USA PATRIOT Act of 2001) and resisted disclosure of information about persons being held at the U.S. naval base at in Guantánamo Bay, Cuba, which was mandated by a federal district judge in July 2002. His decision to hold terror suspects such as Yaser Esam Hamdi as "unlawful combatants" will, if upheld by the courts, leave them in a sort of legal limbo.

Mohammed Atta is believed to be the principal organizer of the terrorist attacks of September 11, 2001. Atta was born September 1, 1968, in Kafr al-Sheikh, Egypt, the son of a lawyer. He is remembered as a quiet boy, overshadowed by his two older sisters one of whom became a zoology professor and the other a medical doctor. Atta graduated from Cairo University with a degree in architectural engineering. Atta appeared to be a loner who, while apparently not very interested in religion, could indulge in outbursts when he saw someone do something that he considered wrong. In 1992, Atta went to Germany and enrolled in the Technical University of Hamburg-Harburg to study urban planning, and he wrote a well-regarded thesis on the conflict between Islam and modern secularism as reflected in the architecture of Aleppo, Syria. However, in the later 1990s, he was increasingly absent from school and work and took on more of the appearance and mannerisms of an Islamic fundamentalist. He also apparently made contact with a number of al-Qaeda operatives. He spent much of 2000 in the United States, clean-shaven and dressed in American style. Apparently his attention had turned toward planning an air-based terrorist attack; later it would be reported that he had asked about getting a government loan to buy a crop-dusting plane. Atta and another future hijacker, Marwan al-Shehhi, took flying lessons and earned their basic pilot's licenses, then took further training on Boeing 727 simulators. Atta is believed have gradually assembled and coordinated the team of 19 hijackers throughout 2001, and on the morning of September 11, it is believed that he was at the controls of the Boeing 757 that crashed into the North Tower of the World Trade Center.

Osama bin Laden (Usama bin Laden) is believed to be the head of the al-Qaeda terrorist network and the person ultimately responsible for the terrorist attacks of September 11, 2001. Born in 1957, the son of a Saudi Arabian multimillionaire, bin Laden emerged by the end of the 1990s as the financial power behind terrorist attacks including the 1998 bombings of American embassies in Africa. Bin Laden first became involved in militant conflict when the Soviets invaded Afghanistan in 1979. He moved his construction company and workers into the country and built the training infrastructure for the guerrilla resistance to the invasion. He and other Afghan leaders received substantial covert support from the CIA, which saw the conflict as an opportunity to mire the Soviets in their own "Vietnam." After the Soviets were defeated, bin Laden and his trained veterans went back to Saudi Arabia, where they turned their radical Islamist focus to fighting the country's secularist government. Around 1990, bin Laden formed a group called al-Qaeda, meaning "the Base." In 1994, the Saudi government expelled bin Laden and his group, and he moved to Sudan, where he set up extensive bases staffed by his fellow Afghan veterans. In 1996, however, with Sudan seeking better relations with the United States, bin Laden moved again—back to Afghanistan. In February 1998, bin Laden announced a new group called "The Islamic World Front for the struggle against the Jews and the Crusaders" and declared that U.S. citizens throughout the world would be fair game for terrorist attack. In August 1998, bin Laden's terrorists bombed U.S. embassies in Nairobi, Kenya, and Dar es Salaam, Tanzania.

Retaliatory U.S. attacks on a factory in Sudan that bin Laden had allegedly used to manufacture chemical weapons and the al-Qaeda bases in Afghanistan aroused controversy while doing little to damage al-Qaeda. In October 2000, the terrorist group demonstrated its tactical resourcefulness by badly damaging the U.S. destroyer *Cole* with a bomb-laden boat, killing 12 American sailors. After the September 11, 2001, attacks, bin Laden appeared on several videotapes made at undetermined times and locations, in which he praised the attacks, essentially took responsibility for them, and suggested that he had used his knowledge of construction and engineering to plan them. On November 12, 2002, and again in February 2003, new tapes surfaced, confirming that Osama bin Laden was in fact still alive.

George W. Bush, 43rd president of the United States, elected in 2000. Born on July 6, 1946, in New Haven, Connecticut, to Barbara and George Herbert Walker Bush, 41st president of the United States. George Bush, Jr., grew up in Midland and Houston, Texas, and frequently identifies himself as a Texan. He majored in history at Yale University and then joined the Air National Guard as an alternative to the Vietnam draft, serving as a pilot. After his term at service, he attended Harvard University, where he earned an MBA. Following graduation he entered the oil business, as had his father. His first political attempt, a run for Congress as a Republican in 1978, was unsuccessful. He also struggled with alcoholism, ending his drinking apparently after an experience of Christian conversion. He was somewhat more successful as managing partner of a group that bought the Texas Rangers Major League Baseball team. In 1994, Bush was elected to the first of two terms as governor of Texas, defeating the popular and feisty Democratic incumbent, Ann Richards. During his years as governor, Bush focused on themes that he later highlighted in the 2000 presidential campaign: education reform and tax cuts. Although the Democratic candidate Al Gore attacked Bush vigorously on issues such as capital punishment and environmental pollution, Bush's personal touch and appeal to bipartisan cooperation seemed to connect with many people, while the more strident Gore did not. The disputed election vote was the closest in presidential history, and Bush began his term without a mandate and with questions about his intellectual capacity, since his speeches frequently included stumbling or awkward phrasing. Bush emerged after the September 11, 2001, attacks, however, as a strong, reassuring leader who vowed that the nation would meet the terrorist challenge and mount a comprehensive "war on terrorism." This new campaign was marked by a steady, methodical diplomatic and military approach that led to the removal of the Taliban in Afghanistan and an at least temporary neutralization of al-Qaeda by the end of 2001. The following year, Bush faced both the question of how to continue a broader struggle against terrorism and resurfacing domestic issues, particularly regarding the struggling economy and corporate corruption. In early 2003, domestic and foreign concerns about Bush's bellicose stance toward Iraq as well as continuing economic malaise the United States threatened to erode Bush's popular support. Once the war began, the majority of Americans rallied behind him, although protests also grew.

Rudolph Giuliani, as mayor of New York City (1993–2001), had to deal with the brunt of the September 11, 2001, attack on the World Trade Center in Manhattan. Born May 28, 1944, in Brooklyn, New York as a youngster he often worked in his parents' restaurant; however, his parents encouraged him to seek a higher education. Although Giuliani seriously considered the Catholic priesthood, he decided to go to law school, New York University. Giuliani's early public career in the 1980s was marked by his emergence as a tough U.S. attorney who took on Mafia bosses as well as Wall Street inside traders. In 1993, he ran for mayor of New York as a Republican, viewed as an uphill battle in the heavily Democratic city. However, widespread fear and disgust about the city's high crime rate and shabby, dangerous public spaces propelled him into City Hall. As mayor, Giuliani won praise in many quarters for his tough policing and the greatly reduced crime rate, as well as making the streets and subways clean and safer. However, liberals and minority activists accused him of ignoring police brutality and not caring about the marginalized. Giuliani also had to deal with marital scandal and a bout of prostate cancer. When the planes hit the World Trade Center he rushed to the scene and narrowly escaped injury when the towers collapsed. His calm, resolute statements to the people of New York won great praise even from political opponents, as well as *Time* magazine's award as 2001 Person of the Year.

Yaser Esam Hamdi, known as the second "American Taliban" (the first being John Walker Lindh), was born on September 26, 1980, in Baton Rouge, Louisiana, a fact that somewhat disconcerted U.S. officials when they reviewed his case at the prison camp at Guantánamo Bay, Cuba. Although little is known of his background, Hamdi apparently grew up in Saudi Arabia. In Afghanistan, he was captured by Northern Alliance forces in and turned over to the Americans. After his citizenship was discovered, he was flown from Guantánamo to a naval brig in Norfolk, Virginia. Although U.S. citizens presumably have a constitutional right to be charged and given access to legal representation, authorities have thus far held Hamdi as an "unlawful combatant," allowing them to hold Hamdi without charge for the duration of hostilities. When a habeas corpus petition was filed, a federal district judge in Norfolk ordered that Hamdi be provided an attorney; however, when the government appealed, a panel of the fourth U.S. circuit court returned the case to the lower court in July 2002, stating that sufficient deference had not been paid to the government's interest in protecting national security against terrorism. In January 2003, the court further said that the president's war powers gave him the right to detain enemy combatants, such as Hamdi, and that courts should defer to such decisions.

Saddam Hussein, Iraqi dictator and frequent target of U.S. military and diplomatic efforts to oust him. Hussein was born April 28, 1937, near Takrit, Iraq. He attended law school at the University of Cairo but soon became involved in politics. As a young member of the Ba'ath Party, Hussein fled Iraq after helping in an attempt to assassinate the country's prime minister, Abd al-Karim Qasim, in 1959. In the 1960s, Hussein returned to Iraq as a Ba'ath Party activist, eventually playing a key role in the 1968 revolution that gave the party control of the country. He became the country's president in 1979. During the 1980s, he embroiled the country in a bloody but inconclusive war with neighboring Iran. In 1990, he sent troops to occupy the small but oil-rich nation of Kuwait; however, in early 1991 a massive military effort by the United States and its allies expelled Iraqi forces from Kuwait and considerably weakened the Iraqi military and infrastructure, although Hussein was not removed from power. Indeed, he was able to brutally contain a Kurdish rebellion in the northern part of the country while suppressing a Shiite rebellion in the south. In a tug of war with the United States and United Nations, Hussein demanded removal of UN economic sanctions while resisting UN arms inspectors, whom he expelled in 1998. Although the United States has been unable to find direct evidence of Iraqi support for Osama bin Laden or involvement in the September 11, 2001, attacks, George W. Bush and other U.S. officials have expressed increasing concern that Hussein has been using the time since the end of inspections to revive his development of weapons of mass destruction (WOMD)—biological, chemical, and possibly nuclear. In late 2002, speculation increasingly turned toward a new full-scale U.S. military action against Iraq, this time aimed at removing Hussein from power. In early 2003, the crisis came to a head. In the United Nations, Security Council permanent members France, Germany, and, to a lesser extent, China and Russia favored strengthening arms inspections and monitoring within Iraq but giving the process more time to work. The Bush administration, however, remained adamant that Iraq had continued to develop and amass weapons of mass destruction in disregard of United Nations resolutions, and on March 19 began an offensive against Iraq. Three weeks later, on April 9, Baghdad fell and Hussein's reign ended. U.S. forces pulled down statues of him and rummaged through his places. The Iraqi people first celebrated and then began widespread looting, starting with the homes and palaces of Hussein and his sons. During the war, U.S. forces bombed specific sites several times on intelligence that Hussein might be there. In late April, nearly two weeks after the fall of Baghdad, however, most believed that Hussein was still alive. U.S. forces continued the manhunt for him—as well as his sons and top staff—both inside and outside Iraq.

Hamid Karzai, elected leader of Afghanistan following the overthrow of the Taliban and the convening of the Loya Jirga, or Grand Council in June 2002. A member of the country's dominant Pashtun ethnic group, Karzai was born December 24, 1957, in Kandahār, Afghanistan, and studied in India and the United States. After the country's former king, Mohammad Zahir Shah, was deposed in 1973, Karzai and his family went abroad. In 1982, with Soviet invaders trying to establish a puppet government in Afghanistan, Karzai returned and participated in the resistance. When the Soviets left in 1992, Karzai became foreign minister in the government of Burhanuddin Rabbani. By the late 1990s, however, the Taliban had become the dominant force, and Karzai began to organize a movement from Pakistan to overthrow it and restore the former monarchy. After the September 11, 2001, attacks on the United States, Karzai slipped back into Afghanistan and organized anti-Taliban forces around Kandahār, which they captured. In December 2001, Karzai became prime minister of the interim government, which was later made official as the Transitional Authority by the Loya Jirga. Having already survived at least one assassination attempt, the articulate Karzai faces the continuing challenge of keeping the peace among often contentious ethnic groups and the warlords who still effectively control much of the country. At the same time, he must marshal foreign assistance (particularly from the United States) to rebuild the country and to establish an army, police force, and other institutions.

John Philip Walker Lindh became known as the "American Taliban" when he was captured while fighting against U.S. forces in Afghanistan. Lindh was born on February 9, 1981, in Silver Spring, Maryland, but his family moved to San Anselmo, California, when he was 10 years old. Friends remember both the boy and the family to be very typical Americans. (His father was an attorney for the U.S. Department of Justice.) In high school Lindh studied world history and cultures and apparently was first exposed to Islam. His parents seemed open to spiritual exploration, thus Lindh's increasing interest in Islamic religion and culture was not discouraged. It is believed he fully committed himself to the faith after reading *The Autobiography of Malcolm X.* (Lindh is white.) He began to attend regular prayer services in nearby Mill Valley. Upon his graduation from high school, he asked to have the name on his diploma changed to Sulayman Al-Lindh. In December 1998, Lindh decided to go to Yemen to study Arabic. Although he returned home for a time, he had clearly transferred his allegiance to militant Islam, studying at a *madrassa* and apparently joining the Taliban forces as well as receiving training at an al-Qaeda camp. Following the September 11, 2001, attacks, the Taliban became a military enemy of the United States. After his capture, Lindh was charged with 10 terrorism-related counts, including conspiracy to kill Americans; however, in July 2002, he and the Justice Department arrived at a plea bargain. Lindh pled guilty to two charges, and the rest were dismissed. He received a 20-year prison sentence—considered by some a harsh fate for a misguided, idealistic youth and by others an insufficient punishment for traitorous deeds.

Norman Y. Mineta, U.S. secretary of transportation since January 2001. Mineta, a Japanese American, was born November 12, 1931, in San Jose, California. In 1942, his all-American life as a Boy Scout and enthusiastic baseball player in southern California was abruptly ended when he and his family along with 120,000 other Japanese Americans were transported to wartime internment camps. After the war Mineta studied at the University of California, Berkeley. He joined the army in 1953 and served as an intelligence officer in Japan and Korea. After returning to California and serving a stint at his father's insurance agency, Mineta began his political career first as a city council member for San Jose and then as the city's mayor, becoming the first Asian-American mayor of a major city. Mineta next served in the House of Representatives from 1975 to 1995, where he was viewed as a very effective legislator and committee chairperson who was knowledgeable about many policy areas including technology, transportation, and aviation. This experience proved valuable when Mineta, who had also been a top executive at Lockheed Martin, was chosen as secretary of commerce in President Bill Clinton's administration. Mineta, a Democrat with strong bipartisan support, then became secretary of transportation under President George W. Bush. The attacks on September 11, 2001, struck a paralyzing, devastating blow to the air transportation network and threatened to destroy an already struggling airline industry. Bush decided to create the Transportation Security Administration (TSA) within the Department of Transportation to overhaul airport security in the face of the terrorist threat. Mineta and TSA director John Magaw face great pressure to install new screening equipment, train the now federalized airport security personnel, and provide additional security for the nation's seaports, highways, pipelines, and other connecting infrastructure.

Zacarias Moussaoui is believed to be the only surviving member of the 20-person hijacking team that carried out the September 11, 2001, attacks on the World Trade Center and Pentagon. He is a French citizen of Moroccan descent born May 30, 1968, who lived for some time in the United Kingdom. Little is known about his background. He was arrested on August 16, 2001, when teachers at a Minnesota flight school became suspicious of Moussaoui's interest in flying jumbo jets but not necessarily in landing them. He was held first on immigration charges, then as a material witness, and ultimately indicted in December 2001 for six forms of conspiracy involving the 9/11 attacks, air piracy, use of weapons of mass destruction, and other charges. The indictment accused Moussaoui of carrying out a number of actions similar to those of other hijackers such as Mohammed Atta, including taking flying lessons, inquiring about crop dusting, and obtaining knives. Moussaoui has also been linked specifically with Ramzi bin al-Shibh, who authorities believe was originally intended to be the 20th hijacker. The extensive indictment does not include a "smoking gun" tying Moussaoui to the attacks but represents a comprehensive outline of al-Qaeda's activities that the government believes will cumulatively prove that Moussaoui was part of a terrorist conspiracy. During preliminary legal proceedings, Moussaoui has behaved erratically, firing his lawyers (whom he says he does not trust) and receiving, provisionally, the right to defend himself. At first he attempted to plead guilty, apparently as a form of unilateral plea bargain intended to avoid the death penalty. When the judge rejected the plea, citing Moussaoui's apparent confusion about the legal system, Moussaoui then changed the plea to not guilty. Some analysts believe the government's case is not very strong, and it remains to be seen if a plea bargain of some sort may be reached with the volatile defendant. Meanwhile, in early February 2003, a new wrinkle entered the case in the form of an order from a secret federal court that granted Moussaoui the right to question bin al-Shibh. U.S. intelligence agencies interrogating bin al-Shibh strongly resist bringing bin al-Shibh to court for fear that he could pass on sensitive information or otherwise compromise terrorism investigations. If the government does not agree to comply with the court order, it may have to try Moussaoui in a military tribunal rather than in a civilian court.

Robert S. Mueller, director of the Federal Bureau of Investigation since September 4, 2001. Born August 7, 1944, in New York City, Mueller attended Princeton University, then served as a marine in the Vietnam War (1967–70), receiving many commendations. Afterward, he attended law school at the University of Virginia, followed by private practice. He entered public service as a federal prosecutor and then a U.S. attorney in Boston, building an increasingly formidable reputation. In 1990, Mueller became assistant attorney general for the criminal division of the Department of Justice. His most notable case involved the prosecution of the B.C.C.I. (Bank of Credit and Commerce International) scandal. Although he returned to private practice briefly at the start of the Clinton administration, he missed the fray and returned as an ordinary prosecutor in the District of Columbia, an area with a very high murder rate. Moving back up the ladder in 1995 as the U.S. attorney in San Francisco,

Mueller won respect for his prosecutorial effectiveness and for recruiting more women and minorities to the department. While some praise his directness, critics have described the high-powered Mueller as overbearing and prone to becoming involved in "turf battles." In the first half of 2001, Mueller served as deputy attorney general and was then nominated and confirmed as director of the FBI, taking office only a week before the 9/11 terrorist attacks. Mueller, who already faced the challenge of reforming an agency that had suffered considerable embarrassment such as quality control problems in the FBI labs, had to change the priorities of the organization to deal with the terrorist threat while building coordination with the CIA and later with the newly organized Department of Homeland Security. Meanwhile, Mueller and the FBI have had to respond to numerous accusations that the FBI had known, or should have known, that a big attack on the United States was in the works. Testifying before a congressional intelligence committee, Mueller assured Congress that he appreciated the efforts of whistle-blower Rowley, an FBI special agent based in Minneapolis who had written a memo warning of possible airline-related attacks prior to September 11, 2001.

Pervez Musharraf, president of Pakistan, the nation most directly related to the U.S. military campaign in Afghanistan in 2001–2. Musharraf was born in Delhi, India, on August 11, 1943, and his middle-class family moved to the newly created nation of Pakistan in 1948. He was considered to be an intelligent, outgoing boy as well as a good student. In 1961, Musharraf entered the Pakistan Military Academy, and in 1965 he saw combat in the second flareup of war between India and Pakistan, receiving a medal for gallantry. By the time of the next war in 1971 Musharraf had become a company commander and soon rose to the rank of brigadier general. While generally secular in outlook, Musharraf did help train Afghani refugees and Islamic fighters in camps on the Pakistani border during the conflict with the Soviets in Afghanistan in the 1980s. During the 1990s, he moved up the ranks of the nation's generals until he became chairman of the Joint Chiefs of Staff Committee; however, he found himself increasingly at odds with Prime Minister Nawaz Sharif. In 1999, Musharraf was leading a Pakistani invasion of Indian-administered territory in Kashmir, when Sharif, bowing to international pressure, halted the invasion. Musharraf loudly objected, and Sharif fired him, leading the military to launch a coup. Musharraf then became the head of government, suspending the constitution and declaring a state of emergency; however what might have been perceived as a problematic dictatorship took on a different complexion following the September 11, 2001, attacks on the United States. The United States badly needed Pakistan as a base of operations for driving the Taliban and al-Qaeda out of Afghanistan. Musharraf agreed to provide the airspace, intelligence, and other support that the United States needed. In exchange, Musharraf ensured that he would receive a growing stream of U.S. aid and improve the international standing of his regime, but he also angered the militant Muslims who make up a significant part of the Pakistani population. Musharraf suppressed the militant demonstrations while making an effort to explain his policy to the population and suggesting eventual democratization.

Abdullah al-Muhajir (Jose Padilla) accused by U.S. authorities of conspiring to build and use a radioactive "dirty bomb," although little detailed evidence has been released publicly. A former Chicago gang member, Jose Padilla converted to Islam and took the name Abdullah al-Muhajir. He was arrested on May 8, 2002, at Chicago's O'Hare International Airport. At first he was moved to New York and held as a material witness in connection with post–September 11 terrorism investigations. However, apparently to keep his case out of the civilian courts and to protect sensitive information, the Justice Department moved al-Muhajir to a naval prison in South Carolina on June 9, asserting that even though he was a U.S. citizen he could be held indefinitely without charge as an "unlawful combatant." Meanwhile, the attorney that had been appointed for him by a New York federal court attempted to have the court assert jurisdiction and require that al-Muhajir be charged or released. Al-Muhajir's defense scored a partial victory on December 4, 2002, when a New York federal judge ruled that al-Muhajir could challenge his detention, though not the government's right to detain unlawful combatants, even those who, like al-Muhajir, were U.S. citizens.

Colin Powell, U.S. secretary of state since 2001 and former chairman of the Joint Chiefs of Staff in the 1990–91 Persian Gulf War. The son of Jamaican immigrants, Powell has become the highest ranked African-American officer in U.S. history as well as one of the few blacks to serve as a member of a presidential cabinet. Powell was born in Harlem in New York City on April 5, 1937, and attended the City College of New York, where he earned an MBA. In 1958, he joined the army and served two tours of duty in Vietnam. In the 1970s and 1980s, Powell moved steadily up the ranks, serving in South Korea, West Germany, and the United States. He became a general in 1986. Powell had also gained civilian experience by serving in the White House, including the Office of Management and Budget (1972–73). In 1989, Powell became a four-star general and chairman of the Joint Chiefs of Staff. In 1990, Iraq invaded and occupied Kuwait, and Powell was in charge of the logistics and ultimate coordination of the massive force of 300,000 soldiers who would be deployed and used to expel the invaders and strike deep into Iraq. Despite, or perhaps because of, his military experience, Powell has consistently counseled restraint in the use of U.S. military force, insisting that it be a last resort, only in areas of vital national interest and with defined objectives. Following the 1991 Gulf War, Powell's popularity and stature as an African-American role model made him attractive to both major parties as a potential national candidate. Powell maintained his lack of interest in such a candidacy, however, and some conservative Republicans objected to his moderate positions on social issues such as abortion and affirmative action. Following the terrorist attacks of September 11, 2001, and the apparently successful conclusion of the first stage of the "war on terrorism" in Afghanistan, some voices in the administration (including President George W. Bush and Vice President Dick Cheney) increasingly urged that military action be taken to remove Iraq's Saddam Hussein once and for all. Powell, consistent with his long-held views, argued against such military action before exhausting diplomatic efforts. However, by 2003, the Bush administration seemed headed toward war, with Powell having to take on the role of conveying what sounded increasingly like an ultimatum to Iraq to disarm and to the UN Security Council to act decisively. In early February, Powell spoke before the Security Council, presenting photographic and intercepted communications evidence supporting the charges that Iraq had WOMD. After the war began in March, Powell's role lessened. In late April, Powell was planning a trip to Syria for May to hold Mideast peace talks.

Sheikh Omar Abdel Rahman, Islamic fundamentalist cleric convicted of directing terrorist attacks. Born in 1938 in Egypt, Rahman, though blind and not a direct participant, was implicated in the assassination of Egyptian president Anwar Sadat in 1981 because he had issued an Islamic judicial decree authorizing the killing. After his acquittal, the Sheikh founded a group, al-Gama'at al-Islamiyya, with the purpose of overthrowing the regime of Hosni Mubarak and replacing it with an Islamic state. He entered the United States and became leader of a small mosque in Jersey City, New Jersey. Following the World Trade Center bombing in February 1993, Rahman was implicated in both the bombing and a wider conspiracy to bomb key installations in New York including the Holland and Lincoln Tunnels and the United Nations building, as well as a plot to assassinate Senator Alfonse d'Amato of New York and UN secretary general Boutros Boutros-Ghali. On October 1, 1995, Rahman was convicted of directing these conspiracies. Legal barriers prevented officials from providing information about Rahman developed by the grand jury to the CIA and other intelligence agencies. The need to remove there barriers was often cited after the September 11, 2001, attacks.

Richard Reid, the convicted "shoe bomber," was prevented by fellow airline passengers and attendants from lighting explosives concealed in his shoes on a flight from Paris to Mianni. Reid is a British citizen of Jamaican descent. He encountered Islam in 1995 while serving a prison sentence for petty theft. Once out of jail, he began to worship at an Islamic mosque and cultural center in the London neighborhood of Brixton that would later become the focus of a terrorism investigation. While some investigators initially considered Reid to be a loner with few ties to terrorist groups, a number of new theories about him have emerged. One is that in July 2001 Reid went to Israel and possibly obtained the explosives and training from Palestinian terrorist groups. Another theory suggests that he met up with al-Qaeda operative Zacarias Moussaoui back in London and then went to an al-Qaeda cell in the Netherlands. Still another theory points to Paris. The investigation continues, and it appears more likely than not that Reid was part of a terrorist network of which much may still be in place. On October 4, 2002, Reid pleaded guilty to all eight counts, including attempted use of a weapon of mass destruction, attempted homicide, and placing an explosive device on an aircraft. On January 31, 2003, Reid was sentenced to life in prison. At his sentencing, he defiantly declared allegiance to Osama bin Laden, Saying, "I am at war with your country."

Ahmed Ressam was convicted of entering the United States with the intent of planting bombs. An Algerian born in 1967, Ressam, using the name Benni Noris, was arrested as he debarked from a car ferry in Port Angeles, Washington, in December 1999, having crossed from Vancouver, Canada. In the trunk of his car U.S. Customs officials found urea, nitroglycerine, and other bomb materials and components including timers fashioned from Casio watches. The turn of the millennium had already raised anxiety about possible computer problems, but Ressam's arrest fueled fears that Osama bin Laden and al-Qaeda had planned a ghastly accompaniment to the scheduled millennial celebrations in large cities. In January 2002, Ressam was convicted of aiding the terrorist bombing plot, which also involved a man named Mokhtar Haouari, whom Ressam testified against. Haouari was convicted of supplying Ressam with fake identification and $3,000 in cash.

Condoleezza Rice, U.S. national security advisor since 2001 and foreign affairs expert specializing in the Soviet Union and Russia. Born on November 14, 1954, in Birmingham, Alabama, Rice's earliest childhood spanned segregation and the growing turmoil of the civil rights struggle. Her father was a minister and educator, and her mother was an accomplished pianist and music teacher. She was bright student with many interests. Rice's family moved to Colorado where she attended high school and then enrolled in the University of Denver at the age of 15. At first Rice aspired to a career in classical music, but she decided she lacked the very high degree of talent needed to be competitive. At school, she met professor Josef Korbel, a former Czech diplomat who had fled the Nazis and the subsequent communist successor. Rice admired Korbel greatly and came to be intrigued by the nuances of political power and diplomatic relations. (Korbel's daughter, Madeleine

Albright, would become secretary of state under President Bill Clinton.) Rice received her degree in international relations in 1974, then earned a master's in economics at the University of Notre Dame, and finally a Ph.D. in international studies back in Denver. Her specialty was the Soviet Union, the "hottest" area of interest in the field during the continuing cold war. Rice would later recall that it was the "Byzantine" complexity of the Soviet system that especially appealed to her. In 1981, Rice became an assistant professor at Stanford University and advanced her career through the decade, winning two distinguished teaching awards. In 1993, she entered Stanford's administration as provost, a position that combined academic and financial duties, and became the youngest person, as well as the first woman and the first African American to hold the post. In George H. W. Bush's administration, Rice served in several advisory capacities, working closely with both National Security Advisor Brent Scowcroft and General Colin Powell. During this tumultuous period Rice and her colleagues tried to understand and deal with the rapid changes that culminated in the collapse of the Soviet Union. During the 1990s, Rice returned to Stanford, but when the younger Bush, George W., ran for president, Rice became the campaign's foreign policy adviser, advising a candidate who had little foreign experience. The newly elected Bush then turned to her to fill the national security advisor slot in the cabinet. Rice saw herself as a hard-headed pragmatist in foreign policy matters, although more liberal on domestic issues. During most of the president's first year, foreign policy was a continuation of the campaign's insistence that the nation limit its involvement in foreign affairs and try to avoid peacekeeping commitments except where directly related to U.S. interests. However, the terrorist attacks of September 11, 2001, suddenly demanded both military and diplomatic involvement on many levels and in many places. In an ongoing behind-the-scenes debate Rice, Colin Powell, Donald Rumsfeld, and Vice President Dick Cheney continue to try to agree on the scope of the war against terrorism, including the question of potential military action against others besides Iraq.

Thomas J. Ridge, director of the Office of Homeland Security, created in late 2001, and former governor of Pennsylvania. Ridge was born to a working-class Pennsylvania family on August 26, 1945, and grew up in the industrial city of Erie. His academic ability took him to Harvard University, where he graduated with honors in government studies in 1967. He then went to law school but was drafted in 1969 into the army where he served as an infantry staff sergeant during the Vietnam War and was awarded three medals including a Bronze Star for valor. After returning from the war, he completed his law degree in 1972. He next served as an assistant district attorney in Erie County until 1982, when he ran for and won a seat in the House of Representatives. Having won as a Republican in a predominately

Democratic district, Ridge established bipartisanship early in his political career. First as representative and then in 1994 as governor of Pennsylvania, Ridge's tough-on-crime attitude appealed to hard-core Republican conservatives, but his support for gun control and abortion rights did not. Despite Ridge's popularity and his ability to help Republicans in the key swing state of Pennsylvania, conservative opposition killed consideration of Ridge as a Republican vice presidential candidate in 1996 and 2000. The terrorist attacks in September 2001 gave Ridge a unique new opportunity; on October 8, 2001, he became the director of Homeland Security, a newly created cabinet-level post. This position would allow him both to serve as a communicator to the public about the terrorist threat and as a coordinator of intelligence and security efforts across dozens of federal agencies. Critics soon questioned the ill-defined nature of the job and whether Ridge had been given enough power to force entrenched bureaucrats to adopt a new agenda. In fall 2002, the legislation establishing the Department of Homeland Security was still stalled in Congress by a dispute between Senate Republicans and Democrats over civil service rights for the affected federal workers. However, following the 2002 elections in which the Republicans regained control of the Senate, Congress passed the homeland security legislation. On January 25, 2003, Ridge was sworn in as head of the new agency. The challenge of merging more than two dozen agencies (or portions of agencies) into the new department is formidable, as is the establishment of coordination with groups outside the agency such as the CIA and the FBI.

Donald H. Rumsfeld, U.S. secretary of defense since 2001. Rumsfeld has what might be considered two separate careers separated by more than two decades. He was born on July 9, 1932, in Evanston, Illinois and grew up in nearby Winnetka. He earned a scholarship to Princeton University and graduated in 1954 with a degree in political science. Rumsfeld next entered the navy and served as a pilot and flight instructor until 1957, when he became an administrative assistant in Congress and then a banker and broker. In 1962, however, Rumsfeld challenged the incumbent in the Thirteenth Congressional District and defeated his scandal-plagued opponent. He served in Congress for three terms, then became Richard Nixon's campaign manager in 1968. Nixon made Rumsfeld director of the Office of Economic Opportunity, a difficult position involving the aid and civil rights programs that had been established during the Lyndon B. Johnson administration, and his pragmatic attitude encountered opposition from both conservatives who were trying to scale down the programs and civil rights and welfare activists. Moving on, Rumsfeld served as U.S. ambassador to NATO and as secretary of defense in Gerald Ford's administration. In 1977, he embarked on more than two decades in the pharmaceutical industry, where he built up the drug company Searle and then sold it to the giant Monsanto Corporation. When George W. Bush's administration came into office in 2001, the relatively inexperienced Bush looked for the reinforcement of highly experienced cabinet members and chose Rumsfeld to be secretary of defense. At first, Rumsfeld faced a Pentagon that was still trying to deal with the end of the cold war, the reconfiguration of forces, and the new Bush administration's relatively isolationist viewpoint. However, in September 2001, Rumsfeld together with the rest of the administration suddenly found themselves embarking on a war of uncertain objectives and duration. The fight against the diffuse enemy of international terrorism would perhaps become a challenge as difficult as, but very different from, the arrayed powers that had faced one another during the cold war. In the debate over whether to attack Iraq, Rumsfeld was a hawk in comparison to the more cautious secretary of state, Colin Powell. When the U.S. offensive began in March, however, Rumsfeld's side clearly prevailed.

Ramzi Ahmed Yousef, Islamic terrorist and associate of Sheikh Omar Abdel Rahman. While Rahman, a blind cleric provided theological inspiration for the New York World Trade Center bombing in 1993 and related terrorist plots, Yousef, an electrical engineer who learned bomb making in an Afghanistan terrorist training camp, actually constructed and planted the bomb. Besides the bombing in New York City, Yousef bombed an airliner in the Philippines in December 1994, while plotting to assassinate Pope John Paul II during his visit there in January 1995. Philippine police uncovered Yousef's bomb-making operation but he fled to Islamabad, Pakistan. When Yousef tried to recruit South African Muslim theology student Istiaque Parker in 1995, the latter refused to smuggle a bomb into the United States and, fearing reprisal, went to U.S. authorities in Islamabad. U.S. and Pakistani agents arrested Yousef in his room and quickly flew him back to the United States, where he was convicted, with two coconspirators, and sentenced to life without parole.

Abu Mussab al-Zarqawi, a senior al-Qaeda leader operating in Iraq and other parts of the Middle East who emerged in 2003 as part of an alleged nexus between al-Qaeda and Iraq's leader Saddam Hussein. Al-Zarqawi, a Jordanian of Palestinian origin, fought in Afghanistan in the 1980s with the mujahideen forces against the Soviet invaders. After that conflict ended, al-Zarqawi began to work more closely with Osama bin Laden in Afghanistan, running one of his training camps in the late 1990s and presumably becoming affiliated with al-Qaeda. In 2001, al-Zarqawi may have been injured during the conflict with the U.S.-backed Northern Alliance. At any rate, he fled from Afghanistan to Iraq, and, according to U.S. officials, apparently went to Baghdad and began training an extremist Muslim group called Ansar-al-Islam, drawing upon his experience with explosives and chemical weapons. The group established a camp in a part of northeastern Iraq controlled neither by the Iraqi government nor by nearby Kurdish groups. There they possibly engaged in the production and testing of chemical weapons. These and other activities were revealed by U.S. authorities after investigation and a lucky cell-phone intercept by American and other cooperating intelligence agencies led to the capture and interrogation of al-Zarqawi's deputy, who is as yet unnamed. Al-Zarqawi is accused of having supplied money and weapons to his deputy, who purportedly assassinated U.S. diplomat Lawrence Foley in October 2002. The revelations of al-Zarqawi's alleged activities took on particular significance in early 2003 as the United States sought to bolster its case against Iraq by showing cooperation between Saddam Hussein's government and al-Qaeda.

CHAPTER 5

GLOSSARY

The following names of organizations, titles of legislation, and other terms are often found in discussion of the terrorist attacks on the United States and subsequent events.

Abu Sayyaf A Philippine Islamic extremist group that has conducted kidnappings and guerrilla raids since the 1990s. It is believed to have connections to al-Qaeda. As part of the post September 11 war on terrorism, the United States has sent aid and military advisers to help the Philippine government cope with Abu Sayyaf and other indigenous terrorist groups.

anthrax Carried by *Bacillus anthracis,* this disease is endemic to livestock at a low level but can also occur among humans. The cutaneous (skin) form of the disease is easily treatable, but the inhaled form can be deadly. The bacteria form spores that can last for many years and can be turned into a very fine, dispersible powder, making anthrax an attractive weapon for terrorists. In the fall of 2001, a series of anthrax-laced letters from an unknown terrorist resulted in five deaths in the United States.

Antiterrorism and Effective Death Penalty Act of 1996 This law was passed in the wake of the Oklahoma City bombing of 1995. Its many different provisions include broadened law enforcement powers against terrorists, stronger prohibitions against terrorist funding, procedures for removing immigrants accused of terrorism, and increased sanctions against the use of biological and chemical weapons.

antiterrorism assistance (ATA) A U.S. State Department program that provides assistance, such as training for border guards and customs officials and the strengthening of airport security, to more than 40 foreign governments for fighting terrorism.

assassination The deliberate murder of a politically or socially prominent person, especially when done for political purposes. It is illegal for the U.S. government to target individuals for assassination, but military raids (as in the attack on the home of Libya leader Muammar al-Qaddafi in

1986) have been launched that might be expected to kill terrorist leaders. The November 4, 2002, missile attack on a top al-Qaeda leader in Yemen has also been likened by critics to an assassination, but defenders view it as a legitimate military action.

attentat clause A provision of an extradition treaty in some nations that says that a nation holding the accused murderer of a head of state (or a head of state's family member) will not treat the accused as a "political" criminal and will extradite without considering any appeals on grounds of political protest or persecution.

Aviation and Transportation Security Act A 2001 law establishing a new Transportation Security Administration within the Department of Transportation. The new administration is charged with protecting airports, highways, waterways, pipelines, and other transportation systems, with particular attention to the newly federalized airport screening workers.

"axis of evil" President Bush has used this term to refer to Iraq, Iran, and North Korea as nations believed to be developing nuclear or other weapons of mass destruction.

biometrics Methods for using very precise physical characteristics or measurements to identify individuals. Examples include eye (retinal) scanning and hand geometry scanning.

bioterrorism The use of pathogens (disease-causing viruses or bacteria) as an instrument of terrorist attack. It has been an increasing concern in recent years.

Border Patrol, U.S. The agency charged with preventing illegal immigrants from crossing U.S. borders.

Camp X-Ray The location within the U.S. military base in Guantánamo Bay, Cuba, where the first facilities were built for holding hundreds of Taliban and al-Qaeda detainees from the war in Afghanistan.

cell The smallest unit of organization of a guerrilla or terrorist group, usually consisting of five or fewer people. Typically, a cell member has no knowledge of or contact with other cells, thus minimizing vulnerability to exposure or infiltration.

Central Intelligence Agency (CIA) The principal U.S. foreign intelligence agency founded in 1947 as the successor to the wartime Office of Strategic Services (OSS). It has primary responsibility for gathering terrorism-related intelligence abroad. The CIA is legally precluded from becoming involved in activities within the United States, although this line may become blurred in the current war against terrorism. The CIA is overseen by the National Security Council (NSC).

Coast Guard, U.S. The branch of the U.S. military tasked with patrolling coastal and harbor areas and with sea rescue services. The Coast Guard was established in 1790. In peacetime it is part of the Department of Transportation. In wartime, however, the Coast Guard becomes part of the Department of the Navy. Its functions may be subsumed into the proposed Department of Homeland Security.

COINTELPRO (Counterintelligence Program) An FBI "active measures" effort during the 1960s and early 1970s. In 1974, the Church Committee found that COINTELPRO had illegally conducted surveillance and disinformation campaigns against dissident leaders such as Dr. Martin Luther King, Jr. The program is often cited as a cautionary example in debates about expanding powers of the FBI and other agencies.

combatant A person encountered as an enemy fighter in a war. A "lawful combatant," who is in uniform, carrying weapons openly, and acting according to the rules of war, is entitled to be treated as a prisoner of war under the Geneva Convention. U.S. officials have decided that al-Qaeda and other terrorists are "unlawful combatants," who do not meet these criteria and can be held without trial.

commando tactics Use of small, highly trained and motivated armed forces inserted into enemy territory. Many nations have elite antiterrorism forces trained in commando tactics, while terrorists themselves could be said to be irregular commandos.

counterinsurgency Military, political, legal, economic, or other measures taken by a government to suppress or defeat revolutionaries. Counterinsurgency forces seek to gain intelligence about guerrilla activity and also to win the support of the public so it will turn against or expose the guerrillas.

counterterrorism The attempt to prevent terrorist attacks and root out and punish terrorist leaders and groups. As with counterinsurgency, intelligence is of key importance. Use of military or paramilitary forces and extrajudicial actions is commonplace in many nations but problematic in democratic societies that support basic civil liberties.

cyberterrorism The damaging or compromising of computer systems by hackers working as or for terrorists. Such activities can include introducing computer viruses, stealing sensitive information, and flooding web sites with bogus information requests.

Delta Force The elite counterterrorist task force of the U.S. Army based in Fort Bragg, North Carolina. The Delta Force has had only limited success against terrorists. In 1980, its attempt to mount an airborne rescue of American hostages in Iran failed when a helicopter and a plane collided.

denial of service attack (DOS attack) A hacking technique in which a flood of requests (often generated from virus-infected computers) bombards a web site, blocking legitimate access to it.

"dirty bomb." *See* **radiological weapon.**

extradition The legal process of transferring a prisoner from the country in which he or she is arrested to the country that has brought criminal charges against that prisoner. Countries often resist requests for extradition of accused terrorists, either because they fear reprisals from terrorist groups or out of concern for the civil liberties of the accused.

Federal Bureau of Investigation (FBI) The primary federal law enforcement agency, also charged with detecting and preventing espionage and terrorist attacks within the United States. The FBI was founded in 1924 as a reorganization of the earlier Bureau of Investigation. The FBI is part of the Department of Justice and is responsible to the attorney general.

Federal Emergency Management Agency (FEMA) The federal agency charged with responding to natural disasters or other widespread emergencies. It is now working on plans to cope with terrorist attacks.

first responders Persons such as police officers, firefighters, and paramedics who are responsible for containing and ameliorating a terrorist attack. Training and vaccination of first responders is now considered a high priority.

fissionables Materials such as uranium (U-238) and plutonium that are capable of causing a nuclear chain reaction or, if sufficiently refined and contained, a nuclear explosion. Such materials are a high-value target for terrorists.

Geneva Convention International agreement on the protection of the rights of prisoners and civilians in time of war. The version currently in force was enacted in 1949 and has been signed by more than 150 nations. Two protocols were added in 1977, dealing with guerrilla combatants. Those protocols were signed by only about half as many nations, not including the United States and Great Britain. Terrorist acts against civilians by states or groups violate the Geneva Convention. *See also* **combatant.**

globalization The increasing economic interdependence of nations and the growing tendency of large multinational corporations to overwhelm local or even national interests. Some analysts believe that opposition to economic globalization as well as Western cultural dominance may be an underlying cause of terrorism.

gross domestic product (GDP) The total value of goods and services produced within the country. GDP is a common measure of a nation's overall economic growth.

Ground Zero The area around the destroyed World Trade Center in New York City, where painstaking excavations were carried out for many months after the September 11, 2001, attack.

guerrilla warfare Military operations carried out by irregular forces against a government or occupying power. Guerrillas try to avoid direct, large-scale confrontations with forces that outmatch them and instead try to control the countryside and gain popular support while raiding government installations and supply convoys. While operating on a larger scale than terrorists and usually enjoying greater popular support, guerrillas frequently resort to terrorist acts such as killing people who collaborate with the government, using bombings and shootings to demonstrate that the government cannot protect the people, or extorting "taxes" from businesses or farms in areas that they control.

habeas corpus A legal writ that requires that a prisoner be produced for arraignment or released. Attempts have been made in a number of recent cases to obtain such a writ for persons accused of terrorism who are being held without filed charges.

Homeland Security Act of 2002 This act, passed in July 2002, establishes the new Department of Homeland Security, which unites all or part of 22 formerly separate federal agencies as a coordinated defense against terrorism.

Immigration and Naturalization Service (INS) The agency charged with processing the various kinds of legal immigrants and visa holders and with preventing illegal entry into the United States. The INS was created as a unification of the immigration and naturalization (citizenship) functions in 1935. It is part of the Department of Justice. After the September 11, 2001, attacks, several thousand immigrants and visa holders were held on immigration-related charges in order to prevent possible terrorist activity while they were questioned about terrorist ties.

infrastructure The networks and facilities a society uses to provide governance, distribute resources, maintain communications, and otherwise function. Terrorists and guerrillas often attack infrastructure targets such as railroads, power plants, police stations, and, perhaps in the future, computer facilities. Infrastructure can also refer to the training camps, weapons and supply caches, and other facilities used by a terrorist group.

insurgency An armed uprising against a government, usually carried on by means of guerrilla warfare tactics.

intifada Arabic for "uprising," this term refers to the spontaneous outbreak of unrest that was triggered in December 1987 by the killing of several Arabs in the Gaza Strip when their vehicle collided with an Israeli vehicle. Rumors that the killing was deliberate inflamed riots and demonstrations, and attempts by the Israeli occupation forces to suppress the demonstrations further heightened and expanded the intifada. Some critics of proposed U.S. military action against Iraq fear that it may trigger similar spontaneous uprisings against Israel or against Arab governments allied with the United States.

jihad An Arabic term usually translated as "holy war." While Islamic terrorists frequently invoke this concept to justify their violent campaigns against the enemies of Islam, some Islamic scholars believe that such use is illegitimate. They point to the term's broader meaning, which includes spiritual purification through the inner struggle with evil, as well as non-violent preaching or teaching.

Loya Jirga The traditional Grand Council of Afghanistan, which met in June 2002 to establish a new government for the country following the overthrow of the Taliban.

madrassa A Muslim school that emphasizes study of the Qur'an (Koran) and other religious teachings, sometimes to the exclusion of secular subjects. Madrassas are sometimes run by Islamic extremists in order to indoctrinate young people against Israel and Western nations.

military tribunal A court conducted by the military separate from and under different rules than a normal civilian court. Normally, military tribunals are used only to try members of the armed forces, but they have been used in wartime (including the Civil War and World War II) to try civilians involved in war-related activities. The extent to which military tribunals may be used following the September 11, 2001, attacks remains unclear.

mujahideen (mujahedeen, mujahadeen) Arabic for "holy warriors." In Afghanistan,the original mujahideen were a loosely organized group of Afghans who rebelled against their country's Soviet-backed government in the late 1970s. After the Soviets invaded in 1979, the mujahideen fought effectively as a guerrilla force, aided by weapons and training provided by the United States and other countries. During the 1980s, Osama bin Laden first emerged as a mujahideen leader who attracted a particularly radical Islamic following; his organization eventually became al-Qaeda. Meanwhile, the Taliban emerged as an alternative to the many warring bands of mujahideen; by the mid-1990s, the Taliban had consolidated its control of Afghanistan and become increasingly extremist.

narcoterrorism The concept that international drug traffickers and terrorists are natural allies who groups in their clandestine nature, use of weapons, and killing and intimidation of opponents. The term is also applied to acts of terrorism carried out by drug lords, such as the Extraditables, the terrorist arm of the Colombian Medellín cartel.

National Security Agency (NSA) A large, highly secretive agency established in 1952 within the Department of Defense, that uses high-tech means to intercept worldwide communications, including cell phone messages and e-mail. The NSA also tries to decrypt coded messages while protecting American encryption systems. (Since the government refused to publicly acknowledge its existence for many years, a common joke is that the initials really stand for "No Such Agency.")

nationalism The development of a national identity in culture, politics, and society. The development of such an identity by an ethnic group living in a country controlled by another group frequently results in guerrilla warfare or terrorism when the national aspirations of the smaller group are not accepted by the dominant group.

Northern Alliance A loosely knit coalition that had been fighting the Taliban and al-Qaeda in Afghanistan prior to the September 11, 2001, attacks on the United States. After 9/11, the United States provided extensive aid to the Northern Alliance and coordinated several air attacks with it.

nuclear terrorism The potential use of nuclear weapons by terrorists. Unsettled conditions in the former Soviet Union during the early 1990s fueled speculation that impoverished or disgruntled Soviet military or nuclear experts would be willing to sell their expertise or even nuclear materials or warheads to terrorist groups. While there seems to be little concrete evidence of such activities, the potentially devastating consequences of terrorists obtaining nuclear weapons have kept nuclear terrorism high on the agenda of counterterrorist planners.

Office of Homeland Security The White House office created by President Bush in October 2001 to provide public communication and agency coordination in response to the ongoing threat of terrorist attack. Former Pennsylvania governor Tom Ridge was appointed its first director. This office was succeeded by a cabinet-level Department of Homeland Security in 2003, with Ridge confirmed as its head.

Operation Anaconda The ground combat effort by U.S. forces against the al-Qaeda stronghold in eastern Afghanistan, in conjunction with the Northern Alliance during February–March 2002.

Operation Enduring Freedom The overall U.S. effort against the Taliban and al-Qaeda in Afghanistan beginning in October 2001 and including both ground operations and air strikes.

plastic explosive A putty-like explosive substance that can be easily shaped and embedded in innocuous objects. Manufactured under designations such as C-4 and Semtex, it is hard to detect, even with X rays, vapor sniffers, or other technologies. Under Muammar al-Qaddafi, Libya obtained a large amount of plastic explosive and distributed it to a variety of terrorist groups.

Posse Comitatus Act The law that prohibits the use of U.S. military forces for civilian law enforcement duties except in narrowly defined circumstances of emergency, insurrection, or invasion. There have been proposals to relax some of these restrictions in the name of counterterrorism.

profiling The identification of individuals as potential terror suspects on the basis of characteristics defined by appearance or behavior. Racial or ethnic profiling is opposed by many people but supported by some as a way to make security operations more efficient.

al-Qaeda (al-Qaida) Meaning "the Base" in Arabic, the name of the terrorist network believed to be organized by and under the ultimate control of Osama bin Laden. Estimates of its size range up to thousands of operatives organized into cells in more than 50 countries around the world.

radiological weapon Sometimes called a "dirty bomb" or a "poor man's nuke," a bomb that disperses radioactive material such as nuclear waste. The explosion is relatively small, but radioactive contamination can kill or sicken people nearby and render an area unsafe for an extended period.

safe house A house or building where a terrorist group can reside or store weapons while remaining concealed from authorities.

separatist General term for a person or group who seeks political independence or autonomy.

Shiites Followers of a sect that split off from the mainstream Sunni sect of Islam in the seventh century in a dispute over who would inherit spiritual leadership. Their theology and minority status (only about one-tenth of the world's Muslims are Shiites) have encouraged them to be militant. In Iran, the only Muslim state where Shiites are the majority, this militancy has been embodied in a fundamentalist government that at least until recently aggressively promoted both fundamentalist movements in neighboring countries and terrorist action against the United States and its allies.

skyjacking Hijacking of aircraft, a common terrorist practice in the 1960s and early 1970s. Tighter airport security and resistance of governments to negotiating with skyjackers had greatly reduced the incidence of skyjacking by the 1980s. The September 11, 2001, attacks in New York City and Washington, D.C., demonstrated, however, a new use of skyjacking—obtaining control of a large jetliner and crashing it into a building. *See also* **suicide bombing.**

smallpox A virulent and potentially deadly viral disease that can spread rapidly in populated areas. Smallpox was the first disease for which an effective vaccination was developed (in the 18th century). By the late 20th century, the disease had been eradicated as a public health threat. At that time, widespread inoculation against the disease ceased, leaving much of the population increasingly vulnerable if smallpox were to be reintroduced by terrorists. Vaccines are currently being stockpiled against the threat of a possible terrorist attack using smallpox, and some areas have begun to inoculate medical and emergency personnel.

smart card A card with an embedded computer chip that can store detailed identifying information about an individual. Combined with biometric information, a smart card could be an effective tool for infrastructure security.

state-sponsored terrorism The support (through training, weapons, money, or provision of safe haven) of terrorism as a means to carry out a nation's foreign policy. Libya, for example, has provided extensive support to a variety of Palestinian and European terrorist groups.

Sunni The orthodox sect of Islam. Sunnis are in the majority in all Islamic countries except Iran. There is often tension between the Sunni majority and the Shiite minority.

Taliban A movement of Islamic extremists that controlled much of Afghanistan from the mid-1990s until it was overthrown by the United States and its allies in late 2001. The Taliban imposed harsh laws and restrictions, particularly on women.

TIPS (Terrorism Information and Prevention System) A proposed program to encourage Americans to report suspicious activity that might be related to terrorism. A particular effort would be made to enroll workers such as mail carriers and utility meter readers. Civil libertarians are concerned about possible abuses of privacy and potential harassment. The program has never really been implemented.

Transportation Security Administration The new federal agency established to handle security for airports and other transportation infrastructure.

undetectable firearms Guns such as the Glock-17 that are mainly plastic with few metal parts. Although not really "undetectable," such guns are a problem for counterterrorism because they are hard to pick up in airport X-ray screenings.

USA PATRIOT Act (Uniting and Strengthening America by Providing Appropriate Tools Required to Intercept and Obstruct Terrorism Act) A 2001 law that goes considerably further than the Antiterrorism and Effective Death Penalty Act of 1996 in expanding the government's surveillance and investigatory powers in dealing with terrorism suspects. Civil libertarians have expressed concerns about many of its provisions, especially with regard to their potential effect on legitimate political activity.

War Powers Act A law passed in 1973 in response to what were perceived to be excesses in the Vietnam War era. It limits the president's use of military force without congressional consent except in emergencies.

weaponized Refers to the processing of an agent (such as anthrax spores) in such a way as to make it effective for use as a terrorist or military weapon.

weapons of mass destruction (WOMD, WMD) Weapons capable of killing large numbers of people at one time, including large conventional or nuclear bombs, chemical weapons such as nerve gases, or biological weapons such as infectious diseases or toxins. The threat of terrorists gaining access to such weapons is a major focus of modern counterterrorism.

PART II

GUIDE TO FURTHER RESEARCH

CHAPTER 6

HOW TO RESEARCH TERRORISM ISSUES

This chapter presents a selection of resources, techniques, and suggestions for researching issues related to the September 11, 2001, attack on the United States and the war on terrorism. Although the approach of a given researcher will depend on his or her interests, objectives, and the amount of time available, the following general approach should be suitable for most purposes.

- Gain a general orientation by reading the first part of this book. Chapter 1 can be read as a narrative, while Chapters 2–5 are best skimmed to get an idea of their coverage and then used as a reference resource.
- Review several of the general overview books and web resources given in the bibliography (Chapter 7).
- Skim a selection of the government, academic, advocacy, and media web sites (see discussion in this chapter), following links that seem likely to be relevant to your research topic
- Use the relevant sections of Chapter 7 to find more books, articles, and web sites on particular topics of interest.
- Find the most recent materials by using bibliographic tools such as the library catalogs and periodical indexes discussed in this chapter.
- To keep up with current events and breaking news, regularly check media web sites and periodically search the catalogs and indexes for recent material.

The chapter is organized according to the various types of resources and tools. The three major categories are online resources, print resources, and the special source area of law, legislation, and legal research.

ONLINE RESOURCES

With the abundance of information available online today, most researchers will begin by looking for relevant web sites. The terrorist attacks of September 11, 2001, the aftermath, and the ongoing war against terrorism have generated a flood of information from many sources: government agencies, academic departments, libraries, advocacy groups, and web sites maintained by major print and broadcast media outlets. These sites generally have the advantage of being authoritative and timely, although some academic or library sites may not be updated as often as government or media outlets.

GOVERNMENT WEB SITES

Numerous federal, state, and even local government agencies have some concern with the terrorist threat; however, certain federal agencies are vitally involved with this problem and thus offer particularly extensive resources. The following are some good starting points:

- CIA main page and its special War on Terrorism section: http://www.odci.gov/
- FBI's War on Terrorism page: http://www.fbi.gov/terrorinfo/terrorism.htm
- U.S. Department of Justice statements and information relating to the aftermath of the September 11, 2001, attacks: http://www.usdoj.gov/ag/terrorismaftermath.html
- U.S. Department of State Counterterrorism Office, which includes a link to the annual report "Patterns of Global Terrorism" and the official list of designated terrorist organizations: http://www.state.gov/s/ct/
- The new Department of Homeland Security web site: http://www.dhs.gov/dhspublic/

ACADEMIC WEB SITES

A number of scholarly sites are devoted to aspects of terrorism research, including sites maintained by universities, libraries, and think tanks. While most sites have considerable information relating to the post–September 11 environment, many have a more global focus. Some of the more extensive academic resource sites include the following:

- Air University Library & Press, of Maxwell Air Force base, Alabama, compiles links to Internet resources on topics of current military interest, including homeland security, the post–September 11 threat, and weapons of mass destruction: http://www.au.af.mil/au/aul/bibs/bib97.htm

- Dudley Knox Library, of the Naval Postgraduate School, also offers an extensive list of links: http://library.nps.navy.mil/home/terrorism.htm
- Terrorism Research Center, a consultancy group, has links to many other organizations and agencies: http://www.terrorism.com/index.shtml
- University Library of the California State University, Northridge, supplies terrorism research resources: http://library.csun.edu/llampert/terrorism/

Any of the above sites will lead the researcher to many of the core resources needed to research the 9/11 attacks, the reaction to them, and ongoing military and diplomatic efforts.

ADVOCACY SITES

Unlike the academic sites, advocacy sites generally espouse a particular concern or point of view, such as the defense of civil liberties (see also the section on "Researching Legal Issues" below). Advocacy sites often include updates on legislation and court cases as well as position statements.

The American Civil Liberties Union has a number of "issues" pages that are relevant to terrorism from a civil liberties standpoint. See, for example,

Criminal Justice: http://www.aclu.org/issues/criminal/hmcj.html
Free Speech: http://www.aclu.org/issues/freespeech/hmfs.html
Immigrants' Rights: http://www.aclu.org/issues/immigrant/hmir.html
National Security: http://www.aclu.org/issues/security/hmns.html

Since the enacted and proposed antiterrorism legislation in the wake of September 11 often includes provisions involving electronic eavesdropping or monitoring, civil liberties groups that focus on computer-related issues are also relevant here. These include

Center for Democracy and Technology: http://www.cdt.org/
Electronic Frontier Foundation: http://www.eff.org/
Electronic Privacy Information Center: http://www.epic.org/

MEDIA WEB SITES

The major broadcast and cable networks, news (wire) services, most newspapers, and many magazines have web sites that include news stories and links to additional information. For breaking news, the following are particularly useful:

Associated Press (AP): http://wire.ap.org/public_pages/WirePortal.pcgi/us_portal.html
Cable News Network (CNN): http://www.cnn.com
New York Times: http://www.nytimes.com
Reuters: http://www.reuters.com
Time magazine: http://www.time.com
Wall Street Journal: http://online.wsj.com/public/us
Washington Post: http://www.washingtonpost.com/

In addition, Yahoo! maintains a large set of links to many newspapers that have web sites or online editions at http://dir.yahoo.com/News_ and_Media/Newspapers/Web_Directories/

OTHER VENUES: NETNEWS AND LISTS

Netnews is a decentralized system of thousands of newsgroups, or forums organized by topic. Most web browsers have an option for subscribing to, reading, and posting messages in newsgroups by connecting to the news feed from your Internet Service Provider (ISP). The Google Groups site (http://groups.google.com) also provides free access and an easy-to-use interface to newsgroups. Although discussion of terrorism-related issues can be found in many newsgroups via a Google news message search, the "alt.security.terrorism" group is specifically devoted to this topic.

Mail lists offer another way to keep up with and discuss recent developments. Some organizations offer a mail list that keeps members posted about current developments. Check the organization's web site for information on how to subscribe to the list.

Netnews and mail lists are generally most valuable when they have a moderator who keeps discussions focused and discourages "flaming," consisting of heated or personally insulting statements.

FINDING MORE ON THE WEB

This chapter has highlighted web sites that appear to be comprehensive and frequently updated; however, no one can compile more than a tiny fraction of the links that might possibly be useful. To find more web sites, the researcher can turn to general web indexes, or portals, or use one of many available search engines.

WEB PORTALS

A web guide, or index, or portal, is a site that offers what amounts to a structured, hierarchical outline of subject areas. This enables the researcher to zero in on a particular aspect of a subject and find links to web sites for further exploration. The links are constantly being compiled and updated by a staff of researchers.

The best known and largest web index is Yahoo! (http://www. yahoo.com). The home page gives the top-level list of topics, and the researcher simply clicks to follow them to more specific areas. In addition to following Yahoo!'s outlinelike structure, there is also a search box where the researcher can type one or more keywords and receive a list of matching categories and sites.

Web indexes such as Yahoo! have two major advantages over undirected surfing. First, the structured hierarchy of topics makes it easy to find a particular topic or subtopic and then explore its links. Second, Yahoo! does not make an attempt to compile every possible link on the Internet (a task that is virtually impossible, given the size of the Web). Rather, sites are evaluated for usefulness and quality by Yahoo!'s indexers. This means that the researcher has a better chance of finding more substantial and accurate information. The disadvantage of web indexes is the flip side of their selectivity: The researcher is dependent on the indexer's judgment for determining what sites are worth exploring.

To explore terrorism via Yahoo!, the researcher should click "Society and Culture" from the home page listing of options, then continue to "Crime," "Types of Crime," and finally "Terrorism." From there, a variety of sites selected by the editors are available for browsing. A brief summary of available subtopics at the time of writing includes

- September 11th Attacks
- Bioterrorism
- Blast-Resistant Structural Design
- Counter-Terrorism
- Dirty Bombs
- Nuclear Terrorism
- Suicide Terrorism
- Terrorist Organization Profiles

The Yahoo! page also includes a list of featured sites and some links to current news, and Yahoo!'s "Full Coverage" news service page covers the subject of terrorism (http://fullcoverage.yahoo.com/Full_Coverage/US/Terrorism/).

In addition to news stories and related web links, the latter features audio and video versions of stories that can be viewed online.

About.com (http://www.about.com) is rather similar to Yahoo! but gives a greater emphasis to overviews or guides prepared by experts in various topics. To find information about terrorism on About.com, type a keyword such as "terrorism" into the "Find it now" box, which will produce a page that has links to subtopics and featured sites.

New guide and index sites are constantly being developed, and their capabilities improve as the Web matures. One example is AskJeeves (http://www.ask.com). This site attempts to answer a researcher's plain-English question, such as "How many died in the attack on the Pentagon?" by providing links to web sites that are likely to contain the answer. The user simply types his or her query into the "Ask" box.

SEARCH ENGINES

Search engines take a very different approach to finding materials on the Web. Instead of organizing topically in a "top-down" fashion, search engines work their way from the bottom up, scanning through web documents and indexing them. There are hundreds of search engines, but some of the most widely used include the following:

- AltaVista: http://www.altavista.com
- Excite: http://www.excite.com
- Google: http://www.google.com
- Hotbot: http://www.hotbot.com
- Lycos: http://www.lycos.com
- Northern Light: http://www.northernlight.com/news.html
- WebCrawler: http://www.WebCrawler.com

Search engines are generally easy to use by applying the same sorts of keywords as those employed in library catalogs. There are a variety of web search tutorials available online (try typing in "web search tutorial" in a search engine to find some). One good search tutorial is published by Bright Planet at http://www.brightplanet.com/deepcontent/tutorials/search/index.asp

Here are a few basic rules for using search engines:

- When looking for something specific, be specific: Use the most precise term or phrase. For example, when looking for information about extradition, type in "extradition," since this is the specific, standard term.

- Phrases (made up of two or more words) should be put in quotes to be matched as phrases rather than as individual, separate words. A good current example is "war on terrorism."
- When looking for a general topic that might be expressed using various different words or phrases, use several descriptive words—nouns are more reliable than verbs—for example, "international terrorism statistics." (Most engines will automatically list first pages that match all three terms.)
- Use wild cards, or symbols (usually an asterisk) to represent letter characters, when a desired word may have more than one ending. For example, "terroris*" matches both *terrorism* and *terrorist.*
- Most search engines support Boolean operators that can be used to broaden or narrow a search: Use "AND" to narrow a search (for example, "chemical AND weapon" will match only pages that have both terms); use OR to broaden a search ("information warfare' OR cyberterrorism" will match any page that has either term); use NOT to exclude unwanted results ("bombings NOT Israel" finds articles about bombings except those in or relating to Israel).

Since each search engine indexes somewhat differently and offers somewhat different ways of searching, it is a good idea to use several different search engines, especially for a general query. Several "metasearch" programs automate the process of submitting a query to multiple search engines. These include Metacrawler (http://www.metacrawler.com) and SurfWax (http://www.surfwax.com/). Note that metasearch engines tend to have two drawbacks: They may overwhelm the user with results (and insufficiently prune duplicates), and they often do not use some of the more popular search engines (such as Google or Northern Light).

Finally, there exist search utilities that can be run from the researcher's own computer rather than through a web site. A good example is Copernic (http://www.copernic.com).

FINDING ORGANIZATIONS AND PEOPLE

Chapter 8 of this book provides a list of organizations and agencies that are involved in the issue of terrorism, the war on terrorism, and homeland security, but new organizations do emerge. Good places to look for information and links to organizations are the State Department, Terrorism Research Center, and other resource sites mentioned at the beginning of this chapter. If a researcher seeks a specific organization and such sites do not yield its name, try the name in a search engine. Generally, the best approach is to put the name of the organization in quotation marks, such as "National Committee Against Repressive Legislation."

Another approach is to take a guess at the organization's likely web address. For example, the American Civil Liberties Union is commonly known by the acronym ACLU, so it is not a surprise that the organization's web site is at http://www.aclu.org. (Note that the web sites of noncommercial organization normally use the ".org" suffix; government agencies, ".gov"; educational institutions, ".edu"; and businesses, ".com.") This technique can save time but does not always work. In particular, watch out for "spoof" sites that mimic or parody organizational sites. Such a site might, for example, have the same name as that of a government agency but end in ".org" instead of ".gov." (Of course, such sites may be of interest in themselves as forms of criticism or dissent.)

There are several ways to find a person on the Internet:

- Put the person's name (in quotes) in a search engine and possibly find that person's home page on the Internet.
- Contact the person's employer (such as a university for an academic or a corporation for a technical professional). Most such organizations have web pages that include a searchable faculty or employee directory.
- Try one of the people-finder services, such as Yahoo! People Search (http://people.yahoo.com) or BigFoot (http://www.bigfoot.com). This may yield contact information such as e-mail address, regular address, and/or phone number.

PRINT RESOURCES

As useful as the Web is for quickly finding information and the latest news, in-depth research still requires trips to the library or bookstore. Getting the most out of the library requires the use of bibliographic tools and resources, such as catalogs, indexes, bibliographies, and other guides that identify the books, periodical articles, and other print material that deal with a particular subject. They are essential tools for the researcher.

LIBRARY CATALOGS

Most researchers are familiar with the basics of physically using a library catalog may not realize that many catalogs can be searched online. Access to the largest library catalog, that of the Library of Congress (LOC), is available at http://catalog.loc.gov. This page includes a guide to using the catalog and both basic and advanced catalog searches.

Yahoo! offers a categorized listing of libraries at http://dir.yahoo.com/Reference/Libraries/. Most catalogs can be searched in at least the following ways:

- An author search is most useful when a researcher suspects a person has written a number of works of interest. However, it may fail if the author's exact name is not used. (Cross-references are intended to deal with this problem, but cannot cover all possible variations.)
- A title search is best when the exact title of the book is known, and the researcher just wants to know if the library has that title. Generally, only the first few words of the title are necessary, excluding initial articles *(a, an, the)*.
- A keyword search will match words found anywhere in the title. It is thus broader and more flexible than a title search, although it may still fail if all keywords are not present.
- A subject search will find all works that have been assigned that subject heading by the library. The big advantage of such a search is that it does not depend on certain words being in the title. However, using a subject search requires knowledge of the appropriate subject headings.

Relevant Library of Congress subject headings relating to the September 11, 2001, attacks and their aftermath include September 11 Terrorist Attacks, 2001 and War on terrorism, 2001 –. Note that Homeland Security is not currently an LOC heading. Materials on this subject may be found under Civil Defense—United States or under National Security—United States. The most general LOC heading is Terrorism, which can be subdivided by region or country, such as the United States. Other subdivisions include

Terrorism and Mass Media
Terrorism—Bibliographies
Terrorism—Cases
Terrorism—Case Studies
Terrorism—Computer Network Resources
Terrorism—Congresses
Terrorism—Databases
Terrorism—Directories
Terrorism—Encyclopedias
Terrorism—Government Policy [subdivided by country]
Terrorism—History [many chronological and other subdivisions]
Terrorism in Literature

Terrorism in Mass Media
Terrorism—Law and Legislation [subdivided by country]
Terrorism—Moral and Ethical Aspects
Terrorism—Political Aspects
Terrorism—Press Coverage
Terrorism—Prevention [in other words, counterterrorism—many subdivisions]
Terrorism—Psychological Aspects
Terrorism—Religious Aspects
Terrorism—Security Measures
Terrorism—Social Aspects
Terrorism—Statistics
Terrorism Victims' Families

Related but narrower LOC terms include the following:

Bioterrorism
Bombings
Chemical Terrorism
Children and Terrorism
Cyberterrorism
Hostages
Nuclear Terrorism
Sabotage
State-sponsored Terrorism
Terrorists [many subdivisions including Biography]
Trials (Terrorism)

In addition, the following general terms may be relevant in some situations:

Crimes against peace
Genocide
Mass murder
Security, international

Once the record for a book or other item is found, it is a good idea to see what additional subject headings and name headings have been assigned to it. These in turn can be used for further searching.

AN ALTERNATIVE: BOOKSTORE CATALOGS

Many people have discovered that online bookstores such as Amazon.com (http://www.amazon.com) and Barnes & Noble (http://www.barnesandnoble.

com) are convenient ways to shop for books. A less-known benefit of online bookstore catalogs is that they often include publisher's information, book reviews, and reader's comments about a given title. They can thus serve as a form of annotated bibliography.

BIBLIOGRAPHIES, INDEXES, AND DATABASES

Bibliographies in various forms provide a convenient way to find books, periodical articles, and other materials. How far to go back in one's reading depends, of course, on one's research topic and goals. Some subjects, such as cyberterrorism or information warfare will not have useful materials more than a few years old. Obviously, September 11, 2001, is a watershed date after which much more material will be found on topics such as homeland security and the war on terrorism, so in some cases researchers may want to limit searches to materials published in 2001 or later.

Popular and scholarly articles can be accessed through periodical indexes that provide citations and abstracts. Abstracts are brief summaries of articles or papers. They are usually compiled and indexed (originally in bound volumes, but increasingly, online). Some examples of printed indexes containing literature related to terrorism are the following:

- Criminal Justice Abstracts
- Criminal Justice Periodical Index
- Index to Legal Periodicals and Books
- Social Sciences Citation Index
- Social Sciences Index
- Sociological Abstracts

Some of these indexes are available online (at least for recent years). Generally, however, they can be accessed only by a library cardholder and not over the Internet (except on a college campus). Consult with a university reference librarian for more help.

Two good indexes have unrestricted search access. UnCover Web (http://www.ingenta.com/) contains brief descriptions of about 13 million documents from about 27,000 journals in just about every subject area. Copies of complete documents can be ordered with a credit card, or they may be obtainable for free at a local library. The other and perhaps the most valuable index for topics related to criminal justice, including terrorist acts in the United States, is the National Criminal Justice Reference Service Justice Information Center (http://www.ncjrs.org). It offers a searchable abstract database containing 150,000 criminal justice publications, and it can be a real gold mine for the more advanced researcher.

PERIODICAL INDEXES

Most public libraries subscribe to database services such as InfoTrac and EBSCO that index articles from hundreds of general-interest periodicals (and some moderately specialized ones). The database can be searched by author or by words in the title, subject headings, and sometimes words found anywhere in the article text. Depending on the database used, "hits" in the database can produce a bibliographical description (author, title, pages, periodical name, issue date, etc.), a description plus an abstract (a paragraph summarizing the contents of the article), or the full text of the article itself. Before using such an index, it is a good idea to view the list of newspapers and magazines covered and determine the years of coverage.

Many libraries provide dial-in, Internet, or telnet access to their periodical databases as an option in their catalog menu. However, licensing restrictions usually mean that only researchers who have a library card for that particular library can access the database (by typing in their card number). Check with local public or school libraries to see what databases are available.

For periodicals not indexed by InfoTrac or another index, or for which only abstracts rather than complete text is available, check to see whether the publication has its own web site (most now do). Some scholarly publications are putting all or most of their articles online. Popular publications tend to offer only a limited selection. Some publications of both types offer archives of several years' back issues that can be searched by author or keyword.

LEGAL RESEARCH

It is important for researchers to be able to obtain the text and summary of laws and court decisions relating to terrorism, particularly given the spate of developments after September 11, 2001. Because of the specialized terminology of the law, legal research tools can be more difficult to master than bibliographical or general research tools. Fortunately, the Internet has also come to the rescue in this area, offering a variety of ways to look up laws and court cases without having to pore through huge bound volumes in law libraries (which may not be easily accessible to the general public).

FINDING LAWS

Most legislation relating to terrorism is federal, as terrorism is usually national or international in scope. When federal legislation passes, it eventually becomes part of the United States Code, a massive legal compendium. Title 18 of the U.S. Code deals with Crimes and Criminal Procedure. Part I of this title defines crimes and penalties and can be used together with this book's summary in Chapter 2 "Legislation, Laws, and Court Cases Relating to the War on Terrorism" to look up specific sections relating to terrorism. (Since so many new provisions and amendments have been passed, it may be better to start with the summaries of the Antiterrorism and Effective Death Penalty Act of 1996 and the USA PATRIOT Act of 2001 in Chapter 2 and the complete legislative summaries in the appendixes before turning to the existing sections of the U.S. Code.)

The U.S. Code can be searched online at several locations, but the easiest site to use is probably that of Cornell Law School (http://www4.law.cornell.edu/uscode/). The fastest way to retrieve a law is by its title and section citation, but phrases and keywords can also be used.

KEEPING UP WITH LEGISLATIVE DEVELOPMENTS

Pending legislation is often tracked by advocacy groups, both national and those based in particular states. See Chapter 8 for contact information.

Proposed federal legislation on terrorism often turns up as part of a large bill often called an omnibus crime bill, although provisions can also be added to appropriations bills for defense, intelligence, or other activities. Terrorism can also be the subject of individual bills (such as the USA PATRIOT Act of 2001).

The Library of Congress Thomas web site (http://thomas.loc.gov/) includes files summarizing legislation by the number of the Congress (each two-year session of Congress has a consecutive number; for example, the 107th Congress was in session in 2001 and 2002). Legislation can be searched for by the name of its sponsor(s), the bill number, or by topical keywords. (Laws that have been passed can be looked up under their Public Law number.) For example, selecting the 106th Congress and typing the phrase "airport security" into the search box retrieved, at the time of writing, a list that began as follows:

*Listing of **39** bills containing your phrase **exactly as entered.***

1. *Airport Security Personnel Protection Act (Introduced in Senate) [S.1829.IS]*
2. *Airport Security Personnel Protection Act (Introduced in House) [H.R.3505.IH]*
3. *Military Standards for Airport Security Screeners Act (Introduced in House)[H.R.3959.IH]*

4. *Military Standards for Airport Security Screeners Act (Introduced in House)[H.R.4058.IH]*
5. *To amend title 49, United States Code, to permit individuals who are nationals of the United States to be hired as airport security screening personnel. (Introduced in House)[H.R.3467.IH]*
6. *Airport and Seaport Terrorism Prevention Act (Introduced in Senate)[S.1429.IS]*
7. *Airline Passenger Safety Enhancement Act of 2001 (Introduced in Senate)[S.1461.IS] . . .*

Clicking on the bill number (in brackets) open a page that includes the text of the legislation and a link to the bill summary and status. For example, the summary for the first bill listed above began as follows:

> ***S.1829***
> *Sponsor: Sen Feinstein, Dianne (introduced 12/14/2001)*
> *Related Bills: H.R.3505*
> *Latest Major Action: 12/14/2001 Referred to Senate committee. Status: Read twice and referred to the Committee on the Judiciary.*
> *Title: A bill to provide for transitional employment eligibility for qualified lawful permanent resident alien airport security screeners until their naturalization process is completed, and to expedite that process*

Further details include sponsors, committee action, and amendments.

Finding Court Decisions

Legislation is only part of the story, of course. The Supreme Court and state court make important decisions every year that determine how the laws are interpreted. Legal decisions are organized using a particular system of citations. The general form is *Party1 v. Party2 volume reporter* [optional start page] *(court, year)*. Here are a couple of examples:

Brandenburg v. Ohio, 395 U.S. 44 (1969): Party 1 is Brandenburg, the defendant who is appealing his case from a state court, and Party 2 is the state of Ohio. The case is in volume 395 of the *U.S. Supreme Court Reports*, beginning on page 44. The case was decided in 1969. (For the Supreme Court, the name of the court is omitted.)

Fierro v. Gomez 77 F.3d 301 (9th Circ. 1996). The two parties are Fierro and Gomez, and the case was in the U.S. Court of Appeals for the Ninth Circuit, decided in 1996.

A state court decision can generally be identified because it includes the state's name. For example, in *State v. Torrance*, 473 (S.E.2d. 703, S.C. 1996), "S.E.2d" means that the second Southeast reporter published the decision, while "S.C." refers to the state (in this case, South Carolina). Note that there are several regional reporters, each covering a group of states.

Once the jurisdiction for the case has been determined, the researcher can then go to a number of places on the Internet to find cases by citation and sometimes by the names of the parties or by subject keywords. Among the most useful sites are the following:

- Legal Information Institute (http://supct.law.cornell.edu/supct/) has all Supreme Court decisions since 1990, plus 610 of "the most important historic" decisions.
- Washlaw Web (http://www.washlaw.edu/) lists many courts, all the states, and legal topics, making it a good jumping-off place for many sorts of legal research; however, the actual accessibility of state court opinions (and the formats they are provided in) varies widely.

LEXIS AND WESTLAW

Lexis and Westlaw are commercial legal databases that have extensive information including an elaborate system of notes, legal subject headings, and ways to show relationships between cases. Unfortunately, these services are too expensive for use by most individual researchers except through a university or corporate library.

MORE HELP ON LEGAL RESEARCH

For more information on conducting legal research, visit Legal Research FAQ (http://www.cis.ohio-state.edu/hypertext/faq/usenet/law/research/top.html). After a certain point, however, the researcher who lacks formal legal training may need to consult with or rely on the efforts of professional researchers or academics in the field.

A FINAL WORD

Thanks to the World Wide Web, more information from more sources is available than ever before. There is also a greater diversity of voices, since any person or group with a computer and Internet service can put up a web site—in some cases one that looks as polished and professional as that of an established group. One benefit is that dissenting views can be found in abundance, including those on sites maintained by terrorist groups or their supporters.

The other side of the coin, however, is that the researcher—whether journalist, analyst, teacher, or student—must take extra care to try to verify facts and to understand the possible biases of each source. Some good questions to ask oneself when doing research on the Internet are the following:

- Who is responsible for this web site?
- What is the background or reputation of the person or group?
- Does the person or group have a stated objective or agenda?
- What biases might this person or group have?
- Do a number of high-quality sites link to this one?
- What is the source given for a particular fact? Does that source actually say what is quoted? Where did the source get that information?

In a sense, in the information age each person must be his or her own journalist.

CHAPTER 7

ANNOTATED BIBLIOGRAPHY

This chapter presents a representative selection of books, articles, and Internet documents and sources relating to the September 11, 2001, terrorist attacks on the United States and the ensuing war on terrorism. Materials have been selected where possible to be accessible, substantial, and diverse in viewpoint. The bibliography is divided into six broad categories that are further divided into subtopics. They are as follows:

Reference and Background
General References
Sourcebooks and Anthologies
Introductions and Overviews
The Attacks of September 11, 2001

The War on Terrorism
Background to the Terrorist Attacks
U.S. Military Campaign Against Terrorism
International Situation, Foreign Policy, and Diplomacy
Intelligence Agencies: Failure and Reform

Homeland Security
General Considerations
Airline and Other Transportation Security
Other Infrastructure Protection
Cyberterrorism

Terrorism and Weapons of Mass Destruction
General Considerations
Nuclear Terrorism
Biological and Chemical Terrorism

Legal Issues
General Legal and Civil Liberties Issues
Investigation, Surveillance, and Screening
Treatment and Prosecution of Suspects

Terrorism and American Society
Economic Effects of September 11 and Aftermath
Political and Social Aspects
Psychological, Philosophical, and Spiritual Dimensions

Within each topic, the listings are divided according to books, articles, and web resources. Note that although all web addresses (URLs) have been checked, web pages are often moved or removed. If an address is not found, a keyword search using a search engine is recommended. See Chapter 6 for more information about Internet research and resources.

REFERENCE AND BACKGROUND

GENERAL REFERENCES

This section focuses on reference works on terrorism in general, including encyclopedias, dictionaries, bibliographies, and chronologies.

Books

Alali, A. Oadasuo, and Gary W. Byrd. *Terrorism and the News Media: A Selected, Annotated Bibliography.* Jefferson, N.C.: McFarland, 1994. Contains entries for more than 600 works (print and electronic) dealing with the often symbiotic relationship between terrorism and the media. Entries are divided into three main areas: understanding terrorism, terrorism and the electronic media, and terrorism and the print media.

Anderson, Sean, and Stephen Sloan. *Historical Dictionary of Terrorism.* Metuchen, N.J.: Scarecrow Press, 1995. This dictionary and reference handbook provides an alphabetical listing of terrorist groups and incidents, as well as a brief chronology and a bibliography.

Babkina, A. M. *Terrorism: An Annotated Bibliography.* 2d ed. Huntington, N.Y.: Nova Science Publishers, 2001. This bibliography covers selected books and journal articles from 1993 to 2001. Books are listed from reproduced Library of Congress catalog records, with no annotation other than the occasional summary included in the cataloging. Journal articles are covered in records from the CRS Public Policy Literature (PPLT) database, and the records include brief notes or summaries.

Overlook Press, 2002. A collection of 15 in-depth reports from BBC reporters around the world. Some topics include the challenges faced by U.S. president Bush and by President Musharraf of Pakistan and the connection between the Arab-Israeli conflict and al-Qaeda. This anthology provides an English-language but not America-centric viewpoint that can broaden the perspective of readers who are normally exposed only to U.S. media.

Calhoun, Craig J., Ashley Timmer, and Paul Prince, eds. *Understanding September 11.* New York: New Press, 2002. Published under the sponsorship of the Social Science Research Council, this wide-ranging anthology includes writings by historians, sociologists, anthropologists, economists, and others. Topics covered include the role of Islam and the situation in the Middle East and Central Asia, as well as military aspects of the war on terrorism.

Dudley, William, ed. *The Attack on America: September 11, 2001.* San Diego, Calif.: Greenhaven Press, 2002. An anthology of articles about the attacks and American response, selected to highlight opposing viewpoints on various issues. Topics include the motivations of the terrorists; whether U.S. policies helped cause the attacks; the applicability of military, law enforcement, and diplomatic responses; and other implications of the attacks.

Egendorf, Laura K., ed. *Terrorism: Opposing Viewpoints.* San Diego, Calif.: Greenhaven Press, 2000. This collection of periodical articles, interviews, and book excerpts presents pro and con viewpoints on a variety of issues relating to terrorism. Topics discussed include the seriousness of the terrorist threat, motivations and justifications for terrorism, and appropriateness of counterterrorism measures.

Hoge, James F., Jr., and Gideon Rose, ed. *How Did This Happen? Terrorism and the New War.* New York: Public Affairs, 2001. A wide-ranging collection of essays by experts in various fields, such as religious scholar Karen Armstrong and terrorism expert Walter Laqueur. Topics include the religious and other motivations for the attacks, historical background for Afghanistan and neighboring areas, various areas of domestic security (including aviation and bioterrorism), and the historical significance of the attacks.

Kegley, Charles W., and William D. Stanley, eds. *The New Global Terrorism: Characteristics, Causes, Controls.* Upper Saddle River, N.J.: Prentice Hall, 2002. A collection of essays by experts analyzing the new "terrain" of the war on terrorism. The book breaks its essays into three groups covering the changing characteristics of emerging terrorism, causes of terrorism old and new, and principles to guide action in the new arena.

Kushner, Harvey W. *Essential Readings on Political Terrorism: Analyses of Problems and Prospects for the 21st Century.* Lincoln, Neb.: Gordian Knot

Books, 2002. An anthology of recent articles on various aspects of global terrorism, grouped into the following topics: defining terrorism; the mind of the terrorist (psychosocial aspects); state, culture, and terrorism; media, communications, and terrorism; the victims of terrorism; chemical and biological warfare agents and terrorism.

Kushner, Harvey W., ed. *The Future of Terrorism: Violence in the New Millennium.* Thousand Oaks, Calif.: Sage Publications, 1998. An overview of the current status and emerging trends in terrorism. Part 1 deals with foreign terrorism, mainly of Islamic origin. Part 2 deals with American domestic terrorism, including hate crime and militant antigovernment groups. Part 3 gives legislative, law enforcement, and technological recommendations for fighting terrorism. Part 4 looks at future terror threats including weapons of mass destruction and the use of the Internet for terror attacks.

Lesser, Ian O., ed. *Countering the New Terrorism.* Santa Monica, Calif.: Rand Corporation, 1999. Contributors characterize a "new terrorism" in which emerging groups with new sponsors, motives, agendas, and weapons have made the traditional cold war analysis of terrorist conflict largely obsolete. The new terrorists are more loosely organized and flexible than the traditional groups and are gaining access to weapons far more lethal than bombs and guns.

Miller, Diana, ed. *Terrorism: Are We Ready?* Huntington, N.Y.: Nova Science Publishers, 2002. A compilation of papers and congressional testimony discussing responses to the threat of terrorism following the attacks of September 11, 2001. The major topic areas discussed are bio/chemical terrorism, infrastructure protection, aviation security, and homeland security (including legal issues arising out of counterterrorism measures).

Perry, Gabrielle, ed. *Terrorism Reader.* Huntington, N.Y.: Nova Science Publishers, 2001. A collection of papers on various aspects of counterterrorism and possible measures to be taken. Topics include foreign policy options, border security systems, the use of the military in homeland security, and legal aspects of counterterrorist measures.

Prados, John, ed. *America Confronts Terrorism: Understanding the Danger and How to Think About It, a Documentary Record.* Chicago: Ivan R. Dee, 2002. A collection of documents relating to anti-American terrorism in recent years including the attacks of September 11, 2001. Includes assessments, projections, reports of the National Commission on Terrorism, a profile of and statement by Osama bin Laden, and reports on such attacks as the Khobar barracks bombing, the African embassy bombings, and the U.S. destroyer *Cole* bombing. The final section looks at some recent executive and legislative responses to terrorism.

Roleff, Tamara, ed. *America Under Attack: Primary Sources.* San Diego, Calif.: Lucent Books, 2002. A collection of articles and excerpts from the media relating to the attacks of September 11, 2001, and the subsequent response. Includes news accounts, speeches, and interviews, as well as statements by President George W. Bush and Osama bin Laden.

Rubin, Barry, and Judith Colp Rubin, eds. *Anti-American Terrorism and the Middle East: A Documentary Reader.* New York: Oxford University Press, 2002. Following the attacks of September 11, 2001, the main focus of U.S. efforts and of the American public has been Osama bin Laden, al-Qaeda, and Afghanistan. However, this collection of 100 key documents reminds readers that there are many other terrorist groups and movements in the Middle East that share a hostile view of the United States and have the resources and capabilities to carry out major terrorist attacks. The collection also includes a variety of responses to September 11 within the Islamic world. A chronology, glossary, and helpful background material for each selection is provided.

Silvers, Robert B., and Barbara Epstein, eds. *Striking Terror: America's New War.* New York: New York Review of Books, 2002. A collection of 16 articles published in the *New York Review of Books* in the weeks following the attacks of September 11, 2001. The authors explore a wide range of issues including the causes and motivations of Islamic terrorism, the activities of al-Qaeda and Osama bin Laden, and conflicts between antiterrorist efforts and civil liberties. Some articles were originally written before or just after the attacks but epilogues have been added to bring them up to date.

Talbott, Strobe, and Nayan Chanda, eds. *The Age of Terror: America and the World after September 11.* New York: Basic Books, 2001. Presents essays by historians and policy experts including Paul Kennedy and Niall Ferguso. Topics include the global historical context, the clash of civilizations and the problems of the "American empire," the failure of intelligence, and the priorities for national security and counterterrorism in a changed world.

Ward, Richard H., and Cindy S. Moors, eds. *Terrorism and the New World Disorder.* Chicago: University of Illinois at Chicago, 1998. A collection of articles by law enforcement experts with a variety of local, national, and international criminal justice perspectives. The first part deals with worldwide trends in the motivation of terrorist and the nature of their potential targets. The second part examines intelligence gathering by law enforcement agencies such as Chicago's Terrorist Task Force. The third part deals with a variety of incidents including the 1995 Oklahoma City bombing, threats to aviation, terrorism by organized crime and drug groups, and other types of terrorism such as religious, left-wing, eco-, and nationalistic. The final art deals with the threat of biological terrorism and law enforcement tactics.

INTRODUCTIONS AND OVERVIEWS

This section includes general introductions to and overviews of terrorism, such as textbooks and popular works.

Books

Combs, Cynthia C. *Terrorism in the 21st Century.* 2d ed. Upper Saddle River, N.J.: Prentice-Hall, 2000. An introductory survey geared toward college undergraduates. Discusses the anatomy of modern terrorism, the actors, and their methods; the organization of national and international counterterrorist agencies; and predictions about future trends. Each discussion concisely presents and assesses the key factors.

Hoffman, Bruce. *Inside Terrorism.* New York: Columbia University Press, 1998. Provides a historical perspective on the development of terrorism from its origins in the French Revolution to anarchist and socialist movements of the 19th century and the nationalism and postcolonialism of the 20th century. The author argues that a new terrorism can be seen in the emergence of groups such as fanatical Muslim and Jewish extremists in the Middle East, the extremist fringe of American militia movements, and apocalyptic sects such as Japan's Aum Shinrikyo. He also argues that this new terrorism is at the same time less tractable and predictable and potentially more dangerous because of the groups' access to weapons of mass destruction and willingness to use them.

Mullins, W. C. *Sourcebook on Domestic and International Terrorism: An Analysis of Issues, Organizations, Tactics and Responses.* 2d ed. Springfield, Ill.: Thomas, 1997. A general handbook on terrorism directed to law enforcement personnel. Areas covered include definitions of terrorism, motivations and psychology of terrorists, dynamics of leadership and organization in terrorist groups, terrorist tactics and weapons, and approaches to counterterrorism.

National Issues Forums. *Terrorism: What Should We Do Now?* Dubuque, Iowa: Kendall/Hunt Publishing, 2003. National Issues Forums, which provides structured materials for discussion groups, organizes this discussion into three different approaches that are simultaneously interrelated "prongs"—an all-out war against terrorism, a focus on homeland security, and an effort to win the hearts and minds of people in areas where terrorism arises. The advantages, tradeoffs, and opposing arguments for each of these three courses of action are outlined and explored.

Piszkiewicz, Dennis. *The Evolution of Terror: Terrorism's War with America.* Westport, Conn.: Praeger Publishers, 2003. A detailed account and analysis of 40 years of developments in world terrorism and U.S. response. In recent years, politics, ideology, and tactics on both sides have changed in important ways.

Simon, Jeffrey D. *The Terrorist Trap: America's Experience with Terrorism.* 2d ed. Bloomington: Indiana University Press, 2001. A history of terrorism against the United States from the Barbary pirates of the early 19th century to September 11, 2001, this book provides good historical context, describing how various U.S. leaders have coped with terrorist threats. It argues that the psychological, ideological, and social elements that make modern terrorism unique require new tactics, and policymakers must avoid being trapped by grandiose rhetoric that blinds them to practical, achievable goals.

Simonsen, Clifford E., and Jeremy R. Spindlove. *Terrorism Today: The Past, the Players, the Future.* Upper Saddle River, N.J.: Prentice-Hall, 2000. A survey textbook for college and law-enforcement training courses. The first part discusses the definition, history, and typology of terrorism; the second discusses terrorism in nine geographical regions; and the third addresses counterterrorism and trends for the 21st century.

White, Jonathan R. *Terrorism: An Introduction.* 2d ed. Belmont, Calif.: West/Wadsworth, 1998. A good introductory textbook approach to the nature, scope, and expression of terrorism. Topics covered include definitions and typologies of terrorism, ways in which terrorist groups justify their activities, structure and dynamics of terrorist groups, and regional surveys of terrorism in Latin America, the Middle East, Europe, and the United States. Each regional section includes background about the ideologies, groups, and conflicts as well as differing interpretations by experts.

Internet Resources

Council on Foreign Relations. "Terrorism: Questions and Answers." Available online. URL: http://cfrterrorism.org/home/. Downloaded August 15, 2002. Offers a "question of the day" and a detailed answer, as well as links to many other topics related to terrorist groups and the war on terrorism, and a weekly news summary.

THE ATTACKS OF SEPTEMBER 11, 2001

The following works deal with the terrorist attacks in New York City and Washington, D.C., and their domestic aftermath. The attackers themselves and the implications of the attacks for intelligence and homeland security are covered in later sections.

Books

Baravalle, Giorgio, and Cari Modine, eds. *New York September Eleven Two Thousand One.* Milbrook, N.Y.: de.Mo, 2001. A collection of photographs, narratives, essays, poems, and other writing that conveys both the immediate impact of the attacks and the intellectual and emotional attempt to come to terms with the crisis. Contributors come from a variety of backgrounds and include spiritual writers, politicians, journalists, and actors.

Bernstein, Richard, and *New York Times* staff. *Out of the Blue: A Narrative of September 11, 2001.* New York: Times Books, 2002. Veteran *New York Times* reporter and former bureau chief Richard Bernstein and his investigative staff create a detailed, interwoven account that brings together the lives of the al-Qaeda terrorists, the victims, and the many heroes who emerged on September 11, as well as describing the national reaction to the attacks.

Editors of *One Nation. The American Spirit: Meeting the Challenge of September 11.* New York: Time, Inc., 2002. The *Life* team that chronicled the attacks in *One Nation: America Remembers September 11, 2001* provides a continuation, using photography and narrative to explore the impact of the attacks on a variety of Americans during the following months, as well as showing recovery efforts at the World Trade Center site and the national display of patriotism.

Frank, Mitch. *Understanding September 11: Answering Questions About the Attack on America.* New York: Viking Childrens Books, 2002. The author, a reporter for *Time* magazine, begins with an account of his rushing from his home in Brooklyn Heights to the scene of the disaster at the World Trade Center. After sharing and acknowledging the emotional impact of the events, he presents a series of questions and answers that give background explanations to the attacks, including Osama bin Laden, al-Qaeda, the situation in Afghanistan and the Middle East, and the religion of Islam. He then looks at the actions of the U.S. government in response to the attacks. Although written at a young adult reading level, this book would also be helpful to parents whose children have asked questions about the events.

Hagen, Susan, and Mary Carouba. *Women at Ground Zero: Stories of Courage and Compassion.* Indianapolis, Ind.: Alpha Books, 2002. A collection of first-person accounts by women firefighters, police officers, paramedics, EMTs, and others who responded to the attack on the World Trade Center on September 11, 2001. Whereas the face of the "typical" 9/11 hero was portrayed as that of a male firefighter or police officer, this book reveals the surprising number of women who were on the front lines.

Halberstam, David. *Firehouse.* New York: Hyperion, 2002. Halberstam, a Pulitzer Prize–winning popular historian, creates a vivid, moving narrative that focuses on the experience of Engine 40, Ladder 35, a New York city firehouse that sent 13 men in response to the World Trade Center attacks. Only one survived. The narrative describes what is known to have happened to each man and the grueling work of recovering their bodies after the towers collapsed. The tightly knit community and culture of firefighters and their families is also highlighted.

Kornbluth, Jesse, and Jessica Pain, eds. *Because We Are Americans: What We Discovered on September 11, 2001.* New York: Warner Books, 2001. A collection of poignant postings from AOL message boards in the days following the terrorist attacks, representing people from many backgrounds.

Life magazine staff, eds. *One Nation: America Remembers September 11, 2001.* Boston: Little, Brown, 2001. A moving, detailed narrative woven from striking photographs and accounts of the attacks and their aftermath. Includes a minute-by-minute description of the events in New York City, although there is little coverage of the Pentagon attack or the crash in Pennsylvania. Includes accounts by survivors and the family members of victims.

Longman, Jere. *Among the Heroes: United Flight 93 and the Passengers and Crew Who Fought Back.* New York: HarperCollins, 2002. Based on extensive interviews with the families of passengers and crew of Flight 93, the author creates a vivid, detailed account of how the passengers decided to fight back against the hijackers. Many of the passengers talked with family members on air phones or cell phones before the final struggle erupted, sending the plane crashing into a Pennsylvania field. Like the firefighters and police of New York City, these passengers emerged as "ordinary American heroes" who may have saved thousands of lives by thwarting the hijackers.

Newseum, with Alicia Shepard and Cathy Trost. *Running Toward Danger: Stories Behind the Breaking News of 9/11.* With an introduction by Tom Brokaw. Lanham, Md.: Rowman & Littlefield, 2002. The Newseum, "America's first interactive museum of news" presents accounts of how more than 100 reporters and photographers raced to the scenes of the attacks in New York City and at the Pentagon, while network anchors and staff struggled to keep up with events and present them in a coherent fashion to a stunned nation.

New York Times staff, eds. *Portraits 9/11/01: The Collected "Portraits of Grief" from the* New York Times. New York: Times Books, 2002. A compilation of the series of portraits in the months following the attacks that introduced *New York Times* readers to the recollections of lives lost and lives forever changed.

Picciotto, Richard. *Last Man Down: A New York City Fire Chief and the Collapse of the World Trade Center.* Berkeley Books, 2002. "The building was shaking like an earthquake . . . but it was the rumble that struck me still with fear. The sheer volume of it. The way it coursed right through me . . . like a thousand runaway trains speeding toward me." This narrative is by a fire chief who, together with a few random colleagues and a civilian, desperately fought to rescue people from the first collapsing tower and then became one of a handful of survivors saved by a pocket in the second tower.

Poynter Institute, eds. *September 11, 2001.* Kansas City, Mo.: Andrews McNeel, 2001. A compilation of 150 front pages of major newspapers throughout the world on the day following the attacks. Prepared by the Poynter Institute, a prestigious journalism school. Useful for observing immediate media reactions, journalistic priorities, and differences in perception of the events around the world.

Reuters staff, eds. *September 11: A Testimony.* Upper Saddle River, N.J.: Prentice Hall, 2001. A collection of photographs assembled by the staff of Reuters news service. According to Reuters, "the guiding principle in assembling these images was one of documenting scenes of endurance, resolve, and determination. Finding the pictures that capture courage and fortitude in the heat and the dust." The images focus on individuals and their reactions to the events.

Sammon, Bill. *Fighting Back: The War on Terrorism from Inside the Bush White House.* Washington, D.C.: Regnery, 2002. A detailed account by a White House correspondent of President George W. Bush's activities and conduct of the war on terrorism from September 11, 2001, through his speeches to rally the nation and successful military campaign against the Taliban in Afghanistan. Sammon, who appears to be an unabashed supporter of the president, had extensive access and opportunities to interview him in detail.

Vanden Heuvel, Katrina, ed. *A Just Response:* The Nation *on Terrorism, Democracy and September 11, 2001.* New York: Thunder's Mouth Press/Nation Books, 2002. A collection of editorials, narratives, columns, and articles that appeared in *The Nation* in the weeks following the terrorist attacks. Contributors include Alexander Cockburn, Christopher Hitchens, and Katha Pollitt. Offers a range of left-liberal opinion, generally calling for a restrained response abroad and the safeguarding of civil liberties at home.

What We Saw: The Events of September 11, 2001 in Words, Pictures, and Video. With an introduction by Dan Rather. New York: Simon & Schuster, 2002. A rich narrative woven from a tapestry of excerpts from news coverage, showing the immediate impact of the events of September 11, 2001, on the people trying to understand and cover them. There is also a collection of newspaper columns and magazine articles by writers such as Anna Quindlen and Pete Hamill. Includes DVD with extensive video footage.

Woodward, Bob. *Bush at War.* New York: Simon and Schuster, 2002. The award-winning journalist of Watergate fame delves into the conception and implementation of the war on terrorism in the weeks and months following the September 11, 2001 attacks. Given extensive access to President George W. Bush and other key figures, Woodward quotes from National Security Council meetings as well as other conversations at the White House, Camp David, and the Pentagon. The author has been praised by some critics for his vivid, detailed inside view of the Bush administration at war but criticized by others for lacking critical perspective because of the extent of his dependence on the administration.

Articles and Papers

Balz, Dan. "Afghan Campaign's Blueprint Emerges." *Washington Post*, January 29, 2002, p. A1. (Third article in an eight-part series, the rest of which are cowritten with Bob Woodward.) After refusing to leave the White House following reports of a possible attack, President Bush and his cabinet settle down to plan the war in Afghanistan. CIA director George Tenet offers an integrated plan involving intelligence assets, CIA covert operatives, and special and military forces working in conjunction with the anti-Taliban Northern Alliance. Meanwhile, Pakistan agrees to seven U.S. demands for aid in fighting terrorism and for cutting off support to the Taliban.

Balz, Dan, and Bob Woodward. "America's Chaotic Road to War: Bush's Global Strategy Began to Take Shape in First Frantic Hours after Attack." *Washington Post*, January 27, 2002, p. A1. (First in a series of eight articles.) A vivid narrative describing just what the president, vice president, cabinet, and Congress did in the hours and days following the attacks of September 11, 2001. This article describes the immediate reactions to the attacks, the attempt to assess the damage and the threat, and the grounding of the nation's air fleet.

———. "Bush Awaits History's Judgment; President's Scorecard Shows Much Left to Do." *Washington Post*, February 3, 2002, p. A1. In the eighth and last article in this *Washington Post* series, both President Bush and the American people are trying to assess how successful the military campaign has been, come December 2001. The campaign has liberated Afghanistan from the Taliban, but Osama bin Laden and many other top al-Qaeda leaders remain at large. A new emphasis has emerged: preventing the "axis of evil" (Iran, Iraq, and North Korea) from developing or obtaining weapons of mass destruction. Domestically, recriminations have begun as evidence emerges that the FBI and other intelligence agencies had significant clues before September 11 that a big terrorist attack was being planned.

———. "At Camp David, Advise and Dissent: Bush Aides Grapple with War Plan." *Washington Post*, January 31, 2002, p. A1. (Number five in a series of eight articles.) Bush and his cabinet begin to flesh out the war campaign against terrorism. CIA director George Tenet said his agency already had assets in place and wanted expanded powers to carry out covert operations in Afghanistan; he is supported by Secretary of Defense Donald Rumsfeld. Secretary of State Colin Powell supported a robust military action in Afghanistan but opposed the desire of President Bush and others to widen the war into an attack on terrorist organizations in other countries.

———. "Combating Terrorism: 'It Starts Today.'" *Washington Post,* February 1, 2002, p. A1. (Sixth in an eight-part series.) The meeting of the war cabinet continues. President Bush agrees to give the CIA the lead in ground operations in Afghanistan, with special forces troops and supplies to arrive in bases near the Afghanistan border in the next few weeks. The priority for the FBI and other agencies is to be homeland defense—preventing further attacks, rather than investigation and prosecution. Attorney General John Ashcroft is to prepare a legislative package for increased surveillance and prosecutorial powers—what will become the USA PATRIOT Act.

———. "A Pivotal Day of Grief and Anger: Bush Visits Ground Zero and Helps Move the Country from Sorrow to War." *Washington Post,* January 30, 2002, p. A1. (Fourth installment in a series of eight articles.) Struggling with his emotions, President Bush gives a Winston Churchill–like speech in the National Cathedral, vowing that the United States will overcome its sorrow and prevail. Bush then visits Ground Zero in Manhattan, letting people know, "I can hear you. The rest of the world hears you. And the people who knocked these buildings down will hear all of us soon!"

———. "A Presidency Defined in One Speech: Bush Saw Address as Both Reassurance and Resolve to a Troubled Nation." *Washington Post,* February 2, 2002, p. A1. In this seventh article of an eight-part series, Bush prepares for a pivotal speech before a joint session of Congress, where he must explain the coming war to the American people. He believes he must stress that the war will be total and take an indefinite period of time. He struggles to preserve "direct and simple" language while fine-tuning and sometimes changing phrasing to avoid offending allied nations.

———. "'We Will Rally the World': Bush and His Advisors Set Objectives, but Struggled with How to Achieve Them." *Washington Post,* January 28, 2002, p. A1. The second article in a series, this installment recounts the day following the September 11 attacks: President Bush receives condolences and offers of support from many nations; Bush and British prime minister Tony Blair form a close partnership and begin a diplomatic campaign to build support for eventual military action against the Taliban and al-Qaeda in Afghanistan.

Annotated Bibliography

"The Collapse of the NY World Trade Centre (Structural)." *Steel Times International*, vol. 26, March 2002, n.p. An analysis of the collapse of the twin towers, which were able to withstand the impact of the planes but succumbed when the lightweight steel floor trusses collapsed under the intense heat of the fire. The result was a cascading failure as floors collapsed and their weight crashed into the floors below.

Gibbs, Nancy. "Person of the Year." *Time*, vol. 158, December 31, 2001, p. 34 ff. "For leading that lesson [about America's strength], for having more faith in us than we had in ourselves, for being brave when required and rude where appropriate and tender without being trite, for not sleeping and not quitting and not shrinking from the pain all around him, Rudy Giuliani, Mayor of the World, is TIME's 2001 Person of the Year."

Ratnesar, Romesh, and Joel Stein. "Out of the Ruins: Ground Zero Today Is Part Spectacle, Part Shrine—and Quintessentially New York." *Time*, vol. 158, December 31, 2001, p. 90 ff. A report on the changing work and life at the Ground Zero site in Manhattan, where workers from around the country mingle with volunteers, uniformed officers, itinerants, passersby, vendors, and tourists.

"The Real Story of Flight 93." *Newsweek*, December 3, 2001, p. 54. A vivid narration of how passengers fought to take their plane back from the hijackers on September 11. Some of the passengers who are believed to have led the counterattack are described and conversations with their families recalled. "The hijackers had been training for two years; the passengers came together in a few minutes. But the odds were not hopeless."

Whitman, David. "Day of Infamy: A Timeline of Terror." *U.S. News & World Report*, September 14, 2001, p. 18. Provides a chronology of the events of September 11, 2001, from 7:58 A.M., when the first plane departed Boston for Los Angeles, to 10:00 P.M., when New York City mayor Rudolph Giuliani ends what must have been the longest day of his life.

Internet Resources

CNN.com. "In-Depth Special: War Against Terror." Available online. URL: http://www.cnn.com/SPECIALS/2001/trade.center/index.html. Downloaded August 15, 2002. This site now serves as an archive for news (including audio and video) related to the attacks on the World Trade Center and the Pentagon plus links to features on related topics such as Afghanistan, anthrax, Osama bin Laden, and airport screening.

Documents Center, University of Michigan. "America's War Against Terrorism: World Trade Center/Pentagon Terrorism and the Aftermath." Available online. URL: http://www.lib.umich.edu/govdocs/usterror.html. Updated July 19, 2002. Provides a variety of links on the terrorist attacks of September 11, 2001; related previous attacks; subsequent attacks; events in other countries; and background research.

New York Newsday.com. "New York City Rebuilds." Available online: http://www.newsday.com/other/special/ny-rebuilds-main.htmlstory. Downloaded August 15, 2002. This site is dedicated to the World Trade Center site, the recovery and rebuilding effort, and future plans for the sites. Includes videos, slides, and a live Ground Zero webcam.

Poynter Institute. "Covering the Attack." Available online. URL: http://www.poynter.org/Terrorism/default.htm. Downloaded August 14, 2002. An archive of the journalism and critical analysis of the coverage of the September 11, 2001, attacks. Includes the text of a large number of stories by journalists, indexed by topic and contributor, a collection of front pages of newspapers from the day after the attacks, and related web links.

Public Broadcasting Service. "Looking for Answers." *Frontline.* Available online. URL: http://www.pbs.org/wgbh/pages/frontline/shows/terrorism/. Downloaded August 15, 2002. Home page for a television documentary cosponsored by the *New York Times.* Provides expanded material and links for topics covered in the program.

"September 11 Digital Archive." Available online. URL: http://911digitalarchive.org/. Downloaded August 15, 2002. A site devoted to preserve digital text (including weblogs and e-mail), imagery, video, audio, and other data relating to the attacks of September 11, 2001. Sponsored by the American Social History Project at the City University of New York and the Center for History and New Media at George Mason University.

THE WAR ON TERRORISM

BACKGROUND TO THE TERRORIST ATTACKS

This section is devoted to works dealing with the terrorists responsible for the attacks, such as Osama bin Laden and al-Qaeda, as well as related subjects, such as militant Islam.

Books

Alexander, Yonah, and Michael S. Swetnam. *Usama bin Laden's al-Qaida: Profile of a Terrorist Network.* Ardsley, N.Y.: Transnational Publishers, 2001. Describes the origins, ideology, operation, and structure of the al-Qaeda network, from its founding in 1989 to its reach into 55 countries today. Includes details of where and how al-Qaeda gets its money and of the attacks it has carried out. (Note that the book was written before September 11, 2001.) Includes a time line. There is also a collection of statements by and documents concerning bin Laden.

Annotated Bibliography

Anonymous. *Through Our Enemies' Eyes: Osama Bin Laden, Radical Islam and the Future of America.* Washington, D.C.: Brassey's, 2002. An anonymous member of the U.S. intelligence community paints a picture of Osama bin Laden and other Islamic extremists as they see themselves rather than as we might like to see them. According to the author, Islamic extremists see the United States as an enemy who has been aggressing against Islamic nations for decades while supporting Israel and secularist Arab governments. They also see U.S. culture as both weak minded and arrogant. The author warns that bin Laden is only the tip of the iceberg, and that eliminating him or even destroying al-Qaeda will not end the war against determined extremists who have a considerable base of support.

Armstrong, Karen. *Islam: A Short History.* New York: Modern Library, 2000. One of the most accessible introductions to the development of Islam, with a vivid narrative that runs from Muhammad, the eruption of Islam from the desert, and the flowering of Islamic civilization, to its decline and subjection to Western colonialism and imperialism, and the Islamic reaction against the modern West.

Benjamin, Daniel K., and Steven Simon. *The Age of Sacred Terror: Radical Islam's War Against America.* New York: Random House, 2002. A book by two former senior members of the National Security Council, begun about a year before the September 11, 2001, attacks. With passionate urgency the authors explain how the intensity of al-Qaeda's determination had been underestimated before the 9/11 attacks and American officials and agents had failed in other ways to grasp the seriousness of the threat. Drawing on a detailed history of al-Qaeda, the authors suggest how the group will adapt to the post–September 11 environment and the measures that must be undertaken to counter it.

Bergen, Peter L. *Holy War, Inc.: Inside the Secret World of Osama bin Laden.* New York: Free Press, 2001. The author, CNN's resident authority on terrorism, begins with an account of his 1997 interview with Osama bin Laden and then fills in details about the terrorist leader's life and aspirations. Bergen dispels what he calls popular misconceptions about bin Laden; for example, he says the CIA never aided bin Laden directly but gave money to Pakistan for the Afghan struggle against the Soviet Union, and the Pakistan intelligence service in turn gave money to bin Laden. Bergen also lays out the global scope and infrastructure of al-Qaeda, comparing it to a multinational corporation.

Corbin, Jane. *Al Qaeda: In Search of the Terror Network That Shook the World.* New York: Thunder's Mouth Press/Nation Books, 2002. A senior BBC correspondent presents the results of her four years of investigations and interviews on four continents. She describes how al-Qaeda built upon the training its members received as U.S.-backed anti-Soviet fighters in

Afghanistan and developed a facility for concealment and "tradecraft" comparable to that found in professional intelligence agencies.

Dennis, Anthony J. *Osama bin Laden: A Psychological and Political Portrait.* Bristol, Ind.: Wyndham Hall Press, 2002. The author, who has studied and written about militant Islam for many years, felt dissatisfied with lurid, simplistic accounts of Osama bin Laden. Instead, he offers what he calls "a more three-dimensional 'psychological portrait' . . . that would in some credible fashion explain the man we see and hear so much about today." Dennis explains the basis for bin Laden's charismatic appeal among many people in the Islamic world and discusses his strengths and limitations.

Dwyer, Jim, et al. *Two Seconds Under the World: Terror Comes to America, the Conspiracy Behind the World Trade Center Bombing.* New York: Crown Publishers, 1994. A vivid and suspenseful account of the World Trade Center bombing in 1993, including a moment-by-moment reconstruction of events surrounding the explosion, accounts by survivors, and questions about the FBI investigation and whether authorities could have prevented the attack by responding to information they had received earlier.

Emerson, Steven. *American Jihad: The Terrorists Living Among Us.* New York: Simon & Schuster, 2002. Emerson, who had been studying the infiltration of Islamic terrorist groups into American society in recent years, says that their ability to mount large-scale operations in this country should not have come as a surprise. Emerson cites the establishment of a significant presence by groups such as Hamas and Islamic Jihad, and how an Islamic center in Tucson, Arizona, became the unlikely source for two of Osama bin Laden's most promising recruits. Emerson believes that "political correctness" may be inhibiting, even post–September 11, the investigation of the full extent of such terrorist penetration.

Esposito, John L. *Unholy War: Terror in the Name of Islam.* New York: Oxford University Press, 2002. A history and exploration of Islam, focusing on elements that emerge in al-Qaeda and other terrorist groups. The concept of jihad is revealed to have many facets, ranging from the benign to the murderous. The author, a professor of religion and international affairs at Georgetown University, discusses particular Islamic thinkers who have influenced terrorist movements and observes careful distinctions between mainstream and extremist Islam.

Fregosi, Paul. *Jihad in the West: Muslim Conquests from the 7th to the 21st Centuries.* Amherst, N.Y.: Prometheus Books, 1998. A sweeping account of the conflict between Islamic fundamentalism, which seeks to convert the nations of the world to Islam, and the nations of the West. In medieval times, the expanding Islamic civilization made both geographical and cultural inroads into the West, but in recent centuries the West has penetrated the Islamic world in turn, first through colonialism and then through the exercise of economic power and cultural influence. Although the book lacks detail on some matters, it provides a broad historical context for understanding recent events and the modern reinterpretations of jihad.

Gohari, M. J. *The Taliban: Ascent to Power.* New York: Oxford University Press on Demand, 2001. Describes the origins and doctrine of the Taliban, its rise to power, life in Afghanistan under Taliban rule, and relations among the Taliban, neighboring countries, and the United Nations and United States. Also includes a chapter on Osama bin Laden and his attitudes.

Gunaratna, Rohan. *Inside Al Qaeda: Global Network of Terror.* New York: Columbia University Press, 2002. Based on extensive interviews and research, the author develops a highly detailed picture of the structure, aims, and strategies of al-Qaeda. He reveals the group's extensive infrastructure and its web of worldwide contacts that developed over nearly 30 years. Finally, he shows the chain of events that led al-Qaeda to move up its plan to attack the United States. The author, a highly reputed terrorism expert, is a research fellow at the Centre for the Study of Terrorism and Political Violence at the University of St. Andrews in Scotland. While the book is generally comprehensive and authoritative, some critics have questioned certain assertions and noted areas that appear poorly organized.

Jess, Sara, and Gabriel Beck. *American Taliban: John Walker Lindh, a Psychological Study.* Berkeley: University of California Press, 2002. The authors trace the life of John Walker Lindh, an American teenager who resolved his adolescent confusion and violent and sexual urges by converting to Islam to become a "holy warrior" and fight for the Taliban. The authors' disturbing portrait, developed in part from reading extensive Internet postings from Lindh's young years, is considerably at odds with the "innocent idealist gone astray" presented by Lindh's lawyers and parents.

Katz, Samuel M. *Relentless Pursuit: The DSS and the Manhunt for the Al-Qaeda Terrorists.* New York: Forge/Tom Doherty Associates, 2002. The author, editor of the journal *Special Ops* and a writer of many other works on international terrorism, looks in this book at the role of the Diplomatic Security Service (DSS), a little-known agency founded in 1985 to protect U.S. diplomats and installations from terrorist attack. He recounts instances where the DSS was able to prevent assassinations or attacks, as well as its capture of Ramzi Yousef, who was later convicted for his role in organizing the 1993 World Trade Center bombing.

Rashid, Ahmed. *Taliban: Militant Islam, Oil and Fundamentalism in Central Asia.* New Haven, Conn.: Yale University Press, 2001. A Pakistani journalist gives an insider's view on the Taliban government, its oppression and corruption (including involvement in the heroin trade), its relationship to Osama bin Laden, and its role in the complex politics of the region.

Reeve, Simon. *The New Jackals: Ramzi Yousef, Osama bin Laden, and the Future of Terrorism.* Boston: Northeastern University Press, 2002. The author, a British investigative journalist, explores the origins, motivations, and activities of Ramzi Yousef, mastermind of the 1993 World Trade Center bombing, and Osama bin Laden, the al-Qaeda leader believed to be responsible for the 1998 U.S. embassy attacks in Africa. Reeves traces the rise of Yousef and bin Laden to the massive support given by the United States to anti-Soviet mujahideen in Afghanistan during the 1980s. Originally published in 1999, this paperback edition includes an epilogue dealing with the attacks of September 11, 2001.

Robinson, Adam. *Bin Laden: Behind the Mask of a Terrorist.* New York: Arcade Publishing, 2002. The author, a journalist who has worked in the Middle East for many years, reveals numerous little-known details about the life of the terrorist leader. Readers learn how Osama bin Laden, who grew up in a wealthy family and became a playboy who indulged in many kinds of excesses, transformed himself into the self-appointed scourge of the secular world. The author then describes how bin Laden painstakingly created the terrorist network and planned devastating attacks against the United States.

Venzke, Ben N., ed. *The al-Qaeda Documents: Vol. 1.* Boston, Mass.: Tempest Publishing, 2002. A compilation of documents by and about al-Qaeda, including extensive excerpts from the al-Qaeda training manual that describe the sophisticated communications, reconnaissance, and operational security measures that enabled the September 11 hijackers to work concealed in the United States for many months as they chose their targets and coordinated the attack plan. There are also excerpts from an al-Qaeda videotape and court documents relating to trials of al-Qaeda members.

Articles and Papers

Abdelkarim, Riad Z. "Why Do They Hate Us? The Question That Won't Go Away." *Washington Report on Middle East Affairs*, vol. 21, March 2002, p. 84. A communications director for the Council on American-Islamic Relations gives a measured answer: There is no religious justification for the terrorist attacks, which have been condemned by all major American Muslim organizations. Most Muslims and Arabs do not hate America per se; indeed, many would like to immigrate to the United States, the author points out. There are aspects of American culture, however, particularly as promoted by the media, that are disliked by many Muslims, and there is a minority of extremists who are willing to take violent action.

Baldauf, Scott. "Latest Al Qaeda Recruits: Afghans Seeking Revenge." *Christian Science Monitor*, vol. 95, January 13, 2003, p. 1. Baldauf reports that the "collateral damage" of Afghan civilians killed in U.S. attacks during the war against the Taliban and al-Qaeda may have created a fertile ground for recruiting suicide terrorists. Surviving family members have not received the kind of apology considered acceptable in traditional Afghan culture, and some are willing to seek vengeance, another traditional remedy. Afghan officials and war victims are quoted.

Emerson, Stephen. "Islamic Terror: From the Midwest to the Mideast." *Wall Street Journal*, August 28, 1995, n.p. A description and diagram of the Hamas terror network, its penetration into the heart of the United States, and the activities leading up to the World Trade Center bombing of 1993. These activities include those of Mousa Abu Marzuk, founding leader of Hamas and a key figure in terrorist planning.

Fennell, Tom, John Donnelly, and Julian Beltrane. "The Invisible Man." *Maclean's*, vol. 115, December 2, 2002, n.p. While about half of the 15 top al-Qaeda leaders have been captured or slain, the number-one target, Osama bin Laden, remains elusive despite the expenditure of vast resources, including a $25 million reward. Bin Laden's videotapes offer few clues other than to confirm that he is still alive and intends to launch further attacks. The CIA places its hope in aggressive cooperation with local intelligence agencies in areas such as Pakistan, Yemen, Indonesia, Malaysia, and the Philippines as well as in the use of unpiloted Predator surveillance and attack drones, such as in Yemen.

Fried, Joseph P. "Sheik and 9 Followers Guilty of a Conspiracy of Terrorism." *New York Times*, October 2, 1995, pp. A1, A11. Reports on the conviction of Sheik Omar Abdel Rahman and nine other militant Muslims for a conspiracy to carry out a terrorist campaign of bombings against the United States and United Nations in an attempt to force U.S. officials to stop supporting Israel and Egypt. Includes backgrounds of all 10 conspirators.

Johnston, David. "Evidence Is Seen Linking Bin Laden to Algerian Group." *New York Times*, January 27, 2000. Available online. URL:http://www.nytimes.com. Reports that investigators have uncovered links between Osama bin Laden and a group of Algerians and others accused of plotting a terrorist attack in the United States. One of the accused, Mohambedou Ould Slahi (a citizen of Mauritania), being held in Senegal, is the brother of one of bin Laden's key lieutenants. Border agents in Port Angeles, Washington, have meanwhile discovered Ahmed Ressam, an Algerian, smuggling a bomb and detonators over the border from Canada.

Kaplan, David E., et al., eds. "The CEO of Terror Inc." *U.S. News & World Report*, October 1, 2000, p. 19. Osama bin Laden called himself "the Contractor," and much of his activity has been the building of a terrorist infrastructure, including a network of camps in Afghanistan. Al-Qaeda consists of two circles: a loose outer one where local extremists and terrorists are funded and trained and a closely held inner circle that plans the most ambitious operations.

McCarthy, Andrew C. "Prosecuting the New York Sheikh." *Middle East Quarterly*, March 1997. Available online. URL:http://www.counterror.org.il/ (link from *Terrorist Organization Profiles: Al Gama'a al-Islamiyya*). The U.S. attorney who led the successful prosecution of Sheikh Omar Abdel Rahman for the 1993 World Trade Center bombing and related conspiracies describes the background of Rahman's group and the transplanting of a jihad onto American soil. Includes chronology.

Smith, Patricia. "America's Most Wanted." *New York Times Upfront*, vol. 134, October 15, 2001, p. 14 ff. An accessible biographical article about Osama bin Laden written for students, with questions and lesson plan.

Smith, Paul J. "Transnational Terrorism and the al Qaeda Model: Confronting New Realities." *Parameters*, vol. 32, Summer 2002, p. 33 ff. Describes al-Qaeda's ambitious plans (including an aborted 1995 plan to bomb multiple airliners), the weaknesses that it exploits in Western societies, and its "multi-cellular terror model with a horizontal structure of 24 organizations combined with a vertical structure culminating in Osama bin Laden." As a truly national organization, Al-Qaeda has penetrated many organizations, including Islamic charities.

Tyre, Peg, Tara Pepper, and Mark Hosenball. "Meet the bin Ladens. They Had It All: Money, Power—and Now the Most Wanted Man on Earth. A Family Affair." *Newsweek*, October 15, 2001, p. 55. A profile of the bin Laden family, Saudis who mainly became secularized, wealthy businesspersons. The exception, Osama, was viewed by the family as a "black sheep." Now the family feels "shattered, . . . abused, . . . tortured."

Internet Resources

bin Laden, Osama, and John Miller. "Talking with Terror's Banker." ABC News transcript. Available online. URL: http://more.abcnews.go.com/sections/world/dailynews/terror_980609.html. Posted August 20, 1998. In an interview, Osama bin Laden defends the violent struggle (jihad) against the United States and its allies. He says that his goal is to "purify Muslim land of all non-believers" and claims that events show that America lacks the will to fight a protracted war.

Annotated Bibliography

U.S. Military Campaign Against Terrorism

This section deals with the U.S. military effort against terrorists abroad, particularly the war in Afghanistan during 2001–2 but also actual and potential involvements in other countries, such as the Philippines and Iraq.

Books

Clancy, Tom, with General Carl Stiner and Tony Koltz. *Shadow Warriors: Inside the Special Forces.* New York: G.P. Putnam, 2002. This book by the best-selling suspense novelist deals with the elite, little-known special forces that made up much of the U.S. military assistance to the Northern Alliance forces that overthrew the Taliban in Afghanistan in late 2001. It traces the development of modern special forces operations to the perceived need for "unconventional warfare" capabilities in the 1970s and the formation of the U.S. Special Operations Command (SOCOM) in 1987. The author describes a number of counterterrorist operations, both successful and unsuccessful, and looks at particular special forces groups such as the SEALs (U.S. Navy) and Rangers and Green Berets (both U.S. Army). The book concludes with a look at the kinds of operations (including PSYOPS, or psychological warfare operations) likely to be needed in the ongoing war on terrorism.

Friedman, Norman. *Terrorism, Afghanistan, and America's New Way of War.* Annapolis, Md.: U.S. Naval Institute, 2003. The author, a noted defense analyst, argues that decisive action by the United States thwarted Osama bin Laden's hopes that the U.S. reaction to the September 1, 2001, attacks would get bogged down and give time to create a massive anti-Western movement in the Islamic world. Instead, the American tactics effectively targeted the Taliban and al-Qaeda despite the latter's decentralized network. Afghanistan thus served as the first test of the new "network-centric" U.S. war-fighting doctrine. Attention is also given to implications for the use of naval and amphibious power.

Haney, Eric L. *Inside Delta Force: The Story of America's Elite Counterterrorist Unit.* New York: Delacorte Press, 2002. The author, a founding member and leader of the army's shadowy Delta Force, describes his harrowing training and even more harrowing assignments, including the aborted attempt to rescue American hostages in Iran. Haney has a number of less than complimentary things to say about other U.S. services, particularly the CIA.

Katman, Kenneth. *Afghanistan: Current Issues and U.S. Policy Concerns.* Washington, D.C.: Congressional Research Service, 2002. An update of events in Afghanistan and an overview of continuing U.S. policy objectives, including stabilization, developing the national army, humanitarian aid, and reconstruction.

Malley, William. *The Afghanistan Wars.* New York: Palgrave Global Publishing, 2002. A history of Afghanistan's recent wars, including its conflict with the Soviet Union and the civil war after the Soviets left. The cumulative impact of these conflicts on the social, cultural, and political institutions of the country is dissected, suggesting the complexity of the task of rebuilding the country after the latest war—the war on terrorism.

Margesson, Rhoda. *Afghanistan's Path to Reconstruction: Obstacles, Challenges, and Issues for Congress.* Washington, D.C.: Congressional Research Service, 2002. Discusses the coordination of efforts by the United States and its allies to rebuild Afghanistan, including both short-term and long-term efforts.

Margolis, Eric S. *War at the Top of the World: The Struggle for Afghanistan, Kashmir and Tibet.* New York: Routledge, 2000. The author describes how these locations, both remote and strategic, have become the focus of modern conflict. The vivid narrative introduces both the key players and the historical background and context, producing a solid introduction to areas that are likely to remain in the news for many years to come.

McGeough, Paul. *Manhattan to Baghdad.* Crows Nest, Australia: Allen & Unwin, 2003. One of Australia's leading foreign correspondents reports from the battlefields of the war on terror, starting with the morning of September 11, 2001, on the streets of downtown Manhattan and his interviews with survivors and families of victims. During the war in Afghanistan in the months that followed, McGeough witnessed the deaths of three of his colleagues in a Taliban ambush, and he interviewed a variety of players in the war, including Northern Alliance commanders and would-be suicide bombers.

McRaven, William H. *Spec Ops: Case Studies in Special Operations Warfare: Theory and Practice.* Novato, Calif.: Presidio Press, 1998. The author, a SEAL team commander, highlights a selection of eight classic cases including six from World War II and two in the 1970s, the successful Israeli airport rescue at Entebbe in 1976 and the unsuccessful U.S. raid on the Son Tay Prisoner-of-War camp in Vietnam in 1970. These varied operations show the techniques of special forces such as the U.S. SEALs and Green Berets, the British Special Air Service, and the Russian Spetsnaz. In considering these cases, he shows how they embodied the six core principles of special operations doctrine: simplicity, security, repetition, surprise, speed, and purpose.

el-Nawawy, Mohammed et al. *Al Jazeera: How the Free Arab News Network Scooped the World and Changed the Middle East.* Boulder, Colo: Westview Press, 2002. As U.S. forces began to hunt for Osama bin Laden after the

September 11, 2001, attacks, television viewers saw bin Laden and heard his messages, courtesy of a new media presence, the Arab-run al-Jazeera television news network based in Qatar. This book explores the impact of the first Arab network not controlled by a government, the response of viewers and Arab governments, and the relationship to CNN and other global media.

Niksch, Larry. *Abu Sayyaf: Target of Philippine-U.S. Anti-Terrorism Cooperation.* Washington, D.C.: Congressional Research Service, 2002. An overview of the emerging policy and program for U.S. military aid to the Philippines to fight the Abu Sayyaf guerrilla/terrorist group.

Peters, Ralph. *Beyond Terror: Strategy in a Changing World.* Mechanicsburg, Pa.: Stackpole Books, 2002. A retired military officer and expert on urban warfare looks at the changing mission of the U.S. military and intelligence services and the tactics needed to fight terrorism and unconventional warfare. (Some of the essays were written prior to September 11, 2001.) The author takes a hard line, urging that when in doubt more force be used rather than less, and that terrorists be killed in battle if possible to avoid creating imprisoned martyrs.

Tanner, Stephen. *Afghanistan: A Complete History from Alexander the Great to the Fall of the Taliban.* New York: Da Capo Press, 2002. A comprehensive military history of a land of forbidding terrain that has been an arena for war more than 2,500 years. The final two chapters describe the rise of the Taliban and the entry of the United States to expel it in late 2001.

Articles and Papers

Hylton, William S. "Dick and Don Go to War." *Esquire*, vol. 137, February 2002, p. 80 ff. A lengthy but vivid biographical account of Vice President Dick Cheney and Secretary of Defense Donald Rumsfeld, who first worked together in the Nixon White House more than 30 years ago and are presently playing a very hands-on role in the war on terrorism.

Klare, Michael T. "Waging Postindustrial Warfare on the Global Battlefield." *Current History*, vol. 100, December 2001, p. 433ff. The author believes that September 11, 2001, has changed modern warfare as radically as did Pearl Harbor (naval airpower) and Hiroshima (nuclear weapons). Al-Qaeda's attack on the United States typifies "postindustrial warfare" through the use of irregular forces and unconventional tactics. The author also discusses the related subjects of guerrilla and insurgent warfare. He asserts that economic globalization has created poverty and social/cultural disruption, thus supplying new grievances for terrorists.

Loeb, Vernon, and Bradley Graham. "Defense Budget: Tough Choices Skirted? Pentagon Critics Say Bush's Proposed Increase Blunts Drive to

Reform the Military." *Washington Post,* February 10, 2002, p. A6. A look at the proposed new defense budget. Despite increased funding, the war on terrorism is forcing budget planners to make difficult choices. The new war has boosted spending for certain high-tech devices such as unpiloted surveillance drones, but money must also be diverted to pay for conventional forces and supplies deployed abroad. Under this pressure the military has changed its requirement to be able to fight two major regional wars to that of pursuing one war while taking a defensive posture in the other.

Pan, Philip P. "Rural Filipinos Welcome U.S. Troops: Special Forces Deployment on Southern Island Is First Since World War II." *Washington Post,* January 28, 2002, p. A13. Describes life in a rural Philippine town where farmers try to avoid being killed by the Abu Sayyaf, a Muslim extremist group. Hundred U.S. troops have arrived to help train the Philippine army, and another 500 are on the way. Public opinion supports the U.S. effort, although there are some vocal critics.

Struck, Doug. "Casualties of U.S. Miscalculations: Afghan Victims of CIA Missile Strike Described as Peasants, not Al Qaeda." *Washington Post,* February 11, 2002, p. A1. Describes the latest in a series of incidents where U.S. forces, possibly relying on faulty intelligence, have attacked and killed groups of civilians. For example, a convoy heading from Khost to Kabul for the inauguration of President Hamid Karzai was mistakenly attacked, and a village in Uruzgan Province was raided. The United States has begun to pay reparations for the latter incident.

Internet Resources

Conetta, Carl. "Strange Victory: A Critical Appraisal of Operation Enduring Freedom and the Afghanistan War." Project on Defense Alternatives. Available online. URL: http://www.comw.org/pda/0201strangevic.html. Posted January 30, 2002. Tallies up the achievements of the war in Afghanistan and the cost in human lives and damage. Although the Taliban was destroyed and al-Qaeda fragmented, there is a cost in casualties, social disruption, and possibly the exacerbation of regional conflicts. Some of these costs might have been avoided by undertaking a more narrowly focused military campaign accompanied by a more robust political and diplomatic effort.

Jane's database service. Available online. URL: http://www.janes.com/. Downloaded August 15, 2002. Provides access to information and articles from a variety of Jane's publications. (Jane is one of the foremost providers of military and intelligence materials to the general public.)

Some summaries and excerpts are free; full information requires a paid subscription. Publications related to counterterrorism include *Jane's Islamic Affairs Analyst* and *Jane's Terrorism and Security Monitor.*

INTERNATIONAL SITUATION, FOREIGN POLICY, AND DIPLOMACY

This section deals with international affairs with reference to the campaign against terrorism as well as foreign policy and diplomatic efforts.

Books

Alexander, Yonah. *Combating Terrorism: Strategies of Ten Countries.* Ann Arbor: University of Michigan Press, 2002. A textbooklike but interesting collection of essays by experts who work in a variety of countries in Europe, the Middle East, Asia, and Latin America. The discussion of how terrorism is fought in countries that differ considerably in their culture and politics provides a needed perspective for Americans who are not often exposed to other points of view.

Campbell, Kurt M., and Michèle A. Flournoy. *To Prevail: An American Strategy for the Campaign Against Terrorism.* Washington, D.C.: Center for Strategic and International Studies, 2001. A comprehensive plan from a task force of scholars at the CSIS convened in response to the September 11, 2001, attacks. Although military, intelligence, and homeland security aspects are discussed, the primary emphasis is on forging a diplomatic campaign. This includes coalition building, public diplomacy, and the expanded use of foreign assistance. The concluding sections give specific regional strategies, findings, and recommendations.

Carr, Caleb. *The Lessons of Terror: A History of Warfare Against Civilians, Why It Has Always Failed and Why It Will Fail Again.* New York: Random House, 2002. A novelist and military historian examines the use of terror tactics throughout history, from ancient conquerors to Crusaders to the modern doctrine of "total war" that first emerged during the American Civil War. Carr argues that any short-term successes using such tactics have been bought at the price of long-term resistance and unrest. He suggests that the war on terrorism must be conducted with vigor but also with thoughtfulness and tactical discrimination if it is to have lasting success.

Chomsky, Noam. *9–11.* New York: Seven Stories Press, 2001. A collection of interviews with the noted American linguist and prominent critic of U.S. foreign policy. While condemning the attacks, Chomsky believes they can only be understood in the context of U.S. foreign policy and how it is perceived in the Islamic world, including support for Israel, U.S. troops in Saudi Arabia, and largely ineffective military strikes against alleged terrorist states or bases. Other more tangential topics relating to globalization and the anti–World Trade Organization movement are also discussed.

Cooley, John K. *Unholy Wars.* 3rd ed. With a foreword by Edward W. Said. Sterling, Va.: Pluto Press, 2002. The emergence of Osama bin Laden and al-Qaeda is examined in the context of years of problematic relations between the United States and radical Islam. Key events include U.S. aid to the anti-Soviet Islamic fighters in Afghanistan in the 1980s, the rise of the Taliban in Afghanistan, and broader struggles between Islamic and secularist forces such as those in Algeria and Pakistan. Additionally, the ties between the "moderate" Saudi state and terrorist groups have produced a volatile mix that has been handled poorly by the U.S. State Department and the CIA. This new edition is thoroughly revised and includes coverage of the September 11, 2001, attacks and the U.S. campaign in Afghanistan.

Dagne, Theodros. *Africa and the War on Terrorism.* Washington, D.C.: Congressional Research Service, 2002. A survey of attitudes and the degree of cooperation of African nations with the U.S.-led war on terrorism. Africa is expected to become more important as the war in Afghanistan winds down and some al-Qaeda members seek refuge in such nations as Somalia.

———. *Sudan: Humanitarian Crisis, Peace Talks, Terrorism, and U.S. Policy.* Washington, D.C.: Congressional Research Service, 2002. Describes ongoing problems in Sudan including war, instability, and state-sponsored terrorism.

Friedman, Thomas L. *Longitudes and Attitudes: Exploring the World after September 11.* New York: Farrar, Straus & Giroux, 2002. The author, the foreign affairs columnist for the *New York Times,* presents a collection of his columns about the September 11, 2001, attacks and the immediate aftermath. Rather than editing them in the light of later events, Friedman wants them to stand as a record of how he and others tried to grapple with the unfolding events.

Gilbert, Paul. *Terrorism, Security, and Nationality.* New York: Routledge, 1995. The author tackles difficult philosophical questions that are often ignored but are necessary for looking objectively at the causes and possible cures for terrorism. These questions revolve around the concepts of national identity and nationalism, the role of the state as seen in various political communities, and the nature of human rights. Principles of political philosophy are applied to assess the justifications given for terrorist and counterterrorist action.

Annotated Bibliography

Grosscup, Beau. *The Newest Explosions of Terrorism: Latest Sites of Terrorism in the 1990s and Beyond.* Far Hills, N.J.: New Horizon Press, 1998. The author argues that the conventional wisdom that sees terrorism diminishing after the end of the cold war may well be mistaken; instead, he says, terrorism may be emerging in many new and troubling forms, as shown in recent developments in Europe (including Ireland and Germany), the Middle East, and India, as well as in American right-wing groups that strike out against facilities associated with globalism and the New World Order. The authoritarian response to terrorism, first evident in President Ronald Reagan's administration, is also critiqued, as well as the limitation of conventional definitions. A middle view of terrorism is proposed, in which terrorism is seen as a changing, multifaceted, and permanent challenge.

Guelke, Adrian. *The Age of Terrorism and the International Political System.* New York: I. B. Tauris, 1995. This book focuses on the origin of "the age of terrorism" as a way of thinking about small group violence during the postcolonialist cold war era of roughly 1960–90. One side of the discussion looks at how the activities of the terrorist groups reflected a transition in world politics, while the other side looks at the characterization of acts as terrorism in the media and by governments during this time. The ending of the cold war has challenged the established paradigm and points to both instability and some hope for resolving conflicts.

Hunter, T. Shireen. *The Future of Islam and the West: Clash of Civilizations or Peaceful Coexistence?* Westport, Conn.: Praeger, 1998. The author takes on Samuel P. Huntington's "clash of civilizations" thesis and marshals evidence to refute it. She argues that the role of "civilizational factors" is not decisive and that modern Islam contains elements of flexibility and progress that make improvement in relations between Islam and the West possible. Shireen is a senior associate in Islamic studies at the Center for Strategic and International Studies in Washington, D.C.

Huntington, Samuel P. *The Clash of Civilizations and the Remaking of World Order.* New York: Simon & Schuster, 1996. Noted Harvard political scientist proposes that the deepest source of international conflicts is not nationalism but the clash between the world's "great civilizations" and their conflicting values, particularly those stemming from religion. Further, the author believes that the United States has often blundered by becoming involved in deep-seated conflicts that it does not understand and cannot resolve. This implies limitations on the traditional American impulse toward internationalism, peacekeeping, and "nation building." The attacks of September 11, 2001, brought renewed interest to this controversial thesis, with opponents suggesting that those same attacks show that the United States is inextricably bound to the world and cannot retreat into a new isolationism.

LePoer, Barbara Leitch. *Pakistan-U.S. Relations.* Washington, D.C.: Congressional Research Service, 2002. Cooperation between the United States and Pakistan has been vital for the military campaign in Afghanistan and for ongoing counterterrorist operations. This report discusses the pressing issues that affect the overall relationship between the two nations, including nuclear proliferation, the activity of Pakistan-based groups in Kashmir, overall relations with India, and democratization and reform within Pakistan.

Lewis, Bernard. *What Went Wrong: Western Impact and Middle Eastern Response.* New York: Oxford University Press, 2001. A noted historian looks at the centuries-long encounter of Islamic civilization with the West, including the dominant role of the Islamic world in the Middle Ages, the resurgence of Europe, the imposition of European colonialism and imperialism on the Middle East, and the often bitter and sometimes fanatical Islamic reaction. An important perspective for understanding the attitudes of both modern and extremist Muslims toward the United States today.

Perl, Raphael, and Kenneth Katzman. *State-Supported Terrorism.* Washington, D.C.: Congressional Research Service, 2002. An updated review of policies and issues with regard to U.S. treatment of states whose governments sponsor or support terrorism.

Pillar, Paul R. *Terrorism and U.S. Foreign Policy.* Washington, D.C.: Brookings Institution Press, 2001. This book suggests that policymakers pay less attention to grandiose military plans and predictions of catastrophic mass destruction and more to a methodical, integrated approach that encompasses law enforcement, international cooperation, and addressing the root conditions—such as poverty and lack of freedom—that feed the recruitment of terrorists. There is also a critique of the U.S. government designation of terrorist groups and sponsor states.

Snow, Donald M. *Distant Thunder: Patterns of Conflict in the Developing World.* 2d ed. Armonk, N.Y.: M. E. Sharpe, 1997. This book provides a broad background on the kinds of conflicts that have erupted throughout the developing world, explaining how they differ from the proxy wars of the cold war era. The author goes on to look at the dynamics of insurgency and counterinsurgency, internal (civil) war, the role of the narcotics trade, the problems of counterterrorism, and a critique of the so-called New World Order.

Tanter, Raymond. *Rogue Regimes: Terrorism and Proliferation.* New York: St. Martins Press, 1999. Examines the new landscape of foreign policy, in which the polarized world of the cold war era has been replaced by the challenge of establishing an international legal order in the face of "rogue states" such as Iraq, Iran, Libya, Syria, and North Korea. Such states threaten the legal order and U.S. national security by sponsoring terrorism and producing (or trying to produce) weapons of mass destruction. The relationship between rogue states and terrorist groups (and "freelancers" such as Osama bin Laden) is discussed, as well as policy options for the future.

Tucker, David. *Skirmishes at the Edge of Empire: The United States and International Terrorism.* Westport, Conn.: Praeger, 1997. An analysis of the evolution of U.S. antiterrorism policy, based on interviews with key decision makers from the Nixon to the Clinton administrations. Includes discussion of both broad strategic principles and tactics for responding to incidents.

Zinn, Howard. *Terrorism and War.* New York: Seven Stories Press, 2002. A collection of interviews with noted leftist historian Howard Zinn. Zinn argues that the U.S. investment in the military of more than $300 billion every year cannot buy security against terrorism. Rather, the degree of terrorism correlates with the involvement in international power struggles, particularly in the Middle East. Much of the anger tapped by Osama bin Laden and al-Qaeda results from U.S. policies, particularly the stationing of troops in Saudi Arabia (near the holy place of Mecca) and what is perceived as a one-sided support for Israel. Zinn urges a reduction in investment in the military and a redirection of resources to alleviating poverty and disease around the world.

Articles and Papers

Bowman, Robert. "Truth Is, We're Terrorized Because We're Hated." *National Catholic Reporter,* vol. 34, October 2, 1998, p. 17. According to the author, a bishop and former Vietnam combat pilot, the unpleasant truth is not, as President Bill Clinton claimed, that the U.S. is attacked by terrorists because it stands for freedom. Rather, it is attacked because it has too often stood for dictatorship and human exploitation. (A number of examples are given, including the installation of the shah in Iran and a right-wing dictator in Chile.) Terrorism springs from this hatred. To end terrorism, we should offer the world aid to rebuild rather than sending troops or weapons.

Bush, George W. "Six Month Anniversary of the September 11 Attacks: World Coalition for Anti-Terrorism." *Vital Speeches,* vol. 68, April 1, 2002, p. 354 ff. In a speech marking the six-month anniversary of the attacks, President George W. Bush asserts the continuing strength of the international coalition against terrorism. He points out that nations as diverse as Japan, Turkey, and Australia have joined in the ongoing war effort in Afghanistan. He also describes the further expansion of the war on terrorism to the Philippines, the Republic of Georgia, and Yemen.

Byford, Grenville. "The Wrong War." *Foreign Affairs*, vol. 81, July-August 2002, p. 34. The problem with the formulation "war against terrorism" begins with the problem of defining the latter. Each type of definition—by goals, by means, by legality, by choice of targets or by effect—leads to contradictions. For example if terrorists are those who act to create fear to achieve a goal, how is the terrorist differentiated from the pilot who dropped the atomic bomb on Hiroshima? In practice definitions usually draw from several elements in an attempt to separate terrorism from "legitimate" government action, and actions are ultimately validated in terms of national interest. The attempt to strike a clear, simple moral tone of good versus evil will inevitably prove unsatisfying.

Choharis, Peter. "The Rule of Law: Indispensable to a Wider War." *Washington Post*, January 6, 2002, p. B1. The author, an expert on international law, argues that if the United States is to expand its war effort beyond Afghanistan, it must show that its actions have legitimacy under widely accepted national law. Only this will keep allies on board, particularly those among the moderate Islamic nations. While the case against the Taliban was straightforward, the argument that nations can be attacked for "supporting terrorism" or for posing a future threat is not. Thus far, the United Nations has not authorized the use of force in such situations.

Cody, Edward. "Defining Terrorism Tricky for Pakistan." *Washington Post*, January 7, 2002, p. A14. Pakistan president Pervez Musharraf struggles to maintain his alliance with the U.S. antiterrorism effort—and the increased aid it brings—while managing domestic Islamic dissent. He also strives to distinguish between supporting terrorism and supporting the "legitimate" struggle of pro-Pakistani people in disputed Kashmir, while trying to accommodate pressure from India and the United States.

DeYoung, Karen. "Bush Lays Down a Marker for 3 'Evil' States." *Washington Post*, January 30, 2002, p.A1. Using rhetoric that some critics have found disturbing and others unproductive, President George W. Bush refers to Iran, Iraq, and North Korea as an "axis of evil" that must be prevented from obtaining nuclear or other weapons of mass destruction. The mention of Iran is viewed as puzzling because relations between that country and the United States had been thawing in recent months.

Eland, Ivan. "Defending Other Nations: The Risk to America's Homeland." *USA Today Magazine*, vol. 127, September 1998, p. 12ff. The author suggests that the risk of terrorist attacks on American soil is proportional to the extent of U.S. interventions in foreign conflicts. With the growing ability of even small terrorist groups to unleash mass destruction in America, the United States should limit its foreign military interventions to cases that involve vital national interests.

Hoffmann, Stanley. "Why Don't They Like Us? How America Has Become the Object of Much of the Planet's Genuine Grievances—and Displaced Discontents." *American Prospect*, vol. 12, November 19, 2001, p. 18 ff. The author suggests that the virulence that erupted on September 11, 2001, must be understood in the context of a collapse of the old world of states, diplomats, and soldiers—a world in which movements of "ordinary" people are driving much of the conflict and change in the world. Although the United States retains dominant power, it finds itself increasingly dealing with governments that no longer represent the people and is thus out of touch with the powerful emerging currents such as that in the Islamic world. The alliance of American with globalist forces further complicates matters. The United States can reduce terrorism by altering its approach to the world and thus the negative images it has for many people around the world.

Kaufmann, Greg. "Orchestrating Foreign Policy: US Interagency Decisions Post–September 11." *Harvard International Review*, vol. 24, Summer 2002, p. 20 ff. Describes the interplay between the diplomatic, military, economic, and informational interests of national power as embodied in the response to the attacks of September 11, 2001. President George W. Bush and Secretary of State Colin Powell were able to work together to craft international support for the war on terrorism, which in turn paved the way for the military effort under Secretary of Defense Donald Rumsfeld. Rumsfeld also became a very effective spokesperson for the war effort; however, the coming formation of the Department of Homeland Security will challenge the ability of these leaders with their different interests and constituencies to work together effectively.

LeFranchi, Howard. "U.S. Unpopular Among Key Allies." *Christian Science Monitor*, vol. 95, December 6, 2002, n.p. America's image around the world seems to be eroding as the war on terrorism continues, writes the author. According to a survey by the Pew Research Center, the favorability rating for the United States has slipped most markedly in Muslim countries, including such allies as Pakistan and Turkey. Ratings have slipped to a lesser extent in many European countries.

Rollins, Karina. "No Compromise: Why We're Going to Lose the War on Terrorism . . . and How We Could Win." *American Enterprise*, vol. 14, January–February 2003, p. 18 ff. The author argues that political correctness may well lead to the failure of the war on terrorism. The refusal to focus on the most likely terrorists—males from certain Islamic countries—has made airport security a joke. The author believes, however, that the deeper problem is failure to recognize the significance of the religious identity and motivation of the terrorists for fear of offending notions of "religious tolerance." A number of other controversial proposals by the author include giving countries an ultimatum to dismantle terrorist training camps, drastically tighten border and immigration control, and view Saudi Arabia as part of the terrorist problem rather than as an ally.

Tolson, Jay. "The New American Empire?" *U.S. News & World Report*, vol. 134, January 13, 2003, p. 34 ff. Critics disagree over whether *imperialism* is the right word to use for the latest trends in U.S. foreign policy in the war on terrorism which include seeking a "regime change" in Iraq, preemptive action against potential rogue states and terrorists, and a possible cultural offensive seeking to liberalize (or Westernize) Islamic countries. The modern American effort shares the idea of exceptionalism (that America has a unique identity and mission in the world) with the imperialistic impulse in the late 19th century, but it does not seek territorial expansion or direct domination of foreign countries. A variety of other attitudes and roles for the United States in the world are discussed in historical and present terms.

Tyler, Patrick E. "Threats and Responses: The Middle East. Yemen, an Uneasy Ally, Proves Adept at Playing Off Old Rivals." *New York Times*, December 19, 2002, p. A1. This article describes the complex relationship between the U.S. war on terrorism and the current regime in Yemen. Yemen has used ties with Iraq to fend off pressure from nearby Saudi Arabia, while buying missiles from North Korea with tacit U.S. approval. In return, Yemen has allowed the United States to fly Predator drone missions over Yemen territory in search of al-Qaeda targets and cooperates with CIA and special forces teams on the ground. However, Yemen seems to be still providing sanctuary to some terrorist cells.

Internet Resources

Central Intelligence Agency. *The World Factbook 2002.* Available online. URL: http://www.odci.gov/cia/publications/factbook/. Downloaded November 15, 2002. This useful reference source, published annually and updated periodically online, provides basic information on the geography, demographics, economics, and infrastructure of each of the world's countries. It is a good first step in researching an area involved with the war on terrorism.

Washingtonpost.com. "Afghanistan." Available online. URL: http://www.washingtonpost.com/wp-srv/world/afghanistan/front.html. Downloaded August 15, 2002. A basic introduction to Afghanistan and recent events there in connection with the war on terrorism. Includes an interactive map.

———. "Iraq and the War on Terrorism." Available online. URL: http://www.washingtonpost.com/wp-srv/world/iraq/front.html. Downloaded August 15, 2002. This basic introduction discusses Iraq's relationship to terrorism, whether it has nuclear or biological weapons, and the possibility of war with the United States.

———. "Pakistan." Available online. URL: http://www. washingtonpost. com/wp-srv/world/pakistan/front.html. Downloaded August 15, 2002. Introduction to Pakistan, its support for terrorism and cooperation with the United States, and difficult relations with India. Includes an interactive map.

———. "The Philippines and the War on Terrorism." Available online. URL: http://www.washingtonpost.com/wp-srv/world/philippines/front. html. Interactive map and links for background to the war on terrorism in the Philippines, including description of the Abu Sayyaf terrorist group.

———. "Somalia and the War on Terrorism." Available online. URL: http://www.washingtonpost.com/wp-srv/world/somalia/front.html. Downloaded August 15, 2002. Interactive map and links for background on Somalia including ties to al-Qaeda, the story of the events portrayed in the movie *Black Hawk Down*, and possible future U.S. military involvement.

"UN Actions Against Terrorism." Available online. URL: http://www.un. org/terrorism. Downloaded February 10, 2003. This portion of the United Nations web site gives background and recent developments in the UN effort against terrorism, including treaties, proposals, and debates in the General Assembly.

INTELLIGENCE AGENCIES: FAILURE AND REFORM

This section deals with intelligence agencies such as the CIA and FBI, their performance in counterterrorism, critiques of intelligence failures, and proposals to reform or improve intelligence gathering.

Books

Baer, Robert. *See No Evil: The True Story of a Ground Soldier in the CIA's War on Terrorism*. New York: Crown Publishers, 2002. The author, a retired field officer who worked more than 20 years in the Middle East, describes what it's like to "run agents" to get intelligence on the ground—something very difficult to do with regard to Islamic extremist groups.

Coulson, Danny O., and Elaine Shannon. *No Heroes: Inside the FBI's Secret Counter-Terror Force*. New York: Pocket Books, 1999. Coulson, the FBI agent who founded the bureau's Hostage Rescue Team, recounts his years of pursuing criminals and terrorists, including right-wing extremists and Middle Eastern bombers. He gives a vivid insider's account of such domestic events as the 1992 Ruby Ridge and 1993 Waco incidents and the 1993 World Trade Center and 1995 Oklahoma City bombings. While acknowledging mistakes (particularly with regard to Ruby Ridge and Waco) and problems of bureaucracy and politicization in the agency, he takes an uncompromising position in favor of law enforcement.

Cuddy, Dennis Laurence. *September 11 Prior Knowledge: Waiting for the Next Shoe to Drop.* Oklahoma City, Okla.: Hearthstone, 2002. The author recounts evidence and warnings received prior to the September 11, 2001, attacks, including Project Bojinka, a plan discovered on a laptop computer in the Philippines in 1995 that called for setting off bombs on some airliners and hijacking airliners and crashing them into the World Trade Center, Pentagon, and other targets. (There is some controversy about the actual extent of what was contemplated in this project.) As September 11, 2001, approached a number of other warnings and intercepted transmissions suggested that terrorists were planning something big for that day, but the author says that nothing was done—a monumental intelligence failure.

Gertz, Bill. *Breakdown: How America's Intelligence Failures Led to September 11.* Washington, D.C.: Regnery, 2002. The chief defense and national security reporter for the *Washington Times* draws on recently declassified documents to lay out the anatomy of what he considers to be not a single failure but massive multiple failures of U.S. intelligence leading up to the September 11, 2001, attacks. Gertz, a conservative, argues that political pressure in the Clinton administration led to the resignation or reassignment of some of the CIA's and NSA's best people, leaving the agencies unprepared for the growing menace of Osama bin Laden and al-Qaeda. Gertz also believes that congressional legislation and oversight of the intelligence community has severely restricted or compromised its effectiveness in combating terrorism.

Johnson, Loch K. *Bombs, Bugs, Drugs, and Thugs: Intelligence and America's Quest for Security.* New York: New York University Press, 2000. A survey and analysis of the U.S. intelligence community, which is populated not only by the CIA, FBI, and NSA but also by many lesser-known agencies. The author believes that the fragmentation of intelligence efforts among so many agencies and the lack of effective coordination limit the ability to respond to emerging crises such as bioterrorism. This analysis gained new cogency after September 11, 2001, with the debate about reforming and reorganizing intelligence and homeland security functions.

Miller, John, and Michael Stone. *The Cell: Inside the 9/11 Plot, and Why the FBI and CIA Failed to Stop It.* New York: Hyperion, 2002. Recounts what the authors consider to be intelligence failures and missed opportunities in the late 1990s that if properly handled could have alerted American authorities to the impending attack of September 11, 2001. For example, the authors say that the investigation of the 1993 World Trade Center bombing was essentially shut down for bureaucratic reasons without coming to an understanding of how al-Qaeda worked. They believe that the problems continued with the failure to properly understand the role of Ramzi Yousef and Omar Abdel Rahman and to connect them with subsequent developments.

Mizell, Louis R., Jr., and James Grady. *Target U.S.A. The Inside Story of the New Terrorist War.* New York: John Wiley & Sons, 1998. A former intelligence agent highlights the many ways in which terrorists have penetrated deep into the heart of America, including a group of Libyan terrorists who set up a secret training camp in Colorado. The author uses anecdotes and detailed evidence from interrogation reports to paint a picture of U.S. vulnerability to terrorist attack.

Wallis, Rodney. *Combating Air Terrorism.* Washington, D.C.: Brassey's, 1993. Describes the need for international cooperation in preventing bombing, skyjacking, and other crimes of terrorism against aviation. The author suggests further steps that can be taken to improve security and incident response.

Articles and Papers

Bamford, James. "Our Best Spies Are in Space." *New York Times,* August 20, 1998, p. A23. Because close-knit, highly committed terrorist groups are hard for American intelligence agencies to penetrate on the ground, the NSA's spy satellite and computer surveillance facilities are vital to the counterterrorist effort. The agency's biggest challenge is not gathering data, but sifting through the tremendous amount of information it receives.

Duffy, Michael, and Nancy Gibbs. "How Far Do We Want the FBI to Go?" *Time,* vol. 159, June 10, 2002, p. 24 ff. As the FBI gears up to make fighting terrorism its highest priority, it has been given broad new powers to uncover evidence. Agents can begin preliminary investigations without getting approval from headquarters, and they are free to "surf" web sites, chat rooms, and other public places in cyberspace. However, can the FBI change its internal culture so that it responds to, organizes, and shares information more effectively? What's more, the existing, bureaucratically defensive culture is largely the result of fear of recriminations from

Congress, and the civil liberties implications of the agency's new powers might well bring such scrutiny.

Elliott, Michael. "They Had a Plan: Long Before 9/11, the White House Debated Taking the Fight to al-Qaeda." *Time*, vol. 160, August 12, 2002, p. 28 ff. Available online. URL: http://www.time.com/time/covers/1101020812/story.html#. This feature describes individuals in both the Clinton and Bush administrations who wanted to do much more about al-Qaeda and the opportunities that were ultimately squandered. It begins with Bill Clinton's national security advisor, Sandy Berger, who warned the incoming Condoleezza Rice that Osama bin Laden and terrorism were likely to be the most important thing on the new administration's agenda.

Isikoff, Michael, and Daniel Klaidman. "The Hijackers We Let Escape." *Newsweek*, June 10, 2002, p. 20. The authors question why the United States let two suspected terrorists, Nawaf Alhazmi and Khalid Almihdhar, enter the United States after attending an al-Qaeda summit in Malaysia. In what may be the biggest intelligence failure of all, the CIA did not pass on information about the terrorists to the INS, which could have denied them entry or to the FBI, which could have tracked them to learn more about their mission and attending of flight school. They later flew the jet into the Pentagon on September 11. The FBI believes that if they had known about the presence of these two terrorists, it could have unraveled the entire plot.

Miller, Judith. "Planning for Terror but Failing to Act." *New York Times*, December 30, 2001, p. A1 ff. An extensive account that outlines what the government knew about Osama bin Laden and al-Qaeda before September 11, 2001. Bin Laden was perceived to be a major threat (particularly after the 1998 embassy bombings) and repeated proposals were made for dealing with him in a more systematic way, but none came to fruition. Further, evidence arising from the activities of Ramzi Yousef and the first World Trade Center bombing in 1993 was not used effectively, and investigations petered out.

Ratnesar, Romesh, and Michael Weisskopf. "How the FBI Blew the Case: The Inside Story of the FBI Whistle-Blower Who Accuses Her Bosses of Ignoring Warnings of 9/11." *Time*, vol. 159, June 3, 2002, p. 24 ff. Provides background on FBI whistle blower, Coleen Rowley, who achieved her childhood goal and became a pioneer FBI woman agent. Her memo provides a devastating critique of the agency's failure to recognize and properly follow up on the suspicious flight school activities of Zacarias Moussaoui, who is now awaiting trial as the 20th hijacker. The Rowley memo eventually led to a promise of reform and nonreprisal by FBI director Robert Mueller.

"A Systematic Failure: George Bush and September 11." *Economist*, May 25, 2002, n. p. The author holds that while it is not reasonable to think

President George W. had definite knowledge of an attack and failed to act, administration characterizations of what was known or could be known are problematic. For example, the possibility of using hijacked airliners as missiles should have been considered, given that two plots to crash aircraft into the Eiffel Tower and CIA headquarters had been foiled previously. The FBI also received reports that suspicious individuals had enrolled in flight schools.

Internet Resources

Office of the Director of Central Intelligence. "United States Intelligence Community." Available online. URL: http://www.odci.gov/ic/icagen2.htm. Downloaded August 15, 2002. Official site giving links to the CIA, Defense Intelligence Agency, and other military and departmental intelligence agencies.

HOMELAND SECURITY

GENERAL CONSIDERATIONS

This section covers general considerations of vulnerabilities in the national infrastructure and attempts to improve defenses against terrorism. It also covers the proposed organization of the Department of Homeland Security.

Books

Canada, Ben. *State and Local Preparedness for Terrorism: Policy Issues and Options.* Washington, D.C.: Congressional Research Service, 2002. Assesses state and local preparedness for terrorist attacks and gives an overview of federal policy and legislation to support this effort. Gives examples of specific federal policies and their application to local governments.

Cordesman, Anthony H. *Terrorism, Asymmetric Warfare, and Weapons of Mass Destruction: Defending the U.S. Homeland.* Westport, Conn.: Praeger, 2002. Cordesman, codirector of the Middle East program at the Center for Strategic and International Studies and author of a number of works on international security, provides a manual for defending the homeland against a variety of existing and emerging unconventional threats. He explains the variety of possible sources for threats (including both independent terrorists and proxies of rogue states) and then discusses how to evaluate the seriousness of threats and how to intelligently prioritize and allocate resources to create the most effective homeland defense.

Decker, Ronald Ray. *Bomb Threat Management.* Boston: Butterworth-Heinemann, 1998. The author, an attorney and security consultant, provides procedures and tools for security personnel to use when confronted by bomb threats. Gives examples of forms for evaluating threats, and procedures for reacting to incidents and recovering from the effects of an explosion.

Jane's Counter Terrorism. Alexandria, Va.: Jane's Information, 2002. A desktop reference to procedures and planning for a variety of possible terrorist attacks. Includes scene and incident management, personnel training, and media relations. Designed for security specialists and facilities managers.

Knezo, Genevieve. *Federal Research and Development for Counter Terrorism: Organization, Funding, and Options.* Washington, D.C.: Congressional Research Service, 2002. Discusses the adequacy of federal funding for scientific research and development of counterterrorism applications and the organization and priority-setting mechanisms of relevant government agencies.

Krouse, William J., and Raphael F. Perl. *Terrorism: Automated Lookout Systems and Border Security Options and Issues.* Washington, D.C.: Congressional Research Service, 2002. Discusses new and proposed technology and procedures for detecting known or suspected members of terrorist organizations and excluding them from entry into the United States.

Relyea, Harold C. *Homeland Security: Department Organization and Management.* Washington, D.C.: Congressional Research Service, 2002. Discusses the issues faced by Congress and the president in designing and implementing the new Department of Homeland Security. These include organization, management structure, labor issues and what to do with the functions of existing agencies that are unrelated to homeland security.

Articles

Becker, Elizabeth. "Brookings Study Calls Homeland Security Plan Too Ambitious." *New York Times,* July 14, 2002, p. 21 ff. In a report on the proposed Department of Homeland Security, the Brookings Institution says that bringing together so many agencies that have unrelated responsibilities (such as environmental cleanup and marine rescue) may make the new organization unwieldy and poorly focused. Ivo H. Daalder, one of the authors of the Brookings study, argues that "The proposal put on the table is too big; it needs to focus on just those functions directly related to homeland security like the Coast Guard, customs, intelligence analysis and protecting public and private infrastructure that doesn't really exist today."

———. "Bush to Propose Broad New Powers in Domestic Security." *New York Times.* July 16, 2002, p. A1 ff. Describes new government powers accompanying the proposed Department of Homeland Security. These include standardizing state driver's licenses, establishing "red teams" to test defenses against terrorist attack, inspecting more shipping containers before they enter the United States, and improving communications between government agencies. But Congress has raised concerns that the administration may be trying to revamp the Posse Comitatus Act, which prohibits the use of the military in domestic law enforcement.

Graham, Bradley, and Bill Miller. "Pentagon Debates Homeland Defense Role: Sept. 11 Attacks Challenge Reluctance to Use Troops for Civil Law Enforcement." *Washington Post*, February 11, 2002, p. A6. Defense officials are rethinking the possible use of U.S. troops to bolster homeland security. Already, about 7,200 National Guard troops have been deployed to airports, and thousands more have been involved with border patrols; supporting the air cover over Washington, D.C., and New York City; and in providing security for the 2002 Winter Olympics. However, the deployment of troops for more direct law enforcement missions runs into legal problems, including whether they would remain under state control or be under federal control, and the Posse Comitatus Act, an 1878 statute that bars the use of troops for making domestic arrests or conducting searches and seizures.

Gourevitch, Alex. "Alien Nation: The Justice Department Takes on Immigrants, er, Terrorists." *American Prospect*, vol. 13, January 13, 2003, n.p. The author reports that the many directives coming from the Justice Department in the wake of September 11, 2001, have created chaos and confusion both among federal (INS) officers and local officials and among immigrants themselves. Although an expanding number of immigrants are being contacted and registered under the new rules, without expensive verification procedures the actual value of the information being obtained is questionable.

Miller, Bill, and Paul Duggan. "Security Worries Bring a Costly Shift in Priorities." *Washington Post*, February 12, 2002, p. A3. Local police face difficult choices when they receive nonspecific terrorist warnings. How many officers should a department divert to guarding high-value targets such as bridges or public gatherings, and how much will this impact the traditional focus of police—preventing or deterring crime? Departments called upon to help federal agencies investigate local immigrant groups also face worsening their community relations. Meanwhile, departments face new expenses such as buying protective gear for biological or chemical attacks.

O'Beirne, Kate. "The DHS Debacle: A Department We'll Spend a Lifetime Criticizing." *National Review*, vol. 54, August 12, 2002, n.p. Available online. URL: http://www.nationalreview.com/12aug02/kob081202.asp. As both conservative and liberal critics see the proposed Department of Homeland Security as being unwieldy, the Bush administration displays "turf battles, and overall lack of enthusiasm for the enterprise." And as large as it would be, the proposed organization leaves out many security-related organizations while incorporating agencies with unrelated functions.

O'Hanlon, Michael. "Protecting the American Homeland: Governor Ridge's Unfinished Work." *Brookings Review*, Summer 2002, p. 13 ff. While there have been no new major terrorist attacks to date, a scorecard for Tom Ridge and the homeland security record is mixed at best. According to the author and Brookings analysts, the proposed new efforts are too narrowly focused on preventing recurrences of the specific kinds of attacks experienced in 2001. Brookings has developed an alternative plan that differs from the Bush administration's in some respects, including expanded use of information technology, improving the U.S. Coast Guard and U.S. Customs Service together with developing comprehensive new systems for cargo inspection, protecting major buildings and facilities, and improving security for nuclear power plants and other facilities containing hazardous materials.

Pell, Eve. "Homeland Security x 50: State Officials Rush to Declare Their Own Versions of the 'War on Terror.'" *Nation*, vol. 274, June 3, 2002, p. 20. Most people are aware of homeland security as a national issue and perhaps of some local measures, but the sum total of state antiterrorism and security initiatives and proposals is staggering. The author gives examples of hastily drafted laws that could lead to the arrest of people engaged in innocuous activities as well as laws directed against certain groups, such as environmentalists, in the guise of fighting terror.

"Poor Tom." *Economist*, April 20, 2002, n.p. An evaluation of Homeland Security director Tom Ridge. Ridge has been battered by bureaucratic turf wars, and he is starting to be bombarded by the media as well. His color-coded terrorism alert system has been essentially discarded, and his suggestions for border security disregarded. However, it is possible that he may be able to reemerge as director of the new Homeland Security Department being considered by Congress.

Walker, Jesse. "Panic Attacks: Drawing the Thin Line Between Caution and Hysteria After September 11." *Reason*, vol. 33, March 2002, p. 36ff. With the nation on hair-trigger alert following the September 11 and anthrax attacks in 2001, there have been many overreactions to innocuous objects or circumstances. While understandable, there is danger in the spread of "social panic" that makes people react inappropriately or irrationally. In a democracy, panic leads to government agencies having wrong priorities and wasting resources. Also, temporary panics often result in the permanent enactment of laws that erode people's freedom.

Waller, J. Michael. "Security Blanket: Here Are Details of the Proposed Department of Homeland Security and the Inside Story of How It Was Planned in Utmost Secrecy." *Insight on the News*, vol, 18, July 22, 2002, p. 12 ff. According to the author, the Department of Homeland Security proposal, based on years of think tank research, was crafted in secrecy so that the plan could be sprung suddenly without giving bureaucrats time to defend their turf. The organization's four main functions are border and transportation security, protection against weapons of mass destruction, infrastructure protection, and information analysis. The FBI (which is being reformed separately) and other law enforcement agencies would remain outside the new department.

Internet Resources

ANSER Institute for Homeland Security. Available online. URL: http://www.homelandsecurity.org. Downloaded August 15, 2002. This non-profit institute provides news, documents, and many links to various aspects of homeland security as well as related government and private organizations.

Bush, George W. "The Department of Homeland Security." Available online. URL: http://www.whitehouse.gov/deptofhomeland/book.pdf. The official June 2002 White House proposal for reorganizing various security-related government departments into a unified Department of Homeland Security. The new department would have four divisions: border and transportation security; emergency preparedness and response; chemical, biological, radiological, and nuclear countermeasures; and information analysis and infrastructure protection.

Department of Homeland Security. Available online. URL: http://www.whitehouse.gov/homeland/. Updated August 15, 2002. This is an interim White House site for the proposed Department of Homeland Security. It provides news and links.

Homeland Defense Journal. Available online. URL: http://www.homelanddefensejournal.com. Updated February 5, 2003. This printed and online newsletter is essentially for the homeland defense "industry," highlighting products, services, and issues.

AIRLINE AND OTHER TRANSPORTATION SECURITY

Since the attacks of September 11, 2001, were carried out by means of hijacking, airline security has received enormous attention. This section focuses on coverage of security for both airline and ground transportation (railways and highways).

Books

Cubbin, Ken. *Survival Tactics for Airline Passengers.* Leesburg, Va.: Avionics Communications, 2002. The author, an airline flight officer and aviation writer, explains how airline passengers can defend themselves and the plane during a hijacking. He explains step-by-step how to assess the situation and use simple self-defense techniques and improvised weapons to thwart the hijackers. He also provides suggestions for improving survival chances in case of a crash, water ditching, or fire.

Frittelli, John. *Maritime Security: Overview of Issues.* Washington, D.C.: Congressional Research Service, 2002. Discusses issues relating to current maritime security legislation, including monitoring and tracking information about cargo and improving the physical security of port facilities.

Morgan, Daniel. *Aviation Security Technologies and Procedures: Screening Passengers and Baggage.* Washington, D.C.: Congressional Research Service, 2001. Describes aviation security issues including technology, funding, and congressional oversight. Outlines proposals in Congress and administration actions since the September 11, 2001, attacks.

Rothberg, Paul F. *Hazardous Materials Transportation: Vulnerability to Terrorists. Federal Activities, and Options to Reduce Risks.* Washington, D.C.: Congressional Research Service, 2001. Assesses the risks of terrorist attack or diversion of the more than 800,000 hazardous material shipments made each day—mostly by truck. Describes preventive measures.

Sweet, Kathleen M. *Terrorism and Airport Security.* Lewiston, N.Y.: Edwin Mellen Press, 2002. A comprehensive look at the subject that includes a history of hijacking/skyjacking, the changing tactics of terrorists, security procedures and equipment, supervision of screeners, special counterterrorism units, and government action in the wake of September 11, 2001.

Wallis, Rodney. *How Safe Are Our Skies? Assessing the Airlines' Response to Terrorism.* Westport, Conn.: Praeger Publishers, 2003. The book discusses and evaluates the new Aviation and Transportation Security Act, the Transportation Security Administration, the FAA, and airline policies.

Articles and Papers

Cottrill, Ken. "New Light on Security: Operation Safe Commerce Brings Together Public, Private Sectors to Analyze Supply Chains." *Traffic World*, vol. 266, July 15, 2002, p. 12 ff. The article reports on a test of Operation Safe Commerce (OSC), a public-private partnership program being developed by the Department of Transportation. The entire supply chain linking a factory making automobile lamps in Nove Zamky, Slovakia, to the Osram-Sylvania facility in Hillborough, VT, was secured by surveillance and data logging, while all the relevant workers were put through security screening. The test, the first of a complete supply chain, was used to find potential gaps in security. OSC pilot projects are currently under way in several U.S. ports including Long Beach, California; Seattle and Tacoma, Washington; and New York/New Jersey.

Janofsky, Michael. "Armed Pilots? Many Travelers Are Gun-Shy." *New York Times*, July 12, 2002, p. A1. The reporter asks travelers what they think about the idea of allowing airline pilots to have firearms in the cockpit. Many oppose arming pilots out of fear of stray bullets, concern that terrorists might gain control of the gun, or a general antipathy toward firearms. Supporters note that pilots are trained, trustworthy individuals who are already responsible for the life of all aboard. A few opponents of firearms suggest that stun guns be used instead.

Rao, Ed, and Frank Binzoni. "Do Detection Technologies Fly?" *Security Management*, vol. 45, October 2001, p. 95. Overview and evaluation of a variety of baggage scanning technologies and the effectiveness of screeners using them.

Robertson, Jack. "U.S. Transportation Chief Pushes Biometrics Adoption—Report Urges Airports to Install Equipment, Screen Passengers Entering Country." *EBN*, October 15, 2001, p. 1. In a report issued by Secretary of Transportation Norman Mineta just after the September 11, 2001, attacks, airports were urged to install biometric passenger-screening systems. Such systems, which have been in limited use by the INS, match physical characteristics (such as fingerprints, the retina, or faces) to identification information. The system could also be used to check in "preapproved" passengers who have been investigated and certified as "safe flyers." Such a passenger would carry a card that would be verified against his or her physical characteristics.

Satchell, Michael. "Everyone Empty Your Pockets?" *U.S. News & World Report*, April 1, 2002, p. 18. Because of opposition to profiling, U.S. airports basically treat each passenger as an equal threat, and then overlay random closer inspections. Besides inconveniencing the public, this policy makes it easier for terrorists to slip "under the radar" since scrutiny is diluted. Use of nonprofile information (such as watch lists) can help, and profiles are not foolproof, since terrorists can learn how to avoid them.

Wood, Daniel B. "Remote Screening Gains, but Will It Help?" *Christian Science Monitor*, July 8, 2002, n.p. Available online. URL: http://www.csmonitor.com/2002/0708/p03s01-usgn.html. The shooting attack at Los Angeles International Airport on July 4, 2002, has renewed interest in developing ways to screen people before they enter the secure area of the airport—perhaps before entering terminals or other crowded public areas. Ironically, one of the largest such programs under development is in Los Angeles, which would screen all passengers at a central facility before transporting them to the various terminals. Supporters of the idea believe that it would improve efficiency and the ability to contain incidents, while critics suggest that it would just relocate the vulnerability.

Internet Resources

Associated Press. "Filling Airport Screening Jobs Proving Difficult." Posted July 28, 2002. Available online. URL: http://www.cnn.com/2002/TRAVEL/NEWS/07/28/airport.screeners.ap/index.html.CNN.com. Despite stepped-up recruiting efforts, the Transportation Security Administration is having trouble finding enough qualified airport screeners to meet the November 19, 2002, deadline. The requirement for English proficiency and a high school education is keeping out many applicants who met preliminary screenings. Because only female screeners are supposed to frisk female passengers, the agency wanted 50 percent female screeners, but finding sufficient numbers of women and minorities is also proving difficult.

Murray, Mark. "In Transportation Security, Blame Game Is in Full Swing." *Government Executive*, August 2, 2002. Available online. URL: http://www.govexec.com/dailyfed/0802/080202nj1.htm. As the deadline for installing explosives detectors in all airports draws near, the administration, Congress, and Transportation secretary Norman Mineta are engaging in a blame game. Mineta blames lack of money, while the Democrats accuse the administration of cutting the funds, and some Republicans are pushing to extend the deadline up to a year.

OTHER INFRASTRUCTURE PROTECTION

This section deals with the vulnerabilities and protection of facilities such as power plants, water systems, agriculture, pipelines, and public buildings.

Books

Abel, Amy, and Mark Holt. *Terrorism: Electric Utility Infrastructure*. Washington, D.C.: Congressional Research Service, 2002. Discusses the physical and cybernetic vulnerability of the complex grid of interlocking components that make up the electrical power system.

Caram, Peter. *The 1993 World Trade Center Bombing: Foresight and Warning*. London: Janus Publishing, 2002. The author, a retired detective and security officer who worked at the World Trade Center, argues that New York Port Authority, which had ultimate responsibility for the building's security, did little to anticipate or attempt to forestall the 1993 attack, despite warnings that terrorists were targeting this potent symbol of U.S. power. After September 2001, the events can be seen in the context of an ever more urgent need to protect vital infrastructure.

Copeland, Claudia, and Betsy Cody. *Terrorism and Security Issues Facing the Water Infrastructure Sector.* Washington, D.C.: Congressional Research Service, 2002. Assesses the adequacy of security for the nation's water supplies and discusses the development and funding of new measures.

Kozlow, Christopher, and John Sullivan. *Jane's Facility Security Handbook.* Alexandria, Va.: Jane's Information Group, 2001. A pocket guide summarizing security considerations and procedures for protecting facilities against terrorism and crime. Includes special sections for hospitals, educational institutions, transportation facilities, utilities, entertainment facilities, and special events.

Rothberg, Paul F. *Pipeline Security: Industry and Federal Efforts and Associated Legislation.* Washington, D.C.: Congressional Research Service, 2002. Discusses the efforts of owners to better secure natural gas pipelines and storage facilities as well as congressional efforts to improve pipeline security.

Articles and Papers

Dreazen, Yochi J. "Ridge Handles Test of Possible Attack at Nuclear Plant." *Wall Street Journal*, October 29, 2001, p. A8. The director of the Office of Homeland Security turned his attention to nuclear power plants amid speculation that they were the next target. Tests and scenarios will be conducted to try to assess vulnerability.

"Protecting the Nation's Dams and Power Systems." *Energy*, vol. 27, Winter 2002, p. 28ff. Describes how managers of hydroelectric dams and power transmission facilities can help resist terrorist attack by a following step-by-step security assessment process developed by the Interagency Forum on Infrastructure Protection (IFIP).

Sevin, Eugene, and Richard G. Little. "Mitigating Terrorist Hazards." *Bridge*, vol. 28, Fall 1998, n.p. Available online. URL:http://www.nae.edu/nae/naehome.nsf/weblinks/NAEW-4NHMEP?opendocument. The authors survey design considerations for making buildings more explosion resistant, with particular focus on the types of bomb attacks typically associated with terrorists (including the attacks on the U.S. embassies in Africa). The main points are minimizing initial casualties, limiting further failure of building structure, and facilitating rescue efforts. Engineers and architects must balance the goal of making buildings more robust and resilient with cost and aesthetics.

Internet Resources

Sirhal, Maureen. "Critical Infrastructure Operators Lack Key Information." *Government Executive*, August 13, 2002. Available online. URL: http://www.govexec.com/dailyfed/0802/081302td1.htm. A report from the FBI's National Infrastructure Protection Center, which conducted simulations to test the ability of various government and private installations (including utilities and communications companies) to recover from damage to their systems. The study found that many organizations had inadequate contingency plans that failed to account for such things as the loss of telephone and Internet connectivity. They also lacked reliable backup communications systems.

CYBERTERRORISM

This section covers vulnerabilities, types of attack, and means of protecting information and communications systems.

Books

Arquilla, John, and David Ronfeldt, eds. *Networks and Netwars: The Future of Terror, Crime, and Militancy.* Santa Monica, Calif: RAND, 2001. A collection of essays on "netwar," attacks carried out by highly networked organizations in and against civil society (as opposed to the military-oriented cyberwar.) A key insight is that both terrorism and organized crime have become increasingly decentralized, relying on communications and information technology as well as social networking to coordinate activities in a fluid way. Thus, the traditional military tactic of trying to cut lines of communication to a central command becomes inapplicable and counterterrorist tactics based on the dynamics of networks must be developed.

Center for Strategic and International Studies. *Cybercrime, Cyberterrorism, Cyberwarfare: Averting an Electronic Waterloo.* Washington, D.C.: Center for Strategic and International Studies, 1998. Summary available online. URL: http://www.csis.org/pubs/cyberfor.html. Report by a task force on the vulnerability of U.S. information systems to hacker and terrorist attack, with recommendations for countering the threat. The United States must develop a comprehensive plan that understands the nature of the information revolution, identifies and secures government functions, understands the needs of the private sector, and provides oversight for the military's use of information warfare.

Dunnigan, James F. *The Next War Zone: Confronting the Global Threat of Cyberterrorism.* New York: Kensington Books, 2002. The author, a wargame designer and consultant on military affairs, tackles the subject of cyberwarfare. Much of the material he covers is generic computer security material, including ways in which ordinary PC users can protect themselves against viruses and Internet-based attacks. However, Dunnigan also covers the development of much more potent cyberweapons by government agencies and their possible use by terrorists or foreign powers. The combination of inherent vulnerability and lack of adequate preparation may prove devastating.

Erbschloe, Michael, and John Vacca. *Information Warfare: How to Survive Cyber Attacks.* New York: McGraw-Hill Professional Publishing, 2001. Geared especially toward managers and security personnel, the book outlines 10 types of attack that might be used by criminals, hackers, or terrorists to attack governments, businesses, or individuals. Both short-term and long-term defensive strategies are given for each threat. Vivid scenarios illustrate the concepts.

Goodman, Seymour E., ed. *The Transnational Dimension of Cyber Crime Terrorism.* Stanford, Calif.: Hoover Institution Press, 2001. A collection of conference papers on many aspects of cyberterrorism including the transnational nature of the problem and the need for an international response, applications to aviation security, cyberspace security and technical capabilities, and the relationship between information security and civil liberties.

Hildreth, Steven A. *Cyberwarfare.* Washington, D.C.: Congressional Research Service, 2001. Discusses current U.S. policies and efforts to combat the threat of foreign agents or terrorists mounting attacks on the American information infrastructure. Includes a glossary.

Smith, Marcia S., et al. *The Internet and the USA PATRIOT Act: Potential Implications for Electronic Privacy, Security, Commerce, and Government.* Washington, D.C.: Congressional Research Service, 2002. Summarizes the application of the USA PATRIOT Act with regard to electronic commerce, security, and privacy.

Yourdon, Edward. *Byte Wars: The Impact of September 11 on Information Technology.* Upper Saddle River, N.J.: Prentice Hall, 2002. A software development guru and futurist outlines strategies for developing software and systems that can withstand cyberterrorism and the likely uncertainty of the post–September 11 world. He suggests that one must build for "survivability" from the ground up rather than trying to harden systems as an afterthought—although he suggests short-term fixes as well.

Articles and Papers

Dizard, Wilson P., III, and William Jackson. "New Strategy Details Homeland IT Goals." *Government Computer News,* vol. 21, July 22,

2002, p. 9. Describes the IT (information technology) budget priorities and allocations in the proposed Department of Homeland Security. The estimated budget for fiscal 2002–3 will be between $1 and $2 billion. Plans call for a "collaborative classified enterprise environment" for sharing security information between agencies, as well as a secure intranet.

Hosenball, Mark. "Al Qaeda's New Life: Bin Laden Loyalists Are Still Hiding and on the Run—but They're Also Ever More Active on the Web." *Newsweek*, December 30, 2002, p. 46. This reports on militant Islamic groups' increasing use of the Internet, including gory games about assassinating Western leaders, propaganda, and what some experts fear might be coded instructions to operatives. CIA agents are surreptitiously roaming Islamic chat rooms trying to trick militants into revealing useful information. Perhaps the ultimate fear is that radical Muslims might gain control of companies vital to the operation of network infrastructure.

Levy, Stephen, and Brad Stone. "Hunting the Hackers." *Newsweek*, vol. 135, February 21, 2000, p. 38. Describes the "denial of service" attacks by hackers who paralyzed major e-commerce sites such as Yahoo! and eBay. While the hackers were not linked to terrorist groups, the attack underscores the vulnerability of the "new economy" to cyberattack.

"Now, Weapons of Mass Disruption? 'Soft Terrorism' Would Be Aimed Against the 'System of Systems' That Is Modern America." *Newsweek*, October 29, 2001, p. 76. Argues that "'Soft,' flexible, pervasive, yet destructive, cyberterrorism lacks the shock value of a collapsing building, but it may be the next 'anthrax' that confronts Americans with their vulnerability."

Internet Resources

Denning, Dorothy. "Activism, Hacktivism, and Cyberterrorism: The Internet as a Tool for Influencing Foreign Policy." Available online. URL: http://www.infowar.com/class_2/00/class2_020400b_i.shtml. Posted February 4, 2000. Describes the emergence of the hacker as political activist during the war in Serbia, where hackers on both sides of the conflict hijacked and defaced web sites. On the positive side, the Internet is an effective tool for activists, but "hacktivists" may find that their destructive electronic protests do not accomplish their foreign policy objectives.

Infowar.com. Available online. URL: http://www.infowar.com. Downloaded August 16, 2002. Site contains articles and links on computer hacking, information warfare, terrorism, legal issues, and related subjects.

TERRORISM AND WEAPONS OF MASS DESTRUCTION

GENERAL CONSIDERATIONS

This section covers concerns that apply to all forms of weapons of mass destruction, including nuclear, biological, and chemical.

Books

Bevelacqua, Armando, and Richard Stilp. *A Citizen's Guide to Terrorism Preparedness.* Albany, N.Y.: Delmar Learning, 2002. A well-organized guide that explains terrorist threats and recommended preparations in nontechnical language. Includes discussion of biological and chemical weapons and tips for security while traveling, as well as step-by-step procedures and charts. The authors have extensive experience in emergency response operations.

———. *Terrorism Handbook for Operational Responders.* Albany, N.Y.: Delmar Publishers, 1998. A concise guide for police, paramedics, firefighters, and other persons who may have to walk into a terrorist situation and deal with the effects of the attack or the demands of the attackers. Coordination of police and firefighting efforts is essential for effectiveness under adverse conditions.

Buck, George. *Preparing for Terrorism: An Emergency Services Guide.* Albany, N.Y.: Delmar Publishers, 1997. A textbook for emergency services personnel. Covers preparing and planning for terrorist attacks, including evaluation of existing plans and procedures. Includes procedures for responding to incidents and minimizing casualties for responders.

Burke, Robert. *Counter-Terrorism for Emergency Responders.* Boca Raton, Fla.: Lewis Publishers, 2000. A handbook for paramedics, police officers, firefighters, and others who are first on the scene and may have to deal with an increasing number of chemical or biological terrorist attacks. The book provides step-by-step procedures for assessing and containing a situation and for aiding victims.

Cilluffo, Frank J., Sharon L. Cardash, and Gordon Nathaniel Lederman. *Combating Chemical, Biological, Radiological, and Nuclear Terrorism: A Comprehensive Strategy.* Washington, D.C.: Center for Strategic and International Studies, 2001. This report from the Homeland Defense Project of the Center for Strategic and International Studies offers an agenda and priorities for high-level federal officials who are seeking to create an integrated national strategy for coping with terrorist attacks using weapons of mass destruction.

Dudonis, Kenneth J., David P. Schultz, and Frank Bolz, Jr. *The Counterterrorism Handbook: Tactics, Procedures, and Techniques.* 2d ed. Grand Rapids, Mich.: CRC Press, 2001. A comprehensive handbook that presents and evaluates procedures for dealing with nearly every type of terrorist attack from hijackings and hostage taking to bombings and use of weapons of mass destruction. The material is organized to meet the needs of first responders who must quickly grasp the essentials of a given situation, as well as managers and planners who must prepare for it.

Falkenrath, Richard A., Robert D. Newman, and Bradley A. Thayer. *America's Achilles' Heel: Nuclear, Biological, and Chemical Terrorism and Covert Attack.* Cambridge, Mass.: MIT Press, 1998. The authors assess current and future capabilities of terrorists to deliver weapons of mass destruction in the United States and consider appropriate policies for intelligence gathering and reaction to specific threats. They suggest that the threat of attacks through chemical, biological, and even nuclear weapons has been underestimated but that a careful, multipronged approach to counterterrorism can mitigate the danger.

Freedman, Lawrence. *Superterrorism: Policy Responses.* Cambridge, Mass.: Blackwell, 2002. The author systematically examines the many different impacts of the September 11, 2001, attacks as a manifestation of a seemingly unprecedented "superterrorism" that might well have been anticipated if not precisely predicted. The impacts will change the views and priorities of policymakers and affect how institutions such as business and the law will operate in years to come.

Hurley, Jennifer A. *Weapons of Mass Destruction: Opposing Viewpoints.* San Diego, Calif.: Greenhaven Press, 1999. Although written for high school students, this anthology of pro-and-con articles provides a useful introduction to the threat of use of weapons of mass destruction by terrorists and rogue states and proposals for countering the threat.

Laqueur, Walter. *The New Terrorism: Fanaticism and the Arms of Mass Destruction.* New York: Oxford University Press, 1999. The author, one of the foremost experts on terrorism, argues that terrorism is taking a new and dangerous form. Traditional terrorist groups, motivated by coherent ideology or nationalism, are giving way to tiny, idiosyncratic groups driven by fanaticism, apocalyptic visions, or the desire for vengeance. At the same time, weapons of mass destruction (chemical, biological, even nuclear) are becoming more available, and the complex information systems at the heart of the modern economy have also become vulnerable to cyberterrorism.

Stern, Jessica. *The Ultimate Terrorists.* Cambridge, Mass.: Harvard University Press, 2001. A vividly written but highly factual account of the threats of terrorist use of weapons of mass destruction, including nuclear, biological, and chemical agents. The author believes that the emergence of a new kind of extremist terrorist and the growing availability of the relevant information and technology have greatly increased the risk of mass destruction attacks. She suggests a variety of legal and protective measures that could make such attacks harder to accomplish.

21st Century Complete Guide to Bioterrorism, Biological and Chemical Weapons, Germ Warfare, Nuclear and Radiation Terrorism. Mount Laurel, N.J.: Progressive Management, 2001. A CD-ROM containing 146 U.S. military and government manuals and other documents relating to biological, chemical, and nuclear attacks, including safety measures and disaster plans. Material is in Adobe PDF format.

Articles and Papers

McGeary, Johanna. "What Does Saddam Have? Iraq May Not Have a Nuclear Bomb, but There's Strong Evidence It Has Chemical and Biological Weapons. Its Past Suggests It Wants a Bigger Arsenal." *Time,* vol. 160, September 26, 2002, p. 26 ff. Although there is considerable debate about what the United States should do about Saddam Hussein, most observers agree that Iraq likely has a considerable stock of chemical and biological weapons and is actively seeking more. However, Hussein is unlikely to be far along toward a nuclear weapon and in general is likely to have only limited means of delivering conventional weapons to targets outside Iraq.

"The Terror Next Time? Nuclear, Chemical and Biological Threats." *Economist,* October 6, 2001, n.p. Modern industrial society creates huge amounts of hazardous substances (there are more than 850,000 hazardous waste sites in the United States alone). However, terrorists face considerable difficulty obtaining the material and creating a weapon (such as a bomb) that would disperse it in the most effective way. Possible state sponsors of nuclear, chemical, or biological terrorism are also discussed.

Sprinzak, Ehud. "The Great Superterrorism Scare." *Foreign Policy,* Fall 1998, p. 110. In a detailed analysis of the risks, the author argues that the apocalyptic scenarios of terrorist attacks with weapons of mass destruction may seem compelling but can lead to bad policy. The high costs and limited effectiveness of countermeasures may actually help terrorists by weakening the state. Such attacks would not meet the goals of most terrorists, and the retaliation would impose unacceptable costs. A more limited approach to counterterrorism emphasizing good intelligence efforts, law enforcement, and a clear doctrine of deterrence would be more appropriate.

Internet Resources

RAND Corporation, eds. "Third Annual Report to the President and the Congress of the Advisory Panel to Assess Domestic Response Capabilities for Terrorism Involving Weapons of Mass Destruction." Available online. URL: http://www.rand.org/nsrd/terrpanel/terror3-print.pdf. Posted December 15, 2001. This detailed report assesses current capabilities for responding to weapons of mass destruction attacks and makes the following recommendations: empowering state and local response, enhancing health and medical capacities, strengthening immigration and border controls, improving security against cyber attacks, and clarifying the roles and missions for use of the military in terrorist situations.

NUCLEAR TERRORISM

This section deals with terrorists' possible use of not only nuclear weapons but also radiological, or dirty, bombs—conventional explosives that disperse radioactive material.

Books

Allison, Graham T., ed. *Avoiding Nuclear Anarchy: Containing the Threat of Loose Russian Nuclear Weapons and Fissile Material.* CSIA Studies in International Security, No. 12. Cambridge, Mass.: MIT Press, 1996. The contributing authors suggest ways to deal with the danger of nuclear weapons (or weapons materials) "leaking" out of Russia, where lack of regulation and oversight combined with opportunism may result in terrorist groups or rogue states obtaining nuclear capability with Russian help. They warn that current American policies in this area are inadequate.

Behrens, Carl E. *Nuclear Powerplants: Vulnerability to Terrorist Attack.* Washington, D.C.: Congressional Research Service, 2002. Discusses vulnerability of nuclear plants to different forms of terrorist attack including seizure of facilities by armed terrorists and crashing a hijacked airliner into a power plant. Also discusses relevant legislative proposals.

Lee, Rennselaer W. *Smuggling Armageddon: The Nuclear Black Market in the Former Soviet Union and Europe.* New York: St. Martin's Press, 1998. The author, an associate with the Foreign Policy Research Institute, investigates and documents the potential and actual illegal movement of nuclear material in Russia. Desperate economic conditions, chaos, and opportunism combine to create a worrisome situation. While many reports of nuclear smuggling turn out to be bogus or unsubstantiated, the possibility that organized crime or terrorists could gain access to some of the former Soviet Union's huge stockpile of nuclear materials or even warheads cannot be dismissed. Efforts by the United States and other governments to cope with the threat are incomplete and poorly coordinated.

Medalia, Jonathan. *Nuclear and Radiological Terrorism.* Washington, D.C.: Congressional Research Service, 2001. Discusses nuclear capabilities that might be available to terrorists (including radiological dirty bombs) and international programs to better secure and reduce stockpiles of nuclear weapons and materials.

Articles and Papers

Keller, Bill. "Nuclear Nightmares." *New York Times*, May 26, 2002, Sec. 6, p. 22. The author describes a variety of devastating scenarios involving terrorist attacks with nuclear weapons or dispersing radioactive material via a dirty bomb or even an aerosol device. All of them were suggested by various American or Russian experts and introduce a discussion of how to deter, detect, or prevent them.

Kluger, Jeffrey. "Defusing the Terror." *Time*, vol. 159, June 24, 2002, p. 30 ff. Using a question-and-answer format, the author explains what a dirty bomb is and what its effects would be. Such a weapon uses a conventional explosion to scatter radioactive material. It is likely to cause only minimal casualties (mainly from the explosion), but fear of radiation would enhance its psychological and economic effects.

——— "The Nuke Pipeline: The Trade in Nuclear Contraband Is Approaching Critical Mass. Can We Turn Off the Spigot?" *Time*, vol. 158, December 11, 2001, p. 40 ff. Smugglers of weapons-grade uranium and other radioactive materials have been arrested trying to sell the material. The main source is Russia, which has more than 100 military facilities, 80 decommissioned nuclear submarines, as well as power plants, all with nuclear material that is being poorly guarded. Although the United States and Russia have been cooperating to try to get a handle on nuclear material, the Bush administration has reduced funding for the program.

Richelson, Jeffrey. "Defusing Nuclear Terror." *Bulletin of the Atomic Scientists*, vol. 58, March–April 2002, p. 38 ff. Describes the capabilities of the Nuclear Emergency Search Team (NEST). NEST first evaluates the credibility of the threat (such as by determining the level of knowledge of nuclear weapons demonstrated by a terrorist group). Teams then use sensors in aircraft and disguised vehicles to track down nuclear bombs or radioactive material and destroy or disarm the bomb. Since its formation in 1975, NEST has investigated approximately 100 cases of possible nuclear terrorism and has actually deployed personnel to the scene in up to 20 or so of these cases.

2002 Radiation Threats: Complete Guide to Federal Documents and Plans on Nuclear and Radioactive Terrorism and Risks. Mount Laurel, N.J.: Progressive Management, 2002. An extensive CD-ROM collection of government manuals, handbooks, self-study courses, and other resources dealing with radioactive materials and effects, nuclear and radiological terrorism, and related matters. Documents are in Adobe PDF format and are readable on both PC and Macintosh computers.

Internet Resources

Nuclear Control Institute. "Nuclear Terrorism." Available online. URL: http://www.nci.org/nuketerror.htm. Downloaded August 16, 2002. This very extensive web site begins with links to topics of current interest (such as whether reactors are adequately protected against terrorist attack and whether dirty bombs are a major terrorist risk). Each question is clearly answered and extensive links to relevant news articles and reports are included.

BIOLOGICAL AND CHEMICAL TERRORISM

These two methods of terrorist attack are usually treated together because of their similar methods of delivery. Currently, most concern relates to biological weapons.

Books

Bartlett, John G., et al. eds. *Bioterrorism and Public Health: An Internet Resource Guide.* Montvale, N.J.: Thomson Medical Economics, 2002. A well-organized organized listing of hundreds of web sites relating to understanding and coping with biological attacks. Although the detailed information would probably be of most use to health professionals, the first part of the book includes advisories and answers to frequently asked questions about bioterrorism.

Buck, George. *Preparing for Biological Terrorism: An Emergency Service Guide.* Albany, N.Y.: Delmar Publishers, 2002. A guide for administrators and managers in the municipal services, public health, education, and industrial areas, it gives many specific procedures for developing emergency response plans. This includes detailed coverage of key topics such as surveillance, detection, diagnosis, and treatment of biological threats, as well as a guide to national infrastructure upon which local agencies might be able to draw.

Cole, Leonard A. *The Eleventh Plague: The Politics of Biological and Chemical Warfare.* New York: W.H. Freeman, 1997. Discusses recent developments in biological and chemical warfare, particularly as they emerged in the Gulf War with Iraq in 1991 and the terrorist nerve gas attack in the Tokyo subway system in 1995. The author suggests that difficulties in detecting and preventing use of chemical and biological agents by rogue states or terrorist groups will prove to be formidable. The book ends with discussion of a proposal to minimize the threat through a multilayered web of detection, defensive efforts, and active response.

Cook, Michelle Stem, and Amy F. Woolf. *Preventing Proliferation of Biological Weapons: U.S. Assistance to the Former Soviet Union.* Washington, D.C.: Congressional Research Service, 2002. Describes the extent and capabilities of biowar-related facilities in the former Soviet Union and U.S. programs aimed at preventing diversion of materials or workers from these facilities to terrorist groups or rogue nations.

Croddy, Eric, Clarisa Perez-Armendariz, and John Hart. *Chemical and Biological Warfare: A Comprehensive Survey for the Concerned Citizen.* New York: Copernicus Books, 2001. The author, a research associate with the Monterey Institute of International Studies, provides a well-organized, authoritative guide to biological agents, how they can be used as weapons, and ways to counteract or minimize their effects.

Graves, Barbara, ed. *Chem-Bio: Frequently Asked Questions.* Boston: Tempest Publishing, 1998. An introduction to biological and chemical agents that may be used by terrorists, including details on detection, delivery methods, effects, treatment of victims, and decontamination procedures. The book is particularly designed for first responders such as paramedics, police, and firefighters.

Jane's Chem-Bio Handbook. 2d ed. Alexandria, Va.: Jane's Information Group, 2002. Designed especially for first responders, this updated edition provides keys for recognizing various forms of chemical or biological attack, essential background information, and checklists for response and management procedures.

Jennings, Christopher. *Biological and Chemical Weapons: Criminal Sanctions and Federal Regulations.* Washington, D.C.: Congressional Research Service, 2001. Discusses regulations and criminal law applicable to biological and chemical weapons (some are also applicable to nuclear, radiological, or other regulated substances).

Miller, Judith, Stephen Engelberg, and William J. Broad. *Germs: Biological Weapons and America's Secret War.* New York: Simon & Schuster, 2001. Three *New York Times* reporters present a history of modern biological warfare beginning with the efforts of an Oregon cult to poison election opponents. Using information gathered from hundreds of interviews, the authors describe the extensive Soviet biological arsenal, the germ warfare stockpiles developed by Iraqi Leader Saddam Hussein, and the accessibility of agents such as anthrax and even smallpox to terrorists.

Moreno, Jonathan D., and Ford Rowan. *In the Wake of Terror: Medicine and Morality in a Time of Crisis.* Cambridge, Mass.: MIT Press, 2003. The authors discuss ethical issues arising from the medical response to terrorism. Topics include the development and distribution of vaccines and antidotes, use of coercive measures in emergencies, the legal and moral obligations of first responders and various institutions, and economic effects and decision making (such as with regard to health insurance).

Novick, Lloyd F., and John S. Marr. *Public Health Issues in Disaster Preparedness: Focus on Bioterrorism.* Gaithersburg, Md.: Aspen Publishers, 2001. An overview and collection of articles by experts on the characteristics of bioterrorism agents and the necessary response procedures. This book is primarily directed to first responders and local health planners and administrators.

Osterholm, Michael T., and John Schwartz. *Living Terrors: What America Needs to Know to Survive the Coming Bioterrorist Catastrophe.* New York: Delacorte, 2001. Written by an epidemiologist and a *Washington Post* science reporter for a popular audience, this book begins each chapter with a chilling scenario showing the results of using a different agent and method of attack. One such example is a disgruntled scientist using a crop-dusting plane to spread anthrax over a sports stadium during a game. The heart of the book explains the nature, effectiveness, and availability of many biological agents that could be used by terrorists, and the difficulties in tracking down the perpetrators. The need to have adequate supplies and training to respond to an attack is stressed, as well as the need to quickly identify and contain the disease. The authors conclude with an "eight-point plan."

Potomac Institute for Policy Studies, Counter Biological Terrorism Panel. *Countering Biological Terrorism in the U.S.* Dobbs Ferry, N.Y.: Oceana Publications, 1999. An evaluation by both military and civilian experts of America's readiness to cope with potential biological terrorist attacks. Current programs within the Department of Defense designed to detect and respond to such attacks are evaluated.

Redhead, C. Stephen, and Donna U. Vogt. *Bioterrorism: Legislation to Improve Public Health Preparedness and Response Capacity.* Washington, D.C.: Congressional Research Service, 2002. Summarizes new bioterrorism preparedness legislation in the House and Senate in 2002, as well as new funding for bioterrorism defense.

Segarra, Alejandro E. *Agroterrorism: Options for Congress.* Washington, D.C.: Congressional Research Service, 2001. Describes possible attacks on American agriculture by terrorists using biological or other weapons, current defensive measures, and proposals for strengthening America's food security.

Stevens, Nye. *Anthrax in the Mail.* Washington, D.C.: Congressional Research Service, 2002. Assesses the ability of the U.S. Postal Service to deal with bioterrorism threats such as the anthrax distributed by mail in fall 2001.

Venzke, Ben N., ed. *First Responder Chem-Bio Handbook.* Boston: Tempest Publishing, 1998. A succinct, practical guide to dealing with chemical or biological attacks. Topics include assessment, treatment, decontamination, and precautions for workers on the scene.

Wood, M. Sandra, ed. *Bioterrorism and Political Violence: Web Resources.* Binghamton, N.Y.: Haworth Press, 2002. A collection of web resources covering background on terrorism, the attacks of September 11, 2001, and sections on specific topics including anthrax, biological agents in general, nuclear terrorism, the psychological impact of terrorism, and disaster preparedness. Also includes general news sites and tips for using the Web.

Articles

Christopher, George W., et al. "Biological Warfare: A Historical Perspective." *Journal of the American Medical Association*, Special Communications, vol. 278, August 6, 1997, pp. 412–417. Available online. URL: http://jama.ama-assn.org/issues/v278n5/ffull/jsc7044.html. Describes and assesses the use of biological warfare tactics from medieval to modern times. Focuses particularly on developments since World War II, the U.S. biological warfare program, the 1972 treaty prohibiting the development of biological weapons, and recent events in Iraq and elsewhere.

Danitz, Tiffany. "Terrorism's New Theater." *Insight*, January 26, 1998, p. 8 ff. Biological agents such as anthrax and botulin toxin are increasingly available to and deliverable by terrorists and rogue nations such as Saddam Hussein's Iraq. Indeed, such agents can be created at home using readily available materials. The U.S. military is inoculating its troops against anthrax, but civilians will remain unprotected.

Holloway, Harry C. et al. "The Threat of Biological Weapons: Prophylaxis and Mitigation of Psychological and Social Consequences." *Journal of the American Medical Association*, vol. 278, August 6, 1997, p. 425 ff. Explores the psychological and social consequences of a biological attack. Panic, post-traumatic stress disorder, depression, and survivor guilt are all likely psychological effects. The invisible nature of the microbial threat enhances fear. Social consequences might include a breakdown of institutions and loss of trust and cooperation. Psychiatric casualties among survivors must be promptly treated.

"The Hunt for the Anthrax Killer: The FBI Still Doesn't Have Enough Evidence to Arrest Anyone, but Agents Do Have Intriguing New Clues." *Newsweek*, August 12, 2002. Agents' (literal) bloodhounds led them to Stephen J. Hatfill, an eccentric scientist who seems prone to exaggeration, but the FBI has been unable to find any solid evidence. The article includes a minibiography of Hatfill, who had been cooperating fully with the agents, although he subsequently filed a complaint against the FBI and held a press conference to assert his innocence.

Lucier, James P. "We Are What We Eat—and That Makes the United States Vulnerable." *Insight on the News*, vol. 14, November 16, 1998, p. 6. Experts at a conference of the National Consortium for Genomic Resources Management and Services (GenCon) have pointed out that the United States food supply is extremely vulnerable to accidental or intentional contamination. Because the U.S. has about a five-day local food supply, any attack that either disrupted food shipment or contaminated the food (such as with disease pathogens) could cause hoarding and severe economic losses. Attack on crops and food animals could also destroy markets for U.S. food exports.

Senkowsky, Sonya. "Building Better Biosensors: If You Think You're Nervous in Airports These Days, You Should Talk to Fred Milanovich." *BioScience*, vol. 52, April 2002, p. 332 ff. Describes the work of Fred Milanovich, program leader for chemical and biological national security at Lawrence Livermore National Laboratory. His team is trying to find ways to thwart terrorists who might surreptitiously spread deadly pathogens in a public place—particularly an airport, where travelers might spread the disease for thousands of miles. The potential solution is a "biodetector" that, like a smoke alarm, would give instant warning as soon as a pathogen is detected. Building a detector that is fast and accurate enough is difficult, but two technologies—immunoassay and DNA-based polymerase chain reaction (PCR)—might be confined and refined sufficiently.

Terry, Rob. "The Biowar: Last Year's Anthrax Attacks Spurred Record Research Spending on Biodefenses, but Most Solutions Are Still Years Away." *Washington Techway*, October 14, 2002, p. 26 ff. Although a concerted effort is under way to confront biological terrorism systematically, the challenge to bring together epidemiology, public health, and vaccine research remains daunting. A number of experts are quoted concerning the remaining problems.

Tucker, Jonathan B., and Amy Sands. "An Unlikely Threat." *Bulletin of the Atomic Scientists*, vol. 55, July 1999, p. 46. The authors suggest the hype by both media and government leaders about the seriousness of the threat of chemical or biological terrorism may be unwarranted. A detailed study by the authors at the Center for Nonproliferation Studies at the Monterey Institute of International Studies in California states that there have been no really significant chemical or biological terrorist attacks on U.S. soil and only one actual fatality. (Since then, there have been five deaths from anthrax attacks in 2001.) Yet government planners seeking big budget increases for fighting terrorism have played up worst-case scenarios, and such attacks have become a staple of movie thrillers. The authors' studies indicate that conventional political terrorists are unlikely to use weapons they view as unreliable or likely to cause massive governmental retaliation, but that terrorists motivated by fanatical or apocalyptic ideas may be more likely to embrace such weapons.

"Who Will Build Our Biodefenses? Vaccines Against Bioterrorism." *Economist (U.S.)*, vol. 366, February 1, 2003, n.p. The recently highlighted threat of terrorist-delivered smallpox brings up serious problems that must be solved before drug companies will wholeheartedly join the effort to create new vaccines against biological terrorism. The firms need their concerns about legal liability for side effects, which may emerge only many years later, allayed. There is also concern that the government will be tempted to abrogate patents or force down prices.

Internet Resources

Animal Science Department, Cornell University. "Ricin Toxin from Castor Bean Plant: Ricinus Communis." Available online. URL: http://www.ansci.cornell.edu/plants/toxicagents/ricin/ricin.html. Downloaded February 11, 2003. This provides an introduction and facts about ricin, a deadly plant toxin that had occasionally been used by spy-assassins during the cold war and in late 2002 was found in an alleged terrorist safe house in London.

Friedlander, Arthur M. "Anthrax." Available online. URL: http://www.nbc-med.org/SiteContent/HomePage/WhatsNew/MedAspects/Ch-22electrv699.pdf. Downloaded August 15, 2002. A chapter from *Medical Aspects of Chemical and Biological Warfare.* Describes the organism, its epidemiology, pathology, possible effects, diagnosis, and treatment.

Tucker, Jonathan B. "Historical Trends Related to Bioterrorism: An Empirical Analysis." *Emerging Infectious Diseases,* Special Issue, vol. 5, July–August 1999. Available online. URL: http://www.cdc.gov/ncidod/EID/vol5no4/tucker.htm An analysis of a database from the Chemical and Biological Weapons Nonproliferation Project at the Monterey Institute's Center for Nonproliferation Studies. A total of 415 incidents from 1900 to January 31, 1999, are classified according to materials used (chemical, biological, radiological), type of event (conspiracy to acquire, possession, threat, hoax, etc.), type of terrorist organization involved, motivation, and other factors. In general, motivation seems to have shifted from protest to separatist sentiment, retaliation, revenge, or apocalyptic prophecy. Symbolic buildings and the general population are more likely to be targeted.

LEGAL ISSUES

GENERAL LEGAL AND CIVIL LIBERTIES ISSUES

This section deals with the legal and legislative aspects of terrorism and with general issues that do not fit into the more specific topics of "Investigation, Surveillance, and Screening" and "Treatment and Prosecution of Suspects," which have their own sections later in this bibliography.

Books

Ackerman, David. *Suits Against Terrorist States.* Washington, D.C.: Congressional Research Service, 2002. Describes legislation and issues relating to the ability of American victims of terrorism to sue states that sponsor the attacks. Discusses the payment of judgments and the use of frozen assets.

Alexander, Yonah, and Edgar H. Brenner, eds. *U.S. Federal Legal Responses to Terrorism.* Ardsley, N.Y.: Transnational Publishers, 2002. A compilation of the sections of the U.S. Code dealing with terrorism including Aliens and Nationality, Crimes and Criminal Procedure, and Foreign Relations and Intercourse. Also includes the USA PATRIOT Act of 2001.

Bazan, Elizabeth B. *Assassination Ban and E.O. 12333. A Brief Summary.* Washington, D.C.: Congressional Research Service, 2002. Discusses the applicability of the executive order banning assassination (direct targeting of foreign leaders) to the current war on terrorism.

Dershowitz, Alan. *Why Terrorism Works.* New Haven, Conn.: Yale University Press, 2002. The author, a prominent attorney generally associated with civil liberties issues, takes a surprisingly hard-line approach to terrorism. He argues the "terrorism problem" is largely of our own making, arising from the international community's failure to effectively confront terrorists and terrorist states who are developing weapons of mass destruction. He further argues that civil liberties have to be yielded to an extent in order for the society itself to survive coming attacks and reduce their incidence. His proposed measures include a national ID card, tightened border security, and even the use of a warrant that would allow torture in extreme circumstances.

Doyle, Charles. *Antiterrorism and Effective Death Penalty Act of 1996: A Summary.* Washington, D.C.: Congressional Research Service, 1996. Although this law has been expanded and superceded by the 2001 USA PATRIOT Act, in some respects the earlier legislation is still important.

———. *The USA PATRIOT Act: A Legal Analysis.* Washington, D.C.: Congressional Research Service, 2002. Provides a detailed analysis of the new law, which includes far-reaching extensions of federal law enforcement and investigation powers with regard to terrorism.

Etzioni, Amitai, and Jason H. Marsh. *Rights vs. Public Safety after 9/11: America in the Age of Terrorism.* Lanham, Md.: Rowman and Littlefield, 2003. A group of scholars and legal experts attempts to strike a balance between liberty and security in the post–September 11 world, discussing a wide range of issues from racial profiling to the use of military tribunals to determining what types of actions might be justifiable in an emergency situation. The contributors take a generally communitarian approach. (Communitarianism, a political philosophy pioneered by Etzioni, seeks to make policy based on the interdependence of individuals and the community.)

Heymann, Philip B. *Terrorism and America: A Commonsense Strategy for a Democratic Society.* Cambridge, Mass.: MIT Press, 1998. An introduction to the development of policy with regard to terrorism in the United States and other democratic societies. Using shocking incidents such as the 1993 World Trade Center and 1995 Oklahoma City bombings as starting points, the author explores the limits of action against terrorism in a democratic society. Better intelligence gathering is crucial, particularly with regard to the emerging threats of chemical, biological, and nuclear weapons, but government actions must not compromise liberty to the point where they destroy people's ability to trust their institutions. Foreign terrorism and state-sponsored terrorism require somewhat different approaches than domestic terrorism, and military action (such as President Bill Clinton's cruise missile strikes against Afghanistan) is often unsuccessful and counterproductive.

Higgins, Rosalyn, and Maurice Flory. *Terrorism and International Law.* New York: Routledge, 1997. A comprehensive collection of documents, including laws and treaties, reflecting the response of the British, French, and international legal system to terrorism. Includes discussion of the extent and existing limitations of international cooperation against terrorism.

Rehnquist, William H. *All the Laws but One: Civil Liberties in Wartime.* New York: Vintage Books, 2000. In his study of civil liberties in wartime, Chief Justice William Rehnquist acknowledges that liberty can be seriously infringed, as during the Civil War and World War I, or as by the internment of Japanese Americans in World War II. Although his assessment is nuanced, Rehnquist ultimately comes down in favor of the necessity of curtailing liberties in some cases in order to prevent a greater evil—namely, the fatal disruption of the country. The account deals mainly with Civil War cases but includes others up to about 1950, with an explanation of the issues and how the Supreme Court ruled in each case.

Articles and Papers

Belluck, Pam. "Threats and Responses: The Bomb Plot, Unrepentant Shoe Bomber Is Given a Life Sentence for Trying to Blow Up Jet." *New York Times*, January 31, 2003, p. A13. The judge sentencing Richard Reid, the convicted shoe bomber, uses the life sentence as an occasion to affirm U.S. resolve against terrorism, while Reid defiantly declares his allegiance to Osama bin Laden and al-Qaeda, stating "I am at war with your country."

Davis, Derek H. "The Dark Side to a Just War: The USA PATRIOT Act and Counterterrorism's Potential Threat to Religious Freedom." *Journal of Church and State*, vol. 44, Winter 2002, p. 5 ff. An evaluation of the effects of the USA PATRIOT Act on civil liberties, free expression, and religious freedom. The author is particularly concerned with the impact on "faith groups" that may find themselves defined as terrorists according to secret criteria, in a process that necessarily involves the government determining the boundaries of permissible religious activity.

Padgett, Tim, and Rochelle Renfor. "Fighting Words: Can a Tenured Professor Be Fired for His Pro-Muslim Views? In a Post-Sept. 11 America, All Bets Are Off." *Time*, vol. 159, February 4, 2002, p. 56. Describes the case of Sami al-Arian, a computer science professor at the University of South Florida who was dismissed for expressing stridently anti-Israel and pro-*intifada* (Palestinian resistance) views. The university argues that death threats against the professor were creating a security risk, while angry alumni might stop donating to the institution. Al-Arian is fighting the dismissal with the support of civil liberties groups.

Internet Resources

American Civil Liberties Union. "National Security." Available online. URL: http://www.aclu.org/issues/security/hmns.html. Downloaded August 15, 2002. This web site features links to news and issues relating to civil liberties implications of the war on terrorism, as well as access to the ACLU News Database and advocacy resources.

Constitutional Rights Foundation. "America Responds to Terrorism." Available online. URL: http://www.crf-usa.org/terror/America%20Responds%20to%20Terrorism.htm. Downloaded February 11, 2003. A series of online lessons designed to help teachers and students deal with feelings and concerns arising from the September 11, 2001, attacks. Includes sections on media awareness and critical thinking, civil liberties issues (with historical background), Islamic issues, and international law and organizations.

Department of State, U.S. "International Conventions and Other Treaties Relating to Terrorism." Available online. URL: http://www.state.gov/r/pa/ho/pubs/fs/6093.htm. Posted November 13, 2001. Gives titles and links to terrorism-related treaties to which the United States is a signatory.

FindLaw. "Special Coverage: War on Terrorism." Available online. URL: http://news.findlaw.com/legalnews/us/terrorism/. Downloaded August 15, 2002. Provides extensive links to news, documents, laws, and cases related to terrorism in general and the post–September 11 war on terrorism in particular. The Laws section provides direct links to the text of legislation, orders, and specific titles of the United States Code.

JURIST Legal Education Network. "Terrorism Law and Policy." Available online. URL: http://jurist.law.pitt.edu/terrorism.htm. Downloaded August 15, 2002. Links to terrorism-related law and policy. Major subdivisions are Terrorism and Terrorists; Counterterrorism Policy; U.S. Anti-terrorism Laws; World Anti-Terrorism Laws; Civil Liberties; Bioterrorism: Legal Issues; Commentary; and Bibliography.

Legal Information Institute. "LII Backgrounder on National Security Law and Counter-Terrorism." Available online. URL: http://www.law.cornell.edu/background/warpower/. Downloaded August 15, 2002. Provides references to the legal underpinnings of the war on terrorism and legislation and executive orders subsequent to September 11, 2001. Divided into sections for the executive, legislative, and judicial branches.

Library of Congress, THOMAS Service. "Legislation Related to the Attack of September 11, 2001." Available online. URL: http://thomas.loc.gov/home/terrorleg.htm. Updated October 30, 2002. Provides links (by bill number) to legislation, joint resolutions, and other resolutions and proposed bills related to the attacks and the war on terrorism.

"NCJRS Abstracts Database." Available online. URL: http://abstractsdb.ncjrs.org/content/AbstractsDB_Search.asp. Updated August 15, 2002. This service, provided by the National Criminal Justice Reference Service, is a searchable database that has abstracts for more than 170,000 books and articles on all aspects of criminal justice, including thousands of publications relating to terrorism, counterterrorism, and related topics. Some abstracts include links to the full-text document.

INVESTIGATION, SURVEILLANCE, AND SCREENING

This section deals with civil liberties issues arising from information gathering by law enforcement or intelligence agencies. This includes surveillance (such as wiretapping), identification and tracking systems, monitoring of the Internet, use of subpoenas, and similar matters.

Books

Dempsey, James X., and David Cole. *Terrorism and the Constitution: Sacrificing Civil Liberties in the Name of National Security.* 2d ed. Los Angeles: First Amendment Foundation, 2002. Discusses the impact of federal counterterrorist laws and policies on civil liberties. Parts I and II discuss the implications of FBI investigations and actions during the 1980s and early 1990s against groups such as Amnesty International, Earth First!, and U.S. supporters of left-wing insurgencies in Central America, as well as the agency's attempt to enlist the aid of librarians in tracking potential terrorists. Part III is devoted to the 1996 Antiterrorism Act and 2001 USA PATRIOT Act, discussing their core provisions and their implications.

Eaton, Joseph W. *The Privacy Card: A Low-Cost Strategy to Combat Terrorism.* Lanham, Md: Rowman and Littlefield, 2003. This revised (and retitled) edition of a 1986 book surveys the issue of whether to implement a "national ID card" in light of the new threats posed by global terrorism. The advantages of a tamper-proof ID system are balanced against potential threats to privacy and ease of abuse in tracking innocent citizens. Suggestions for reconciling security and privacy concerns are offered.

Giroux, Henry A. *Public Spaces, Private Lives: Democracy Beyond 9/11.* Landham, Md.: Rowman and Littlefield, 2003. Although many of the author's essays included in this book were written before September 11, 2001, this only helps show how the terrorist attacks fit into broader trends in the conflict between individual privacy and the growing and pervasive operation of government and private agencies in the gathering of personal information. The author argues that market-based ideology is supplanting the older democratic ideology as a basis for thinking about privacy, especially in relation to new technology.

Smith, Alison M. *National Identification Cards: Legal Issues.* Washington, D.C.: Congressional Research Service, 2002. Summarizes the legal background and controversy over the proposed use of some form of uniform national identification, perhaps incorporating biometric data.

Articles and Papers

Berkowitz, Bill. "AmeriSnitch." *Progressive*, vol. 66, May 2002, p. 27 ff. A critique of Attorney General John Ashcroft's promotion of Neighborhood Watch programs expanded to watch for terrorists, and the proposed TIPS (Terrorist Information and Prevention System), which is supposed to enlist workers such as mail carriers, utility workers, and train conductors to watch for suspicious activity. Civil liberties groups are beginning to speak out against the idea of "turning the information society into an informant society."

Demmer, Valerie L. "Civil Liberties and Homeland Security." *Humanist*, vol. 62, January–February 2002, p. 7 ff. A critique of the USA PATRIOT Act, particularly its impact on the First Amendment rights of expression and association. Democrat Russ Feingold from Wisconsin, the only senator to vote against the bill, is quoted as follows: "Of course there is no doubt that, if we lived in a police state, it would be easier to catch terrorists. If we lived in a country that allowed the police to search your home at any time for any reason; if we lived in a country that allowed the government to open your mail, eavesdrop on your phone conversations, or intercept your email communications; if we lived in a country that allowed the government to hold people in jail indefinitely based on what they write or think, or based on mere suspicion that they are up to no good, then the government would no doubt discover and arrest more terrorists. But that probably would not be a country in which we would want to live. And that would not be a country for which we could, in good conscience, ask our young people to fight and die. In short, that would not be America."

Dreyfuss, Robert. "Colin Powell's List: The Targeting of 'Terrorist' Groups Harks Back to Earlier Repression of Dissent." *Nation*, vol. 274, March 25, 2002, p. 16. The proliferation of government lists that designate foreign terrorist organizations threatens to stifle dissent in a maze of regulations that leave people who simply want to express political views uncertain as to where they stand. Historically, the lists conjure up earlier periods of repression such as the post–World War I Red Scare and the McCarthy hysteria of the 1950s. Further, the criteria by which some organizations are listed but others are not remain unclear.

Kandra, Anne. "National Security vs. Online Privacy: The New Antiterrorism Law Steps Up Electronic Surveillance of the Internet." *PC World*, vol. 20, January 2002, p. 37 ff. The author expresses concern about provisions of the new USA PATRIOT Act as they apply to Internet use. E-mail and web activities of persons unrelated to a particular investigation might be "swept up," and the secret technology for Internet surveillance (formerly known as "Carnivore") remains obscure but troubling.

McGee, Jim. "Fighting Terror with Databases: Domestic Intelligence Plans Stir Concern." *Washington Post*, February 16, 2002, p. A27. Federal authorities are building powerful new investigative tools by linking databases containing information about, for example, immigrants and resident aliens. Local police are being given increased access to information from federal agencies, and often carrying out interviews on their behalf. As a sort of pilot program, 5,000 Middle Eastern men who share some characteristics with the September 11, 2001, hijackers have been "voluntarily" interviewed. Some civil libertarians believe that an open-ended database system may suck in thousands of innocent citizens, subject them to harassment and employment difficulties, and serve to deter legitimate political dissent as happened in the 1950s and 1970s.

Oder, Norman. "Libraries, Universities Meet with Lawyers on Patriot Act: Questions about Patron Confidentiality Heating Up; After TV Controversy, ALA Issues Distancing Statement." *Library Journal*, vol. 117, January 2002, p. 16. Library and academic organizations meet with the Justice Department to discuss the implications of the new USA PATRIOT Act for information about patrons' library use. The American Library Association is preparing specific guidelines for dealing with subpoenas and other government demands and for determining their legality. One difficult area is determining when a library is allowed to tell a patron that his or her records have been requested by the government; another problem is potential conflicts with state confidentiality laws that may be superceded.

Waller, J. Michael. "Fears Mount Over 'Total' Spy System." *Insight on the News*, vol. 19, December 24, 2002, n.p. The revelation of an experimental Pentagon research program called Total Information Awareness has provoked alarm from civil libertarians. While reports that the program intended to build lengthy dossiers on each individual in the United States are apparently unfounded, the massive "data mining" involved raises concerns, nevertheless, of privacy advocates. The fact that the program was being run by retired admiral John Poindexter (who had been central in the Iran-contra affair) does not reassure critics. Defenders of the system say that data will not be identified with specific individuals, and other safeguards will be put in place.

TREATMENT AND PROSECUTION OF SUSPECTS

This section deals with the arrest and detention of suspected terrorists. Issues covered include use of military tribunals, combatant status, use of immigration laws, applicability of habeas corpus, the right to an attorney, access to the courts, and so on. Specific recent cases and investigations (such as that of John Walker Lindh) are also included.

Books

Chadwick, Elizabeth. *Self-Determination, Terrorism, and the International Humanitarian Law of Armed Conflict.* Boston: M. Nijhoff, 1996. Focuses on terrorism conducted as part of a popular struggle for self-determination, a complex area that often blurs the distinction between terrorism and guerrilla war. Discusses the problem of applying International Humanitarian Law to such actions and the broader question of the strategy behind such terrorism and the failure of states to deter it.

Elsea, Jennifer. *Terrorism and the Law of War: Trying Terrorists as War Criminals Before a Military Commission.* Washington, D.C.: Congressional Research Service, 2001. Discusses principles, precedents, issues, and considerations involved in treating terrorists as war criminals and trying them for violating the laws of war.

Fisher, Louis. *Military Tribunals: The Quirin Precedent.* Washington, D.C.: Congressional Research Service, 2002. Discusses the procedures used in the military tribunal that tried eight German saboteurs during World War II and the issues and precedents arising from the Supreme Court appeal in *Ex Parte Quirin.*

Halstead, T.J. *Monitoring Inmate-Attorney Communications: Sixth Amendment Implications.* Washington, D.C.: Congressional Research Service, 2001. Describes the interim order authorizing prisons to monitor conversations between suspects and their attorneys when "reasonable suspicion" exists that the communications may facilitate terrorism. Discusses relevant Sixth Amendment issues.

Latham, Peter S., and Patricia H. Latham. *Terrorism and the Law: Bringing Terrorists to Justice.* Washington, D.C.: JKL Communications, 2002. The authors discuss the application of the law of war and military tribunals for trying suspects connected to the September 11, 2001, attacks. They include historical background and legal precedents arising from the use of military tribunals during the Civil War and particularly during World War II, when eight German saboteurs were captured and tried on American soil. They conclude by suggesting that military tribunals may have significant advantages compared to civilian courts and that their use is in keeping with the magnitude of the war on terrorism.

Reisman, M., and Chris T. Antoniou. *The Laws of War: A Comprehensive Collection of Primary Documents on International Laws Governing Armed Conflict.* New York: Vintage Books, 1994. Because terrorist acts often arise during wars (particularly civil war and ethnic conflicts), this useful collection of sources on the law of armed conflict is also relevant to the student of terrorism.

Articles and Papers

Anderson, Martin Edwin. "Is Torture an Option in War on Terror? Interrogators Increasingly Frustrated with Hardened al-Qaeda Terrorists

Are Considering the Use of Tactics Once Unthinkable for U.S. Law-Enforcement Officers." *Insight on the News*, vol. 18, June 17, 2002, p. 21 ff. Potential scenarios such as a hidden suitcase nuclear bomb have heightened the debate about whether the use of "truth drugs" or even torture might be justified in extreme circumstances. The use of CIA-backed paramilitary forces who might torture by proxy is also discussed.

Cohen, Adam. "Rough Justice: The Attorney General Has Powerful New Tools to Fight Terrorism. Has He Gone Too Far?" *Time*, vol. 158, December 10, 2001, p. 30 ff. Describes a number of civil liberties issues arising from the new initiatives and powers being used by the Justice Department against terrorism suspects. The most controversial is the proposed use of military tribunals that bypass many key protections of the regular courts. The danger also exists that broad powers (such as being able to hold persons without charges or conduct secret proceedings) first used against noncitizen terrorist suspects might be extended to citizens and beyond the context of terrorism. Finally, there is the question of whether the balance of powers between the executive and judiciary branches may be dangerously tilted toward the former if the courts are unable or unwilling to review cases involving extraordinary powers in "wartime."

Crumley, Bruce. "Terror's Track: New Information About Shoe-Bomber Richard Reid Provides Some Answers—and Raises More Questions." *Time International*, vol. 159, February 11, 2002, p. 18. While initial speculation about Richard Reid held that he was a mentally unstable loner, further investigation suggests that he met with other terrorists in Paris shortly before boarding the plane with explosives in his shoes. The sophistication of the explosives and traces found on them strongly suggest the shoe bomb was provided to Reid. The explosives are also similar to those found in some other thwarted al-Qaeda plots.

Gerstein, Josh. "Under Charge—The Real 9/11 Civil Liberties Problem." *New Republic*, April 22, 2002, p. 22. Holding suspects without charges and carrying out secret legal proceedings are the two most serious civil liberties issues arising from the war on terrorism. Recently, the government has started holding persons indefinitely as "material witnesses," such as Anwar Almirabi, who was held at first only for a visa violation but now has been in prison for seven months. The secrecy of the proceedings and the lack of access to communications facilities for most prisoners makes it very difficult to defend such cases, and thus far the appeals courts have generally not scrutinized them.

Isikoff, Michael. "The Case Against Moussaoui: Internal Doubts—Evidence Against the '20th Hijacker' Mostly Circumstantial." *Newsweek*, August 5, 2002, p. 6. After trying to plead not guilty in a strange attempt at a plea bargain, Moussaoui changed his plea to guilty. The government's case may be weak, though it is still scheduled for trial.

Johnston, David. "A Plea Suited to Both Sides." *New York Times*, July 16, 2002, p. A1. John Walker Lindh's plea bargain gained him an expected 20-year sentence in a climate where a jury might well have sentenced him to life. But it also rid the government of a case that was weak on evidence and might possibly reveal mistreatment.

Peabody, Bruce G. "In the Wake of September 11: Civil Liberties and Terrorism." *Social Education*, vol. 66, March 2002, p. 90 ff. Considers three major civil liberties issues raised by executive and legislative action after September 11, 2001: expanded power to eavesdrop between prisoners and their attorneys, the possible use of military tribunals, and the ability to deport aliens "reasonably believed" to be connected to terrorist organizations or to hold them indefinitely without trial.

Santora, Marc. "Threats and Responses: The Buffalo Case, 6 Indicted on Charges of Providing Material Aid to a Terrorist Group." *New York Times*, October 22, 2002, p. A19. Describes the arrest of six Yemeni immigrants who are accused of having received training from al-Qaeda and having contact with Osama bin Laden. The case could lead to another court challenge to provisions of the Antiterrorism and Effective Death Penalty Act of 1996 that prohibit providing "material aid" to a designated terrorist group.

Seelye, Katherine Q. "Judge Questions Detention of American in War Case." *New York Times*, August 14, 2002, p. A19. Despite the great deference of the appeals court to the government's wartime interest, federal district judge Robert G. Doumar remains skeptical about the legality of holding Yaser Hamdi without charges or access to an attorney. Judge Doumar is called upon to determine whether a bare statement from a government official is sufficient to brand Hamdi an "enemy combatant" without legal rights.

———. "War on Terror Makes for Odd Twists in Justice System: Flexible Rules Raise Constitutional Issues." *New York Times*, June 23, 2002, p. 16 ff. A survey of recent cases that expose the contradictory processing of terrorism suspects. While two Americans (Yaser Hamdi and Jose Padilla) are held in military brigs (jails) without access to lawyers, two foreigners (Zacarias Moussaoui and Richard Reid) are provided the protections of the normal civilian courts. Following the plea bargain for John Walker Lindh, the intentions of prosecutors with regard to the other cases remain uncertain.

Tyrangiel, Josh. "The Taliban Next Door." *Time*, vol. 158, December 17, 2001. The strange story of John Walker Lindh, the "sweet, quiet boy" who became a troubled teenager, a fervent Muslim, and a fighter for the Taliban.

Internet Resources

Dorf, Michael C. "What Is an 'Unlawful Combatant,' and Why It Matters." FindLaw Corporate Counsel Center. Available online. URL: http://writ.corporate.findlaw.com/dorf/20020123.html. Posted January 23, 2002. The author argues that neither al-Qaeda nor Taliban fighters meet the requirements for treatment as prisoners of war under the Geneva Convention. It is plausible to classify them as "unlawful combatants" and detain them until the (indefinite) cessation of hostilities. However, even if they were deemed prisoners of war, they could also be held.

Human Rights Watch. "Legal Issues Arising from the War in Afghanistan and Related Anti-Terrorism Efforts." Available online. URL: http://www.hrw.org/campaigns/september11/ihlqna.htm. Downloaded August 15, 2002. A series of questions and answers about the applicability of international humanitarian and human rights law to the prosecution of the war on terrorism. Topics include the nature of international humanitarian law, the use of law enforcement versus military action, how persons captured can be prosecuted or treated, and what forms of war making are lawful.

"Legal Group Opposes Enemy Combatant Policy." *New York Times*, February 10, 2003. Available online. URL: http://www.nytimes.com/reuters/news/news-rights-lawyers.html. The American Bar Association (ABA) at its midyear meeting voted overwhelmingly to support the right of U.S. citizens held as enemy combatants to have access to an attorney and to legal review of their status. The ABA also urges Congress to establish clear standards and procedures for designating individuals as enemy combatants. However, a U.S. attorney argues that such a policy might fatally undermine the effort to obtain critical information about possible future terrorist attacks.

TERRORISM AND AMERICAN SOCIETY

ECONOMIC EFFECTS OF SEPTEMBER 11 AND AFTERMATH

This section deals with the direct or indirect economic impact of the September 11, 2001, attacks themselves, measures taken in response to the attacks (such as the air shutdown), and subsequent attacks such as the anthrax letters. Business opportunities arising from the needs of the war on terrorism are also covered.

Books

Alexander, Dean C., and Yonah Alexander. *Terrorism and Business: The Impact of September 11, 2001.* Ardsley, N.Y.: Transnational Publishers, 2002.

Discusses the many economic impacts of the attacks in New York City and Washington, D.C., as well as the subsequent anthrax mail attacks and other concerns. Begins with the state of the economy before September 11, 2001, then summarizes the immediate impact on the regions directly hit. Next, the authors discuss impacts on specific industries including aviation, hotels, conventions and tourism, real estate, and technology. This is followed by a survey of new business opportunities brought about by the war on terrorism and the needs of homeland security. These areas include manufacturers of security equipment, defense contractors, communications and data processing, biotechnology, and transportation. The book concludes with consideration of effects on the labor force and a summary of U.S. legislative and other response to the terrorist attacks.

Linden, Edward V. *Focus on Terrorism.* New York: Nova Publishers, 2002. Describes the economic effects of the September 11, 2001, terrorist attacks and the implications and opportunities involved in the national response. Subjects include assistance to workers in the airline and other industries, assistance to small business, the market for terrorism insurance, and congressional legislation for victim assistance and funding for counterterrorism and military action.

Articles and Papers

Fletcher, Meg. "Sept. 11 Creates Challenges for Work Comp." *Business Insurance*, November 5, 2001, p. 1. Explores the problems in obtaining worker's compensation insurance renewals in the uncertain atmosphere following the September 11, 2001, attacks. Covering workers for the effects of terrorist attacks is difficult because the extent of such attacks is so unpredictable. Employer safety records cannot fairly be charged with events that are so much beyond the employer's control.

Lewis, Richard P. "September 11, 2001: How Insurance Can Help." *Corporate Counsel*, vol. 8, November 2001, p. A9. Summarizes insurance coverage issues arising from the terrorist attacks. These include the use of war risk (or specifically terrorism risk) exclusions, which are relatively uncommon and which some companies have already promised not to use in connection with the September 11, 2001, attacks. However, reinsurance companies (which spread the risk for insurers) may be more willing to use such exclusions, causing a problem for primary insurers. Advice is also given to businesspeople about claims based on property and business property insurance.

Miller, Bill, and Eric Pianin. "Corporations Target Homeland Security: Patriotism and Capitalism Meet in Rush to Cash in on New Funds for Solutions." *Washington Post*, February 11, 2002, p. A7. Companies that make surveillance, screening, security, communications, and information management devices are poised to cash in on the vastly expanded homeland security budget (at least $38 billion in 2002). Particular areas of demand for new, expensive technology include bioterrorism detection and vaccination, explosives "sniffing" devices, and revamping large information processing systems. Products of several defense contractors are described.

Internet Resources

National Center for Policy Analysis. "Terrorism and the Economy." Available online. URL:http://www.ncpa.org/iss/ter/econ.html. Updated July 9, 2002. Provides links to articles and reports on the various economic impacts of the September 11, 2001, attacks as well as the effectiveness of economic policy, stimulus packages, and other measures for dealing with the faltering economy.

POLITICAL AND SOCIAL ASPECTS

This section covers the relationship of terrorism to political or social issues, such as competing ideologies or tolerance of dissent.

Books

Bennett, William J. *Why We Fight: Moral Clarity and the War on Terrorism.* New York: Doubleday, 2002. Bennett, former secretary of education and a popular writer on civic virtue, provides a spirited defense for the American values that he believes were targeted by the terrorists and undermined by an intellectual elite that espouses cultural relativism. Critics, however, see what Bennett calls self-doubt to be necessary self-criticism.

Berman, Paul. *Terror and Liberalism.* New York: W. W. Norton, 2003. The author, who has written extensively about the totalitarian movements of the 20th century, argues that the terrorist challenge is really the latest challenge to liberalism by totalitarianism. In fighting terrorism, however, the United States should learn from its mistakes in the cold war era and not undermine liberal values in the process of defending them.

Collins, John, and Ross Glover, eds. *Collateral Language: A User's Guide to America's New War.* New York: New York University Press, 2002. A collection of essays that analyze and deconstruct the "loaded" terms such as *evil* or *vital interests* that have become part of the national rhetoric since September 11, 2001. Besides describing the evolving usage of terms, the essays offer general tools or techniques for analyzing political language.

Denzin, Norman K., and Yvonna S. Lincoln. *9/11 in American Culture.* Landham, Md.: Rowman and Littlefield, 2003. A collection of essays by cultural and "qualitative research" scholars, who share their personal and intellectual responses to the terrorist attacks and the aftermath.

Hachten, William A., and James F. Scotton. *The World News Prism: Global Media in an Age of Terrorism.* 6th ed. Ames: Iowa State Press, 2002. This highly regarded text uses the issues raised by global terrorism and the post–September 11, 2001, world to illustrate issues relating to the practice of journalism. It offers both the practitioners of journalism and its consumers (the rest of us) a way to understand how current events are covered in the global media.

Hanson, Victor Davis. *An Autumn of War: What America Learned from September 11 and the War on Terrorism.* New York: Anchor Books, 2002. The author, a classics professor and columnist for *National Review Online*, presents a collection of essays written during the months following the 9/11 attacks. In them he explores the idea of war coming to America from a military historical perspective and argues that September 11, 2001, is the latest chapter in the West's long struggle against barbarism. He describes how Americans of different classes and backgrounds responded to the challenge. His conservative analyses challenge leftist critics of the war effort.

Kellner, Douglas. *From 9/11 to Terror War: The Dangers of the Bush Legacy.* Lanham, Md.: Rowman and Littlefield, 2003. The author focuses on the Bush administration's response to the September 11, 2001, attacks, both in terms of homeland security (and related domestic policies) and in foreign policy. He argues that Bush has successfully used the shock of 9/11 to enact many reactionary laws and policies that probably would have remained blocked in a peacetime Congress. The Bush administration is also taken to task for its previous neglect of the terrorism threat as well as entanglements involving supporters in the oil industry.

Knezo, Genevieve. *Possible Impacts of Major Counter Terrorism Security Actions on Research, Development, and Higher Education.* Washington, D.C.: Congressional Research Service, 2002. Discusses the possible negative impacts of the USA PATRIOT Act and other terrorism-related legislation and regulation on institutions of higher education and research. Areas of concern include the newly tightened requirements and tracking for holders of immigrant student visas.

Mahajan, Rahul. *The New Crusade: America's War on Terrorism.* New York: Monthly Review Press, 2002. The author, a peace activist, offers a comprehensive critique of the war on terrorism. He explores what he says is systematic distortion by government officials and the media of the reasons for the terrorist attack and U.S. war aims, as well as events in Afghanistan. The war on terrorism is put in the context of ongoing American foreign policy that has protected elite interests while leading to the deaths of thousands of innocent people.

Maher, Bill. *When You Ride Alone, You Ride with Bin Laden: What the Government Should Be Telling Us to Help Fight the War on Terrorism.* New Millennium Press, 2002. The acerbic host of the *Politically Incorrect* cable show aroused outrage when he pointed out that "cowardly" was not really an accurate epithet to describe terrorists who were willing to die for their beliefs. Maher continues his provocative ways in this collection of humorous yet telling observations about what is wrong with current American attempts to fight terrorism. Maher uses clever illustrations, including new renditions of World War II posters such as the gas-saving poster that gives its title to the book. Among other observations Maher notes that a country that could reach the Moon in a decade should also be able end its dependence on (and entanglement with) foreign oil and that random airport searches sacrifice common sense to political correctness.

Merrill, Robert, ed. *Enduring Freedom or Enduring War? Prospects and Costs of the New American 21st Century.* University Park, Md.: Maisonneuve Press, 2002. A collection of essays critical of various aspects of the new American war on terrorism. Generally the authors argue that the U.S. government is not fighting for "enduring freedom" but for the continued untrammeled exercise of global capitalism abroad, regardless of the physical and economic casualties it inflicts. Domestically, the war is seen as a war on civil liberties.

Schechter, Danny. *Media Wars: News at a Time of Terror.* Landham, Md.: Rowman and Littlefield, 2003. A leading media analyst (and founder of MediaChannel), Schechter dissects thousands of media accounts of the war on terror. He concludes that the media has largely become an echo chamber or megaphone for the military and U.S. policy, with dissenting views being largely ignored.

Scraton, Phil. *Beyond September 11: An Anthology of Dissent.* Sterling, Va.: Pluto Press, 2002. An anthology of personal accounts and political dissents by critics of the U.S. war on terrorism, including Noam Chomsky, Robert Fisk, and Naomi Klein. The varied critiques include challenges to the legal basis of the government's actions, deconstruction of language used to justify the war against terrorism, and criticism of the media, especially the lack of coverage of civilian deaths in Afghanistan.

Vidal, Gore. *Perpetual War for Perpetual Peace.* New York: Thunder's Mouth Press/Nation Books, 2002. In this collection of articles mainly from *Vanity Fair* and the *Nation*, the acerbic novelist and essayist criticizes the American media and public for self-righteousness, complacency, and unwillingness to come to terms with the connection between U.S. foreign and domestic policies and terrorism at home and abroad. Vidal goes on to criticize what he sees as an escalating attack on civil liberties by the government following the attacks of September 11, 2001.

Annotated Bibliography

Articles and Papers

Chaddock, Gail Russell. "In Politics, It's About 'Security.'" *Christian Science Monitor*, vol. 95, January 16, 2003, p. 1. This article reports on the political use of homeland security concerns as the new Congress opens. The Republicans, who won control of the Senate in the 2002 midterm election, are trying to frame virtually every domestic issue (including rollbacks of some environmental regulations) around security concerns. The Democrats suffered electorally because they followed the traditional political wisdom of not challenging national security concerns in a time of crisis. This has ended up with them scrambling for viable issues not connected with security; however, the Democrats have begun to take advantage of security concerns by proposing new spending on infrastructure such as ports and water treatment plants, where expansion (and jobs for union workers) can be framed around security needs.

Jervis, Robert. "An Interim Assessment of September 11: What Has Changed and What Has Not?" *Political Science Quarterly*, vol. 117, Spring 2002, p. 37 ff. A lengthy assessment of changes in social and political realities following the September 11, 2001, attacks. Aspects discussed include the vulnerability of the nation and its economy, the declining relevance and power of states (as opposed to the federal government), the limitations of the ability to understand terrorist grievances that cannot be addressed, the characterization and scope of the war on terrorism and the use of war rhetoric, and the opportunity of nations to forge closer bonds against a common threat.

Kinsley, Michael. "Listening to Our Inner Ashcrofts." *Washington Post*, January 4, 2002, p. A27. In an editorial, liberal editor and writer Kinsley recounts how both academics and TV pundits such as Bill Maher have been blasted for disagreeing with the prevailing prowar rhetoric, even in minor ways. In reaction to White House press secretary Ari Fleishcher's comment that Americans "need to watch what they say," Kinsley fears that many people are doing just that—censoring themselves and crippling the possibility for healthy political debate while hiding government malfeasance.

Lindsey, Brink. "Terrorism's Fellow Travelers Bash the U.S." *USA Today*, vol. 130, May 2002, p. 22 ff. A conservative and senior fellow at the Cato Institute decries an assortment of liberal intellectuals and movements for what he considers to be a pathological anticapitalist and anti-American sensibility. He argues that their totalitarianism and fanaticism is not unlike that of the terrorists themselves.

"The New Age of Terrorism: Futurists Respond." *Futurist*, vol. 36, January–February 2002. Contains excerpts from analysis by futurists of the

September 11, 2001, attacks, including consideration of the effects on war making, globalization, and society.

Podhoretz, Norman. "The Return of the 'Jackal Bins.'" *Commentary*, vol. 113, April 2002, p. 29 ff. This lengthy essay looks at the reaction of America's largely left-leaning intellectual and artistic community to September 11, 2001. Podhoretz wonders whether the Left will eventually mobilize against the prowar consensus (as it did in Vietnam), or perhaps translate the new surge of patriotism into an adequate intellectual defense of the war effort.

Internet Resources

Chomsky, Noam, and William Bennett. "CNN Debate on 'Terrorism': Chomsky v. Bennett." Available online. URL: http://www.counterpunch.org/chomsky0530.html. Posted May 30, 2002. Transcript of a broadcast debate between the two public intellectuals. Moderator Paula Zahn asks them to defend their respective books *9–11* and *Why We Fight*. Chomsky maintains that the United States is the world's worst "terrorist nation," while Bennett asserts that America, while guilty of some bad things in the past, has done more good than any other nation.

PSYCHOLOGICAL, PHILOSOPHICAL, AND SPIRITUAL DIMENSIONS

This section deals with the psychological effects of terrorism, treatment of victims, and application of spiritual insights or understanding to the events of September 11, 2001.

Books

Coady, Tony, and Michael O'Keefe, eds. *Terrorism and Justice: Moral Arguments in a Threatened World*. Carlton South, Australia: Melbourne University Press, 2002. This collection provides a variety of philosophical perspectives on whether terrorism can ever be justified, the status of "noncombatants," and what is appropriate or defensible in the name of counterterrorism. Topics for the papers include a definition of terrorism; terrorism as a just war and supreme emergency, terrorism as a weapon for the powerless state terrorism, terrorism and collective responsibility, terrorism in relation to "liberation ideology"; changing understandings of jihad; terrorism and the right to wage war, the just response to terrorism, and the war against terrorism as a war of good against evil.

Annotated Bibliography

Elshtain, Jean Bethke. *Just War Against Terror: The Burden of American Power in a Violent World.* New York: Basic Books, 2003. The author undertakes a philosophical defense of the "just war" doctrine as applied to current terrorist threats. She argues that pacifism is not tenable in the face of terrorist fanatics and that attempts to "understand" and excuse terrorists through "root causes" are misguided. The responsibility to deal with terrorism effectively must not be avoided.

Findley, Paul. *Silent No More: Confronting America's False Images of Islam.* Beltsville, Md.: Amana Publications, 2001. The author, a congressman who has extensive experience with Middle East affairs, presents mainstream Islamic principles, beliefs, and practices and dispels common stereotypes about the religion. He points out that Muslims are an increasingly important part of the U.S. political landscape, with a growing number of Muslims being elected to office.

Gehring, Verna V., ed. *War after September 11.* Lanham, Md.: Rowman and Littlefield, 2002. Six contributors from the Institute for Philosophy and Public Policy at the University of Maryland discuss what is permissible in terms of actions and targets in the war against terrorism. Three pairs of essays look at the limits of the traditional paradigms (such as war and retaliation), the ultimate risks of the war on terrorism (such as to human rights), and possible constructive alternatives.

Juergensmeyer, Mark. *Terror in the Mind of God: The Global Rise of Religious Violence.* Updated ed. Berkeley: University of California Press, 2001. A sociologist of religion argues that it is simplistic to say that the appeal of violence or terror is not part of legitimate religion but only the province of cults or fanatics. Rather, he says, violence can be part of the enactment of "cosmic war"—struggles of ultimate significance that become linked with urgent political and ideological issues and are embodied in religious imagery—so that religion and violence are mysteriously and perhaps inextricably intertwined. This updated edition includes coverage of the events of September 11, 2001.

Kressel, Neil J. *Mass Hate: The Global Rise of Genocide and Terror.* Reading, Mass.: Perseus Books, 1996. The author, a psychologist specializing in international affairs, addresses the question of why mass terrorism and genocide reached a peak in the 20th century. As case studies, he examines in particular the Holocaust, genocide in Rwanda, the campaign of rape and torture in Bosnia, and the 1993 bombing of the World Trade Center in New York City by Islamic extremists. He suggests that while the ideologies underlying acts of terror differ, the psychological process by which leaders manipulate followers into committing them is essentially the same.

Neuberger, Luisa De Cataldo, and Tiziana Valentini. *Women and Terrorism.* Trans. Leo Hughes. New York: St. Martin's Press, 1996. This Italian work deals with a largely neglected aspect of the terrorism debate: the participation of women in terrorism. Using case studies, the authors point out both the distinctive motivations of female terrorists and the stereotypes that prevent proper consideration of female terrorism by both academic researchers and the criminal justice system. Includes interview and questionnaire transcripts.

Pearlstein, Richard M. *The Mind of the Political Terrorist.* Wilmington, Del.: SR Books, 1991. Taking a Freudian approach to his analysis of terrorists belonging to Weather Underground, the Symbionese Liberation Army, the Baader-Meinhoff gang, and the Italian Red Brigades (active in the 1960s, 1970s, and 1980s), the author concludes that these terrorists suffer from a "narcissistic rage" that creates both self-destructiveness and violence toward others.

Pyszczynski, Thomas A., Sheldon Solomon, and Jeff Greenberg. *In the Wake of 9/11: The Psychology of Terror.* Washington, D.C.: American Psychological Association, 2002. The authors apply recent psychological research to the problem of "terror management," or dealing with the immediate and long-term effects of the trauma of a terrorist attack on society. Terror management theory (TMT) is derived from the work of Ernest Becker in the 1980s, which attempted to place the dynamics of both terrorist and victim in a coherent context. The authors illustrate the application of TMT to many specific examples from the events and news coverage following September 11, 2001. They also include necessary background on the attacks and consider related historical, religious, social, and economic factors.

Reich, Walter, ed. *Origins of Terrorism: Psychologies, Ideologies, Theologies, States of Mind.* Washington, D.C.: Woodrow Wilson Center, 1990. The contributors, experts in history, religion, and behavioral science, discuss a variety of worldviews, motivations, states of mind, and goals for terrorism. They begin with the assumption that terrorism is a complex, multidimensional problem and offer diverse approaches to understanding it.

Silke, Andrew, ed. *Terrorists, Victims, and Society: Psychological Perspectives on Terrorism and Its Consequences.* New York: John Wiley, 2003. A wide-ranging collection of papers on psychological aspects of terrorism divided into three sections: terrorists, victims, and responding to terrorism. Sample topics include the psychology of hostage-taking, psychology of cyberterrorism, psychology of suicidal terrorism, victims of terrorism and the media, impact of terrorism on children, and deterring terrorists.

Stout, Chris E., ed. The Psychology of Terrorism series. Westport, Conn.: Praeger, 2002. According to the publisher, "Outstanding academics, clinicians, and activists worldwide contributed to this multivolume, peer-reviewed set." Titles in the series include *Psychological Dimensions in War and Peace*, *A Public Understanding*, *Clinical Aspects and Responses*, *Programs and Practices in Response and Prevention*, and *Theoretical Understandings and Perspectives*.

Waldman, Steven, ed. *From the Ashes: A Spiritual Response to the Attack on America*. Emmaus, Penn.: Rodale Press, 2001. A collection of postings from the online forum Beliefnet in which spiritual leaders and "ordinary believers" of many faiths try to come to terms with the 9/11 attacks. The many contributors include Archbishop Desmond Tutu, Neale Donald Walsch, Reverend Andrew M. Greeley, Charles Colson, Bishop John Shelby Spong, Sri Chinmoy, Billy Graham, Sam Keen, Karen Armstrong, Imam Izak-El Mu'eed Pasha, Rabbi Joseph Telushkin, Pope John Paul II, His Holiness the Dalai Lama.

Wieviorka, Michel. *The Making of Terrorism*. Trans. David Gordon White. Chicago: University of Chicago Press, 1993. A comparative analysis of Italian, Peruvian, Basque, and Middle Eastern terrorist groups. The author gathered his evidence through staged confrontations and extensive interviews, using a method called "interventionist sociology." He argues that terrorism at root represents the alienation of the individual from the very ideology he or she professes as motivation.

Williams, Rowan. *Writing in the Dust: After September 11*. Grand Rapids, Mich.: W. B. Eerdmanns, 2002. In this short book, an Anglican theologian raises the most difficult theological and emotional questions arising from the September 11, 2001, attacks. To deal with the surging fear and anger, he suggests that people avoid grasping at quick solutions, and instead experience the "void" of cataclysmic events as a "breathing space" in which new human connections might be made.

Zacharias, Ravi K. *Light in the Shadow of Jihad*. Sisters, Oreg.: Multnomah Publishers, 2002. A minister and scholar of comparative religion tries to answer questions that have been asked by many people in the wake of September 11, 2001. These include the relationship between Islam and the fanaticism of jihad, how religion interacts with culture and state, the possibility of an apocalyptic future, and whether there is a spiritual path that can bring healing to those wounded by violence.

Articles and Papers

Cox, Harvey. "Religion and the War Against Evil." *Nation*, vol. 273, December 24, 2001, p. 29. When the United States was struck on September

11, 2001, many Americans instinctively turned to religion for some sort of understanding or sustenance. At the same time some right-wing religionists such as Jerry Falwell and Pat Robertson suggested that God himself is angry at our social wickedness and thus allowed the attacks. Meanwhile the terrorists, of course, cited religion as the ultimate reason for their actions. Cox, a noted professor of divinity at Harvard University, suggests that the times call for a rapprochement or even cooperative effort between secularism (or modernity) and religion. Secularism offers a vital critique of religion's pride and power grabbing, while religion can call modernity back from its inhuman tendencies.

"Is Torture Ever Justified?" *Economist*, vol. 366, January 11, 2003, p. 9. This article discusses current U.S. interrogation techniques being used against terrorist suspects, such as "stress and duress," which includes sleep deprivation and forcing prisoners to remain in uncomfortable positions. In the "ticking bomb" scenario, many would justify use of considerable torture to find out the location of the bomb, but even here, there is a question of what the limits should be—for example, would it be OK to threaten someone's family? Some critics fear that once torture is allowed, even under limited circumstances, a line will be crossed that would inevitably create pressure for use of more coercive measures in other circumstances.

Miles, Jack. "Theology and the Clash of Civilizations." *Cross Currents*, vol. 51, Winter 2002, p. 451 ff. If there is indeed a "clash of civilizations" between Islam and the West, then the author believes that two things must happen to be able to resolve it without endless bloodshed. Within the *umma*, or world of Islam, a strong alternative to the fanatic intolerance typified by Osama bin Laden must emerge. But equally important, the West, in which the triumph of secularism has made talk of religion almost impossible in the exercise of statecraft, must be willing to understand and engage the theological worldview and values held by Muslims.

Internet Resources

Hudson, Rex A. "The Sociology and Psychology of Terrorism: Who Becomes a Terrorist and Why?" Federal Research Division, Library of Congress. Available online. URL: http://www.loc.gov/rr/frd/Sociology-Psychology%20of%20Terrorism.htm. Posted August 12, 2002. This study from 1999 surveys psychological and sociological literature and representative examples of terrorist groups and individuals. Its purpose is to develop more accurate profiles that would aid in counterterrorist efforts. The report begins with definitions, typologies, and five different approaches (multicausal, political, organizational, physiological, and psychological). Different hypotheses for explaining the psychology of the terrorist are given, along with different ways of thinking about the terrorist. A profile is then developed and compared to various prominent terrorists.

CHAPTER 8

ORGANIZATIONS AND AGENCIES

Following are listings for selected organizations and agencies involved with terrorism-related issues. They are divided into three groups: government agencies, academic research institutes, and advocacy groups, such as civil liberties and human rights organizations.

GOVERNMENT AGENCIES

Note: Under the new Department of Homeland Security, some existing agencies or functions will eventually be merged into the new cabinet-level office.

Centers for Disease Control and Prevention
URL: http://www.bt.cdc.gov
Phone: 1(888)246-2675
1600 Clifton Road
Atlanta, GA 30333
The Centers for Disease Control and Prevention has, like many other federal agencies, undertaken new initiatives to assess and deal with the threat of biological terrorism. Its Public Health Emergency Preparedness and Response" page includes links to background information on biological agents and response procedures, news, official statements, and emergency services.

Central Intelligence Agency
URL: http://www.cia.gov
E-mail: Use form at web site
Phone: (703) 482-0623
Office of Public Affairs
Washington, DC 20505
The CIA is responsible for obtaining and analyzing intelligence relating to foreign threats against the United States, including terrorist activities. It provides analysis for the executive branch and policymakers as well as engaging in various clandestine activities. The CIA also provides educational resources to the public including the annual *CIA World Factbook.*

Customs Service
URL: http://www.customs.ustreas.gov
Phone: (202) 927-1770
1300 Pennsylvania Avenue, NW
Washington, DC 20229
The U.S. Customs Service is responsible for controlling the movement of persons and goods across the nation's borders, making a key player in homeland defense.

Department of Defense
URL: http://www.dod.gov
E-mail: Use form at http://www.dod.gov/faq/comment.html
Office of the Secretary of Defense (Public Affairs)
Room 3A750, The Pentagon
1400 Defense Pentagon
Washington, DC 20301-1400
The U.S. Department of Defense offers extensive resources relating to the military aspects of the war on terrorism, such as the recently concluded operations in Afghanistan. Its Defense Link web site offers maps, imagery, and publications.

Department of Homeland Security
URL: http://www.whitehouse.gov/deptofhomeland
URL: http://ww.dhs.gov/dhspublic/
E-mail: president@whitehouse.gov or use the "contact us" feature on the DHS web site
Phone: (202) 456-1111
The White House
1600 Pennsylvania Avenue, NW
Washington, DC 20500
The Department of Homeland Security Office at the White House has been given the mission of preventing terrorist attacks within the United States, reducing America's vulnerability to terrorism, and minimizing the damage and recovery from attack that do occur.

Department of Justice
URL: http://www.usdoj.gov
E-mail: AskDOJ@usdoj.gov
Phone: (202) 353-1556
950 Pennsylvania Avenue, NW
Washington, DC 20530-0001
The U.S. Department of Justice is the agency ultimately responsible for all federal law enforcement activities. It is headed by the attorney general of the United States. The FBI is one of its many component agencies. Others include the Civil Rights Division and the Immigration and Naturalization Service.

Department of State
URL: http://www.state.gov
E-mail: publicaffairs@panet.us-state.gov
Phone: (202) 647-4000
2201 C Street, NW
Washington, DC 20520
The U.S. State Department provides a variety of resources dealing with foreign affairs, including annual reports on human rights abuses and terrorism. The web page for the State Department's Office for Counterterrorism (http://www.state.gov/s/ct/ohs/) offers reports and other resources relating to counterterrorism and homeland security.

Federal Aviation Administration
URL: http://www.faa.gov
Phone: (800) 322-7873
800 Independence Avenue, SW
Washington, DC 20591
The new Transportation Security Administration (TSA) has taken over direct responsibility for aviation and transportation security, but as the overall regulator of civil aviation and operator of air traffic control and other systems, the FAA plays a part in the effort to make flying more secure.

Federal Bureau of Investigation
URL: http://www.fbi.gov
Phone: (202) 324-5520
935 Pennsylvania Avenue, NW
Washington, DC 20535
The FBI investigates incidences of terrorism and compiles data on domestic terrorism. Following the September 11, 2001, attacks, the FBI has made terrorism its first priority and increased its proactive investigations. Its home page includes links to news, reports, and background material.

Federal Emergency Management Agency
URL: http://www.fema.gov
E-mail: opa@fema.gov
Phone: (202) 566-1600
500 C Street, SW
Washington, DC 20472
The FEMA is traditionally concerned with providing disaster assistance; however, like many other government agencies, FEMA has been focusing more attention on response to terrorist attacks.

Immigration and Naturalization Service
URL: http://www.ins.gov
Phone: (800) 375-5283
425 I Street, NW
Washington, DC 20536
Part of the Department of Justice, the INS is responsible for regulating immigration and the various statuses available to aliens visiting or residing in the United States. The Border Patrol is its enforcement arm. The web site has news and background material about the agency.

National Infrastructure Protection Center
URL: http://www.nipc.gov
E-mail: nipc.watch@fbi.gov
Phone: (888) 585-9078
J. Edgar Hoover Building
935 Pennsylvania Avenue, NW
Washington, DC 20535-0001
The National Infrastructure Protection Center is an interagency effort whose mission is "to serve as the U.S. government's focal point for threat assessment, warning, investigation, and response for threats or attacks against our critical infrastructures." Its emphasis is protecting the information infrastructure from cyberterrorism.

Transportation Security Administration
URL: http://www.tsa.dot.gov
E-mail: 9-AWA-TELLFAA@faa.gov
400 Seventh Street, SW
Washington, DC 20590

The TSA has taken over responsibility for airport security from the Federal Aviation Administration (FAA). It is also responsible for developing security programs for ground transportation.

ACADEMIC AND RESEARCH ORGANIZATIONS

Center for Defense Information
URL: http://www.cdi.org
E-mail: info@cdi.org
Phone: (202) 462-4559
1779 Massachusetts Avenue, NW
Washington, DC 20036
The Center for Defense Information is "the nation's foremost independent military research organization." Its mission is to provide an independent perspective on military and security matters for policymakers and the public. Its Terrorism Project page (http://www.cdi.org/terrorism/) provides a variety of analyses and studies.

Center for Strategic and International Studies
URL: http://www.csis.org
E-mail: webmaster@csis.org
Phone: (202) 887-0200 1800 K Street, NW
Suite 400
Washington, DC 20006
This center publishes books, reports, and periodicals dealing with foreign policy and national strategy. Relevant topics include arms control, nuclear proliferation, and homeland security.

Centre for the Study of Terrorism and Political Violence (St. Andrews University)
URL: http://www.st-and.ac.uk/academic/intrel/research/cstpv
E-mail: CSTPV@st-andrews.ac.uk
Phone: 44 (0) 1334 462938
Department of International Relations
University of St Andrews
St Andrews KY169AL
SCOTLAND
A British academic research center that provides an extensive database and links to terrorism-related topics at its web site.

Federation of American Scientists
URL: http://www.fas.org
E-mail: fas@fas.org
Phone: (202) 546-3300
1717 K Street, NW
Suite 209
Washington, DC 20036
The Federation of American Scientists provides research and advocacy on many issues involving the use (or abuse) of science and technology. Its Intelligence Resource Program page (http://www.fas.org/irp/threat/terror.htm) offers a variety of links to federation reports and other resources relating to intelligence and counterterrorism.

Institute for Security Technology Studies
URL: http://www.ists.dartmouth.edu/ISTS

E-mail: Stacy.Kollias@ Dartmouth.edu
Phone: (603) 646-0700
Dartmouth College
45 Lyme Road
Suite 200
Hanover, NH 03755
A government-funded institute at Dartmouth College, focusing on "cyber-security and information infrastructure protection research." Includes links to information about cyberterrorism and its relationship to the September 11, 2001, and subsequent attacks.

International Association for Counterterrorism and Security Professionals
URL: http://www.iacsp.com
P.O. Box 10265
Arlington, VA 22210
This organization for professionals involved with security and counterterrorism issues has two member publications the *Journal of Counterterrorism and Security* and the *Counterterrorism and Security Report.* Its web site includes a Terrorism Watch summarizing recent news developments, featured news topics, a Terrorism Information Desk, and special reports.

International Policy Institute for Counter-Terrorism
URL: http://www.ict.org.il
E-mail: mail@ict.org.il
Phone: 972-9-9527277
P.O. Box 167
Herzliya, 461550
ISRAEL
A research institute and think tank in Herzliya, Israel, this organization is primarily concerned with developing public policy and strategies to deal with terrorism as a global issue. Offers publications and holds conferences. The web site includes news updates and background data about terrorist groups and attacks.

Terrorism Research Center
URL: http://www.terrorism.com/index.shtml
E-mail: TRC@terrorism.com
This independent organization conducts research and provides information to the public on terrorism and related issues. The organization's web site provides extensive resource links.

ADVOCACY GROUPS

American Civil Liberties Union
URL: http://www.aclu.org
E-mail: aclu@aclu.org
Phone: (212) 549-2500
125 Broad Street
18th Floor
New York, NY 10004-2400
Originally founded in 1920, the ACLU conducts extensive litigation on constitutional issues including privacy and free speech. This puts the group on a collision course with much antiterrorism legislation.

American Enterprise Institute
URL: http://www.aei.org

E-mail: info@aei.org
Phone: (202) 862-5800
The American Enterprise Institute is a generally conservative, probusiness think tank. Although usually advocating limited government, it is a strong supporter of the military and homeland security efforts against terrorism.

Amnesty International
URL: http://www.amnesty.org (worldwide)
URL: http://www.aiusa.org (United States)
E-mail: admin-us@aiusa.org
Phone: (202) 544-0200
600 Pennsylvania Avenue, SE Fifth Floor
[Washington Office]
This international human rights group publicizes human rights abuses around the world and seeks to mobilize world opinion against oppressive governments. Since human rights abuses are often related to terrorism and counterterrorism, this organization's reports and other resources can be quite useful.

Brookings Institution
URL: http://www.brookings.org
E-mail: brookinfo@brook.edu
Phone: (202) 797-6000
This venerable think tank produces reports and conferences and takes a generally liberal, activist-government approach to public policy issues. It has undertaken a major project on terrorism and American foreign policy to provide analysis and recommendations in the wake of the September 11, 2001, attacks.

CATO Institute
URL: http://www.cato.org
E-mail: Choose from contacts page (http://www.cato.org/people/staff.html#contactus)
Phone: (202) 842-0200
1000 Massachusetts Avenue, NW
Washington, DC 20001-5403
The CATO Institute is a libertarian policy 'think tank' that generally advocates individual liberty and strict limitations on government power. CATO has been critical of a number of the post–September 11, 2001, government initiatives. See its terrorism resource page (http://www.cato.org/current/terrorism/index.html).

Center for Democracy and Technology
URL: http://www.cdt.org
E-mail: webmaster@cdt.org
Phone: (202) 637-9800
1634 I Street, NW
Suite 1100
Washington, DC 20006
The civil liberties group works to "promote democratic values and constitutional liberties in the digital age." It offers a Counter-Terrorism Issues page (http://www.cdt.org/policy/terrorism/) that includes links to news about legislation relating to terrorism, particularly wiretapping and computer surveillance.

Council on American-Islamic Relations
URL: http://www.cair-net.org
E-mail: cair@cair-net.org
Phone: (202) 488-8787

453 New Jersey Avenue, SE
Washington, DC 20003
Relations between the Islamic and other communities in the United States came under increased strain after the September 11, 2001, attacks. The Council on American-Islamic Relations condemns the 9/11 attacks while advocating tolerance and nondiscrimination toward American Muslims.

Electronic Frontier Foundation
URL: http://www.eff.org
E-mail: ask@eff.org
Phone: (415) 436-9333
1550 Bryant Street
Suite 725
San Francisco, CA 94103
Formed in 1990 to maintain and enhance intellectual freedom, privacy, and other values of civil liberties and democracy in networked communications, the foundation publicizes and campaigns against antiterrorism legislation that it considers repressive or threatening to privacy. The group publishes newsletters, Internet guidebooks, and other documents; provides mailing lists and other online forums; and hosts a large electronic document archive.

Electronic Privacy Information Center
URL: http://www.epic.org
E-mail: info@epic.org
Phone: (202) 544-9240
666 Pennsylvania Avenue, SE
Suite 301
Washington, DC 20003
The center was established in 1994 to focus public attention on emerging privacy issues relating to the national information infrastructure. Some of these issues have arisen from antiterrorism legislation. The organization publishes the *EPIC Alert* and leads campaigns on privacy issues.

First Amendment Foundation
URL: http://www.floridafaf.org
E-mail: foi@vashti.net
Phone: (800) 337-3518
336 East College Avenue
Tallahassee, FL 32301
This Florida-based organization seeks to strengthen First Amendment rights and to educate the public about their importance. It expressed serious concerns about the 1996 antiterrorism act, publishing *terrorism and the Constitution*, which among other things reviewed the history of abuses of the rights of dissident groups and immigrants by the FBI and other federal agencies.

Humanitarian Law Project
Phone: (310) 836-6316
8124 West Third Street
Suite 105
Los Angeles, CA 90048
This project supports legal protection for international humanitarian efforts. It became involved with the debate and subsequent litigation over the Antiterrorism and Effective Death Penalty Act of 1996 because the law includes a provision prohibiting Americans from giving

humanitarian aid to or through groups that the federal government has designated as terrorist. It filed a suit, *Humanitarian Law Project v. Reno* seeking to overturn that provision. A U.S. district court did agree that language relating to providing "training" or "personnel" was impermissably vague; the language was subsequently amended.

Human Rights Watch
URL: http://www.hrw.org
E-mail: hrwnyc@hrw.org
Phone: (212) 290-4700
350 Fifth Avenue
34th Floor
New York, NY 10118-3299
This group is dedicated to investigating and publicizing human rights violations around the world and working for reforms that strengthen human rights. The web site offers access by region and country to reports on human right abuses, as well as to the group's annual World Report and an extensive catalog of publications.

PART III

APPENDICES

APPENDIX A

BACKGROUND MATERIALS FOR THE MILITARY CAMPAIGN IN AFGHANISTAN AND ELSEWHERE, 2001–

Operation Enduring Freedom, the military response to the terrorist attacks of September 11, 2001, began on October 7, 2001, with air strikes launched from carriers and land bases in the Persian Gulf and from the base at Diego Garcia in the Indian Ocean. By December 10, 2001, about 12,000 bombs and missiles had been launched against targets in Afghanistan. Meanwhile, a fleet of C-130 and C-17 cargo planes delivered 1,450 tons of heavy equipment to the main ground base (Camp Rhino) in Afghanistan, and by December they had also delivered 2.5 million individual food rations as humanitarian aid.

Comparing the effort in Afghanistan to the Persian Gulf War of 1990–91 (Operation Desert Storm), the rate of sorties flown in Afghanistan was only about 200 per day as opposed to 3,000 a day in the earlier war. However, according to General Tommy Franks, head of U.S. Central Command, each bomber in Afghanistan was able to deal with two targets, while in the Gulf War on average 10 planes were required to take out a single target. Thus, the military believes that advanced technology and improved doctrine have made it possible to do much more with much less.

Operation Anaconda, executed March 1–16, 2002, by a combined force of about 1,700 U.S. soldiers (including both regular infantry battalions and special forces), 1,000–1,500 Afghan soldiers, and 200 soldiers from allied countries (mainly Australia and Europe constituted the bulk of the ground effort). The main attack was made against a concentration of al-Qaeda and Taliban fighters in the Shahi Kot valley, south of Gardez, in eastern Afghanistan. Meanwhile, air strikes continued, with a cumulative total of 21,000 bombs and missiles being used by the end of March 2002.

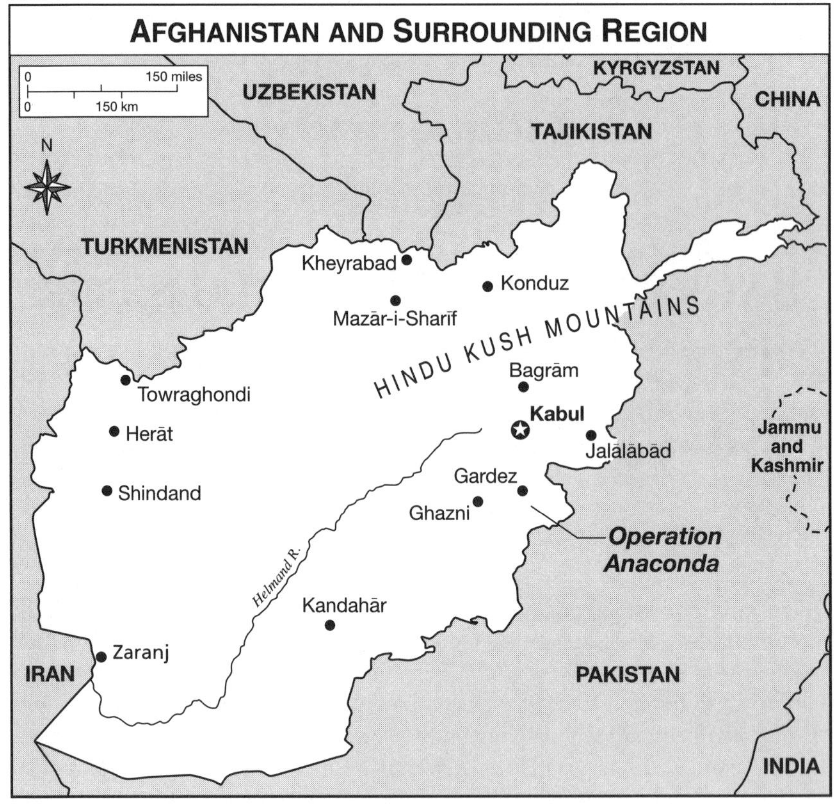

The Taliban as a coherent entity collapsed in a matter of days. Al-Qaeda fighters dispersed, sometimes fighting fiercely when surrounded. U.S. casualties in action totaled 10, while about 40 were wounded (mostly in Operation Anaconda). Twenty six soldiers were also killed in aircraft crashes or other accidents. The estimates for enemy and civilian casualties are less certain and wide ranging. The numbers of al-Qaeda and Taliban killed were probably in the mid-hundreds, with at least an equal number successfully fleeing and hundreds more captured and shipped to U.S. detention facilities in Guantánamo Bay, Cuba. Estimates of civilian casualties—mostly those accidentally killed by U.S. bombing attacks—range from about 400 to several thousand. (The latter number generally comes from sources critical of U.S. policy.)

The Background Notes on countries in this appendix were compiled from the following sources, which are available online as indicated. Minor amendments have been made to reflect events to early 2003.

United States Department of State, Bureau of South Asian Affairs.
"Afghanistan" (http://www.state.gov/p/sa/ci/af/)
"Pakistan" (http://www.state.gov/p/sa/ci/pk/)

United States Department of State, Bureau of Near Eastern Affairs.
"Egypt" (http://www.state.gov/p/nea/ci/c3729.htm)
"Saudi Arabia" (http://www.state.gov/p/nea/ci/c2419.htm)
"Yemen" (http://www.state.gov/p/nea/ci/c2423.htm)

United States Department of State, Bureau of African Affairs.
"Somalia" (http://www.state.gov/p/af/ci/so/)

United States Department of State, Bureau of European and Eurasian Affairs.
"Azerbaijan" (http://www.state.gov/p/eur/ci/aj/)
"Georgia" (http://www.state.gov/p/eur/ci/gg/)

United States Department of State, Bureau of East Asian and Pacific Affairs.
"Indonesia" (http://www.state.gov/p/eap/ci/id/)
"Malaysia" (http://www.state.gov/p/eap/ci/my/)
"Philippines" (http://www.state.gov/p/eap/ci/rp/)

United States Department of State, *Patterns of Global Terrorism 2001* (http://www.state.gov/s/ct/rls/pgtrpt/2001/).

United States Central Intelligence Agency, *CIA World Factbook 2002* (http://www.cia.gov/cia/publications/factbook/).

AFGHANISTAN: A BRIEF OVERVIEW

Until the attacks and war on terrorism in 2001–2002, most Americans knew little about Afghanistan. The following provides a basic summary (with minor amendments) of the embattled nation and its neighbors.

Profile

Official Name

Islamic State of Afghanistan. (The Taliban referred to the country as the Islamic Emirate of Afghanistan.)

Geography

Area: 648,000 sq. km. (252,000 sq. mi.); slightly smaller than Texas.

Cities: *Capital* (1999/2000 UN est.) Kabul—1,780,000. *Other cities* (1988 UN est.; current figures are probably significantly higher)—Kandahār (226,000); Herat (177,000); Mazār-i-Sharīf (131,000); Jalālābād (58,000); Konduz (57,000).

Terrain: Landlocked; mostly mountains and desert.
Climate: Dry, with cold winters and hot summers.

People

Nationality: *Noun and adjective*—Afghan(s).
Population (July 2002 est.): 27,755,775. More than 4 million Afghans live outside the country, mainly in Pakistan and Iran, although almost 1 million have returned since the removal of the Taliban.
Annual population growth rate (2002 est.): 3.43% (*Note:* Main ethnic groups: Pashtun, Tajik, Hazara, Uzbek, Turkmen, Aimaq, Baluch, Nuristani, Kizilbash.)
Religions: Sunni Muslim 84%, Shia Muslim 15%, other 1%. Main languages: Dari (Afghan Persian), Pashto.
Education: Only a small percentage of children attend school. *Literacy* (1999 est.)—31.5% (male: 47.2%, female: 15%), but real figures may be lower given breakdown of education system and flight of educated Afghans. Rates may rise again with restored and sustained stability and foreign aid.
Health: *Infant mortality rate* (2002 est.)—144.76/1,000. *Life expectancy* (2000 est.)—46.62 yrs. (male); 45.1 yrs. (female).
Workforce: Mostly in rural agriculture (perhaps 80%); number cannot be estimated accurately due to conflict.

Government

Type: Afghanistan identifies itself as an "Islamic state."
Independence: August 19, 1919 (from U.K. control over Afghan foreign affairs).
Organization: At a UN-sponsored conference held in Bonn, Germany, in early December 2001, agreement was reached between Afghan political factions to create an interim government and establish a process to move toward a permanent government. The Interim Authority was installed on December 22, 2001, with Hamid Karzai as chairman. In June 2002, the country's grand council, or Loya Jirga, met and confirmed Hamid Karzai as the leader of the country's transitional government, pending elections to be held in June 2004.
Flag: Adopted in 2002, the flag has three vertical bands—black, red, and green—with the great seal of Afghanistan superimposed on the bands. Based on the flag in use from 1930 to 1973.

Economy

GDP: $3 billion (1991 est.) and may well be correct. Purchasing parity power (1999 est.) was $21 billion, or $800 per capita. The economy essentially crashed during the 2001–2002 conflict, and recovery has been slow.

Natural resources: Natural gas, oil, coal, copper, chromite, talc, barites, sulfur, lead, zinc, iron, salt, precious and semiprecious stones.

Agriculture (at least 65% of GDP): *Products*—wheat, corn, barley, rice, cotton, fruit, nuts, karakul pelts, wool, and mutton.

Industry (estimated 20% of GDP): *Types*—small-scale production for domestic use of textiles, soap, furniture, shoes, fertilizer, and cement; handwoven carpets for export; natural gas, precious and semiprecious gemstones.

Trade (1996 est.): *Exports*—$80 million (does not include opium): opium, fruits and nuts, handwoven carpets, wool, cotton, hides and pelts, precious and semiprecious gems. *Major markets*—Central Asian republics, Pakistan, Iran, European Union (EU), India. Estimates show that the figure for 2001 is much reduced, except for opium. *Imports*—$150 million (1996 est.): food, petroleum products, and consumer goods. Estimates show that imports have been severely reduced in 2001. *Major suppliers*—Central Asian republics, Pakistan, Iran.

Currency: The currency is called the afghani. There continue to be problems of separate printing of the afghani in different parts of the country. The afghani is highly inflated with rates fluctuating frequently, although it strengthened markedly with the ouster of the Taliban and the installation of the Interim Authority. The market rate during much of 2001 exceeded 50,000 afghanis to $1. The Pakistani rupee and other foreign currencies are frequently used as legal tender.

People

Afghanistan's ethnically and linguistically mixed population reflects its location astride historic trade and invasion routes leading from central Asia into south and southwest Asia. Pashtuns are the dominant ethnic group, accounting for about 38% of the population. Tajik (25%), Hazara (19%), Uzbek (6%), Aimaq, Turkmen, Baluch, and other small groups also are represented. Dari (Afghan Persian) and Pashto are official languages. Dari is spoken by more than one-third of the population as a first language and serves as a lingua franca for most Afghans, though the Taliban used Pashto. Tajik, Uzbek, and Turkmen are spoken widely in the north. Smaller groups throughout the country also speak more than 70 other languages and numerous dialects.

Afghanistan is an Islamic country. An estimated 84% of the population is Sunni, following the Hanafi school of jurisprudence; the remainder is predominantly Shia, mainly Hazara. Despite attempts during the years of communist rule to secularize Afghan society, Islamic practices pervade all aspects of life. In fact, Islam served as the principal basis for expressing opposition to the communists and the Soviet invasion. Likewise, Islamic religious tradition and codes, together with traditional practices, provide the principal means of controlling personal conduct and settling legal disputes. Excluding urban populations in the principal cities, most Afghans are divided into tribal and other kinship-based groups, which follow traditional customs and religious practices.

History

Afghanistan, often called the crossroads of central Asia, has had a turbulent history. In 328 B.C., Alexander the Great entered the territory of present-day Afghanistan, then part of the Persian Empire, to capture Bactra (present-day Balkh). Invasions by the Scythians, White Huns, and Turks followed in succeeding centuries. In A.D. 642, Arabs invaded the entire region and introduced Islam.

Arab rule quickly gave way to the Persians, who controlled the area until conquered by the Turkic Ghaznavids in 998. Mahmūd of Ghazni (998–1030) consolidated the conquests of his predecessors and turned Ghazni into a great cultural center as well as a base for frequent forays into India. Following Mahmūd's short-lived dynasty, various princes attempted to rule sections of the country until the Mongol invasion of 1219. The Mongol invasion, led by Genghis Khan, resulted in massive slaughter of the population; destruction of many cities, including Herat, Ghazni, and Balkh; and the despoliation of fertile agricultural areas.

Following Genghis Khan's death in 1227, a succession of petty chiefs and princes struggled for supremacy until late in the 14th century, when one of Genghis Khan's descendants, Tamerlane (Timur), incorporated Afghanistan into his own vast Asian empire. Babur, a descendant of Tamerlane and the founder of India's Moghul dynasty at the beginning of the 16th century, made Kabul the capital of an Afghan principality.

In 1747, Ahmad Shāh Durrāni, the founder of what is known today as Afghanistan, established his rule. A Pashtun, Durrāni was elected king by a tribal council after the assassination of the Persian ruler Nāder Shāh at Khabushan in the same year. Throughout his reign, Durrāni consolidated chieftainships, petty principalities, and fragmented provinces into one country. His rule extended from Mashhad in the west to Kashmir and Delhi in the east, and from the Amu Darya River in the north to the Arabian Sea in the south. With the exception of a nine-month period in 1929, all of Afghanistan's rulers until the 1978 Marxist coup were from Durrāni's Pashtun tribal confederation, and all were members of that tribe's Mohammadzai clan after 1818.

European Influence

Collision between the expanding British and Russian Empires significantly influenced Afghanistan during the 19th century in what was termed the "Great Game." British concern about Russian advances in central Asia and growing influence in Persia culminated in two Anglo-Afghan wars. The first (1839–42) not only resulted in the destruction of the British forces, but is remembered today as an example of the ferocity of Afghan resistance to foreign rule. The second Anglo-Afghan war (1878–80) was sparked by Amir Shīr 'Ali Khān's refusal to accept a British mission in Kabul. This conflict brought Amir 'Abdorrahmān to the Afghan throne. During his reign (1880–1901), the British and Russians officially established the boundaries of what would become modern Afghanistan. The British retained effective control over Kabul's foreign affairs.

Afghanistan remained neutral during World War I, despite German encouragement of anti-British feelings and Afghan rebellion along the borders of British India. The Afghan king's policy of neutrality was not universally popular within the country, however.

Habībollāh, 'Abdorrahmān's son and successor, was assassinated in 1919, possibly by family members opposed to British influence. Habībollāh's third son, Amānollāh, regained control of Afghanistan's foreign policy after launching the third Anglo-Afghan war with an attack on India in the same year. During the ensuing conflict, the war-weary British relinquished their control over Afghan foreign affairs by signing the Treaty of Rawalpindi in August 1919. In commemoration of this event, Afghans celebrate August 19 as their independence day.

Reform and Reaction

King Amānollāh (1919–29) moved to end his country's traditional isolation in the years following the third Anglo-Afghan war. He established diplomatic relations with most major countries and, following a 1927 tour of Europe and Turkey—during which he noted the modernization and secularization advanced by Ataturk—introduced several reforms intended to modernize Afghanistan. Some of these, such as the abolition of the traditional Muslim veil for women and the opening of a number of coeducational schools, quickly alienated many tribal and religious leaders. Faced with overwhelming armed opposition, Amānollāh was forced to abdicate in January 1929 after Kabul fell to forces led by Bacha-i-Saqao, a Tajik brigand. Prince Nāder Khān, a cousin of Amānollāh's, in turn defeated Bacha-i-Saqao in October of the same year and, with considerable Pashtun tribal support, was declared king. Four years later, however, he was assassinated in a revenge killing by a Kabul student.

Mohammad Zahir Shah, Nāder Khān's 19-year-old son, succeeded to the throne and reigned from 1933 to 1973. In 1964, King Zahir Shah promulgated a liberal constitution providing for a two-chamber legislature to which the king appointed one-third of the deputies. The people elected another third, and the remainder were selected indirectly by provincial assemblies. Although Zahir's "experiment in democracy" produced few lasting reforms, it permitted the growth of unofficial extremist parties on both the left and the right. These included the communist People's Democratic Party of Afghanistan (PDPA), which had close ideological ties to the Soviet Union. In 1967, the PDPA split into two major rival factions: the Khalq (Masses) faction, headed by Nur Muhammad Taraki and Hafizullah Amin and supported by elements within the military, and the Parcham (Banner) faction, led by Babrak Karmal. The split reflected ethnic, class, and ideological divisions within Afghan society.

Zahir's cousin, Sardar Mohammad Daud, served as his prime minister from 1953 to 1963. During his tenure, Daud solicited military and economic assistance from both Washington, D.C., and Moscow and introduced controversial social policies of a reformist nature. Daud's alleged support for the creation of a Pashtun state in the Pakistan-Afghan border area heightened tensions with Pakistan and eventually resulted in Daud's dismissal in March 1963.

Daud's Republic (1973–1978) and the April 1978 Coup

Amid charges of corruption and malfeasance against the royal family and poor economic conditions created by the severe 1971–72 drought, former prime minister Daud seized power in a military coup on July 17, 1973. Zahir Shah fled the country eventually finding refuge in Italy. Daud abolished the monarchy, abrogated the 1964 constitution, and declared Afghanistan a republic with himself as its first president and prime minister. His attempts to carry out badly needed economic and social reforms met with little success, and the new constitution promulgated in February 1977 failed to quell chronic political instability.

Seeking to exploit more effectively mounting popular disaffection, the PDPA reunified with Moscow's support. On April 27, 1978, the PDPA initiated a bloody coup, which resulted in the overthrow and murder of Daud and most of his family. Nur Muhammad Taraki, secretary general of the PDPA, became president of the Revolutionary Council and prime minister of the newly established Democratic Republic of Afghanistan. Opposition to the Marxist government emerged almost immediately. During its first 18 months of rule, the PDPA brutally imposed a Marxist-style "reform" program, which ran counter to deeply rooted Afghan traditions.

Decrees abolishing usury, forcing changes in marriage customs, and pushing through an ill-conceived land reform were particularly misunderstood by virtually all Afghans. In addition, thousands of members of the traditional elite, the religious establishment, and the intelligentsia were imprisoned, tortured, or murdered. Conflicts within the PDPA also surfaced early and resulted in exiles, purges, imprisonments, and executions.

By the summer of 1978, a revolt began in the Nuristan region of eastern Afghanistan and quickly spread into a countrywide insurgency. In September 1979, Hafizullah Amin, who had earlier been prime minister and minister of defense, seized power from Taraki after a palace shoot-out. Over the next two months, instability plagued Amin's regime as he moved against perceived enemies in the PDPA. By December, party morale was crumbling, and the insurgency was growing.

The Soviet Invasion

The Soviet Union moved quickly to take advantage of the April 1978 coup. In December 1978, Moscow signed a new bilateral treaty of friendship and cooperation with Afghanistan, and the Soviet military assistance program increased significantly. The regime's survival increasingly was dependent upon Soviet military equipment and advisers as the insurgency spread and the Afghan army began to collapse.

By October 1979, however, relations between Afghanistan and the Soviet Union were tense as Hafizullah Amin refused to take Soviet advice on how to stabilize and consolidate his government. Faced with a deteriorating security situation, on December 24, 1979, large numbers of Soviet airborne forces, joining thousands of Soviet troops already on the ground, began to land in Kabul under the pretext of a field exercise. On December 26, these invasion forces killed Hafizullah Amin and installed Babrak Karmal, exiled leader of the Parcham faction, bringing him back from Czechoslovakia and making him prime minister. Massive Soviet ground forces invaded from the north on December 27.

Following the invasion, the Karmal regime, although backed by an expeditionary force that grew as large as 120,000 Soviet troops, was unable to establish authority outside Kabul. As much as 80% of the countryside, including parts of Herāt and Kandahār, eluded effective government control. An overwhelming majority of Afghans opposed the communist regime, either actively or passively. Afghan freedom fighters (mujahideen) made it almost impossible for the regime to maintain a system of local government outside major urban centers. Poorly armed at first, in 1984 the mujahideen began receiving substantial assistance in the form of weapons and training from the United States and other outside powers.

In May 1985, the seven principal Peshawar-based guerrilla organizations formed an alliance to coordinate their political and military operations against the Soviet occupation. Late in 1985, the mujahideen were active in and around Kabul, launching rocket attacks and conducting operations against the communist government. The failure of the Soviet Union to win over a significant number of Afghan collaborators or to rebuild a viable Afghan army forced it to bear an increasing responsibility for fighting the resistance and for civilian administration.

Soviet and popular displeasure with the Karmal regime led to its demise in May 1986. Karmal was replaced by Muhammad Najibullah, former chief of the Afghan secret police (KHAD). Najibullah had established a reputation for brutal efficiency during his tenure as KHAD chief. As prime minister, Najibullah was ineffective and highly dependent on Soviet support. Undercut by deep-seated divisions within the PDPA, regime efforts to broaden its base of support proved futile.

The Geneva Accords and Their Aftermath

By the mid-1980s, the tenacious Afghan resistance movement—aided by the United States, Saudi Arabia, Pakistan, and others—was exacting a high price from the Soviets, both militarily within Afghanistan and by souring the USSR's relations with much of the Western and Islamic world. Although informal negotiations for a Soviet withdrawal from Afghanistan had been under way since 1982, it was not until 1988 that the governments of Pakistan and Afghanistan, with the United States and Soviet Union serving as guarantors, signed an agreement settling the major differences between them. The agreement, known as the Geneva Accords, included five major documents, which, among other things, called for U.S. and Soviet noninterference in the internal affairs of Pakistan and Afghanistan, the right of refugees to return to Afghanistan without fear of persecution or harassment, and, most important, a timetable that ensured full Soviet withdrawal from Afghanistan by February 15, 1989. About 14,500 Soviet and an estimated 1 million Afghan lives were lost between 1979 and the Soviet withdrawal in 1989.

Significantly, the mujahideen were neither party to the negotiations nor to the 1988 agreement and, consequently, refused to accept the terms of the accords. As a result, the civil war continued after the Soviet withdrawal, which was completed in February 1989. Najibullah's regime, though failing to win popular support, territory, or international recognition, was able to remain in power until 1992 but collapsed after the defection of General Abdul Rashid Dostam and his Uzbek militia in March. However, when the victorious mujahideen entered Kabul to assume control over the city and the central government, a new round of internecine fighting began between the various militias, which had coexisted only uneasily during the Soviet occupation. With the demise of their common enemy, the militias' ethnic, clan, religious, and personality differences surfaced, and the civil war continued.

Seeking to resolve these differences, the leaders of the Peshawar-based mujahideen groups established the interim Islamic Jihad Council in mid-April 1992 to assume power in Kabul. Moderate leader professor Sibghatullah Mojaddedi was to chair the council for two months, after which a 10-member leadership council composed of mujahideen leaders and presided over by the head of the Jamiat-i-Islami (Islamic Society), professor Burhanuddin Rabbani, was to be set up for four months. During this six-month period, the Loya Jirga, or Grand Council of Afghan elders and notables, would convene and designate an interim administration that would hold power up to a year, pending elections.

But in May 1992, Rabbani prematurely formed the leadership council, undermining Mojaddedi's fragile authority. In June, Mojaddedi surrendered power to the Leadership Council, which then elected Rabbani as president. Nonetheless, heavy fighting broke out in August 1992 in Kabul between forces loyal to President Rabbani and rival factions, particularly those who supported Gulbuddin Hekmatyar's Hezb-e-Islami (Islamic Party). After Rabbani extended his tenure in December 1992, fighting in the capital flared up in January and February 1993. The Islamabad Accord, signed in March 1993, which appointed Hekmatyar as prime minister, failed to have a lasting effect. A follow-up agreement, the Jalalabad Accord, called for the militias to be disarmed but was never fully implemented. Through 1993, Hekmatyar's Hezb-e-Islami forces, allied with the Shia Hezb-i-Wahdat (Unity Party) militia, clashed intermittently with Rabbani's and Ahmad Shah Masood's Jamiat forces. Cooperating with Jamiat were militants of Abdul Rasul Sayyaf's Ittihad-i-Islami (Islamic Alliance) and, periodically, troops loyal to ethnic Uzbek strongman Abdul Rashid Dostam. On January 1, 1994, Dostam switched sides, precipitating large-scale fighting in Kabul and in northern provinces, which caused thousands of civilian casualties in Kabul and elsewhere and created a new wave of displaced persons and refugees. The country sank even further into anarchy; forces loyal to Rabbani and Masood, both ethnic Tajiks, controlled Kabul and much of the northeast, while local warlords exerted power over the rest of the country.

Rise of the Taliban

In reaction to the anarchy and warlordism prevalent in the country and the lack of Pashtun representation in the Kabul government, a movement called the Taliban of former mujahideen arose. Many of its members had been educated in *madrassas* (Islamic religious schools) in Pakistan and were largely from rural Pashtun backgrounds; the movement's name comes from *talib*, which means "pupil." This group dedicated itself to removing the warlords, establishing order, and imposing Islam on the country. It received considerable support from Pakistan. In 1994 it developed enough strength to capture the city of Kandahar from a local warlord and proceeded to expand its control throughout Afghanistan, occupying Kabul in September 1996. By the end of 1998, the Taliban occupied about 90% of the country, limiting the opposition largely to a small, largely Tajik corner in the northeast and the Panjshir valley. Efforts by the UN, prominent Afghans living outside the country, and other interested countries to bring about a peaceful solution to the continuing conflict came to naught, largely because of intransigence on the part of the Taliban.

The Taliban sought to impose an extreme interpretation of Islam—based in part upon rural Pashtun tradition—upon the entire country and committed massive human rights violations, particularly directed against women and girls, in the process. Women were restricted from working outside the home or pursuing an education were not to leave their homes without an accompanying male relative, and were forced to wear a traditional body-covering garment called the *burka*. The Taliban committed serious atrocities against minority populations, particularly the Shia Hazara ethnic group, and killed noncombatants in several well-documented instances. In 2001, as part of a drive against relics of Afghanistan's pre-Islamic past, the Taliban destroyed two large statues of the Buddha outside of the city of Bāmiān and announced destruction of all pre-Islamic statues in Afghanistan, including the remaining holdings of the Kabul Museum.

From the mid-1990s, the Taliban provided sanctuary to Osama bin Laden, a Saudi national who had fought with them against the Soviets, and provided a base for his and other terrorist organizations. The UN Security Council repeatedly sanctioned the Taliban for these activities. Bin Laden provided both financial and political support to the Taliban. Bin Laden and his al-Qaeda group were charged with the bombing of the U.S. embassies in Nairobi and Dar es Salaam in 1998, and in August 1998, the United States launched a cruise missile attack against bin Laden's terrorist camp in Afghanistan. Bin Laden and al-Qaeda are believed to be responsible for the September 11, 2001, terrorist acts in the United States, among other crimes.

Also in September, agents working on behalf of the Taliban and believed to be associated with bin Laden's al-Qaeda group assassinated Northern Alliance defense minister and chief military commander Ahmad Shah Masood, a hero of the Afghan resistance against the Soviets and the Taliban's principal military opponent. Following the Taliban's repeated refusal to expel bin Laden and his group and end its support for international terrorism, the United States and its partners in the antiterrorist coalition began a campaign on October 7, 2001, targeting terrorist facilities and various Taliban military and political assets within Afghanistan.

Under pressure from U.S. air power and anti-Taliban ground forces, the Taliban disintegrated rapidly and Kabul fell on November 13. Sponsored by the UN, Afghan factions opposed to the Taliban met in Bonn, Germany, in early December and agreed on a political process to restore stability and governance to Afghanistan. In the first step, an Afghan Interim Authority was formed and was installed in Kabul on December 22, 2001. The Interim Authority prepared for the Loya Jirga, which in turn met in June 2002 to form the Transitional Administration to prepare for elections in June 2004. In addition, the Interim Authority worked closely with coalition forces in rooting out remnants of al-Qaeda and the Taliban. The international community has pledged over $4.5 billion in aid for the reconstruction of Afghanistan. On April 18, 2002, former king Zahir Shah returned to Kabul after an exile of 29 years. The 88-year-old former monarch filled a symbolic role of national unity in opening the Loya Jirga.

Government and Political Conditions

During 2002, the Afghanistan Transitional Authority was attempting to bring effective governance to the country although its reach beyond the capital, Kabul, remained tenuous and its ability to deliver necessary social services dependent on funds from the international donor community. Ministries in the government were apportioned with an eye toward balancing the country's different ethnic groups, although continued complaints of imbalance may lead to a restructuring of government in the Transitional Administration following the Loya Jirga.

By the end of 2002, the year-old transitional Afghan government had made some progress. More than 2 million Afghan refugees have returned to Afghanistan, representing a dramatic vote of confidence in a better future for their country. President Karzai has put together a government that now interacts constructively with the 60 nations of the international community assisting in Afghanistan's reconstruction. Roads are being built; schools are now in session. Girls are once again in school, and Afghans are beginning to experience the security that allows for a normal life.

Afghanistan's progress toward becoming a full member of the international community took an important step forward on December 22, 2002, when Afghanistan and six neighboring countries signed the Kabul Declaration on Good Neighborly Relations, a pledge to respect Afghanistan's independence and territorial integrity. The signing ceremony marked one year since the establishment of a representative Afghan government, an achievement of the international community and the Afghans working together.

Afghanistan's domestic security depends on the cooperation, goodwill, and non-interference of Afghanistan's neighbors. The United States strongly supports the efforts of the Afghan government under President Karzai to establish its authority and good governance throughout the country and to secure commitment of both neighboring states and local leaders to this goal.

International efforts to rebuild Afghanistan were addressed at the Tokyo Donors Conference for Afghan Reconstruction in January 2002, when $4.5 billion was collected for a trust fund to be administered by the World Bank. Priority areas for reconstruction include the construction of education, health, and sanitation facilities; enhancement of administrative capacity; the development of the agricultural sector; and the rebuilding of road, energy, and telecommunication links.

Principal Government Officials

Chairman—Hamid Karzai
Minister of Foreign Affairs—Abdullah Abdullah

The United States suspended operation of the Afghan embassy in Washington, D.C., on August 21, 1997. The Embassy of the Afghanistan Interim Authority reopened in January 2002. It is located at 2000 L Street NW, Suite 200, Washington, DC 20036; tel.: (202) 416–1620.

Economy

Historically, there has been a dearth of information and reliable statistics about Afghanistan's economy. The Soviet invasion and ensuing civil war destroyed much of the underdeveloped country's limited infrastructure and disrupted normal patterns of economic activity. Gross domestic product has fallen substantially over the past 20 years because of loss of labor and capital and disruption of trade and transport. Continuing internal strife hampered both domestic efforts at reconstruction as well as international aid efforts.

Agriculture

The Afghan economy continues to be overwhelmingly agricultural, despite the fact that only 12% of its total land area is arable and less than 6% currently is cultivated. Agricultural production is constrained by an almost total dependence on erratic winter snows and spring rains for water; irrigation is primitive. Relatively little use is made of machines, chemical fertilizer, or pesticides.

Grain production is Afghanistan's traditional agricultural mainstay. Overall agricultural production dramatically declined following three years of drought as well as the sustained fighting, instability in rural areas, and deteriorated infrastructure. Soviet efforts to disrupt production in resistance-dominated areas also contributed to this decline, as did the disruption to transportation resulting from ongoing conflict.

The war against the Soviet Union and the ensuing civil war also led to migration to the cities and refugee flight to Pakistan and Iran, further disrupting normal agricultural production. Recent studies indicate that agricultural production and livestock numbers are only sufficient to feed about half of Afghanistan's population. Shortages are exacerbated by the country's already limited transportation network, which has deteriorated further due to damage and neglect resulting from war and the absence of an effective central government.

Opium became a source of cash for some Afghans, especially following the breakdown in central authority after the Soviet withdrawal, and opium-derived revenues probably constituted a major source of income for the two main factions. The Taliban earned roughly $40 million per year on opium taxes alone. Opium is easy to cultivate and transport and offers a quick source of income for impoverished Afghans. Afghanistan was the world's largest producer of raw opium in 1999 and 2000. In 2000 the Taliban banned opium poppy cultivation in part to attract foreign aid and also to control the opium market with large existing stockpiles that earned substantially large price increases. While cultivation of opium poppy was virtually eliminated in Taliban-controlled areas, drug trafficking has continued unabated. Later, in 2001, the Taliban reportedly announced that poppy cultivation could resume. Much of Afghanistan's opium production is refined into heroin and is either consumed by a growing regional addict population or exported, primarily to western Europe. The Afghan Interim Authority began to enact major counternarcotics policies and programs, but more vigilance will be needed to eliminate the Afghan drug trade.

Trade and Industry

Trade accounts for a small portion of the documented Afghan economy, and there are no reliable statistics relating to trade flows. In 1996, exports, not including opium, were estimated at $80 million and imports at $150 million. These figures have probably decreased over time. Since the Soviet withdrawal and the collapse of the Soviet Union, other limited trade relationships appear to be emerging with central Asian states, Pakistan, Iran, the EU, and Japan. Afghanistan trades little with the United States. Afghanistan does not enjoy U.S. most-favored-nation (MFN) trading status, which was revoked in 1986.

Afghanistan is endowed with a wealth of natural resources, including extensive deposits of natural gas, petroleum, coal, copper, chromite, talc, barites, sulfur, lead, zinc, iron ore, salt, and precious and semiprecious stones. In the 1970s the Soviets estimated Afghanistan had as much as 5 trillion cubic feet of natural gas, 95 million barrels of oil and condensate reserves, and 400 million tons of coal. Unfortunately, the country's continuing conflict, remote and rugged terrain, and inadequate transportation network usually have made mining these resources difficult, and there have been few serious attempts to further explore or exploit them.

The most important resource has been natural gas, first tapped in 1967. At their peak during the 1980s, natural gas sales accounted for $300 million a year in export revenues (56% of the total). Ninety percent of these exports went to the Soviet Union to pay for imports and debts. However, during the withdrawal of Soviet troops in 1989, Afghanistan's natural gas fields were capped to prevent sabotage by the mujahideen. Restoration of gas production has been hampered by internal strife and the disruption of traditional trading relationships following the collapse of the Soviet Union. Gas production has dropped from a high of 290 million cubic feet (Mmcf) per day in the 1980s to a low of about 22 Mmcf in 2001.

Trade in goods smuggled into Pakistan once constituted a major source of revenue for Afghan regimes, including the Taliban, and also figured as an important element in the Afghan economy. Many of the goods smuggled into Pakistan originally entered Afghanistan from Pakistan, where they fell under the Afghan Trade and Transit Agreement (ATTA), which permitted goods bound for Afghanistan to transit Pakistan free of duty. When Pakistan clamped down in 2000 on the types of goods permitted duty-free transit, routing of goods through Iran from the gulf increased significantly. Shipments of smuggled goods were subjected to fees and duties paid to the Afghan government. The trade also provided jobs to tens of thousands of Afghans on both sides of the Durand Line, which forms the border between Afghanistan and Pakistan. Pakistan's closing of its border with Afghanistan in September 2001 presumably drastically curtailed this traffic.

Transportation

Landlocked Afghanistan has no functioning railways, but the Amu Darya River, which forms part of Afghanistan's border with Turkmenistan, Uzbekistan, and Tajikistan, has barge traffic. During their occupation of the country, the Soviets completed a bridge across the Amu Darya and built a motor vehicle and railroad bridge between Termez and Jeyretan.

Most road building occurred in the 1960s, funded by the United States and the Soviet Union. The Soviets built a road and tunnel through the Salang Pass in 1964, connecting northern and southern Afghanistan. A highway connecting the principal cities of Herāt, Kandahār, Ghazni, and Kabul, with links to highways in neighboring Pakistan, formed the primary road system.

The highway system requires almost total reconstruction, and regional roads are in a state of disrepair. The poor state of the Afghan transportation and communication networks has further fragmented and hobbled the struggling economy.

Economic Development and Recovery

Afghanistan embarked on a modest economic development program in the 1930s. The government founded banks; introduced paper money; established a university; expanded primary, secondary, and technical schools; and sent students abroad for education. In 1956, the Afghan government promulgated the first in a long series of ambitious development plans. By the late 1970s, these had achieved only mixed results due to flaws in the planning process as well as inadequate funding and a shortage of the skilled managers and technicians needed for implementation.

These constraints on development have been exacerbated by the flight of educated Afghans and the disruption and instability stemming from the Soviet occupation and ensuing civil war. Today, economic recovery and long-term development will depend on establishing an effective and stable political system and an end to more than 22 years of conflict.

The UN and the international donor community continue to provide considerable humanitarian relief. Since its inception in 1988, the umbrella UN Office for the Coordination of Humanitarian Assistance to Afghanistan (UNOCHA) has channeled more than $1 billion in multilateral assistance to Afghan refugees and vulnerable persons inside Afghanistan. The United States, the EU and Japan are the leading contributors to this relief effort. One of its key tasks is to eliminate from priority areas—such as villages, arable fields, and roads—some of the 5 to 7 million land mines and 750,000 pieces of unexploded ordnance, sown mainly during the Soviet occupation, which continue to litter the Afghan landscape. Afghanistan is the most heavily mined country in the world; mine-related injuries number up to 300 per month. Without successful mine clearance, refugee repatriation, political stability, and economic reconstruction will be severely constrained.

Foreign Relations

Before the Soviet invasion, Afghanistan pursued a policy of neutrality and nonalignment in its foreign relations. In international forums, Afghanistan generally followed the voting patterns of Asian and African nonaligned countries. Following the Marxist coup of April 1978, the Taraki government developed significantly closer ties with the Soviet Union and its communist satellites.

After the December 1979 invasion, Afghanistan's foreign policy mirrored that of the Soviet Union. Afghan foreign policymakers attempted, with little success, to increase their regime's low standing in the noncommunist world. With the signing of the Geneva Accords, Najibullah unsuccessfully sought to end Afghanistan's isolation within the Islamic world and in the Non-Aligned Movement.

Most Western countries, including the United States, maintained small diplomatic missions in Kabul during the Soviet occupation. (Throughout the Soviet occupation, the United States did not recognize the Afghan regimes, and its mission was headed by a chargé d'affaires rather than an ambassador.) Many countries subsequently closed their missions due to instability and heavy fighting in Kabul.

Pakistan, Saudi Arabia, and the United Arab Emirates (UAE) recognized the Taliban regime in 1997. Saudi Arabia and the UAE withdrew recognition following the September 11, 2001, bombings. Repeated Taliban efforts to occupy Afghanistan's seat at the UN and Organization of the Islamic Conference (OIC) were unsuccessful.

Pakistan

Two areas—Pashtunistan and Baluchistan—have long complicated Afghanistan's relations with Pakistan. Controversies involving these areas date back to the establishment of the Durand Line in 1893 dividing Pashtun and Baluch tribes living in Afghanistan from those living in what later became Pakistan. Afghanistan vigorously protested the inclusion of Pashtun and Baluch areas within Pakistan without providing the inhabitants with an opportunity for self-determination. Since 1947, this problem has led to incidents along the border, with extensive disruption of normal trade patterns. The most serious crisis lasted from September 1961 to June 1963, when diplomatic, trade, transit, and consular relations between the countries were suspended. The 1978 Marxist coup further strained relations between the two countries.

Pakistan took the lead diplomatically in the United Nations, the Non-Aligned Movement, and the OIC in opposing the Soviet occupation. During the war against the Soviet occupation, Pakistan served as the primary logistical conduit for the Afghan resistance. Pakistan, aided by UN agencies, private groups, and many friendly countries, continues to provide refuge to several million Afghans.

Pakistan initially developed close ties to the Taliban regime, which it believed would offer strategic depth in any future conflict with India, and extended recognition in 1997. This policy was not without controversy in Pakistan, where many objected to the Taliban's human rights record and radical interpretation of Islam. Following the Taliban's resistance to Islamabad's pressure to comply with relevant UN Security Council Resolutions and surrender Osama bin Laden after the September 11 bombings in New York City and Washington, D.C., Pakistan dramatically altered its policy by closing its border and downgrading its ties.

Much of Afghanistan has long relied on Pakistani links for trade and travel to the outside world, and Pakistan views Afghanistan as eventually becoming its primary route for trade with central Asia, though these plans will of necessity await establishment of secure conditions.

Iran

Afghanistan's relations with Iran have fluctuated over the years, with periodic disputes over the water rights of the Helmand River as the main issue of contention. Following the Soviet invasion, which Iran opposed, relations deteriorated. The Iranian consulate in Herāt closed, as did the Afghan consulate in Mashhad. The Iranians complained of periodic border violations following the Soviet invasion. In 1985, they urged feuding Afghan Shia resistance groups to unite to oppose the Soviets. Iran supported the cause of the Afghan resistance and provided limited financial and military assistance to rebel leaders who pledged loyalty to the Iranian vision of Islamic revolution. Iran provides refuge to about 2 million Afghans, though it has refused to accept more in recent years and, indeed, tried to force many to repatriate.

Following the emergence of the Taliban and their harsh treatment of Afghanistan's Shia minority, Iran stepped up assistance to the Northern Alliance. Relations with the Taliban deteriorated further in 1998 after Taliban forces seized the Iranian consulate in Mazār-i-Sharīf and executed Iranian diplomats.

Russia

In the 19th century, Afghanistan served as a strategic buffer state between czarist Russia and the British Empire in the subcontinent. Afghanistan's relations with Moscow became more cordial after the Bolshevik revolution in 1917. The Soviet Union was the first country to establish diplomatic relations with Afghanistan after the third Anglo-Afghan war and signed an Afghan-Soviet nonaggression pact in 1921, which also provided for Afghan transit rights through the Soviet Union. Early Soviet assistance included financial aid, aircraft and attendant technical personnel, and telegraph operators.

The Soviets began a major economic assistance program in Afghanistan in the 1950s. Between 1954 and 1978, Afghanistan received more than

$1 billion in Soviet aid, including substantial military assistance. In 1973, the two countries announced a $200-million assistance agreement on gas and oil development, trade, transport, irrigation, and factory construction. Following the 1979 invasion, the Soviets augmented their large aid commitments to shore up the Afghan economy and rebuild the Afghan military. They provided the Karmal regime an unprecedented $800 million. The Soviet Union supported the Najibullah regime even after the withdrawal of Soviet troops in February 1989. Today, unresolved questions concerning Soviet soldiers missing in action and prisoners of war in Afghanistan remain an issue between Russia and Afghanistan.

Tajik rebels based in Afghanistan in July 1993 attacked a Russian border outpost in Tajikistan, killing 25 Russians and prompting Russian retaliatory strikes, which caused extensive damage in northern Afghanistan. Reports of Afghan support for the Tajik rebels have led to cool relations between the two countries.

Russia became increasingly disenchanted with the Taliban over their support for Chechen rebels and for providing a sanctuary for terrorist groups active in central Asia and in Russia itself. Russia provided military assistance to the Northern Alliance.

Tajikistan

Afghanistan's relations with newly independent Tajikistan have been complicated by political upheaval and civil war in Tajikistan, which spurred some 100,000 Tajiks to seek refuge in Afghanistan in late 1992 and early 1993. Tajik rebels seeking to overthrow the regime of Russian-backed former communist Imamali Rahmanov began operating from Afghan bases and recruiting Tajik refugees into their ranks. These rebels, reportedly aided by Afghans and a number of foreign Islamic extremists, conducted cross-border raids against Russian and Tajik security posts and sought to infiltrate fighters and materiel from Afghanistan into Tajikistan. Also disenchanted by the Taliban's harsh treatment of Afghanistan's Tajik minority, Tajikistan facilitated assistance to the Northern Alliance.

U.S.-Afghan Relations

The first extensive contact of an American with Afghanistan was made by Josiah Harlan, an adventurer from Pennsylvania who was an adviser in Afghan politics in the 1830s and reputedly inspired the British writer Rudyard Kipling's story "The Man Who Would Be King." After the establishment of diplomatic relations in 1934, the U.S. policy of helping developing nations raise their standard of living was an important factor in maintaining and improving U.S.-Afghan ties. From 1950 to 1979, U.S.

foreign assistance provided Afghanistan with more than $500 million in loans, grants, and surplus agricultural commodities to develop transportation facilities, increase agricultural production, expand the educational system, stimulate industry, and improve government administration.

In the 1950s, the United States declined Afghanistan's request for defense cooperation but extended an economic assistance program focused on the development of Afghanistan's physical infrastructure—roads, dams, and power plants. Later, U.S. aid shifted from infrastructure projects to technical assistance programs to help develop the skills needed to build a modern economy. The Peace Corps was active in Afghanistan between 1962 and 1979.

After the April 1978 coup, relations deteriorated. In February 1979, U.S. Ambassador Adolph "Spike" Dubs was murdered in Kabul after Afghan security forces burst in on his kidnappers. The United States then reduced bilateral assistance and terminated a small military training program. All remaining assistance agreements were ended after the Soviet invasion.

Following the Soviet invasion, the United States supported diplomatic efforts to achieve a Soviet withdrawal. In addition, generous U.S. contributions to the refugee program in Pakistan played a major part in efforts to assist Afghans in need. U.S. efforts also included helping Afghans living inside Afghanistan. This cross-border humanitarian assistance program aimed at increasing Afghan self-sufficiency and helping Afghans resist Soviet attempts to drive civilians out of the rebel-dominated countryside. During the period of Soviet occupation of Afghanistan, the United States provided about $3 billion in military and economic assistance to Afghans and the resistance movement.

The U.S. embassy in Kabul was closed in January 1989 for security reasons but officially reopened as an embassy on January 17, 2002. Throughout the difficult and turbulent past 20 years, the United States has supported the peaceful emergence of a broad-based government representative of all Afghans and has been active in encouraging a UN role in the national reconciliation process in Afghanistan. The United States provides financial aid for mine-clearing activities and other humanitarian assistance to Afghans through international organizations. The United States is the largest provider of humanitarian assistance to Afghanistan. The aid effort has continued despite a U.S. cruise missile attack on a terrorist camp in Afghanistan associated with Osama bin Laden in 1998, with the military action taken against terrorist and Taliban targets in October 2001 and the actions of Operation Enduring Freedom in 2001–2002. However, aid has been slow in reaching the people of Afghanistan, both because of lack of larger commitments by donor nations and because much of Afghanistan is still effectively controlled by local warlords who are often embroiled in conflicts with one another.

UN Efforts

During the Soviet occupation, the United Nations was highly critical of the USSR's interference in the internal affairs of Afghanistan and was instrumental in obtaining a negotiated Soviet withdrawal under the terms of the Geneva Accords.

In the aftermath of the accords and subsequent Soviet withdrawal, the United Nations has assisted in the repatriation of refugees and has provided humanitarian aid such as health care, educational programs, and food and has supported mine-clearing operations. The UNDP and associated agencies have undertaken a limited number of development projects. However, the UN reduced its role in Afghanistan in 1992 in the wake of fierce factional strife in and around Kabul. The UN Secretary General has designated a personal representative to head the UNOCHA and the Special Mission to Afghanistan (UNSMA), both based in Islamabad, Pakistan. Throughout the late 1990s, 2000, and 2001, the UN unsuccessfully strived to promote a peaceful settlement between the Afghan factions as well as provide humanitarian aid, this despite increasing Taliban restrictions upon UN personnel and agencies.

OTHER COUNTRIES IN THE WAR ON TERRORISM

In addition to Afghanistan, a number of neighboring and other countries have had varying involvements with both Islamic terrorism and the war on terrorism initiated by the United States.

AZERBAIJAN

Azerbaijan and the United States have a good record of cooperation on counterterrorism issues that predates the September 11, 2001, attacks. Azerbaijan assisted in the investigation of the 1998 East Africa embassy bombings and has cooperated with the U.S. Embassy in Baku against terrorist threats to the mission. In the wake of the September 11 attacks, the government of Azerbaijan expressed unqualified support for the United States and offered "whatever means necessary" to the U.S.-led antiterrorism coalition. To date, Azerbaijan has granted blanket overflight clearance, offered the use of bases, and engaged in information sharing and law-enforcement cooperation.

Azerbaijan also has provided strong political support to the United States. In a ceremony at the U.S. ambassador's residence on December 11, 2001, President Heydar Aliyev reiterated his intention to support all measures taken by the United States in the fight against international terrorism. In early October, the parliament voted to ratify the UN Convention on the Suppression of the Financing of Terrorism, bringing to eight the number of international counterterrorism conventions to which Azerbaijan is a party.

While Azerbaijan previously had been a route for international mujahideen with ties to terrorist organizations seeking to move men, money, and materiel throughout the Caucasus, Baku stepped up its efforts to curb the international logistics networks supporting the mujahideen in Chechnya and has effectively reduced their presence and hampered their activities. Azerbaijan has taken steps to combat terrorist financing. It has made a concerted effort to identify possible terrorist-related funding by distributing lists of suspected terrorist groups and individuals to local banks. In August 2001, Azerbaijani law enforcement arrested six members of the Hizb ut-Tahrir terrorist group who were put on trial in early 2002. Members of Jayshullah, an indigenous terrorist group, who were arrested in 1999 and tried in 2000, remain in prison. In December 2001, Azerbaijani authorities revoked the registration of the local branch of the Kuwait Society for the Revival of the Islamic Heritage, an Islamic nongovernmental organization (NGO) suspected of supporting terrorist groups. After the September 11 attacks, Azerbaijan increased patrols along its southern land and maritime borders with Iran and detained several persons crossing the border illegally. It has deported at least six persons with suspected ties to terrorists, including three to Saudi Arabia and three to Egypt. The Department of Aviation Security increased security at Baku's Bina Airport and has implemented International Civil Aviation Organization recommendations on aviation security.

EGYPT

The Egyptian and U.S. governments continued to work closely together on a broad range of counterterrorism issues in 2001. The relationship was further strengthened in the wake of the September 11 attacks. Key Egyptian government and religious officials condemned the attacks; President Hosni Mubarak was the first Arab leader to support the U.S. military campaign in Afghanistan publicly. Egypt also supported efforts to cut off the flow of terrorism financing by strengthening banking regulations, including preparing a money-laundering bill for this purpose. The government of Egypt renewed its appeals to foreign governments to extradite or return Egyptian fugitives.

Other actions taken by the government of Egypt to support U.S. counterterrorism efforts following the September 11, 2001, attacks included continuing to place a high priority on protecting U.S. citizens and facilities in Egypt from attack; strengthening security for U.S. forces transiting the Suez Canal; implementing aviation security directives; agreeing to participate in the voluntary Advanced Passenger Information System; and granting extensive overflight and canal transit clearances.

Egypt itself has been for many years a victim of terrorism, although this has abated. No terrorism-related deaths were reported in Egypt in 2001, but the Egyptian government continued to regard terrorism and extremist activity as an urgent challenge. The Egyptian government indicted nearly 300 Egyptians and foreigners on terrorism-related charges. They will be tried by a military tribunal. Other terrorists' detentions were extended. Of those arrested, 87 were members of a group Egyptian authorities dubbed "al-Wa'ad" (The Promise). They were accused of planning to assassinate key Egyptian figures and blow up strategic targets; at the time of the arrests, authorities reportedly discovered arms caches and bomb-making materials. Those arrested included 170 al-Gama'at al-Islamiyya (IG) members, accused of killing police and civilians. They also were accused of targeting tourists and robbing banks between 1994 and 1998. Egypt's principal terrorist organizations, the Egyptian Islamic Jihad (EIJ) and the IG, suffered setbacks following September 11. International members of both groups and some suspects were returned to Egypt from abroad for trial. The government renewed its appeals to foreign governments to extradite or return other Egyptian fugitives. In early 2001, IG leader Rifa'i Ahmad Taha Musa published a book in which he attempted to justify terrorist attacks that result in mass civilian casualties. He disappeared several months thereafter, and his whereabouts at the time of this report's publication remained unknown.

GEORGIA

The Georgian government condemned the September 11, 2001, terrorist attacks and supports the international coalition's fight against terrorism. Immediately following the attacks, Georgian troops along the border with Russia went on high alert to monitor the passage of potential terrorists in the area. In early October, Tbilisi offered the United States the use of its airfields and airspace.

Georgia continued to face spillover violence from the Chechen conflict, including a short period of fighting in the separatist region of Abkhazia and bombings by aircraft from Russian territory on Georgia under the guise of antiterrorist operations. Like Azerbaijan, Georgia also contended with international mujahideen using Georgia as a conduit for financial and logistic support for the mujahideen and Chechen fighters. The Georgian government has not been able to establish effective control over the eastern part of the country. In early October, Georgian authorities extradited 13 Chechen guerrillas to Russia, moving closer to cooperation with Russia. President Eduard Shevardnadze in November 2001 promised to cooperate with Russia in apprehending Chechen separatist fighters and foreign mujahideen in the Pankisi Gorge—a region in northern Georgia that Russian authorities accuse Georgia of allowing Chechen terrorists to use as a safe haven—if Moscow furnishes Tbilisi with concrete information on their whereabouts and alleged wrongdoing. The United States has provided training and other assistance to help Georgian authorities implement tighter counterterrorism controls in problem areas.

Kidnappings continued to be a problem in Georgia. Two Spanish businessmen kidnapped on November 30, 2000, and held near the Pankisi Gorge were released on December 8, 2001. A Japanese journalist was taken hostage in the Pankisi Gorge in August 2001 and released on December 9.

INDONESIA

Immediately after the September 11 attacks, President Megawati expressed public support for a global war on terrorism and promised to implement UN counterterrorism resolutions. The Indonesian government, however, said it opposed unilateral U.S. military action in Afghanistan. The government has since taken limited action in support of international antiterrorist efforts. It made some effort to bring its legal and regulatory counterterrorism regime up to international standards. Although often slow to acknowledge terrorism problems at home, Indonesia also has taken some steps against terrorist operations within its borders. Police interviewed Abu Bakar Bashir, leader of the Majelis Mujahidin Indonesia, about his possible connections to Jemaah Islamiyah or Kumpulan Mujahidin Malaysia (KMM). Police arrested a Malaysian in August when he was wounded in an attempt to detonate a bomb at a Jakarta shopping mall. Two Malaysians were arrested in Indonesia thus far in conjunction with the bombing of the Atrium shopping mall. In addition, Indonesia has issued blocking orders on some of the terrorists as required under UN Security Council Resolution 1333, and bank compliance with freezing and reporting requirements is pending. At the end of 2001, the United States remained concerned that terrorists related to al-Qaeda, Jemaah Islamiyah, and KMM were operating in Indonesia.

Radical Indonesian Islamic groups threatened to attack the U.S. embassy and violently expel U.S. citizens and foreigners from the country in response to the U.S.-led campaign in Afghanistan. A strong Indonesian police presence prevented militant demonstrators from attacking the compound in October. One of the most vocal of the Indonesian groups, Front Pembela Islam (Islamic Defenders Front), had previously threatened U.S. citizens in the country.

Press accounts reported more than 30 major bombing incidents throughout the archipelago, including blasts in June and December 2001 at the U.S.-owned ExxonMobil facility in Aceh region. Unidentified gunmen also kidnapped and assassinated several prominent Indonesians during the year, including a Papuan independence activist and a leading Acehnese academic. Officials made little progress in apprehending and prosecuting those responsible for the bombings in 2001, having arrested only five persons. Laskar Jihad, Indonesia's largest radical group, remained a concern at year's end as a continuing source of domestic instability.

Communal violence between Christians and Muslims in the provinces of Maluku and Central Sulawesi continued in 2001. Several villages were razed in Sulawesi in November and December, leading to a major security response from the Indonesian military.

Indonesia and Australia signed a Memorandum of Understanding on counterterrorism cooperation in early 2002, preparing the way for concrete actions against the spread of terrorism in Southeast Asia. Fears of growing terrorist strength in Indonesia were confirmed on October 12, 2002, when two large bombs destroyed a nightclub on the island of Bali, killing more than 180 people. Suspicion soon focused on Jemaah Islamiyah, a regional militant Islamic group whose leader Abu Bakar Bashir has expressed great admiration for Osama bin Laden. It has been suggested that Jemaah Islamyiah, aided by al-Qaeda, may be planning widespread attacks against American and other foreign interests throughout the region during 2003.

MALAYSIA

Malaysian prime minister Mahathir Mohamad condemned the September 11, 2001, attacks as unjustified and made a first-ever visit to the U.S. embassy to sign the condolence book and express solidarity with the United States in the fight against international terrorism. The Malaysian government cooperated with international law enforcement and intelligence efforts, made strides in implementing financial counterterrorism measures, aggressively pursued domestic counterterrorism before and after September 11, and increased security surrounding the U.S. embassy and diplomatic residences. The government in October expressed strong reservations about U.S. military action in Afghanistan.

Malaysia suffered no incidents of international terrorism in 2001, although Malaysian police authorities made a series of arrests of persons associated with regional Islamic extremist groups with al-Qaeda links. Between May and December close to 30 members of the domestic Kumpulan Mujahidin Malaysia (KMM) group and an extremist wing of KMM were arrested for activities deemed threatening to Malaysia's national security. KMM detainees were being held on a wide range of charges, such as planning to wage a jihad, possessing weaponry, carrying out bombings and robberies, murdering a former state assemblyman, and planning attacks on foreigners, including U.S. citizens. Several of the arrested militants reportedly underwent military training in Afghanistan, and several key leaders of the KMM are also deeply involved in Jemaah Islamiyah. Jemaah Islamiyah is alleged to have ties not only to the KMM, but to Islamic extremist organizations in Indonesia, Singapore, and the Philippines; Malaysian police also have been investigating whether Jemaah Islamiyah has connections to September 11 terrorist suspect Zacarias Moussaoui.

Nineteen members of the Malaysian Islamist sect al-Ma'unah who were detained in July 2000 following the group's raid on two military armories in northern Malaysia were found guilty of treason in their bid to overthrow the government and establish an Islamic state. Sixteen members received life sentences while the remaining three were sentenced to death. Ten other members had pleaded guilty earlier to a reduced charge of preparing to wage war against the king and were sentenced to 10 years in prison, although the sentences of two were reduced to seven years on appeal. An additional 15 al-Ma'unah members remained in detention under the Internal Security Act.

PAKISTAN

After September 11, 2001, Pakistan pledged and provided full support for the coalition effort in the war on terrorism. Pakistan has afforded the United States unprecedented levels of cooperation by allowing the U.S. military to use bases within the country. Pakistan also worked closely with the United States to identify and detain extremists and to seal the border between Pakistan and Afghanistan. In February 2002, the United States and Pakistan agreed to institutionalize counterterrorism exchanges as a component of a newly created, wide-ranging Law Enforcement Joint Working Group.

As of November 2001, Islamabad had frozen more than $300,000 in terrorist-related assets in several banks. In December President Pervez Musharraf announced to the government a proposal to bring Pakistan's *madrassas* (religious schools)—some of which have served as breeding grounds for extremists—into the mainstream educational system. Pakistan also began sweeping police reforms, upgraded its immigration control system, and began work on new antiterrorist finance laws.

In December, Musharraf cracked down on "anti-Pakistan" extremists, and by January 2002, Pakistani authorities had arrested more than 2,000 including leaders of the Lashkar-e-Taiba (LT) and Jaish-e-Mohammed (JEM), both designated as Foreign Terrorist Organizations—as well as the Jamiat Ulema-i-Islami (JUI), a religious party with ties to the Taliban and Kashmiri militant groups. Pakistani support for Kashmiri militant groups designated as Foreign Terrorist Organizations waned after September 11. Questions remain, however, whether Musharraf's "get tough" policy with local militants and his stated pledge to oppose terrorism anywhere will be fully implemented and sustained.

In October 2002, a new coalition cabinet was installed, with the new prime minister being Mir Zafarullah Khan Jamali, a close ally of Musharraf. Although a more radical Islamic party had also made gains in the parliament, Musharraf and his civilian allies seem likely to be able to keep Pakistan reasonably aligned with U.S. interests in the war on terrorism.

PHILIPPINES

Philippine president Gloria Macapagal-Arroyo has been Southeast Asia's staunchest supporter of the international counterterrorism effort, offering medical assistance for coalition forces, blanket overflight clearance, and landing rights for U.S. aircraft involved in Operation Enduring Freedom. After marathon sessions, the Philippine Congress passed the Anti–Money Laundering Act of 2001 on September 29, 2001. This legislation overcame vocal opposition and passed quickly as the congress took steps to support the international effort to freeze terrorist assets throughout the world. In addition, the Philippine military, with U.S. training and assistance, in October intensified its offensive against the terrorist Abu Sayyaf Group (ASG), which has been involved in high-profile kidnappings for many years.

Small radical groups in the Philippines continued attacks against foreign and domestic targets in 2001. The ASG, designated a Foreign Terrorist Organization by the U.S. government in 1997 and redesignated in 1999 and 2001, kidnapped three U.S. citizens and 17 Filipinos in May from a resort on Palawan Island in the southern Philippines. Of the original 20 hostages kidnapped, 15 escaped or were ransomed; three hostages (including Guillermo Sobero, a US citizen) were murdered; and two U.S. citizens remained captive at year's end. The "Pentagon Gang" kidnap-for-ransom group, which is responsible for the kidnap and/or murder of Chinese, Italian, and Filipino nationals in 2001, was added to the U.S. Terrorism Exclusion List (TEL) in December.

Peace talks with the Communist Party of the Philippines/New People's Army (CPP/NPA) began in April 2001 but broke down in June after the NPA, the military wing of the CPP, claimed responsibility for the assassination on June 12 of a Philippine congressman from Cagayan. The Alex Boncayao Brigade (ABB)—a breakaway CPP/NPA faction—engaged in intermittent fighting with Philippine security forces during the year.

During the first half of 2002, the United States sent about 1,000 troops to assist the Philippine government in rooting out the Abu Sayyaf terrorists. Because of historic resentment of American colonialism, the U.S. troops were not allowed to fight, except in self-defense; their activities were restricted to providing training and technical support. The United States also offered a $5 million reward for capture of five top Abu Sayyaf leaders. By the time the withdrawal of the U.S. forces began in July, one major Abu Sayyaf leader had been killed, and the terrorists had been largely driven from the province of Basilan and parts of Mindanao. However, the group continued to operate in other areas. In one operation Philippine forces tried to rescue hostages, including Gracia and Martin Burnham, a Christian missionary couple who had been kidnapped the previous year. Gracia was among those freed, but Martin was killed in the fighting.

In October 2002, a number of small bomb and grenade attacks struck the capital at Manila. In response, President Arroyo called for strong new measures including a national ID card and the use of a plainclothes force of 500 "secret marshals." However, the government was embarrassed when it arrested perpetrators who turned out to have had little to do with the attacks.

In February 2003, the Pentagon announced a renewal of the antiterrorism offensive in the Philippines, which includes about 750 U.S. special forces and ground troops in an attempt to root out about 250 Abu Sayyaf members in Sulu Province, in the southern part of the country. The combat patrols will be backed up by a reserve force of 1,000 U.S. Marines on ships offshore, plus attack helicopters and aircraft. This effort seems to represent greater willingness of the Philippine government to allow direct U.S. action against terrorists.

Distinguishing between political and criminal motivation for many of the terrorist-related activities in the Philippines continued to be problematic, most notably in the numerous cases of kidnapping for ransom in the southern Philippines. Both Islamist separatists and Communist insurgents sought to extort funds from businesses in their operating areas, occasionally conducting reprisal operations if money was not paid.

SAUDI ARABIA

After September 11, 2001, and the realization that 15 of 19 of the attackers were Saudi citizens, the Saudi government reaffirmed its commitment to combat terrorism and responded positively to requests for concrete action in support of coalition efforts against al-Qaeda and the Taliban. The king, crown prince, government-appointed religious leaders, and official news media publicly and consistently condemned terrorism and refuted the few ideological and religious justifications made by some clerics.

In October, the Saudi government announced it would implement UN Security Council Resolution 1373, which called for, among other things, the freezing of terrorist-related funds. The Saudi government has ratified six of 12 UN conventions relating to terrorism and signed an additional three, including the UN Convention for the Suppression of the Financing of Terrorism. The remaining three conventions are under consideration. The Saudi government also pressed nongovernmental organizations and private agencies to implement existing Saudi laws that govern the soliciting of contributions for domestic or international humanitarian causes. These laws were not scrupulously enforced in the past, and some representatives of international terrorist organizations solicited and collected funds from private citizens and businesses in Saudi Arabia. In December, Saudi authorities agreed to cooperate with U.S. investigators in suspected cases of terrorism financing.

Several threats against U.S. civilian and military personnel and facilities in Saudi Arabia were reported in 2001, but none materialized. By year's end, Saudi authorities had finished an investigation into a series of bombings in Riyadh and the Eastern Province (Ash-Sharqiyah) and determined that the bombings were criminal rather than political in motivation. In October an apparent suicide bombing in al-Khubar killed one U.S. citizen and injured another. The Saudi investigation since revealed that the bomber was a Palestinian, acting alone, for unverified motives relating to the Palestinian *intifada.*

There was only one significant act of international terrorism in Saudi Arabia in 2001—the hijacking of a Turkish plane en route to Russia in March, perpetrated to protest Russian actions in Chechnya. Saudi forces stormed the plane, rescuing most of the passengers. The Saudi government denied requests from Russia and Turkey to extradite the hijackers.

During 2002, the United States put increasing pressure on Saudi Arabia to shut down the financial networks that have made the country such a rich source of funding for al-Qaeda and other terrorist groups. At the same time, however, Saudi Arabia has tried to resist U.S. pressure, particularly with regard to the possible war with Iraq, and there have been suggestions that Saudi Arabia may try to remove or reduce the U.S. military presence in the country.

The government of Saudi Arabia continued to investigate the June 1996 bombing of the Khubar Towers housing facility near Dhahran that killed 19 U.S. military personnel and wounded some 500 U.S. and Saudi personnel. The Saudi government continued to hold in detention a number of Saudi citizens linked to the attack, including Hani al-Sayegh, extradited by the United States in 1999.

SOMALIA

Somalia, a nation with no central government, represents a potential breeding ground as well as safe haven for terrorist networks. Civil war, clan conflict, and poverty have combined to turn Somalia into a "failed state," with no one group currently able to govern the entire country, poor or nonexistent law enforcement, and an inability to monitor the financial sector. Some major factions within Somalia have pledged to fight terrorism. However one indigenous group, al-Ittihad al-Islami (AIAI), is dedicated to creating an Islamic state in Somalia, has carried out terrorist acts in Ethiopia, and may have some ties to al-Qaeda. AIAI remains active in several parts of Somalia.

In July 2001, gunmen in Mogadishu attacked a World Food Program convoy, killing six persons and wounding several others. In March, extremists attacked a Medecins Sans Frontières medical charity facility, killing 11 persons, wounding 40, and taking nine hostages. The hostages were later released.

The need for cooperation among Somalia's neighbors in the Horn of Africa is obvious, given the long borders shared with Somalia by Djibouti, Ethiopia, and Kenya. These countries have—individually and, in cooperation with the United States—taken steps to close their ports of entry to potential terrorists, deny use of their banking systems to transfer terrorist-linked assets, and bring about the peaceful reconciliation and long-term stability that will remove the "failed-state" conditions currently found in Somalia.

YEMEN

Yemen immediately condemned the terrorist attacks of September 11, 2001. The Yemeni government also publicly condemned terrorism "in all its forms and sources," expressing support for the international fight against terror. Moreover, the Yemeni government took practical steps to enhance its intelligence and military cooperation with the United States.

During his official visit to Washington in November 2001, President Ali Abdallah Salih underscored Yemen's determination to function as an active partner in counterterrorism with the United States. Senior U.S. officials welcomed President Salih's commitment but made clear that any counterterrorism cooperation would be judged by its results.

The United States and Yemen continued their joint investigation of the attack in October 2000 on the USS *Cole*. Cooperation was productive, particularly in the aftermath of September 11, and established important linkages among the East Africa U.S. embassy bombings, the USS *Cole* bombing, and the September 11 attacks. The Yemeni government's assistance in providing investigators with key documents, allowing evidence to be processed in the United States and facilitating access to suspects made the discoveries possible.

In 2001, the Yemeni government arrested suspected terrorists and pledged to neutralize key al-Qaeda nodes in Yemen. Increased pressure from security services forced some terrorists to relocate. Yemen enhanced previously lax security at its borders, tightened its visa procedures, and prevented the travel to Afghanistan of potential terrorists. Authorities carefully monitored travelers returning from abroad and cracked down on foreigners who were residing in the country illegally or were suspected of engaging in terrorist activities.

On the education front, the government began integrating formerly autonomous private religious schools—some of which were propagating extremism—into the national educational system and tightened requirements for visiting foreign students. The Yemeni government asked a large number of foreign students from Arab or Islamic backgrounds to leave the country.

Several terrorist organizations maintained a presence in Yemen. HAMAS and the Palestine Islamic Jihad continued to maintain offices in Yemen legally. Other international terrorist groups with members operating illegally in Yemen included al-Qaeda, the Egyptian Islamic Jihad, al-Gama'at al-Islamiyya, Libyan opposition groups, and the Algerian Armed Islamic Group. An indigenous terrorist group, the Islamic Army of Aden, remained active in the country.

In November 2002, it was revealed that the United States had been operating the Predator, an unpiloted armed drone aircraft against suspected al-Qaeda targets in Yemen. In one attack, a Predator fired a Hellfire missile at a car, killing six al-Qaeda suspects.

APPENDIX B

BACKGROUND TO THE ATTACKS OF SEPTEMBER 11, 2001, AND HOMELAND SECURITY

PRECURSORS

Since the 1980s, a relatively low-level war had been fought between the United States and various Islamist terrorist groups, including some Palestinian outfits and the al-Qaeda international network founded by Osama bin Laden. The map indicates some of the major terrorist attacks and U.S. responses prior to September 11, 2001.

ATTACKS OF SEPTEMBER 11, 2001

On the morning of September 11, 2001, four hijacked U.S. airliners were steered toward domestic targets. Two airliners, American Airlines flight 11 and United Airlines flight 175, both originating in Logan Airport, Boston, and bound for Los Angeles, crashed into the twin towers of the World Trade Center in New York City. A third plane, American Airlines flight 77, flying from Washington, D.C.'s Dulles Airport to Los Angeles, was turned back by the hijackers and crashed into the Pentagon in the capital. The fourth aircraft, United Airlines flight 93, out of Newark, New Jersey, and bound for San Francisco, crashed in a field near Shanksville, Pennsylvania, apparently after passengers attacked the hijackers. It was seemingly bound for a target in Washington, D.C., most likely the Capitol. The accompanying map shows the flight paths of the four planes.

The attack on the Pentagon alone, gouging a path of destruction deep into one of the huge building's sides, would have been among the worst terrorist

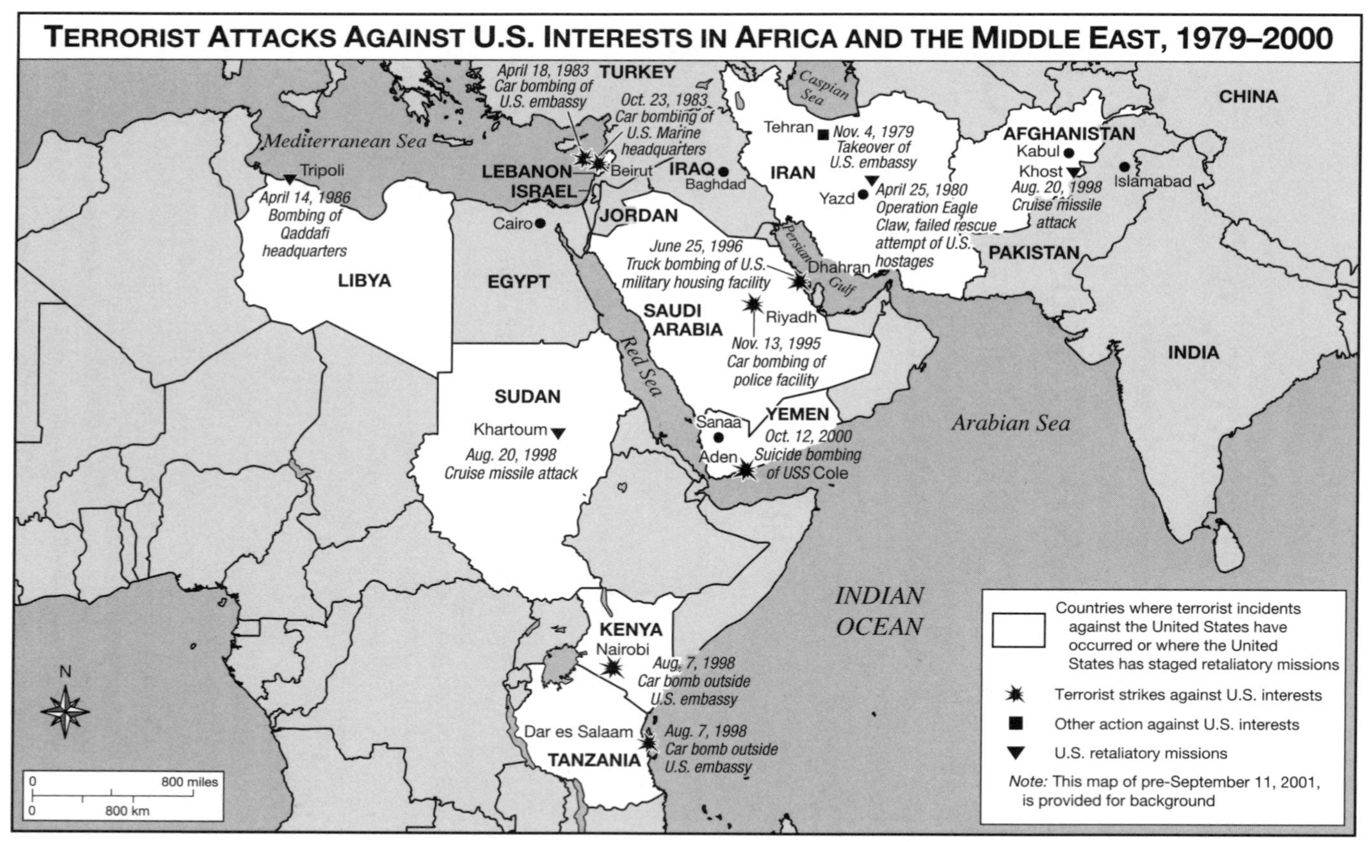
TERRORIST ATTACKS AGAINST U.S. INTERESTS IN AFRICA AND THE MIDDLE EAST, 1979–2000
April 18, 1983
Car bombing of U.S. embassy
TURKEY
Oct. 23, 1983
Car bombing of U.S. Marine headquarters
Caspian Sea
Tehran
Nov. 4, 1979
Takeover of U.S. embassy
AFGHANISTAN
Kabul
Khost
Aug. 20, 1998
Cruise missile attack
Islamabad
CHINA
Mediterranean Sea
Tripoli
April 14, 1986
Bombing of Qaddafi headquarters
LEBANON
ISRAEL
Beirut
IRAQ
Baghdad
IRAN
Yazd
April 25, 1980
Operation Eagle Claw, failed rescue attempt of U.S. hostages
PAKISTAN
Cairo
JORDAN
June 25, 1996
Truck bombing of U.S. military housing facility
Persian Gulf
Dhahran
LIBYA
EGYPT
SAUDI ARABIA
Riyadh
Nov. 13, 1995
Car bombing of police facility
INDIA
Red Sea
SUDAN
Khartoum
Aug. 20, 1998
Cruise missile attack
Sanaa
YEMEN
Oct. 12, 2000
Aden
Suicide bombing of USS Cole
Arabian Sea
INDIAN OCEAN
KENYA
Nairobi
Aug. 7, 1998
Car bomb outside U.S. embassy
Dar es Salaam
TANZANIA
Aug. 7, 1998
Car bomb outside U.S. embassy
N
0
800 miles
0
800 km
Countries where terrorist incidents against the United States have occurred or where the United States has staged retaliatory missions
Terrorist strikes against U.S. interests
Other action against U.S. interests
U.S. retaliatory missions
Note: This map of pre-September 11, 2001, is provided for background

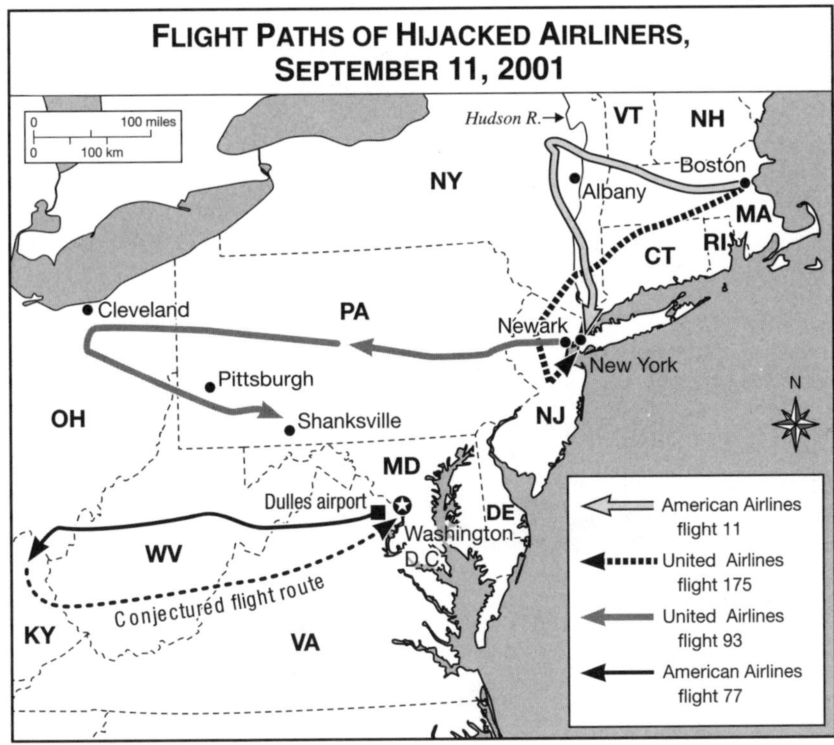

attacks on U.S. soil, comparable to the 1995 Oklahoma City bombing. This attack, however, was dwarfed by the impact of the two airliners on the World Trade Center towers and the consequently damage to the surrounding buildings. The accompanying map shows the buildings in the World Trade Center area destroyed or damaged in the attack.

HOMELAND SECURITY

There were two major responses to the terrorist attacks. The first was the military campaign in Afghanistan (see Appendix A), which has been extended to varying degrees to other countries such as Yemen and the Philippines. The other is the attempt to develop new organizational structures and procedures for detection and defense of terrorist attacks. During the fall of 2002, Congress struggled with the details of President George W. Bush's proposed Department of Homeland Security. Finally, in November, Congress passed legislation establishing the new department, and the president signed it. On January 25, 2003, former Pennsylvania governor Tom Ridge, who had headed the White House Office of Homeland Security following the September 11, 2001, attacks, was sworn in as head of the new cabinet-level department. As of early 2003, many details of the merging of 22 separate agencies into the new department remained to be worked out. The accompanying chart shows proposed Homeland Security expenditures by agency. The tables, provided by the White House Office of Homeland Security, give a breakdown of the 2002, 2002 supplemental, and proposed 2003 fiscal year funding for activities involved in homeland security. (The complete proposal is available online at http://www.whitehouse.gov/homeland/homeland_security_book.pdf.)

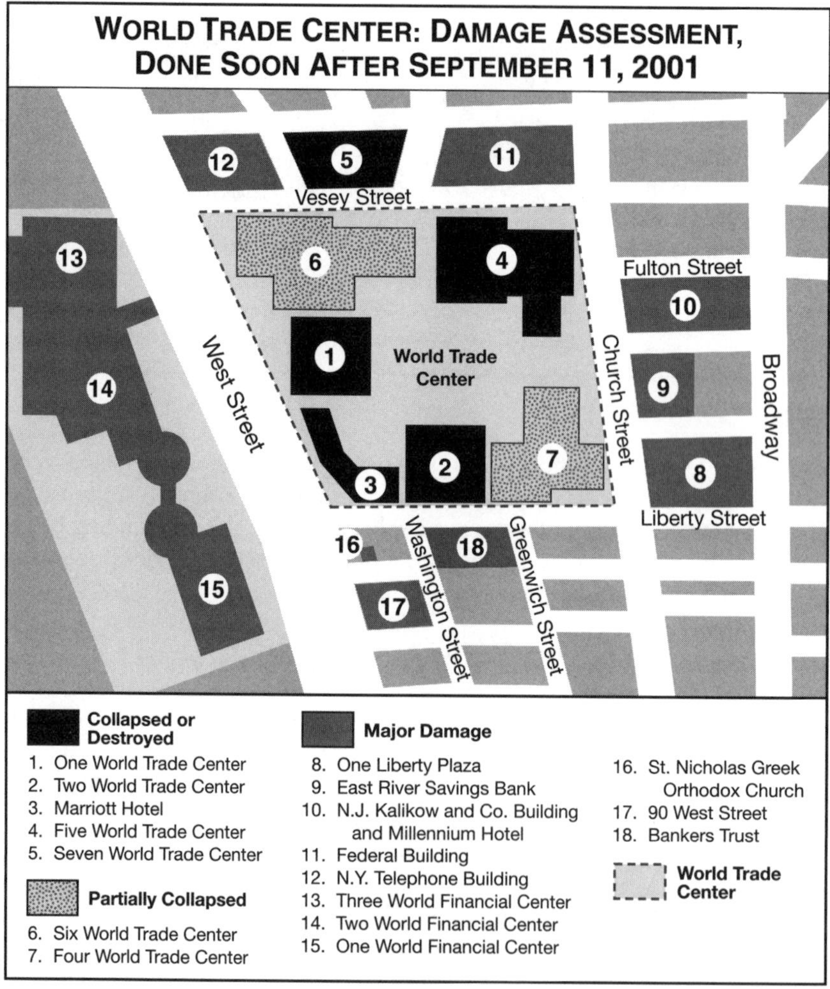

Appendix B

HOMELAND SECURITY: REQUEST BY AGENCY, DISTRIBUTION OF FISCAL YEAR 2003

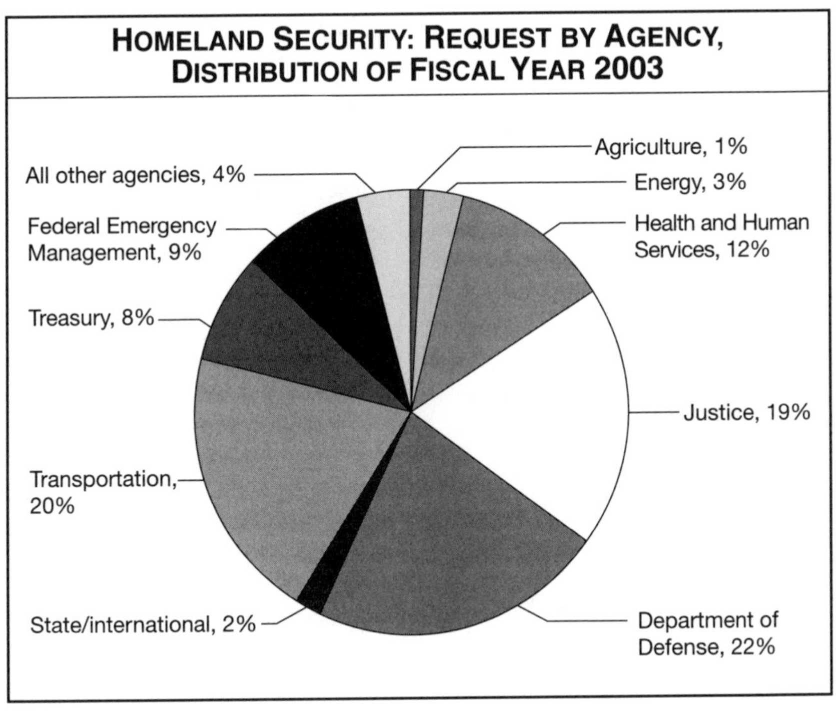

HOMELAND SECURITY—FUNDING BY INITIATIVE AREA (IN MILLIONS OF DOLLARS)

Initiative Area	2002 Enacted Base	Fiscal Year 2002 Supplemental	Fiscal Year 2003 Proposed
Supporting first responders	$291	$651	$3,500
Defending against biological terrorism	$1,408	$3,730	$5,898
Securing America's borders	$8,752	$1,194	$10,615
Using 21st-century technology to defend the homeland	$155	$75	$722
Aviation security	$1,543	$1,035	$4,800
Other non–Department of Defense (DOD) homeland security	$3,186	$2,384	$5,352
DOD homeland security (outside initiatives)	$4,201	$689	$6,815
TOTAL	**$19,535**	**$9,758**	**$37,702**

Source: White House Office of Homeland Security, 2002.

SUPPORTING FIRST RESPONDERS (IN MILLIONS OF DOLLARS)

Type of Support from the Federal Emergency Management Agency and the Justice Department	2002 Enacted Base	Fiscal Year 2002 Supplemental	Fiscal Year 2003 Proposed
Equip first-responder teams	$159	$188	$770
Train state and local first responders	$56	$171	$665
Assist emergency-response planning	$3	$24	$35
Enhance communications infrastructure to support interoperability	$0	$113	$1,365
Improve command and control to ensure effective procedures at response sites	$0	$17	$35
Fund interjurisdictional agreements and mutual aid compacts	$0	$0	$140
Disseminate information regarding emergency response to the public	$0	$0	$35
Provide federal technical assistance to state and local emergency response agencies	$36	$30	$350
Test readiness and provide feedback on performance	$7	$85	$105
Other	$30	$25	$0
TOTAL	**$291**	**$651**	**$3,500**

Source: White House Office of Homeland Security, 2002.

DEFENDING AGAINST BIOLOGICAL TERRORISM (IN MILLIONS OF DOLLARS)

Type	2002 Enacted Base	Fiscal Year 2002 Supplemental	Fiscal Year 2003 Proposed
Enhance medical communications and surveillance capabilities			
Info/communications systems	$34	$40	$202
Center of Research Excellence for Bio T/Emerging Infections (Bldg. O)			
Medical surveillance systems	$0	$0	$175
Epidemiologist exchange program	$0	$0	$10
Media/public information campaign	$0	$0	$5
Total	**$34**	**$40**	**$392**

Appendix B

Type	2002 Enacted Base	Fiscal Year 2002 Supplemental	Fiscal Year 2003 Proposed
Strengthen state and local health systems*			
Hospital infrastructure (labs and decontamination)	$0	$0	$283
State public health lab capacity	$13	$15	$200
Hospital Mutual Aid (planning/coordination)	$5	$135	$235
State epidemiological teams	$0	$0	$80
Educational incentives for curriculum	$0	$0	$60
Hospital training exercises with states	$0	$0	$73
Public health preparedness planning	$29	$810	$210
Metropolitan Medical Response System (MMRS)	$20	$0	$60
Total	**$67**	**$96**	**$1,202**
Research and development			
Basic and applied biodefense research (National Institutes of Health [NIH])	$93	$85	$1,080
Biodefense research infrastructure (NIH)	$0	$70	$336
Anthrax vaccine development (NIH and Centers for Disease Control and Prevention [CDC])	$18	$0	$268
Expedited drug approval/research (Food and Drug Administration [FDA])	$7	$41	$49
Research facility security upgrades (Department of Health and Human Services [HHS])	$0	$84	$100
Bioweapons defense/countermeasures (Department of Defense [DOD])		$120	
Agent identification, detection, and area monitoring (DOD)		$300	
Other research and development (DOD)	$182	$1	$182
Total	**$300**	**$28**	**$2,435**
Improve federal response			
National pharmaceutical stockpile	$52	$593	$300
Upgrade CDC capacity and labs—including BL 4 Lab	$18	$60	$109
Ft. Collins (HHS)	$0	$0	$100
Upgrade USAMRIID BL 4 Lab	$0	$0	$0
Improving decontamination methods (Environmental Protection Agency [EPA])	$0	$0	$75
Federal public health response teams	$6	$45	$43
Federal preparedness planning	$0	$0	$10
Total	**$76**	**$69**	**$637**

(continued)

DEFENDING AGAINST BIOLOGICAL TERRORISM *(CONTINUED)* (IN MILLIONS OF DOLLARS)

	2002 Enacted	Fiscal Year 2002	Fiscal Year 2003
Type	**Base**	**Supplemental**	**Proposed**
Other bioterrorism preparedness			
Smallpox vaccine purchase	$0	$512	$100
FDA food safety	$0	$97	$99
HHS rapid toxic screening	$5	$10	$15
Other HHS	$43	$40	$118
EPA drinking-water safety	$2	$88	$22
Postal Service decontamination	$0	$675	$0
Procurement of biodefense equipment and counterproliferation (DOD)	$337	$63	$337
Other agencies and activities	$544	$266	$542
TOTAL, BIOTERRORISM	**$1,408**	**$3,73**	**$5,898**

* Does not include funding in the first-responder initiative.

Source: White House Office of Homeland Security, 2002.

SECURING AMERICA'S BORDERS (IN MILLIONS OF DOLLARS)

	2002 Enacted	Fiscal Year 2002	Fiscal Year 2003
Activity by Area	**Base**	**Supplemental**	**Proposed**
Immigration and Naturalization Service (Justice Department): Enforcement*	**$4,111**	**$570**	**$4,963**
Select components:			
Border Patrol	$1,256	$68	$1,471
Inspections	$821	$125	$999
Detention and deportation	$1,029	$10	$1,100
Unspecified emergency-response requirements (supplemental funding only)		**$72**	
Entry-exit visa system (non-add)	$17	$13	$380
INS, including entry-exit visa system	$4,128	$583	$5,343
U.S. Customs Service (Treasury): Inspections	**$1,713**	**$364**	**$2,332**
Select components:			
Northern border security	$532	$117	$744
Customs maritime security	$355	$109	$684

Activity by Area	2002 Enacted Base	Fiscal Year 2002 Supplemental	Fiscal Year 2003 Proposed
U.S. Coast Guard (Transportation Department): Enforcement	**$2,631**	**$209**	**$2,913**
Select components:			
Ports, waterways, and coastal security	$473	$209	$1,213
Interdiction activities	$778	$0	$587
Capital programs	$636	$0	$725
Animal and Plant Health Inspection Service (Agriculture Department): Agricultural quarantine program (border inspections)	**$297**	**$50**	**$407**
TOTAL, BORDER SECURITY	**$8,752**	**$1,194**	**$10,615**
TOTAL (including entry-exit visa system)	**$8,769**	**$1,207**	**$10,995**

* For Fiscal Year 2003, includes $615 million proposed to be transferred to the detention trustee.

Source: White House Office of Homeland Security, 2002.

USING 21ST-CENTURY TECHNOLOGY TO DEFEND THE HOMELAND (IN MILLIONS OF DOLLARS)

Activity	2002 Enacted Base	Fiscal Year 2002 Supplemental	Fiscal Year 2003 Proposed
Assure broad access and horizontal sharing across selected federal databases:			
Program office to identify and commence process for information sharing (Commerce Department)	$0	$0	$20
Ensure procedures for and handling of sensitive homeland security information to facilitate information sharing while protecting sources:			
Secure videoconferencing with states (Federal Emergency Management Agency [FEMA])*	$0	$0	$7

(continued)

USING 21ST-CENTURY TECHNOLOGY TO DEFEND THE HOMELAND *(CONTINUED)* (IN MILLIONS OF DOLLARS)

	2002 Enacted	Fiscal Year 2002	Fiscal Year 2003
Activity	**Base**	**Supplemental**	**Proposed**
Entry-exit visa system (also represented as a non-add to the border initiative—funding to Immigration and Naturalization Service)	**$17**	**$13**	**$380**
Assure relevant information about threats is conveyed to state and local officials in a timely manner:	**$3**	**$0**	**$17**
Threat dissemination systems (Justice Department)	$3	$0	$10
Educational program for state and local officials (National Archives and Records Administration)	$0	$0	$7
Cyberspace security—Protecting our information infrastructure:	**$135**	**$62**	**$298**
National Infrastructure Simulation and Analysis Center (Energy Department)**	$0	$0	$20
Cyber Warning Intelligence Network (Department of Defense [DOD])	$0	$0	$30
Priority wireless access (DOD)	$0	$0	$60
GovNet feasibility study (General Services Administration [GSA])	$0	$0	$5
Cybercorps (National Science Foundation)	$11	$0	$11
Federal computer incident response capability (GSA)	$10	$0	$11
National Infrastructure Protection Center, NIPC (Federal Bureau of Investigation)	$72	$61	$125
Computer Security Division (National Institute of Standards and Technology)	$11	$0	$15
Critical Infrastructure Assurance Office (Commerce Department)	$5	$1	$7
Other IT/information sharing	$26	$0	$15
TOTAL, IT/INFORMATION SHARING	**$155**	**$75**	**$722**

* Includes funding under the first-responder initiative.

** Does not include $20 million in supplemental funding provided to DOD for the National Infrastructure Simulation and Analysis Center. Funds are included in the DOD total.

Source: White House Office of Homeland Security, 2002.

Appendix B

HOMELAND SECURITY—NONDEFENSE FUNDING OUTSIDE OF INITIATIVE AREA (IN MILLIONS OF DOLLARS)

	2002 Enacted	Fiscal Year 2002	Fiscal Year 2003
Other Activity	**Base**	**Supplemental**	**Proposed**
Department of Agriculture: Physical and IT security	$12	$106	$94
Department of Commerce: Physical security, IT security, and CIP	$73	$16	$88
Department of Energy: Energy security, physical security, IT security, and R&D (nonbioterrorism)	$744	$142	$884
Department of the Interior: Safeguarding facilities and national landmarks	$26	$89	$94
International agencies: Domestic physical security and visa programs	$618	$80	$814
Department of Justice: Law enforcement and other activities	$585	$809	$1,643
Department of Transportation: Hardening modes (nonaviation) and R&D	$7	$132	$14
Department of the Treasury: Law enforcement and other activities	$386	$251	$521
Corps of Engineers: Hardening and security	$0	$139	$65
Executive Office of the President: Physical and IT security and the Office of Homeland Security	$2	$58	$48
Federal Emergency Management Agency: Salaries and expenses and the Office of National Preparedness	$0	$25	$50
General Services Administration: Federal facilities security	$109	$127	$326
National Aeronautics and Space Administration: Security of assets	$121	$109	$129
National Science Foundation: CIP research and physical and IT security	$198	$0	$197
Social Security Administration: Critical infrastructure protection	$102	$3	$119
Corporation for National and Community Service	$29	$0	$118
District of Columbia: Emergency planning and response for the Capitol region	$13	$200	$15
Nuclear Regulatory Commission	$5	$36	$34
Other Homeland Security	$157	$63	$99
TOTAL, OTHER HOMELAND SECURITY	**$3,186**	**$2,384**	**$5,352**

Source: White House Office of Homeland Security, 2002.

APPENDIX C

USA PATRIOT ACT OF 2001

Title I: Enhancing Domestic Security Against Terrorism—Establishes in the Treasury the Counterterrorism Fund.

(Section 102) Expresses the sense of Congress that: (1) the civil rights and liberties of all Americans, including Arab Americans, must be protected, and that every effort must be taken to preserve their safety; (2) any acts of violence or discrimination against any Americans be condemned; and (3) the Nation is called upon to recognize the patriotism of fellow citizens from all ethnic, racial, and religious backgrounds.

(Section 103) Authorizes appropriations for the Federal Bureau of Investigation's (FBI) Technical Support Center.

(Section 104) Authorizes the Attorney General to request the Secretary of Defense to provide assistance in support of Department of Justice (DOJ) activities relating to the enforcement of Federal criminal code (code) provisions regarding the use of weapons of mass destruction during an emergency situation involving a weapon (currently, chemical weapon) of mass destruction.

(Section 105) Requires the Director of the U.S. Secret Service to take actions to develop a national network of electronic crime task forces throughout the United States to prevent, detect, and investigate various forms of electronic crimes, including potential terrorist attacks against critical infrastructure and financial payment systems.

(Section 106) Modifies provisions relating to presidential authority under the International Emergency Powers Act to: (1) authorize the President, when the United States is engaged in armed hostilities or has been attacked by a foreign country or foreign nationals, to confiscate any property subject to U.S. jurisdiction of a foreign person, organization, or country that he determines has planned, authorized, aided, or engaged in such hostilities or attacks (the rights to which shall vest in such agency or person as the President may designate); and (2) provide that, in any judicial review of a determination made under such provisions, if the determination was based on classified information such information may be submitted to the reviewing court ex parte and in camera.

Title II: Enhanced Surveillance Procedures—Amends the Federal criminal code to authorize the interception of wire, oral, and electronic communications for the production of evidence of: (1) specified chemical weapons or terrorism offenses; and (2) computer fraud and abuse. (Section 203) Amends rule 6 of the Federal Rules of Criminal Procedure (FRCrP) to permit the sharing of grand jury information that involves foreign intelligence or counterintelligence with Federal law enforcement, intelligence, protective, immigration, national defense, or national security officials (such officials), subject to specified requirements.

Authorizes an investigative or law enforcement officer, or an attorney for the Government, who, by authorized means, has obtained knowledge of the contents of any wire, oral, or electronic communication or evidence derived therefrom to disclose such contents to such officials to the extent that such contents include foreign intelligence or counterintelligence. Directs the Attorney General to establish procedures for the disclosure of information (pursuant to the code and the FRCrP) that identifies a United States person, as defined in the Foreign Intelligence Surveillance Act of 1978 (FISA).

Authorizes the disclosure of foreign intelligence or counterintelligence obtained as part of a criminal investigation to such officials.

(Section 204) Clarifies that nothing in code provisions regarding pen registers shall be deemed to affect the acquisition by the Government of specified foreign intelligence information, and that procedures under FISA shall be the exclusive means by which electronic surveillance and the interception of domestic wire and oral (current law) and electronic communications may be conducted.

(Section 205) Authorizes the Director of the FBI to expedite the employment of personnel as translators to support counter-terrorism investigations and operations without regard to applicable Federal personnel requirements. Requires: (1) the Director to establish such security requirements as necessary for such personnel; and (2) the Attorney General to report to the House and Senate Judiciary Committees regarding translators.

(Section 206) Grants roving surveillance authority under FISA after requiring a court order approving an electronic surveillance to direct any person to furnish necessary information, facilities, or technical assistance in circumstances where the Court finds that the actions of the surveillance target may have the effect of thwarting the identification of a specified person.

(Section 207) Increases the duration of FISA surveillance permitted for non-U.S. persons who are agents of a foreign power.

(Section 208) Increases (from seven to 11) the number of district court judges designated to hear applications for and grant orders approving electronic surveillance. Requires that no fewer than three reside within 20 miles of the District of Columbia.

(Section 209) Permits the seizure of voice-mail messages under a warrant.

(Section 210) Expands the scope of subpoenas for records of electronic communications to include the length and types of service utilized, temporarily assigned network addresses, and the means and source of payment (including any credit card or bank account number).

(Section 211) Amends the Communications Act of 1934 to permit specified disclosures to Government entities, except for records revealing cable subscriber selection of video programming from a cable operator.

(Section 212) Permits electronic communication and remote computing service providers to make emergency disclosures to a governmental entity of customer electronic communications to protect life and limb.

(Section 213) Authorizes Federal district courts to allow a delay of required notices of the execution of a warrant if immediate notice may have an adverse result and under other specified circumstances.

(Section 214) Prohibits use of a pen register or trap and trace devices in any investigation to protect against international terrorism or clandestine intelligence activities that is conducted solely on the basis of activities protected by the first amendment to the U.S. Constitution.

(Section 215) Authorizes the Director of the FBI (or designee) to apply for a court order requiring production of certain business records for foreign intelligence and international terrorism investigations. Requires the Attorney General to report to the House and Senate Intelligence and Judiciary Committees semi-annually.

(Section 216) Amends the code to: (1) require a trap and trace device to restrict recoding or decoding so as not to include the contents of a wire or electronic communication; (2) apply a court order for a pen register or trap and trace devices to any person or entity providing wire or electronic communication service in the United States whose assistance may facilitate execution of the order; (3) require specified records kept on any pen register or trap and trace device on a packet-switched data network of a provider of electronic communication service to the public; and (4) allow a trap and trace device to identify the source (but not the contents) of a wire or electronic communication.

(Section 217) Makes it lawful to intercept the wire or electronic communication of a computer trespasser in certain circumstances.

(Section 218) Amends FISA to require an application for an electronic surveillance order or search warrant to certify that a significant purpose (currently, the sole or main purpose) of the surveillance is to obtain foreign intelligence information.

(Section 219) Amends rule 41 of the FRCrP to permit Federal magistrate judges in any district in which terrorism-related activities may have occurred to issue search warrants for searches within or outside the district.

(Section 220) Provides for nationwide service of search warrants for electronic evidence.

(Section 221) Amends the Trade Sanctions Reform and Export Enhancement Act of 2000 to extend trade sanctions to the territory of Afghanistan controlled by the Taliban.

(Section 222) Specifies that: (1) nothing in this Act shall impose any additional technical obligation or requirement on a provider of a wire or electronic communication service or other person to furnish facilities or technical assistance; and (2) a provider of such service, and a landlord, custodian, or other person who furnishes such facilities or technical assistance, shall be reasonably compensated for such reasonable expenditures incurred in providing such facilities or assistance.

(Section 223) Amends the Federal criminal code to provide for administrative discipline of Federal officers or employees who violate prohibitions against unauthorized disclosures of information gathered under this Act. Provides for civil actions against the United States for damages by any person aggrieved by such violations.

(Section 224) Terminates this title on December 31, 2005, except with respect to any particular foreign intelligence investigation beginning before that date, or any particular offense or potential offense that began or occurred before it.

(Section 225) Amends the Foreign Intelligence Surveillance Act of 1978 to prohibit a cause of action in any court against a provider of a wire or electronic communication service, landlord, custodian, or any other person that furnishes any information, facilities, or technical assistance in accordance with a court order or request for emergency assistance under such Act (for example, with respect to a wiretap).

Title III: International Money Laundering Abatement and Anti-Terrorist Financing Act of 2001—International Money Laundering Abatement and Financial Anti-Terrorism Act of 2001—Sunsets this Act after the first day of FY 2005 if Congress enacts a specified joint resolution to that effect.

Subtitle A: International Counter Money Laundering and Related Measures—Amends Federal law governing monetary transactions to prescribe procedural guidelines under which the Secretary of the Treasury (the Secretary) may require domestic financial institutions and agencies to take specified measures if the Secretary finds that reasonable grounds exist for concluding that jurisdictions, financial institutions, types of accounts, or transactions operating outside or within the United States, are of primary money laundering concern. Includes mandatory disclosure of specified information relating to certain correspondent accounts.

(Section 312) Mandates establishment of due diligence mechanisms to detect and report money laundering transactions through private banking accounts and correspondent accounts.

(Section 313) Prohibits U.S. correspondent accounts with foreign shell banks.

(Section 314) Instructs the Secretary to adopt regulations to encourage further cooperation among financial institutions, their regulatory authorities, and law enforcement authorities, with the specific purpose of encouraging regulatory authorities and law enforcement authorities to share with financial institutions information regarding individuals, entities, and organizations engaged in or reasonably suspected (based on credible evidence) of engaging in terrorist acts or money laundering activities. Authorizes such regulations to create procedures for cooperation and information sharing on matters specifically related to the finances of terrorist groups as well as their relationships with international narcotics traffickers.

Requires the Secretary to distribute annually to financial institutions a detailed analysis identifying patterns of suspicious activity and other investigative insights derived from suspicious activity reports and investigations by Federal, State, and local law enforcement agencies.

(Section 315) Amends Federal criminal law to include foreign corruption offenses as money laundering crimes.

(Section 316) Establishes the right of property owners to contest confiscation of property under law relating to confiscation of assets of suspected terrorists.

(Section 317) Establishes Federal jurisdiction over: (1) foreign money launderers (including their assets held in the United States); and (2) money that is laundered through a foreign bank.

(Section 319) Authorizes the forfeiture of money laundering funds from interbank accounts. Requires a covered financial institution, upon request of the appropriate Federal banking agency, to make available within 120 hours all pertinent information related to anti-money laundering compliance by the institution or its customer. Grants the Secretary summons and subpoena powers over foreign banks that maintain a correspondent bank in the United States. Requires a covered financial institution to terminate within ten business days any correspondent relationship with a foreign bank after receipt of written notice that the foreign bank has failed to comply with certain judicial proceedings. Sets forth civil penalties for failure to terminate such relationship.

(Section 321) Subjects to record and report requirements for monetary instrument transactions: (1) any credit union; and (2) any futures commission merchant, commodity trading advisor, and commodity pool operator registered, or required to register, under the Commodity Exchange Act.

(Section 323) Authorizes Federal application for restraining orders to preserve the availability of property subject to a foreign forfeiture or confiscation judgment.

(Section 325) Authorizes the Secretary to issue regulations to ensure that concentration accounts of financial institutions are not used to prevent association of the identity of an individual customer with the movement of funds of which the customer is the direct or beneficial owner.

(Section 326) Directs the Secretary to issue regulations prescribing minimum standards for financial institutions regarding customer identity in connection with the opening of accounts. Requires the Secretary to report to Congress on: (1) the most timely and effective way to require foreign nationals to provide domestic financial institutions and agencies with appropriate and accurate information; (2) whether to require foreign nationals to obtain an identification number (similar to a Social Security or tax identification number) before opening an account with a domestic financial institution; and (3) a system for domestic financial institutions and agencies to review Government agency information to verify the identities of such foreign nationals.

(Section 327) Amends the Bank Holding Company Act of 1956 and the Federal Deposit Insurance Act to require consideration of the effectiveness of a company or companies in combating money laundering during reviews of proposed bank shares acquisitions or mergers.

(Section 328) Directs the Secretary take reasonable steps to encourage foreign governments to require the inclusion of the name of the originator in wire transfer instructions sent to the United States and other countries, with the information to remain with the transfer from its origination until the point of disbursement. Requires annual progress reports to specified congressional committees.

(Section 329) Prescribes criminal penalties for Federal officials or employees who seek or accept bribes in connection with administration of this title.

(Section 330) Urges U.S. negotiations for international cooperation in investigations of money laundering, financial crimes, and the finances of terrorist groups, including record sharing by foreign banks with U.S. law enforcement officials and domestic financial institution supervisors.

Subtitle B: Bank Secrecy Act Amendments and Related Improvements—Amends Federal law known as the Bank Secrecy Act to revise requirements for civil liability immunity for voluntary financial institution disclosure of suspicious activities. Authorizes the inclusion of suspicions of illegal activity in written employment references.

(Section 352) Authorizes the Secretary to exempt from minimum standards for anti-money laundering programs any financial institution not subject to certain regulations governing financial recordkeeping and reporting of currency and foreign transactions.

(Section 353) Establishes civil penalties for violations of geographic targeting orders and structuring transactions to evade certain recordkeeping requirements. Lengthens the effective period of geographic targeting orders from 60 to 180 days.

(Section 355) Amends the Federal Deposit Insurance Act to permit written employment references to contain suspicions of involvement in illegal activity.

(Section 356) Instructs the Secretary to: (1) promulgate regulations requiring registered securities brokers and dealers, futures commission merchants, commodity trading advisors, and commodity pool operators, to file reports of suspicious financial transactions; (2) report to Congress on the role of the Internal Revenue Service in the administration of the Bank Secrecy Act; and (3) share monetary instruments transactions records upon request of a U.S. intelligence agency for use in the conduct of intelligence or counterintelligence activities, including analysis, to protect against international terrorism.

(Section 358) Amends the Right to Financial Privacy Act to permit the transfer of financial records to other agencies or departments upon certification that the records are relevant to intelligence or counterintelligence activities related to international terrorism.

Amends the Fair Credit Reporting Act to require a consumer reporting agency to furnish all information in a consumer's file to a government agency upon certification that the records are relevant to intelligence or counterintelligence activities related to international terrorism.

(Section 359) Subjects to mandatory records and reports on monetary instruments transactions any licensed sender of money or any other person who engages as a business in the transmission of funds, including through an informal value transfer banking system or network (e.g., hawala) of people facilitating the transfer of money domestically or internationally outside of the conventional financial institutions system.

(Section 360) Authorizes the Secretary to instruct the United States Executive Director of each international financial institution to use his or her voice and vote to: (1) support the use of funds for a country (and its institutions) which contributes to U.S. efforts against international terrorism; and (2) require an auditing of disbursements to ensure that no funds are paid to persons who commit or support terrorism.

(Section 361) Makes the existing Financial Crimes Enforcement Network a bureau in the Department of the Treasury.

(Section 362) Directs the Secretary to establish a highly secure network in the Network that allows financial institutions to file certain reports and receive alerts and other information regarding suspicious activities warranting immediate and enhanced scrutiny.

(Section 363) Increases to $1 million the maximum civil penalties (currently $10,000) and criminal fines (currently $250,000) for money laundering. Sets a minimum civil penalty and criminal fine of double the amount of the illegal transaction.

(Section 364) Amends the Federal Reserve Act to provide for uniform protection authority for Federal Reserve facilities, including law enforcement officers authorized to carry firearms and make warrantless arrests.

(Section 365) Amends Federal law to require reports relating to coins and currency of more than $10,000 received in a nonfinancial trade or business.

(Section 366) Directs the Secretary to study and report to Congress on: (1) the possible expansion of the currency transaction reporting requirements exemption system; and (2) methods for improving financial institution utilization of the system as a way of reducing the submission of currency transaction reports that have little or no value for law enforcement purposes.

Subtitle C: Currency Crimes—Establishes as a bulk cash smuggling felony the knowing concealment and attempted transport (or transfer) across U.S. borders of currency and monetary instruments in excess of $10,000, with intent to evade specified currency reporting requirements.

(Section 372) Changes from discretionary to mandatory a court's authority to order, as part of a criminal sentence, forfeiture of all property involved in certain currency reporting offenses. Leaves a court discretion to order civil forfeitures in money laundering cases.

(Section 373) Amends the Federal criminal code to revise the prohibition of unlicensed (currently, illegal) money transmitting businesses.

(Section 374) Increases the criminal penalties for counterfeiting domestic and foreign currency and obligations.

(Section 376) Amends the Federal criminal code to extend the prohibition against the laundering of money instruments to specified proceeds of terrorism.

(Section 377) Grants the United States extraterritorial jurisdiction where: (1) an offense committed outside the United States involves an access device issued, owned, managed, or controlled by a financial institution, account issuer, credit card system member, or other entity within U.S. jurisdiction; and (2) the person committing the offense transports, delivers, conveys, transfers to or through, or otherwise stores, secrets, or holds within U.S. jurisdiction any article used to assist in the commission of the offense or the proceeds of such offense or property derived from it.

Title IV: Protecting the Border—Subtitle A: Protecting the Northern Border—Authorizes the Attorney General to waive certain Immigration and Naturalization Service (INS) personnel caps with respect to ensuring security needs on the Northern border.

(Section 402) Authorizes appropriations to: (1) triple the number of Border Patrol, Customs Service, and INS personnel (and support facilities) at points of entry and along the Northern border; and (2) INS and Customs for related border monitoring technology and equipment.

(Section 403) Amends the Immigration and Nationality Act to require the Attorney General and the Federal Bureau of Investigation (FBI) to provide the Department of State and INS with access to specified criminal history extracts in order to determine whether or not a visa or admissions applicant has a criminal history. Directs the FBI to provide periodic extract updates. Provides for confidentiality.

Directs the Attorney General and the Secretary of State to develop a technology standard to identify visa and admissions applicants, which shall be the basis for an electronic system of law enforcement and intelligence sharing system available to consular, law enforcement, intelligence, and Federal border inspection personnel.

(Section 404) Amends the Department of Justice Appropriations Act, 2001 to eliminate certain INS overtime restrictions.

(Section 405) Directs the Attorney General to report on the feasibility of enhancing the Integrated Automated Fingerprint Identification System and other identification systems to better identify foreign individuals in connection with U.S. or foreign criminal investigations before issuance of a visa to, or permitting such person's entry or exit from, the United States. Authorizes appropriations.

Subtitle B: Enhanced Immigration Provisions—Amends the Immigration and Nationality Act to broaden the scope of aliens ineligible for admission or deportable due to terrorist activities to include an alien who: (1) is a representative of a political, social, or similar group whose political endorsement of terrorist acts undermines U.S. antiterrorist efforts; (2) has used a position of prominence to endorse terrorist activity, or to persuade others to support such activity in a way that undermines U.S. antiterrorist efforts (or the child or spouse of such an alien under specified circumstances); or (3) has been associated with a terrorist organization and intends to engage in threatening activities while in the United States.

(Section 411) Includes within the definition of "terrorist activity" the use of any weapon or dangerous device.

Redefines "engage in terrorist activity" to mean, in an individual capacity or as a member of an organization, to: (1) commit or to incite to commit, under circumstances indicating an intention to cause death or serious bodily injury, a terrorist activity; (2) prepare or plan a terrorist activity; (3) gather information on potential targets for terrorist activity; (4) solicit funds or other things of value for a terrorist activity or a terrorist organization (with an exception for lack of knowledge); (5) solicit any individual to engage in prohibited conduct or for terrorist organization membership (with an exception for lack of knowledge); or (6) commit an act that the actor knows, or reasonably should know, affords material support, including a safe house, transportation, communications, funds, transfer of funds or other material financial benefit, false documentation or identification, weapons (including chemical, biological, or radiological weapons), explosives, or training for the commission of a terrorist activity; to any individual who the actor knows or reasonably should know has committed or plans to commit a terrorist activity; or to a terrorist organization (with an exception for lack of knowledge).

Defines "terrorist organization" as a group: (1) designated under the Immigration and Nationality Act or by the Secretary of State; or (2) a group of two or more individuals, whether related or not, which engages in terrorist-related activities.

Provides for the retroactive application of amendments under this Act. Stipulates that an alien shall not be considered inadmissible or deportable because of a relationship to an organization that was not designated as a terrorist organization prior to enactment of this Act. States that the amendments under this section shall apply to all aliens in exclusion or deportation proceedings on or after the date of enactment of this Act.

Directs the Secretary of State to notify specified congressional leaders seven days prior to designating an organization as a terrorist organization. Provides for organization redesignation or revocation.

(Section 412) Provides for mandatory detention until removal from the United States (regardless of any relief from removal) of an alien certified by the Attorney General as a suspected terrorist or threat to national security. Requires release of such alien after seven days if removal proceedings have not commenced, or the alien has not been charged with a criminal offense. Authorizes detention for additional periods of up to six months of an alien not likely to be deported in the reasonably foreseeable future only if release will threaten U.S. national security or the safety of the community or any person. Limits judicial review to habeas corpus proceedings in the U.S. Supreme Court, the U.S. Court of Appeals for the District of Columbia, or any district court with jurisdiction to entertain a habeas corpus petition. Restricts to the U.S. Court of Appeals for the District of Columbia the right of appeal of any final order by a circuit or district judge.

(Section 413) Authorizes the Secretary of State, on a reciprocal basis, to share criminal- and terrorist-related visa lookout information with foreign governments.

(Section 414) Declares the sense of Congress that the Attorney General should: (1) fully implement the integrated entry and exit data system for airports, seaports, and land border ports of entry with all deliberate speed; and (2) begin immediately establishing the Integrated Entry and Exit Data System Task Force. Authorizes appropriations.

Requires the Attorney General and the Secretary of State, in developing the integrated entry and exit data system, to focus on the use of biometric technology and the development of tamper-resistant documents readable at ports of entry.

(Section 415) Amends the Immigration and Naturalization Service Data Management Improvement Act of 2000 to include the Office of Homeland Security in the Integrated Entry and Exit Data System Task Force.

(Sec. 416) Directs the Attorney General to implement fully and expand the foreign student monitoring program to include other approved educational institutions like air flight, language training, or vocational schools.

(Section 417) Requires audits and reports on implementation of the mandate for machine readable passports.

(Section 418) Directs the Secretary of State to: (1) review how consular officers issue visas to determine if consular shopping is a problem; and (2) if it is a problem, take steps to address it, and report on them to Congress.

Subtitle C: Preservation of Immigration Benefits for Victims of Terrorism—Authorizes the Attorney General to provide permanent resident status through the special immigrant program to an alien (and spouse, child, or grandparent under specified circumstances) who was the beneficiary of a petition filed on or before September 11, 2001, to grant the alien permanent residence as an employer-sponsored immigrant or of an application for labor certification if the petition or application was rendered null because of the disability of the beneficiary or loss of employment due to physical damage to, or destruction of, the business of the petitioner or applicant as a direct result of the terrorist attacks on September 11, 2001 (September attacks), or because of the death of the petitioner or applicant as a direct result of such attacks. (Section 422) States that an alien who was legally in a nonimmigrant status and was disabled as a direct result of the September attacks may remain in the United States until his or her normal status termination date or September 11, 2002. Includes in such extension the spouse or child of such an alien or of an alien who was killed in such attacks. Authorizes employment during such period. Extends specified immigration-related deadlines and other filing requirements for an alien (and spouse and child) who was directly prevented from meeting such requirements as a result of the September attacks respecting: (1) nonimmigrant status and status revision; (2) diversity immigrants; (3) immigrant visas; (4) parolees; and (5) voluntary departure.

(Section 423) Waives, under specified circumstances, the requirement that an alien spouse (and child) of a U.S. citizen must have been married for at least two years prior to such citizen's death in order to maintain immediate relative status if such citizen died as a direct result of the September attacks. Provides for: (1) continued family-sponsored immigrant eligibility for the spouse, child, or unmarried son or daughter of a permanent resident who died as a direct result of such attacks; and (2) continued eligibility for adjustment of status for the spouse and child of an employment-based immigrant who died similarly.

(Section 424) Amends the Immigration and Nationality Act to extend the visa categorization of "child" for aliens with petitions filed on or before September 11, 2001, for aliens whose 21st birthday is in September 2001 (90 days), or after September 2001 (45 days).

(Section 425) Authorizes the Attorney General to provide temporary administrative relief to an alien who, as of September, 10, 2001, was lawfully in the United States and was the spouse, parent, or child of an individual who died or was disabled as a direct result of the September attacks.

(Section 426) Directs the Attorney General to establish evidentiary guidelines for death, disability, and loss of employment or destruction of business in connection with the provisions of this subtitle.

(Section 427) Prohibits benefits to terrorists or their family members.

Title V: Removing Obstacles to Investigating Terrorism—Authorizes the Attorney General to pay rewards from available funds pursuant to public advertisements for assistance to DOJ to combat terrorism and defend the Nation against terrorist acts, in accordance with procedures and regulations established or issued by the Attorney General, subject to specified conditions, including a prohibition against any such reward of $250,000 or more from being made or offered without the personal approval of either the Attorney General or the President.

(Section 502) Amends the State Department Basic Authorities Act of 1956 to modify the Department of State rewards program to authorize rewards for information leading to: (1) the dismantling of a terrorist organization in whole or significant part; and (2) the identification or location of an individual who holds a key leadership position in a terrorist organization. Raises the limit on rewards if the Secretary of State determines that a larger sum is necessary to combat terrorism or defend the Nation against terrorist acts.

(Section 503) Amends the DNA Analysis Backlog Elimination Act of 2000 to qualify a Federal terrorism offense for collection of DNA for identification.

(Section 504) Amends FISA to authorize consultation among Federal law enforcement officers regarding information acquired from an electronic surveillance or physical search in terrorism and related investigations or protective measures.

(Section 505) Allows the FBI to request telephone toll and transactional records, financial records, and consumer reports in any investigation to protect against international terrorism or clandestine intelligence activities only if the investigation is not conducted solely on the basis of activities protected by the first amendment to the U.S. Constitution.

(Section 506) Revises U.S. Secret Service jurisdiction with respect to fraud and related activity in connection with computers. Grants the FBI primary authority to investigate specified fraud and computer related activity for cases involving espionage, foreign counter-intelligence, information protected against unauthorized disclosure for reasons of national defense or foreign relations, or restricted data, except for offenses affecting Secret Service duties.

(Section 507) Amends the General Education Provisions Act and the National Education Statistics Act of 1994 to provide for disclosure of educational records to the Attorney General in a terrorism investigation or prosecution.

Title VI: Providing for Victims of Terrorism, Public Safety Officers, and Their Families—Subtitle A: Aid to Families of Public Safety Officers—Provides for expedited payments for: (1) public safety officers involved in the prevention, investigation, rescue, or recovery efforts related to a terrorist attack; and (2) heroic public safety officers. Increases Public Safety Officers Benefit Program payments.

Subtitle B: Amendments to the Victims of Crime Act of 1984—Amends the Victims of Crime Act of 1984 to: (1) revise provisions regarding the allocation of funds for compensation and assistance, location of compensable crime, and the relationship of crime victim compensation to means-tested Federal benefit programs and to the September 11th victim compensation fund; and (2) establish an antiterrorism emergency reserve in the Victims of Crime Fund.

Title VII: Increased Information Sharing for Critical Infrastructure Protection—Amends the Omnibus Crime Control and Safe Streets Act of 1968 to extend Bureau of Justice Assistance regional information sharing system grants to systems that enhance the investigation and prosecution abilities of participating Federal, State, and local law enforcement agencies in addressing multi-jurisdictional terrorist conspiracies and activities. Authorizes appropriations.

Title VIII: Strengthening the Criminal Laws Against Terrorism—Amends the Federal criminal code to prohibit specific terrorist acts or otherwise destructive, disruptive, or violent acts against mass transportation vehicles, ferries, providers, employees, passengers, or operating systems.

(Section 802) Amends the Federal criminal code to: (1) revise the definition of "international terrorism" to include activities that appear to be intended to affect the conduct of government by mass destruction; and (2) define "domestic terrorism" as activities that occur primarily within U.S. jurisdiction, that involve criminal acts dangerous to human life, and that appear to be intended to intimidate or coerce a civilian population, to influence government policy by intimidation or coercion, or to affect government conduct by mass destruction, assassination, or kidnapping.

(Section 803) Prohibits harboring any person knowing or having reasonable grounds to believe that such person has committed or to be about to commit a terrorism offense.

(Section 804) Establishes Federal jurisdiction over crimes committed at U.S. facilities abroad.

(Section 805) Applies the prohibitions against providing material support for terrorism to offenses outside of the United States.

(Section 806) Subjects to civil forfeiture all assets, foreign or domestic, of terrorist organizations.

(Section 808) Expands: (1) the offenses over which the Attorney General shall have primary investigative jurisdiction under provisions governing acts of terrorism transcending national boundaries; and (2) the offenses included within the definition of the Federal crime of terrorism.

(Section 809) Provides that there shall be no statute of limitations for certain terrorism offenses if the commission of such an offense resulted in, or created a foreseeable risk of, death or serious bodily injury to another person.

(Section 810) Provides for alternative maximum penalties for specified terrorism crimes.

(Section 811) Makes: (1) the penalties for attempts and conspiracies the same as those for terrorism offenses; (2) the supervised release terms for offenses with terrorism predicates any term of years or life; and (3) specified terrorism crimes Racketeer Influenced and Corrupt Organizations statute predicates.

(Section 814) Revises prohibitions and penalties regarding fraud and related activity in connection with computers to include specified cyber-terrorism offenses.

(Section 816) Directs the Attorney General to establish regional computer forensic laboratories, and to support existing laboratories, to develop specified cyber-security capabilities.

(Section 817) Prescribes penalties for knowing possession in certain circumstances of biological agents, toxins, or delivery systems, especially by certain restricted persons.

Title IX: Improved Intelligence—Amends the National Security Act of 1947 to require the Director of Central Intelligence (DCI) to establish requirements and priorities for foreign intelligence collected under the Foreign Intelligence Surveillance Act of 1978 and to provide assistance to the Attorney General (AG) to ensure that information derived from electronic surveillance or physical searches is disseminated for efficient and effective foreign intelligence purposes. Requires the inclusion of international terrorist activities within the scope of foreign intelligence under such Act.

(Section 903) Expresses the sense of Congress that officers and employees of the intelligence community should establish and maintain intelligence relationships to acquire information on terrorists and terrorist organizations.

(Section 904) Authorizes deferral of the submission to Congress of certain reports on intelligence and intelligence-related matters until: (1) February 1, 2002; or (2) a date after February 1, 2002, if the official involved certifies that preparation and submission on February 1, 2002, will impede the work of officers or employees engaged in counterterrorism activities. Requires congressional notification of any such deferral.

(Section 905) Requires the AG or the head of any other Federal department or agency with law enforcement responsibilities to expeditiously disclose to the DCI any foreign intelligence acquired in the course of a criminal investigation.

(Section 906) Requires the AG, DCI, and Secretary of the Treasury to jointly report to Congress on the feasibility and desirability of reconfiguring the Foreign Asset Tracking Center and the Office of Foreign Assets Control to provide for the analysis and dissemination of foreign intelligence relating to the financial capabilities and resources of international terrorist organizations.

(Section 907) Requires the DCI to report to the appropriate congressional committees on the establishment and maintenance of the National Virtual Translation Center for timely and accurate translation of foreign intelligence for elements of the intelligence community.

(Section 908) Requires the AG to provide a program of training to Government officials regarding the identification and use of foreign intelligence.

Title X: Miscellaneous—Directs the Inspector General of the Department of Justice to designate one official to review allegations of abuse of civil rights, civil liberties, and racial and ethnic profiling by government employees and officials.

(Section 1002) Expresses the sense of Congress condemning acts of violence or discrimination against any American, including Sikh-Americans. Calls upon local and Federal law enforcement authorities to prosecute to the fullest extent of the law all those who commit crimes.

(Section 1004) Amends the Federal criminal code with respect to venue in money laundering cases to allow a prosecution for such an offense to be brought in: (1) any district in which the financial or monetary transaction is conducted; or (2) any district where a prosecution for the underlying specified unlawful activity could be brought, if the defendant participated in the transfer of the proceeds of the specified unlawful activity from that district to the district where the financial or monetary transaction is conducted.

States that: (1) a transfer of funds from one place to another, by wire or any other means, shall constitute a single, continuing transaction; and (2) any person who conducts any portion of the transaction may be charged in any district in which the transaction takes place.

Allows a prosecution for an attempt or conspiracy offense to be brought in the district where venue would lie for the completed offense, or in any other district where an act in furtherance of the attempt or conspiracy took place.

(Section 1005) First Responders Assistance Act—Directs the Attorney General to make grants to State and local governments to improve the ability of State and local law enforcement, fire department, and first responders to respond to and prevent acts of terrorism. Authorizes appropriations.

(Section 1006) Amends the Immigration and Nationality Act to make inadmissible into the United States any alien engaged in money laundering. Directs the Secretary of State to develop a money laundering watchlist which: (1) identifies individuals worldwide who are known or suspected of money laundering; and (2) is readily accessible to, and shall be checked by, a consular or other Federal official before the issuance of a visa or admission to the United States.

(Section 1007) Authorizes FY 2002 appropriations for regional antidrug training in Turkey by the Drug Enforcement Administration for police, as well as increased precursor chemical control efforts in South and Central Asia.

(Section 1008) Directs the Attorney General to conduct a feasibility study and report to Congress on the use of a biometric identifier scanning system with access to the FBI integrated automated fingerprint identification system at overseas consular posts and points of entry to the United States.

(Section 1009) Directs the FBI to study and report to Congress on the feasibility of providing to airlines access via computer to the names of passengers who are suspected of terrorist activity by Federal officials. Authorizes appropriations.

(Section 1010) Authorizes the use of Department of Defense funds to contract with local and State governments, during the period of Operation Enduring Freedom, for the performance of security functions at U.S. military installations.

(Section 1011) Crimes Against Charitable Americans Act of 2001—Amends the Telemarketing and Consumer Fraud and Abuse Prevention Act to cover fraudulent charitable solicitations. Requires any person engaged in telemarketing for the solicitation of charitable contributions, donations, or gifts to disclose promptly and clearly the purpose of the telephone call.

(Section 1012) Amends the Federal transportation code to prohibit States from licensing any individual to operate a motor vehicle transporting hazardous material unless the Secretary of Transportation determines that such individual does not pose a security risk warranting denial of the license. Requires background checks of such license applicants by the Attorney General upon State request.

(Section 1013) Expresses the sense of the Senate on substantial new U.S. investment in bioterrorism preparedness and response.

(Section 1014) Directs the Office for State and Local Domestic Preparedness Support of the Office of Justice Programs to make grants to enhance State and local capability to prepare for and respond to terrorist acts. Authorizes appropriations for FY 2002 through 2007.

(Section 1015) Amends the Crime Identification Technology Act of 1998 to extend it through FY 2007 and provide for antiterrorism grants to States and localities. Authorizes appropriations.

(Section 1016) Critical Infrastructures Protection Act of 2001—Declares it is U.S. policy: (1) that any physical or virtual disruption of the operation of the critical infrastructures of the United States be rare, brief, geographically limited in effect, manageable, and minimally detrimental to the economy, human and government services, and U.S. national security; (2) that actions necessary to achieve this policy be carried out in a public-private partnership involving corporate and non-governmental organizations; and (3) to have in place a comprehensive and effective program to ensure the continuity of essential Federal Government functions under all circumstances.

Establishes the National Infrastructure Simulation and Analysis Center to serve as a source of national competence to address critical infrastructure protection and continuity through support for activities related to counterterrorism, threat assessment, and risk mitigation.

Defines critical infrastructure as systems and assets, whether physical or virtual, so vital to the United States that their incapacity or destruction would have a debilitating impact on security, national economic security, national public health or safety, or any combination of those matters. Authorizes appropriations.

APPENDIX D

MAIN DIVISIONS OF THE DEPARTMENT OF HOMELAND SECURITY

DIVISION		FORMER DEPARTMENT OR AGENCY
Border and Transportation Security	Immigration and Naturalization Service enforcement functions	Justice Department
	Transportation Security Administration	Transportation Department
	Customs Service	Treasury Department
	Federal Protective Services	General Services Administration
	Animal and Plant Health Inspection Service (parts)	Agriculture Department
Emergency Preparedness and Response	Federal Emergency Management Agency,	*Independent agency*
	Chemical, biological, radiological, and nuclear response units	Health and Human Services Department
	Nuclear incident response teams	Energy Department
	National Domestic Preparedness Office	Federal Bureau of Investigation
	Office of Domestic Preparedness	Justice Department
	Domestic emergency support teams	*From various departments and agencies*
Science and Technology	Civilian biodefense research programs	Health and Human Services Department
	National Biological Warfare Defense Analysis Center (*Proposed in fiscal 2003 budget*)	N/A
	Plum Island Animal Disease Center	Agriculture Department
	Lawrence Livermore National Laboratory (parts)	Energy Department
Information Analysis and Infrastructure Protection	National Communications System	Defense Department
	National Infrastructure Protection Center	Federal Bureau of Investigation
	Critical Infrastructure Assurance Office	Commerce Department
	National Infrastructure Simulation and Analysis Center	Energy Department
	Federal Computer Incident Response Center	General Services Administration
Management		N/A
Secret Service	Secret Service, including presidential protection units	Treasury Department
Coast Guard	U.S. Coast Guard	Transportation Department
Bureau of Citizenship and Immigration Services	Immigration and Naturalization Service non-enforcement functions	Justice Department

Source: White House/U.S. Department of Homeland Security

INDEX

Locators in **boldface** indicate biographical entries. Locators followed by *g* indicate glossary entries. Locators followed by *m* indicate maps.

Index

Index

Index

Index

Index

Index

S

Index